FOUNDATION Mathematics

Book 4

As per NEP 2020

AF883696

Includes Problems based on:

- Problem Solving Skills
- Creativity Skills
- Reasoning Skills
- Critical Thinking Skills
- Art Integration Skills
- Application Skills

Online Features

- Animated Videos
- Video Lessons
- Assignments

By
R. S. Dhauni
S. S. Sharma

Edited by
Nisha Mudgal

GOYAL BROTHERS PRAKASHAN

GOYAL BROTHERS PRAKASHAN

EDUCATIONAL PUBLISHERS

Sales & Registered Office :

11/1903, Chuna Mandi, Paharganj, New Delhi-110055
Post Box : 5720, Phones : 43551877 & 43561877
E-mail : info@goyal-books.com
Website : www.goyal-books.com

Administrative Office :

D-231, Sector 63, Noida-201301 (U.P.), Phone : 0120-4655555

Edition : 2026

Price: ₹499

STEPS TO ACCESS CONTENT USING QR CODES PRINTED IN THIS BOOK :

Visit www.meritbox.app or Download **"Merit Box"** App from Google Play Store or Apple App Store.

A. For App user
- Register yourself.
- On "Home" screen, Go to "Scan QR Code".
- Scan the QR Codes provided in the book to view the required content.

B. For website user
- Register yourself.
- Go to "Online Support".
- In "Scan, Watch and Learn" section, enter the QR-Code and Click on "Submit" button to view the required content.

For any assistance, please reach us at elearning@goyal-books.com or +91-120-4655555.

Published & Printed by
Roshan Lal Goyal for Goyal Brothers Prakashan, New Delhi

INTRODUCTION

We are pleased to present the revised edition of the series **Foundation Mathematics for Primary Classes** (Books 1—5). This series is based on the latest curriculum prepared and recommended by the **Council for the Indian School Certificate Examinations, New Delhi**. The new curriculum for Classes 1 to 5 is designed to ensure that children build a solid foundation in Mathematics by connecting and applying mathematical concepts in a variety of ways. This curriculum aims to develop a number of mathematical skills and processes among children.

Main objectives of teaching and learning Mathematics at primary level are :

- To develop the mathematical thinking and problem solving skills and apply these to formulate and solve problems.
- To acquire the necessary mathematical concepts and skills for everyday life, and for continuous learning in mathematics and related disciplines.
- To develop the necessary process skills for the acquisition and application of mathematical concepts.
- To create love and interest towards mathematics.
- To make effective use of a variety of mathematical tools in the learning and application of mathematics.
- To reason logically, communicate mathematically, and learn cooperatively and independently.

The present series has been developed and designed keeping the above objectives in mind. This child-friendly series teaches Mathematics in such an interesting and comprehensive manner that even an average child has no difficulty in grasping the fundamental concepts of Mathematics.

The Salient Features of this Series are :

- **Eye-catching illustrations** and **child-friendly** layout to kindle the imagination of the child and create an interest in the subject.
- Each chapter begins with the heading **Learning Target**, which tells about the concrete goal of the chapter.
- The **I Can** in the starting of the chapter describes what the students will be able to do after the chapter.
- **Let Us Recall,** is meant to refresh the concepts learnt in the previous class.
- Under the heading **Explore and Learn**, students will investigate, study or analyse the concepts.
- **Apply and Learn** asks questions to apply the knowledge gained after exploring the concepts.
- The head **Note** provides tips to remember for solving the questions easily.
- The fact box **Remember** highlights the important points.
- Questions under the heading **Challenge** trigger the analytical reasoning of the students.
- **Value Based Questions** are meant to inculcate moral values in the children.
- **Review and Refresh** at the end of each chapter checks the retention capacity and the level of understanding of the students.
- Assignments under the heading **Mental Maths** not only enhance the mathematical and calculation skills of the students but also fortify the concepts already learned.
- **Fun with Maths** contains out of the way questions which challenge the understanding capacity of the students.
- **Maths Lab Activities** are meant to learn mathematical concepts through various activities.
- **Check Your Pace** is meant to revise and revisit the concepts learnt in the last two or three chapters.
- **Two Model Test Papers,** one for Half Yearly Examination and other for Annual Examination have also been added in each book.

It is hoped that the series will meet the requirements of the students, teachers and parents alike. Suggestions and constructive criticism for the improvement of the books would be highly appreciated.

—The Publishers

Inside Features aligned with NEP 2020

Learning Targets are concrete goals written in student friendly language.

Learning Target — To know about Roman Numeration system.

I Can articulate at the beginning what students should know and be able to do.

I Can
- I can **define** a dividend, a divisor and a quotient.
- I can **divide** 2-digit, 3-digit and 4-digit numbers by 1-digit number.
- I can **explain** properties of division.
- I can **solve** word problems on division.

Let Us Recall helps students recapitulate the basics to understand the chapter.

As per NEP

Let Us Recall

In the previous classes, we learnt to read time from a clock. We also learned the relation between hours and minutes. Let us review what we learnt earlier. We learnt that : 1 hour = 60 minutes, 1 day = 24 hours

Explore and Learn enables students to investigate, study or analyse the concepts.

As per NEP

Explore and Learn

Properties of Multiplication

1. **Order Property :** Observe the following :

	3	4	← Multiplicand
×	2	6	← Multiplier
2	0	4	
6	8	0	
8	8	4	← Product

	2	6	← Multiplicand
×	3	4	← Multiplier
1	0	4	
7	8	0	
8	8	4	← Product

Apply and Learn asks questions to apply the knowledge gained after exploring the concept.

As per NEP

Exercise 4C

Apply and Learn

A. Find the sum :

1.

	Th	H	T	O
	5	2	4	0
+	4	6	9	8

2.

	Th	H	T	O
	3	7	2	4
+	2	6	9	8

Notes provide important tips to remember for solving questions easily.

We see that the product of any number and 0 is 0. This property is known as **multiplicative property of 0.**

As per NEP

Challenge helps to trigger the analytical reasoning of the students.

CHALLENGE

My ones digit is 4. My tens digit is 8. My hundreds digit is 2 less than my ones digit. My thousands digit is same as my hundreds digit. What number am I?

Remember provides facts to understand the chapter.

REMEMBER

To find the difference of two numbers, we always subtract the smaller number from the greater number.

Value Based Questions give an opportunity to show the values present in oneself.

As per NEP

Value Based Questions

In a library there are 4,076 books on Literature, 2,536 books on Science and 2,452 books on Mathematics.

1. How many more Literature books are there in the library than that on Science?
2. Are books on Literature more than the books on Science and Mathematics together? If yes, by how many?

Review and Refresh checks the retention capacity and level of understanding.

As per NEP

Review and Refresh

A. Using the tangram pieces, make the letters C, F and H.

B. How many line segments are there in each of the following figures? Name them :

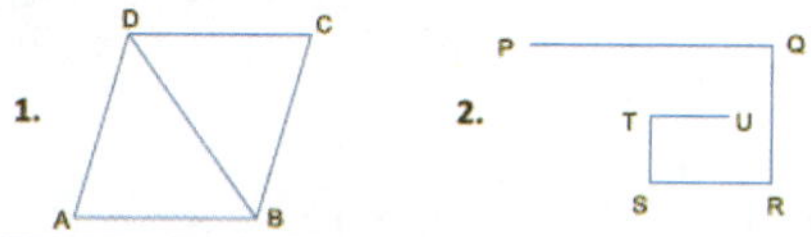

Mental Maths enhances mathematical skills and fortifies the concepts already learnt.

Mental Maths

1. 8 × 6 = 48 gives the division facts ____________ and ____________
2. In a division, remainder is always ____________ than the divisor.
3. 5000 ÷ 5 = ____________

Fun with Maths consists of out of the box questions.

As per NEP

Fun With Maths

1. Here the grid is made up of 17 matchsticks.
   Its area is 6 sq units.
   Remove exactly 5 matchsticks, so that the area of the grid becomes 3 sq cm.

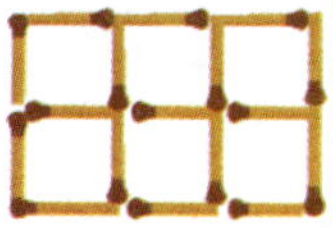

Check Your Pace helps to improve speed and accuracy in solving problems.

As per NEP

CHECK YOUR PACE

(Based on Chapters 13, 14)

A. The number of different subject books in a school library is given in the following table :

Subject	Hindi	English	Science	Mathematics	Social Science
Number of books	120	140	90	80	110

Draw a pictograph to represent the above data.

Maths Lab Activity provides interesting, engaging and interactive learning.

As per NEP

Maths Lab Activity

Objective : Understanding patterns in a calendar.

Materials Required : A calendar of any month.

Procedure/Demonstration :

1. Take a calendar of any month and mark a 3 × 3 box (9 dates) on it.
2. Add the 9 numbers of this box.
   10 + 11 + 12 + 17 + 18 + 19 + 24 + 25 + 26 = 162
3. Find the smallest number of the box Here it is 10.
4. Add 8 to it. So, 10 + 8 = 18.
5. Multiply the sum by 9. So, 18 × 9 = 162.
6. We can get the sum of the numbers of the selected box (obtained in step 2) without adding. To do so, simply multiply the middle number by 9. So, 18 × 9 = 162.
7. Do the above process for another 3 × 3 box and see whether it always works or not.

M	T	W	T	F	S	S
1	2	3	4	5	6	7
8	9	10	11	12	13	14
15	16	17	18	19	20	21
22	23	24	25	26	27	28
29	30	31				

Features of Online Support

Teachers can access **E-Books** easily.

Animated Videos can visually represent abstract ideas.

Video Lessons enable students to learn at their own individual pace.

Teachers can create question paper using **Test Paper Generator** in the simplest and most convenient way.

Teacher's Resource Book gives teachers practical advice, guidance, resource ideas and materials for the classroom.

Assignments enable students to check the progress of their own learning.

Log into **www.study.goyalsonline.com** or download **Merit Box App**.

Components of the Teacher's Resource Book

- Background knowledge
- Objectives
- Overview of the chapters
- New vocabulary
- Teaching/Learning materials
- Teaching/Learning strategies/activities
- Evaluation & Assessment
- Solution to MTP
- Hints to some selected problems

CONTENTS

THEME 1 : NUMBERS

1. Numbers up to 999999 --- 1-19
   - Numbers beyond 9999 • Indian Place-Value Chart • Writing Large Numbers in Figures
   - Face-value • Place-value • Expanded Form • Comparison of Numbers
   - Ascending and Descending Order • Successor and Predecessor of a Number
   - Forming the Greatest and the Smallest Numbers
2. Roman Numerals --- 20-24
3. Fractional Numbers --- 25-53
   - One-half • One-fourth or a Quarter • One-third • Fractional Parts
   - Numerator and Denominator of a Fraction • Parts of a Collection
   - Equivalent Fractions • An Important Property of Equivalent Fractions
   - Fractions in Lowest Terms • Comparison of Fractions
   - Addition and Subtraction of Fractions with the same (like) Denominator
   - Types of Fractions • Proper and Improper Fractions
   - Mixed Number (or Mixed Fraction)
   - Conversion of a Mixed Fraction into an Improper Fraction
   - Conversion of an Improper Fraction into a Mixed Fraction
   - **Check Your Pace** (Based on Chapters 1, 2, 3) --- 54

THEME 2 : NUMBER OPERATIONS

4. Addition --- 55-67
   - Addition without Carrying (or without Regrouping)
   - Addition with Carrying (or with Regrouping) • Properties of Addition
   - Word Problems
5. Subtraction --- 68-78
   - Subtraction without Borrowing (or without Regrouping)
   - Subtraction with Borrowing (or with Regrouping) • Properties of Subtraction
   - Addition and Subtraction Together • Word Problems
6. Multiplication --- 79-98
   - Multiplication Tables
   - Multiplication of a 3-digit and a 4-digit Number by a 1-digit Number
   - Multiplication by 2-digit Number • Multiplication by a 3-digit Number
   - Properties of Multiplication • Multiplication by Tens, Hundreds and Thousands
   - Word Problems • Quick Multiplication • Rounding Numbers
   - Estimation of Sum/Difference/Product
   - **Check Your Pace** (Based on Chapters 4, 5, 6) --- 99
7. Division --- 100-113
   - Terms Associated with Division
   - Dividing a 2-digit, a 3-digit and a 4-digit Number by a 1-digit Number
   - Division by 10 and 100 • Properties of Division • Word Problems

THEME 3 : PLAYING WITH NUMBERS

8. Multiples and Factors --- 114-137
- Multiples • Properties of Multiples • Factors • Properties of Factors • Even and Odd Numbers
- Prime Numbers • Composite Numbers • To Find Prime Numbers between 1 and 100
- Tests for Divisibility • Prime Factorization • Common Factors • Highest Common Factor (HCF)
- HCF by Long Division Method • Properties of HCF • Common Multiples
- Lowest Common Multiples (LCM) • LCM by Long Division Method • Properties of LCM

THEME 4 : GEOMETRY

9. Geometrical Shapes --- 138-166
- Tangram • Tessellation • Open and Closed Curves
- Simple closed curves • Polygons • Rectangle • Square
- Basic Geometrical Concepts • Perpendicular Lines
- Parallel Lines • Drawing Parallel Lines with Set Squares
- Circle • Drawing a Circle • Terms Related to a Circle
- How to Find the Centre of a Given Circle
- Relationship between Radius and Diameter of a Circle
- Symmetry • Reflection • Views of an Object
- **Check Your Pace** (Based on Chapters 7, 8, 9) --- 167

10. Perimeter and Area --- 168-179
- Perimeter • To Find the Perimeter of a Triangle, a Rectangle and a Square
- Area • Units of Area • Area of a Rectangle and a Square

THEME 5 : MEASUREMENT

11. Measurement of Length, Mass and Capacity --- 180-195
- Measurement of Length • Addition and Subtraction in Length
- Measurement of Mass • Addition and Subtraction in Mass
- Measurement of Capacity • Addition and Subtraction in Capacity

12. Time --- 196-210
- Use of a.m. or p.m. • Conversion of Time • Time Duration • Interpreting a Calendar.
- **Check Your Pace** (Based on Chapters 10, 11, 12) --- 211

THEME 6 : DATA HANDLING

13. Data Handling --- 212-220
- Drawing Pictographs • Bar Graphs

THEME 7 : PATTERNS

14. Patterns --- 221-227
- **Check Your Pace** (Based on Chapters 13, 14) --- 228
- **Model Test Paper-1 (For Half Yearly Examination)** --- 229
- **Model Test Paper-2 (For Annual Examination)** --- 231
- **Answers** --- 233

THEME 1 : NUMBERS

Numbers up to 999999

Learning Target To know about numbers up to 999999 (5-digit and 6-digit numbers).

I Can

- **I can read** and write 5-digit and 6-digit numbers.
- **I can find** place value and face value of any digit in a number.
- **I can write** numbers in expanded and short form.
- **I can write** 5-digit and 6-digit numbers in Indian place-value chart.
- **I can find** successor and predecessor of any number.
- **I can form** the smallest and the greatest 5-digit and 6-digit numbers using the given digits.
- **I can compare** numbers up to 6-digits.

Let Us Recall

In Class 3, we have learnt about the numbers up to 9999 (nine thousand nine hundred ninety-nine). In this chapter, we shall study about the numbers greater than 9999. First of all, let us have a quick review of what we have read.

Exercise 1A

A Write the following numbers in words :

1. 4985 ____________________

2. 8120 ____________________

3. 9500 ____________________

B Write the following numbers in figures :

1. Two thousand four hundred twenty-nine ____________
2. Three thousand four hundred seventy ____________
3. Nine thousand five hundred three ____________

C Fill in the blanks :

1. In 2964, 9 is at ____________ place.
2. In 1042, 2 is at ____________ place.
3. In 5720, 5 is at ____________ place.
4. In 8036, 3 is at ____________ place.

D Write the place-value of :

1. 5 in 1536. ____________
2. 8 in 2781. ____________
3. 1 in 1346. ____________
4. 0 in 5047. ____________

E Write the following numbers in the expanded form :

1. 4387 = ____________
2. 2893 = ____________
3. 1400 = ____________

F Write the short form of :

1. 2000 + 500 + 80 + 4 = ____________
2. 6000 + 50 + 8 = ____________
3. 4000 + 60 + 1 = ____________
4. 8000 + 100 + 2 = ____________

G Find the successor of :

1. 8599 ____________
2. 3600 ____________
3. 9998 ____________
4. 2099 ____________

H Find the predecessor of :

1. 3000 ____________
2. 5937 ____________
3. 4010 ____________
4. 9999 ____________

I Arrange the following numbers in ascending order :

1. 4526, 4256, 4569, 4325
2. 1007, 1070, 1700, 1050

J Arrange the following numbers in descending order :

1. 2916, 4531, 9814, 6005
2. 7308, 7338, 7348, 7304

Explore and Learn

Numbers Beyond 9999

We know that the greatest 1-digit number is 9.

If we add 1 to 9, we get 9 + 1 = 10, the smallest 2-digit number.

The greatest 2-digit number is 99.

If we add 1 to 99, we get 99 + 1 = 100, the smallest 3-digit number.

The greatest 3-digit number is 999.

If we add 1 to 999, we get 999 + 1 = 1000, the smallest 4-digit number.

The greatest 4-digit number is 9999.

If we add 1 to 9999, we get 9999 + 1 = 10000, the smallest 5-digit number.

The greatest 5-digit number is 99999.

If we add 1 to 99999, we get 99999 + 1 = 100000, the smallest 6-digit number.

We read 100000 as one lakh. The sixth place from the right is called lakhs place.

As before we may have larger numbers as given below :

400000 — read as four lakh.

539042 — read as five lakh thirty-nine thousand forty-two.

732519 — read as seven lakh thirty-two thousand five hundred nineteen.

999999 — read as nine lakh ninety-nine thousand nine hundred ninety-nine.

999999 is the greatest 6-digit number.

Indian Place-Value Chart

CODE-zVF4

To read and write large numbers, we use the following Indian place-value chart :

Periods →	Lakhs	Thousands		Ones		
Places →	L	T-Th	Th	H	T	O
	Lakhs 100000	Ten thousands 10000	Thousands 1000	Hundreds 100	Tens 10	Ones 1

In the above place-value chart, the six places are grouped into **periods**. The first three places from the right end are grouped under **'ones period'**. The next two places are grouped under **'thousands period'** and the last one place is grouped under **'lakhs period'**.

To read large numbers, we use the periods.

Observe the following place-value chart in which the digits of the numbers 63158, 39846, 251034, 193056 and 100000 are arranged.

Periods →	Lakhs	Thousands		Ones		
Places →	L	T-Th	Th	H	T	O
63158 →		6	3	1	5	8
39846 →		3	9	8	4	6
251034 →	2	5	1	0	3	4
193056 →	1	9	3	0	5	6
100000 →	1	0	0	0	0	0

While reading a number, all the digits in the same period are read together and the name of the period (except the ones) is read along with them.

While writing a number, we put a comma after every period to separate the periods. This helps us to read the number easily.

Example 1 : Write the number name for each of the following numbers :

(a) 38,946 (b) 2,90,534 (c) 4,59,861

Solution :

	Lakhs	Thousands		Ones			
	L	T-Th	Th	H	T	O	
(a)		3	8	9	4	6	→ Thirty-eight thousand, nine hundred forty six.
(b)	2	9	0	5	3	4	→ Two lakh ninety thousand five hundred thirty-four
(c)	4	5	9	8	6	1	→ Four lakh fifty nine thousand eight hundred sixty-one

Note : The plural for the period is not written. For example, instead of writing six lakhs, forty thousands two hundreds, we write six lakh forty thousand two hundred.

Explore and Learn

Writing Large Numbers in Figures

CODE-3ePu

Example 2 : Write the number – 'two lakh five thousand one hundred twenty-four' in figures.

Solution : We proceed as follows :

Step 1 : Make three periods as shown.

L	Th		O		

The first period from right will have three parts, the second will have two parts and the third will have only one part.

Step 2 : Write all the lakhs in the first period from the left.

L	Th		O		
2					

Step 3 : Write all the thousands in the second period from the left. We fill all the parts. For example, if it is 5 thousand, we write 05.

L	Th		O		
2	0	5			

Step 4 : Write the hundreds, tens and ones in the third period from the left.

L	Th		O		
2	0	5	1	2	4

Thus, two lakh five thousand one hundred twenty-four in figures is 2,05,124.

Example 3 : Write each of the following numbers in figures :

(a) Twelve thousand five hundred twenty-one
(b) Forty-one thousand two
(c) Six lakh thirty-six thousand, five hundred ten
(d) Eight lakh three thousand fifty-six.

Solution : (a) Twelve thousand five hundred twenty-one

L	Th		O			
0	1	2	5	2	1	→ 12,521

(b) Forty-one thousand two

L	Th		O			
0	4	1	0	0	2	→ 41,002

REMEMBER

0 at the extreme left position is meaningless. 0413 is actually 413.

(c) Six lakh thirty-six thousand five hundred ten

L	Th		O		
6	3	6	5	1	0

→ 6,36,510

(d) Eight lakh three thousand fifty-six

L	Th		O		
8	0	3	0	5	6

→ 8,03,056

Exercise 1B

Apply and Learn

A Make a place-value chart with six places. Enter in it the digits of the numbers given below :

1. 65,494 **2.** 1,49,206 **3.** 2,51,362 **4.** 3,50,008 **5.** 9,50,004

B Read the numbers written in the place-value chart below. Write them in words:

	Lakhs	Thousands		Ones		
	L	T-Th	Th	H	T	O
1.		5	3	0	2	6
2.	4	8	0	0	0	9
3.	2	1	5	0	6	0
4.	3	0	5	4	0	7
5.	7	0	1	8	2	4

C Write the number names for each of the following numbers :

1. 29,502 **2.** 6,83,527 **3.** 6,53,008 **4.** 7,00,058 **5.** 7,95,326

D Write each of the following numbers in figures :

1. Fifteen thousand five hundred twelve. ____________

2. One lakh twenty-one thousand two hundred nineteen ____________

3. Four lakh thirty thousand six ____________

4. Two lakh five thousand fifty-three ____________

5. Five lakh one ____________

Explore and Learn

Face-Value

Consider the number 2,95,613.

It has six digits 2, 9, 5, 6, 1 and 3.

We say that in 2,95,613, the face value of 2 is 2, 9 is 9, 5 is 5, 6 is 6, 1 is 1 and 3 is 3.

The face-value of a digit in a number is the value of the digit itself regardless of the position of the digit.

Example 1 : Find the face-value of :

(a) 2 in 1,95,263 (b) 5 in 25,134

(c) 8 in 1,63,548 (d) 0 in 60,793

Solution : (a) Face-value of 2 in 1,95,263 is 2.

(b) Face-value of 5 in 25,134 is 5.

(c) Face-value of 8 in 1,63,548 is 8.

(d) Face-value of 0 in 60,793 is 0.

Place-Value

The place-value of a digit in a number depends upon the place it occupies in the place-value chart.

Place-value of a digit = Face-value × Value of the place it occupies in the place-value chart.

Lakhs (L)	Ten-thousands (T-Th)	Thousands (Th)	Hundreds (H)	Tens (T)	Ones (O)
1,00,000	10,000	1,000	100	10	1

Consider the number 6,18,359.

Let us arrange the digits of the above number in the following place-value chart.

L 1,00,000	T-Th 10,000	Th 1,000	H 100	T 10	O 1
6	1	8	3	5	9

From the above place-value chart, we have,

9 is at ones place, so its place-value is 9 ones = 9 × 1 = 9.

5 is at tens place, so its place-value is 5 tens = 5 × 10 = 50.

3 is at hundreds place, so its place-value is 3 hundreds = 3 × 100 = 300.

8 is at thousands place, so its place-value is 8 thousands = 8 × 1,000 = 8,000.

1 is at ten thousands place, so its place-value is 1 ten thousand = 1 × 10,000 = 10,000.

6 is at lakhs place, so its place-value is 6 lakhs = 6 × 1,00,000 = 6,00,000.

Example 2 : Write the place-value of 3 in each of the following numbers :

(a) 13,584 (b) 3,50,962 (c) 6,85,931 (d) 5,93,821

Solution : Arrange the digits of the numbers in the place-value chart.

	L	T-Th	Th	H	T	O
	1,00,000	10,000	1,000	100	10	1
(a)		1	**3**	5	8	4
(b)	**3**	5	0	9	6	2
(c)	6	8	5	9	**3**	1
(d)	5	9	**3**	8	2	1

(a) Place-value of 3 in 13,584= 3 × 1,000 = 3,000.

(b) Place-value of 3 in 3,50,962= 3 × 1,00,000 = 3,00,000.

(c) Place-value of 3 in 6,85,931= 3 × 10 = 30.

(d) Place-value of 3 in 5,93,821= 3 × 1,000 = 3,000.

Example 3 : Write the place-value of 0 in the following numbers :

(a) 25,170 (b) 6,52,701 (c) 3,05,217

Solution : (a) In 25,170, 0 is at ones place, so its place-value is 0 × 1 = 0.

(b) In 6,52,701, 0 is at tens place, so its place-value is 0 × 10 = 0.

(c) In 3,05,217, 0 is at ten thousands place, so its place-value is 0 × 10,000 = 0.

REMEMBER

The place-value of 0 is always 0, whatever place it occupies in the place-value chart.

Explore and Learn

Expanded Form

CODE-KDHN

To express a number as the sum of the place-values of its digits is called its expanded form.

Example 4 : Write the following numbers in expanded form :

(a) 35,126 (b) 3,01,647

Solution : Write the given numbers in the place-value chart.

(a)

L	T-Th	Th	H	T	O
	3	5	1	2	6

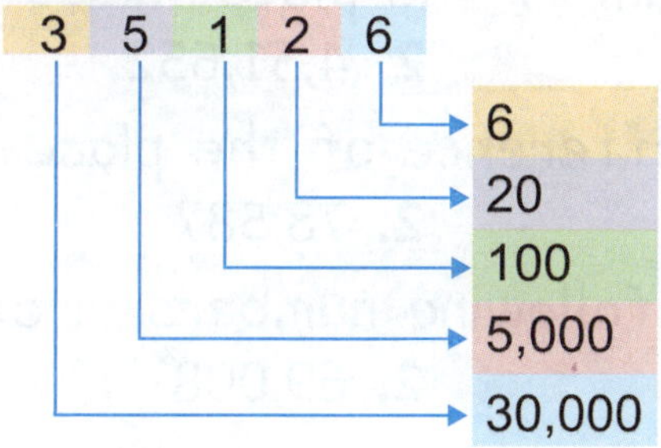

Thus, 35,126 = 30,000 + 5,000 + 100 + 20 + 6.

(b)

L	T-Th	Th	H	T	O
3	0	1	6	4	7

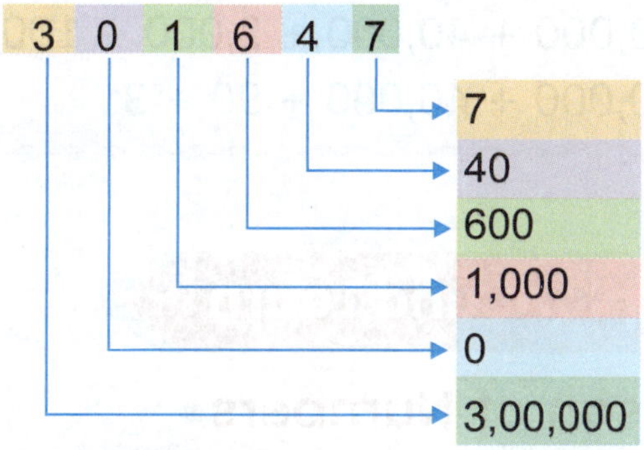

Thus, 3,01,647 = 3,00,000 + 0 + 1,000 + 600 + 40 + 7

= 3,00,000 + 1,000 + 600 + 40 + 7.

CHALLENGE

My ones digit is 4. My tens digit is 8. My hundreds digit is 2 less than my ones digit. My thousands digit is same as my hundreds digit. What number am I?

Exercise 1C

Apply and Learn

A Write the face-value of :

1. 1 in 25,103 **2.** 7 in 75,124 **3.** 6 in 2,01,536 **4.** 3 in 4,00,312

B Find the place-value of :

1. 3 in 25,134 **2.** 6 in 6,43,521 **3.** 4 in 3,49,026 **4.** 0 in 53,019

C Write the place-value of the underlined digits in each of the following :

1. 46,738 **2.** 5,46,201 **3.** 8,00,536 **4.** 8,52,196

D Choose the numbers in which the place-value of 4 is 4,000 :

4,61,290, 9,24,300, 56,004, 64,000, 95,624, 46,521

E Find the sum of the place-values of 5 in :

1. 25,125 **2.** 4,51,652 **3.** 7,50,534 **4.** 51,350

F Find the difference of the place-values of 8 in :

1. 85,218 **2.** 78,587 **3.** 4,68,382 **4.** 9,08,083

G Write the following numbers in expanded form :

1. 6,594 **2.** 69,008 **3.** 1,85,541 **4.** 5,19,030

H Write the short form of :

1. 5,000 + 300 + 40 + 3

2. 2,00,000 + 50,000 + 300 + 90 + 4

3. 6,00,000 + 40,000 + 2,000 + 100 + 7

4. 5,00,000 + 500 + 5

5. 2,00,000 + 40,000 + 90 + 3

6. 9,00,000 + 4,000 + 200

Explore and Learn

CODE-QNGh

Comparison of Numbers

Case 1. When two numbers have different number of digits :

Out of the two numbers, a number having more digits is greater than the other.

Thus, 27 > 9, 324 > 99, 1,291 > 948, 11,468 > 9,274.

Example 1 : Which is greater?

(a) 2,537 or 51,693 (b) 5,12,964 or 291 (c) 1,56,201 or 27,193

Solution : (a) 2,537 has 4 digits and 51,693 has 5 digits.

So, 51,693 is greater than 2,537 or 51,693 > 2,537.

(b) 5,12,964 has 6 digits and 291 has 3 digits.

So, 5,12,964 is greater than 291 or 5,12,964 > 291.

(c) 1,56,201 has 6 digits and 27,193 has 5 digits.

So, 1,56,201 is greater than 27,193 or 1,56,201 > 27,193.

Case 2. When the two numbers have the same number of digits :

In this case, we proceed as follows :

Step 1 : First compare the digits at the left-most place in both the numbers. If they are not equal, then the number which has the greater digit at this place is greater than the other.

Step 2 : If they are equal, then compare the second digits from left in both the numbers. If they are not equal, then the number which has the greater digit at this place is greater than the other.

Step 3 : If they are equal in value, compare their third digits from the left. Continue this process until you come across unequal digits at the corresponding places.

Example 2 : Compare :

(a) 25,306 and 25,419 (b) 6,34,510 and 6,34,578

Solution : (a) Consider 25,306 and 25,419. Both are 5-digit numbers.

We start from the left-most digits. Here, 2 = 2.

Next, we compare the second digits from the left. Here, 5 = 5.

Next, we compare the third digits from the left. Here, 3 < 4

Thus, 25,306 < 25,419 or 25,419 > 25,306.

(b) Consider 6,34,510 and 6,34,578. Both are 6-digit numbers.

Comparing the digits, we have

6 = 6 (left-most digits)

3 = 3 (second digits from the left)

4 = 4 (third digits from the left)

5 = 5 (fourth digits from the left)

1 < 7 (fifth digits from the left)

Thus, 6,34,510 < 6,34,578 or 6,34,578 > 6,34,510.

CODE-gEvc

Ascending and Descending Order

Ascending order means the arrangement of numbers from the smallest to the greatest.

Example 3 : Arrange the following numbers in ascending order :

3,25,102; 5,65,101; 4,32,256; 7,41,212; 4,63,205

Solution : First we arrange the given numbers in a place value chart :

L	T-Th	Th	H	T	O
3	2	5	1	0	2
5	6	5	1	0	1
4	3	2	2	5	6
7	4	1	2	1	2
4	6	3	2	0	5

All the numbers have 6 digits. Comparing the digits at the lakhs place, we get 3 < 4 < 5 < 7.

Now, we compare 4,32,256 and 4,63,205. Both these numbers have the same digits at the lakhs place. So, we compare the digits at the ten-thousands place.

This digit is 3 in 4,32,256 and 6 in 4,63,205.

Since, 3 < 6, so, 4,32,256 < 4,63,205.

Thus, 3,25,102 < 4,32,256 < 4,63,205 < 5,65,101 < 7,41,212

Hence, the given numbers arranged in ascending order are :

3,25,102; 4,32,256; 4,63,205; 5,65,101; 7,41,212.

Descending order means the arrangement of numbers from the greatest to the smallest.

Example 4 : Arrange the following numbers in descending order :

4,69,901; 90,618; 6,06,211; 5,58,690; 6,26,923

Solution : First we arrange the given numbers in a place value chart.

L	T-Th	Th	H	T	O
4	6	9	9	0	1
	9	0	6	1	8
6	0	6	2	1	1
5	5	8	6	9	0
6	2	6	9	2	3

90,618 is a 5-digit number. All others are 6-digit numbers.

So, 90,618 is the smallest number.

Comparing the digits at lakhs place, we get 6 > 5 > 4.

Now, we compare 6,06,211 and 6,26,923. Both the numbers have 6 at the lakhs place. So, we compare their digits at the ten-thousands place.

This digit is 0 in 6,06,211 and 2 in 6,26,923.

So, 6,06,211 < 6,26,923.

Thus, 6,26,923 > 6,06,211 > 5,58,690 > 4,69,901 > 90,618.

Hence, the given numbers arranged in descending order are:

6,26,923; 6,06,211; 5,58,690; 4,69,901; 90,618.

Explore and Learn

Successor of a Number

The number that comes just after a given number is called its successor.

CODE-PrKC

To find the successor of a given number, we add 1 to the given number.

Example 5 : Find the successors of :

(a) 599 (b) 3,500 (c) 31,499

Solution : (a) Successor of 599 = 599 + 1 = 600.

(b) Successor of 3,500 = 3,500 + 1 = 3,501.

(c) Successor of 31,499 = 31,499 + 1 = 31,500.

Predecessor of a Number

CODE-n9to

The number that comes just before a given number is called its predecessor.

To find the predecessor of a given number, we subtract 1 from the given number.

Example 6 : Find the predecessor of :

(a) 270 (b) 6,900 (c) 7,54,196

Solution : (a) Predecessor of 270 = 270 − 1 = 269.

(b) Predecessor of 6,900 = 6,900 − 1 = 6,899.

(c) Predecessor of 7,54,196 = 7,54,196 − 1 = 7,54,195.

Explore and Learn

Forming the Greatest and the Smallest Numbers

CODE-rzed

We know that the greatest number is formed by arranging the given digits from the greatest to the smallest.

The smallest number is formed by arranging the given digits from the smallest to the greatest.

Let us take the digits 5, 9, 4, 6, 3 and 2.

Here, 9 > 6 > 5 > 4 > 3 > 2

So, the greatest 6-digit number formed using these digits is 9,65,432.

So, the smallest 6-digit number formed using these digits is 2,34,569.

But, if we have one of the given digits as 0, then it is not written at the extreme left. So, while writing the smallest number, we write 0 in the second place from the left.

Let us take the digits 7, 6, 0, 2 and 5.

The greatest 5-digit number formed is 76,520.

The smallest 5-digit number formed is 20,567 not 02,567.

Example 7 : Write the smallest and the greatest 4-digit numbers using all the digits 3, 6 and 5. You may repeat the digits.

Solution : The smallest 4-digit number = 3,356

Note that here we repeated the smallest digit.

The greatest 4-digit number = 6,653

Note that here we repeated the greatest digit.

CHALLENGE

I am the smallest 5-digit number with all digits greater than 4 and with all my digits different. Who am I?

Example 8 : Write the smallest and the greatest 4-digit number using two different digits.

Solution : Using two smallest digits are 0 and 1.

Then, the smallest 4-digit number is 1000.

Using two greatest digits are 9 and 8.

Then, the greatest 4-digit number = 9998.

Exercise 1D

Apply and Learn

A Fill in the blanks using >, = or < :

1. 2,506 ________ 286
2. 4,651 ________ 79,512
3. 6,29,103 ________ 4,51,632
4. 6,54,738 ________ 6,54,291
5. 66,329 ________ 6,51,780
6. 95,163 ________ 4,510
7. 37,541 ________ 37,541
8. 6,53,497 ________ 6,53,479

B Ring the largest number in each group :

1. 5,320, 3,520, 2,530, 2,053
2. 3,70,621, 2,06,713, 6,30,271, 3,60,217
3. 8,39,216, 8,93,162, 2,16,893, 6,89,312
4. 7,20,163, 7,20,136, 7,02,163, 6,89,312

C Ring the smallest number in each group :

1. 62,514, 21,951, 41,527, 42,519
2. 9,81,750, 8,91,750, 9,18,750, 8,19,570
3. 6,09,268, 6,90,286, 9,60,268, 6,90,628
4. 2,51,673, 2,51,637, 2,51,768, 2,51,367

D Arrange the following numbers in ascending order :

1. 351; 1,678; 2,500; 6,135; 21,015
2. 3,65,727; 4,78,051; 26,871; 45,341; 19,007

E Arrange the following numbers in descending order :

1. 81,526; 4,54,839; 2,81,263; 7,19,076; 2,35,245

2. 6,53,192; 6,35,294; 68,156; 1,28,193; 6,346

F Write the successor of each of the following numbers :

1. 65,830 **2.** 12,599 **3.** 6,89,959 **4.** 4,99,999

G Write the predecessor of each of the following numbers :

1. 7,36,000 **2.** 5,72,992 **3.** 5,32,600 **4.** 4,00,310

H Write the greatest and the smallest number using the following digits only once:

1. 6, 8, 9, 3, 1 **2.** 3, 0, 1, 7, 2 **3.** 2, 8, 0, 3, 9, 4

I Solve the following :

1. Write the successor of the greatest 5-digit number.

2. Write the predecessor of the smallest 6-digit number.

3. Write the greatest and the smallest 5-digit numbers using all of the following digits. You may repeat the digits.

(a) 7, 5, 2, 8 (b) 4, 0, 1, 8 (c) 9, 3, 7, 4

4. Write the smallest 4-digit number using

(a) only one digit (b) different digits.

5. Write the greatest 5-digit number using

(a) two different digits (b) different digits.

Value Based Questions

The department of Social Welfare did a survey to know the number of literate males and females in a town. The results are given below :

Total number of males = 37,442

Number of literate males = 29,005

Total number of females = 32,309

Number of literate females = 21,896

1. Write the number name for each of the numbers involved.

2. Arrange the four numbers written above in ascending order.

3. What measures should be taken so that maximum number of people of our society become literate?

Review and Refresh

A Write the number names for each of the following numbers :

1. 43,575
2. 6,29,001
3. 5,00,040
4. 5,90,304
5. 8,05,904
6. 1,54,687
7. 32,508
8. 2,00,008

B Write each of the following numbers in figures :

1. Twelve thousand five hundred twenty-four.
2. Twenty thousand eight.
3. Four lakh two hundred twenty-three.
4. Eight lakh fifteen thousand nine hundred five.

C Find the place-value of :

1. 5 in 2,35,019
2. 7 in 7,54,186
3. 0 in 7,03,168

D Write the expanded form of following numbers :

1. 1,25,197
2. 2,83,005
3. 5,41,938

E Write the short form of :

1. 6,00,000 + 3,000 + 800 + 50
2. 5,00,000 + 3,000 + 200 + 10 + 9
3. 7,00,000 + 300 + 8
4. 2,00,000 + 3,000 + 10

F Compare the following numbers using > or < :

1. 25,471 ______ 4,371
2. 53,914 ______ 6,35,914
3. 6,73,019 ______ 7,63,019
4. 6,54,301 ______ 6,54,321

G Arrange the following numbers in ascending order :

1. 15,324; 15,630; 298; 1,13,542
2. 31,854; 1,25,000; 1,85,000; 29,812

H Arrange the following numbers in descending order :

1. 25,192; 1,25,471; 61,832; 94,371
2. 62,917; 1,00,008; 45,132; 36,472

I Write the successor of 99,999.

J Write the smallest 4-digit number using 0, 1, 5, 7 (only once).

Mental Maths

1. Write 'six lakh, four hundred' in figures. ______________
2. Write the face-value of 6 in 2,61,908. ______________
3. Write the place-value of 2 in 7,52,693. ______________
4. Write the short form of 5,00,000 + 2,000 + 70 + 3. ______________
5. Write the predecessor of the smallest 7-digit number. ______________
6. Write the greatest 5-digit number using three different digits. ______________
7. How many 3-digit numbers are there? ______________
8. Place-value and face-value of 0 is always 0. Is it true? ______________
9. How many thousands are there in ten lakhs? ______________
10. Which is greater : 3,69,501 or 3,69,510? ______________

Fun With Maths

1. How many times does the digit 9 occur from 1 to 100?
2. David says to Peter : If you give me one marble, we will both have the same number of marbles.

   Peter says to David : If you give me one marble, I will have twice the number of marbles that you have.

   How many marbles does each one have?
3. Monu's clues about his mystery number are represented inside a box as shown below.

My number has
- 5 tens
- 8 thousands
- 2 ones
- 6 ten thousands
- 0 hundreds

What is Monu's mystery number?

(a) 58,260 (b) 62,850 (c) 68,052 (d) 86,520

4. Reena has 6 blocks with digits 6, 8, 3, 5, 2 and 9 written on them. She wants to make the numbers out of these digits.

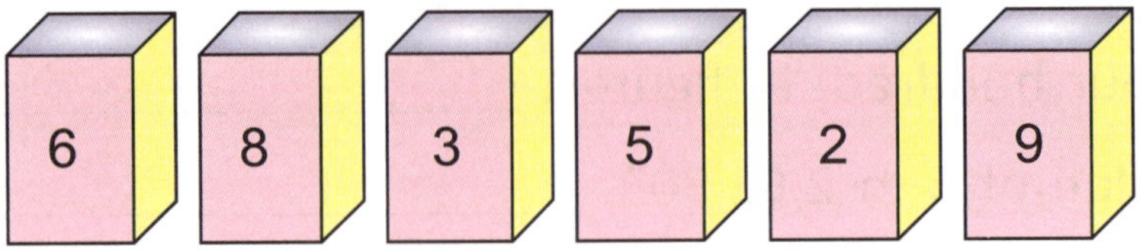

Observe the digits and answer the following questions:

(i) The smallest 6-digit number, using all digits only once is:

(a) 9,58,632 (b) 2,35,869 (c) 2,35,698 (d) 2,35,689

(ii) The place value of 8 in the greatest 6-digit number, using each digit only once is :

(a) 80 (b) 8,000 (c) 800 (d) 80,000

(iii) The predecessor of 9,87,500 is :

(a) 9,87,499 (b) 7,89,499 (c) 9,87,501 (d) 9,87,549

(iv) Which of the following is equivalent to "five lakh one thousand and nine"?

(a) 50109 (b) 501009 (c) 500109 (d) 510090

To get worksheet on this chapter scan this QR code

CODE-Sa8w

Maths Lab Activity

Objective : Understanding place values of digits in 5-digit and 6-digit numbers using paper strips.

Materials Required : Paper strips of dimensions 18 cm × 3 cm (approx.)

Procedure/Demonstration :

1. Take a paper strip and fold it into 6 equal parts as shown.

2. Write 2,00,000 in the first box from left of the strip.

2,00,000					

3. In the next box write 60,000.

2,00,000	60,000				

4. Similarly, in the next boxes, write 4,000; 700, 30 and 9 respectively.

2,00,000	60,000	4,000	700	30	9

5. Now carefully fold the strip as shown below.

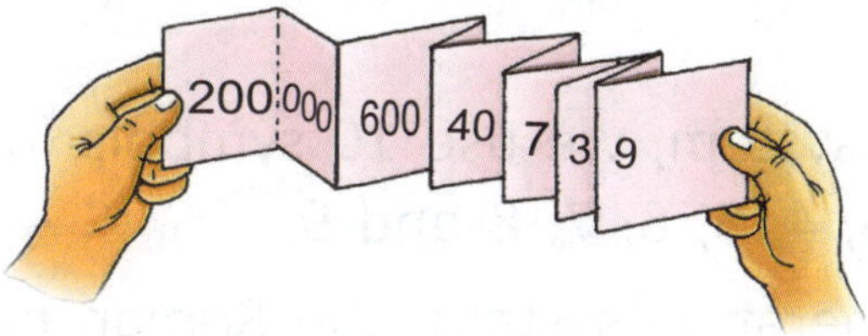

In this way, the folded strip represents the number 264739.

6. If we unfold it, it represents the place value of each digit.

2,00,000	60,000	4,000	700	30	9

7. In the same way we can form other numbers and get the place values of its digits.

Roman Numerals

Learning Target

To know about Roman Numeration system.

I Can

- **I can tell** about rules of Roman Numeration system.
- **I can compare** numbers written in Hindu-Arabic system and Roman Numeration system
- **I can convert** Hindu-Arabic Numerals to Roman Numerals and Vice-Versa.

Explore and Learn

CODE-BS3a

Introduction

In Hindu-Arabic numeration system, we use 10 symbols (digits) to write any number. These symbols are 0, 1, 2, 3, 4, 5, 6, 7, 8 and 9.

Unlike the Hindu-Arabic numeration system, the Roman numeration system uses only seven symbols to write any number.

These symbols are I, V, X, L, C, D and M.

The values of these symbols are given below :

Roman Numerals	I	V	X	L	C	D	M
Hindu-Arabic Numerals	1	5	10	50	100	500	1000

There is no zero in the Roman system. An important difference between the Hindu-Arabic system and the Roman system is that Roman system does not use place value.

Following rules are used to write Roman numerals.

Rule 1. Repetition of a Roman numeral means addition.

For example, III = 1 + 1 + 1 = 3

XX = 10 + 10 = 20

Rule 2. If a smaller Roman numeral is written to the right of a greater Roman numeral, the smaller is always added to the greater one.

For example, VII = 5 + 1 + 1 = 7

XI = 10 + 1 = 11

XXI = 10 + 10 + 1 = 21

XV = 10 + 5 = 15

REMEMBER

In Roman numeration system,
(a) repetition of a symbol is not allowed more than three times.
(b) the symbol V cannot be repeated.
(c) the symbol V is never subtracted.

Rule 3. If a smaller Roman numeral is written to the left of a greater Roman numeral, the smaller is always subtracted from the greater one.

For example, IV = 5 − 1 = 4

IX = 10 − 1 = 9

Given below is the chart showing Hindu-Arabic numerals (up to 40) and corresponding Roman numerals.

Hindu-Arabic numerals	Roman numerals	Hindu-Arabic numerals	Roman numerals	Hindu-Arabic numerals	Roman numerals	Hindu-Arabic numerals	Roman numerals
1	I	11	XI	21	XXI	31	XXXI
2	II	12	XII	22	XXII	32	XXXII
3	III	13	XIII	23	XXIII	33	XXXIII
4	IV	14	XIV	24	XXIV	34	XXXIV
5	V	15	XV	25	XXV	35	XXXV
6	VI	16	XVI	26	XXVI	36	XXXVI
7	VII	17	XVII	27	XXVII	37	XXXVII
8	VIII	18	XVIII	28	XXVIII	38	XXXVIII
9	IX	19	XIX	29	XXIX	39	XXXIX
10	X	20	XX	30	XXX	40	XL

Example 1 : Write the Hindu-Arabic numerals for the following :

(a) XXI (b) IX (c) XXVI

(d) XIII (e) XXXIX

Solution : (a) XXI = 10 + 10 + 1 = 21

(b) IX = 10 − 1 = 9

(c) XXVI = 10 + 10 + 5 + 1 = 26

(d) XIII = 10 + 1 + 1 + 1 = 13

(e) XXXIX = 10 + 10 + 10 + 10 − 1 = 39

CHALLENGE

If you take away one from nineteen, you will get twenty. How?

Example 2 : Write each of the following in Roman numerals :

(a) 8 (b) 14 (c) 25 (d) 31 (e) 37

Solution : (a) 8 = VIII

(b) 14 = 10 + 4 = XIV

(c) 25 = 10 + 10 + 5 = XXV

(d) 31 = 10 + 10 + 10 + 1 = XXXI

(e) 37 = 10 + 10 + 10 + 5 + 1 + 1 = XXXVII

Exercise 2

Apply and Learn

A Write the Hindu-Arabic numerals for each of the following :

1. IV	**2.** IX	**3.** XV	**4.** XVI	**5.** XX
6. XXVII	**7.** XIX	**8.** XIV	**9.** XXXIV	**10.** XXXVIII
11. XXXIX	**12.** XXV	**13.** XXX	**14.** XXIV	**15.** VII

B Write each of the following in Roman numerals :

1. 21	**2.** 14	**3.** 23	**4.** 37	**5.** 27
6. 29	**7.** 36	**8.** 35	**9.** 19	**10.** 33
11. 38	**12.** 26	**13.** 16	**14.** 18	**15.** 15

C Fill in the blanks using <, = or > :

1. XVI ____ 14	**2.** XVIII ____ 18	**3.** XXIV ____ 26
4. XI ____ 9	**5.** XXXIX ____ 39	**6.** XIX ____ 21

D Which of the following are meaningless :

1. XIIII **2.** XIX **3.** XVV **4.** XXV **5.** VX

E Match the numerals of two columns which indicate the same number:

1. 11	(a) XXXIV
2. 23	(b) XXIII
3. 15	(c) III
4. 34	(d) XI
5. 3	(e) XXVII
6. 27	(f) XV

Mental Maths

1. Roman numeration system has no symbol for zero. Is this correct? ____________
2. Which symbol in Roman system can never be repeated? ____________
3. Which symbol in Roman system can never be subtracted? ____________
4. Which is greater : XXII or XII? ____________
5. Which is smaller 37 or XXXV? ____________
6. In all, how many symbols are used in Roman system? ____________
7. Write the Hindu-Arabic numeral for XXIX. ____________
8. XX = 10 + 10 = 20. In the same way, can we write VV = 5 + 5 = 10? ____________
9. Write the Roman numeral for 31. ____________
10. At most, how many times can a symbol be repeated in Roman system? ____________

Fun With Maths

1. What must you do to make the following statement true?

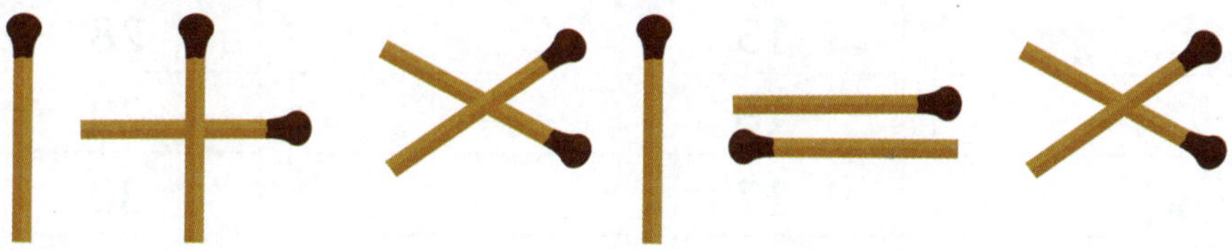

2. Here is information about Roman numerals in two statement, read them carefully. Choose the correct option.

Statement I : Repetition of a Roman numeral means addition.

Statement II : If a smaller Roman numeral is written to the right of a greater Roman numeral, the smaller numeral is always added to the greater one.

(a) Statement I is true but statement II is false

(b) Statement I is false but statement II is true

(c) Both the statements are true

(d) Both the statements are false

To get worksheet on this chapter scan this QR code

CODE-QwrC

Maths Lab Activity

Objective : To build an understanding of Roman numerals.

Materials Required : Matchsticks.

Procedure/Demonstration :

	Each numeral is made of 2 matchsticks.
	Each numeral is made of 3 matchsticks.
	Each numeral is made of 4 matchsticks.

Using matchsticks, make all the Roman numerals up to 39 and complete the following tables.

Number	Matchsticks needed	Number	Matchsticks needed	Number	Matchsticks needed
1		14		27	
2		15		28	
3		16		29	
4		17		30	
5		18		31	
6		19		32	
7		20		33	
8		21		34	
9		22		35	
10		23		36	
11		24		37	
12		25		38	
13		26		39	

Write the number which requires maximum number of matchsticks. ____________

Write the numbers which require 2 matchsticks each. ____________

Write the number between 20 and 30 which requires maximum number of matchsticks. ____________

3

THEME 1 : NUMBERS

Fractional Numbers

Learning Target

To understand fractions

I Can

- **I can explain** what a fraction is.
- **I can explain** what the numerator and denominator are in a fraction.
- **I can define** and write equivalent fractions.
- **I can convert** fractions to lowest terms.
- **I can compare** fractions.
- **I can add and subtract** like fractions.
- **I can explain** different types of fractions.

Explore and Learn

CODE-H8ms

One-Half

Observe the following :

(A) (B) (C)

In figure (B), a cake has been cut into two unequal parts. In figure (C), a cake has been cut into two equal parts.

(A) (B) (C)

In figure (B), an apple has been cut into two unequal parts. In figure (C), an apple has been cut into two equal parts.

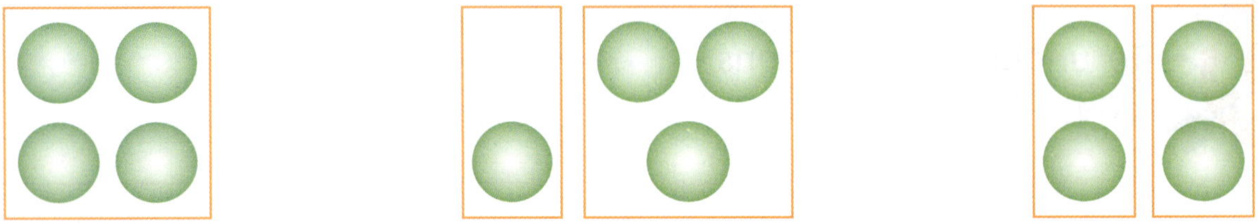

(A) (B) (C)

In figure (A), there are 4 marbles. In figure (B), the marbles are divided into two unequal parts. In figure (C), the marbles are divided into two equal parts.

When we divide one whole into two equal parts, each part is called **one-half** of the whole.

We write one-half as $\frac{1}{2}$. Two-halves make a whole.

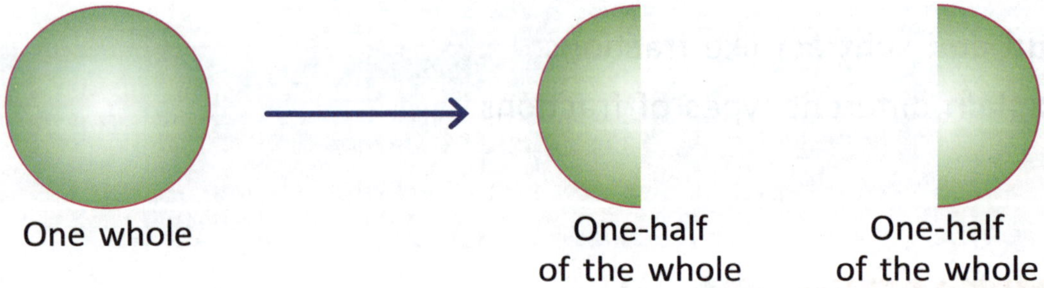

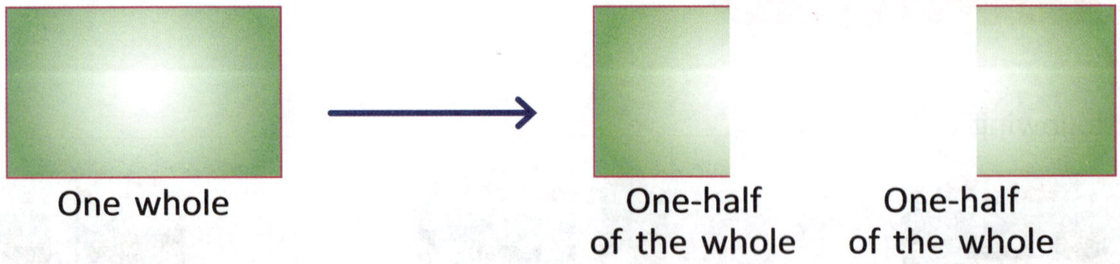

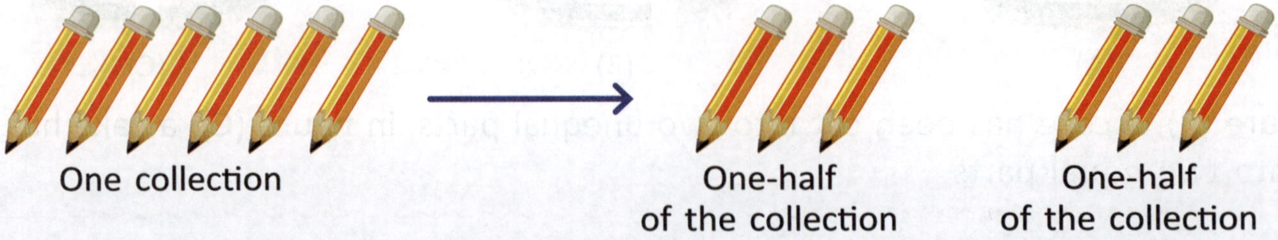

Observe the following figure in which the shaded region is one-half of the figure.

In each of the above figures, what about the unshaded part? Clearly, in each figure the unshaded part is also one-half of one whole figure.

One-Fourth or a Quarter

CODE-ZaxU

Observe the following :

(A) (B) (C)

In figure (B), a cake has been cut into four unequal parts. In figure (C), a cake has been cut into four equal parts.

(A) (B) (C)

In figure (B), a chocolate has been cut into four unequal parts. In figure (C), a chocolate has been cut into four equal parts.

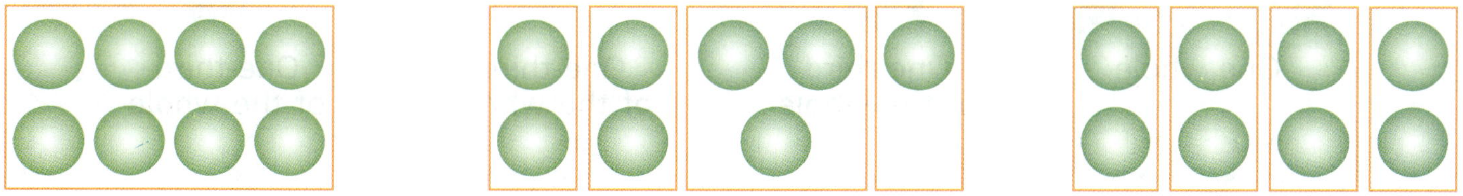

(A) (B) (C)

In figure (A), there are 8 marbles. In figure (B), the marbles are divided into four unequal parts. In figure (C), the marbles are divided into four equal parts.

When we divide one whole into four equal parts, each part is called **one-fourth** or **a quarter** of the whole.

We write one-fourth as $\frac{1}{4}$. Four-fourths make a whole.

One whole | One-fourth of the whole | One-fourth of the whole | One-fourth of the whole | One-fourth of the whole

One whole | One-fourth of the whole | One-fourth of the whole | One-fourth of the whole | One-fourth of the whole

One collection | One-fourth of the collection | One-fourth of the collection | One-fourth of the collection | One-fourth of the collection

CODE-h9bk

One-Third

When a whole is cut or divided into three equal parts, each part is called one-third of the whole.

One whole | One-third of the whole | One-third of the whole | One-third of the whole

One whole | One-third of the whole | One-third of the whole | One-third of the whole

One whole | One-third of the whole | One-third of the whole | One-third of the whole

One-third is written as $\frac{1}{3}$. Three-thirds make a whole.

Exercise 3A

Apply and Learn

A Colour one-half of each figure :

1. 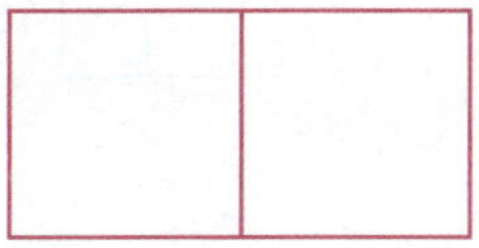	2. 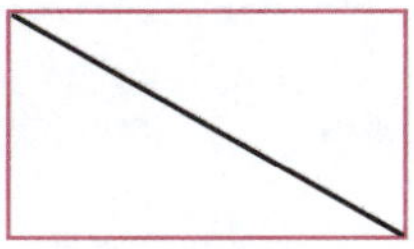	3. 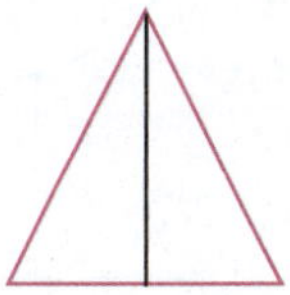	4. 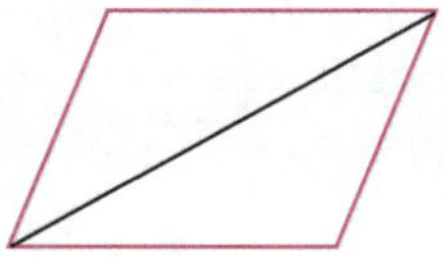
5. 	6. 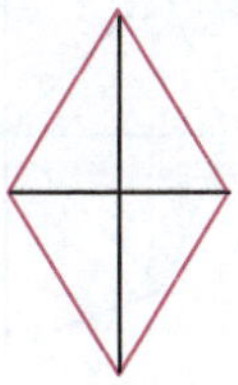	7. 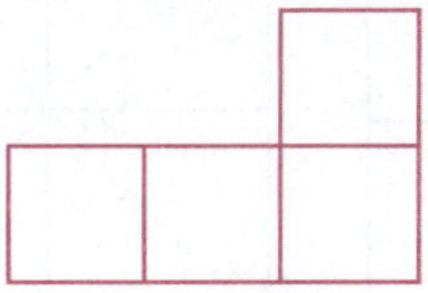	8. 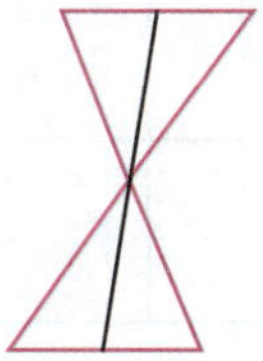

B Divide each collection into two equal parts by dotted lines :

1. 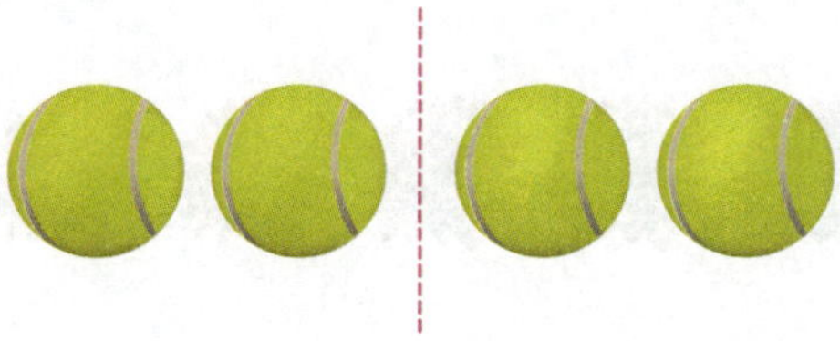	2. 
3. 	4. 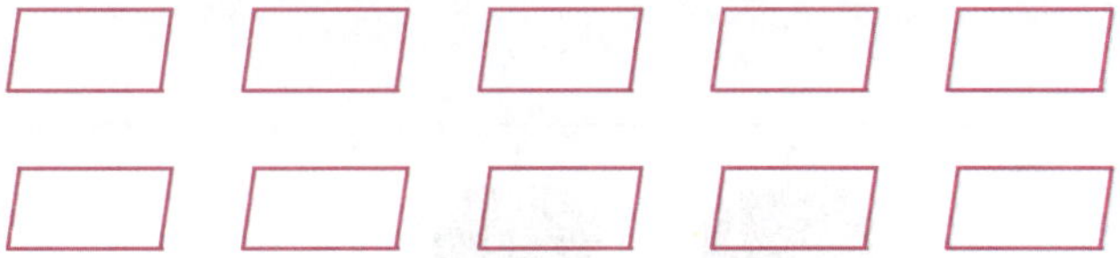
5. 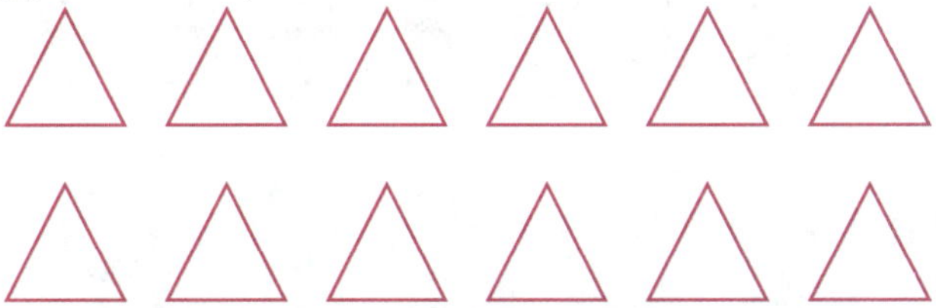	6. 
7. 	8. 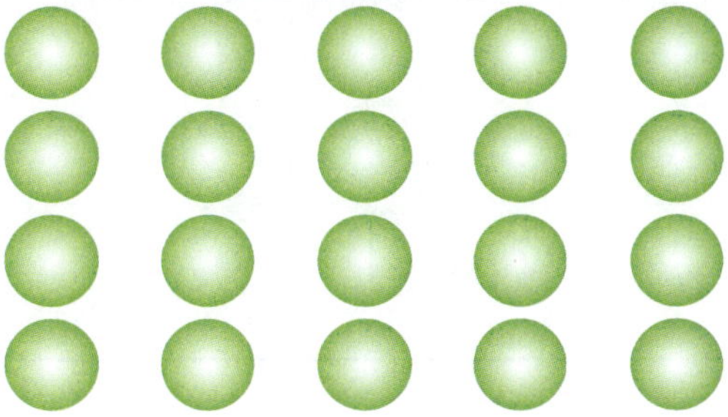

C Colour one-fourth (a quarter) of each figure :

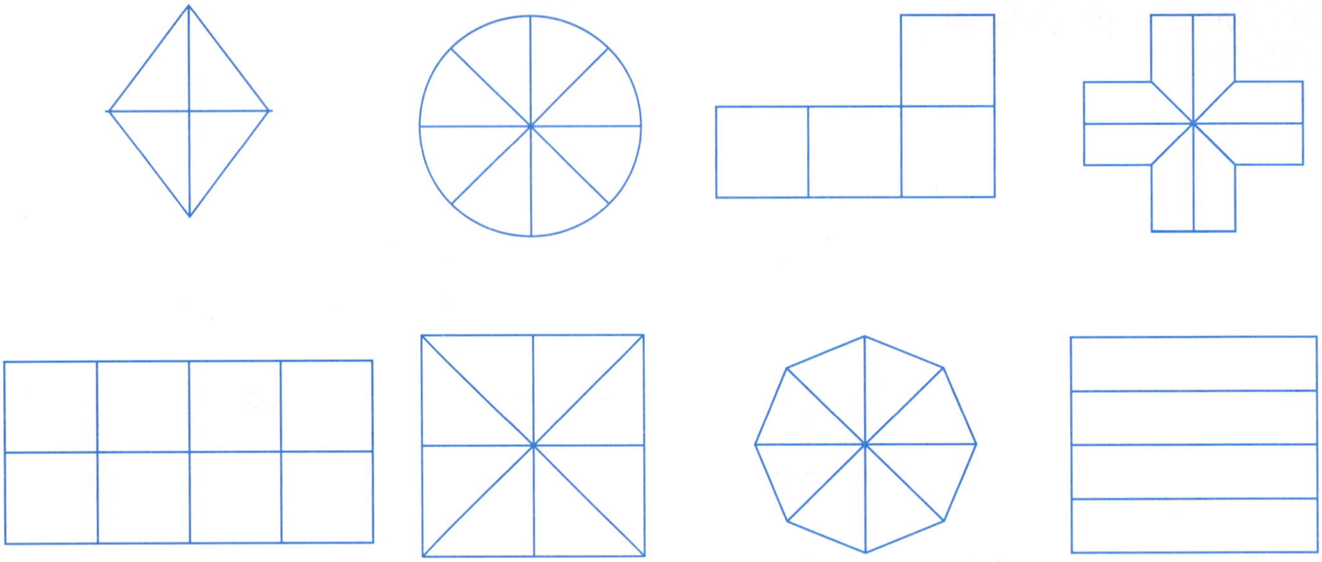

D Divide each collection into four equal parts by dotted lines :

1.
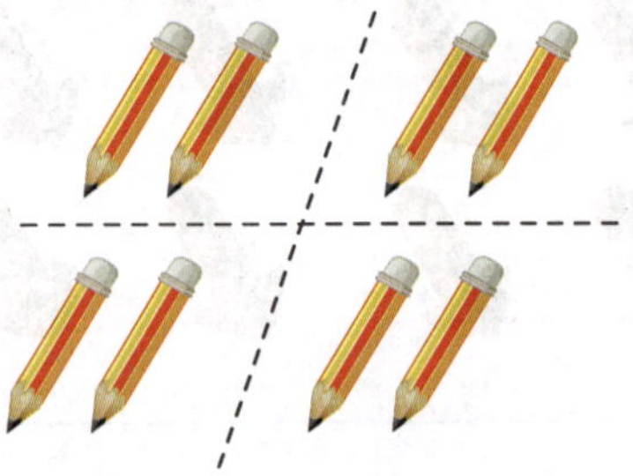

2.

3.

4.

5.
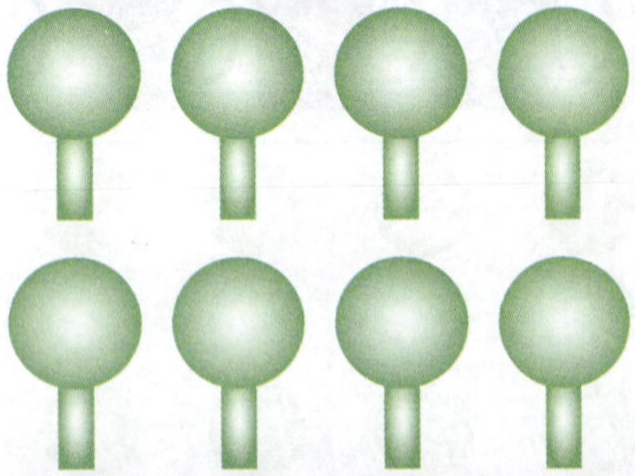

6.
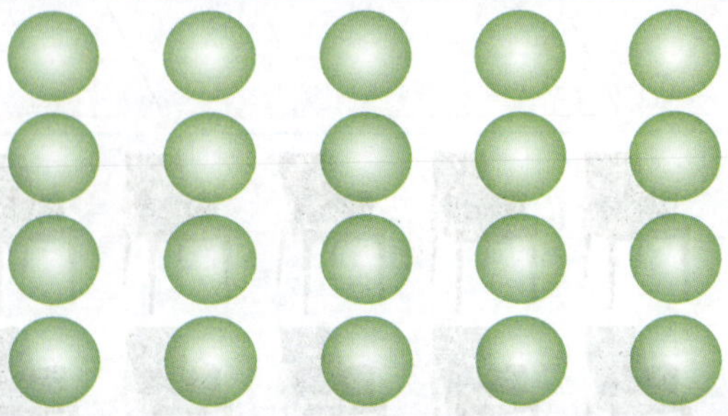

E Colour one-third of each figure :

1. 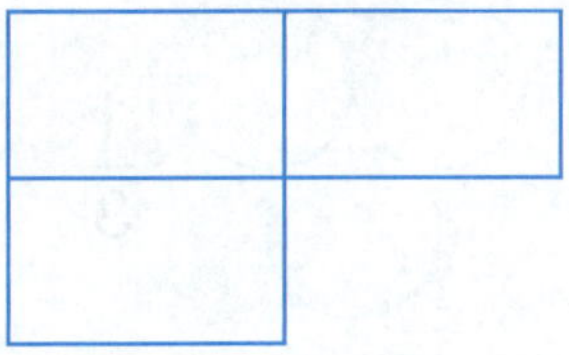

2. 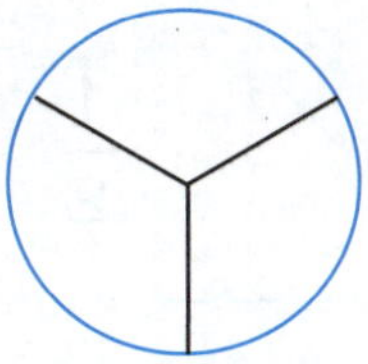

3. 

4. 

F Divide each collection into three equal parts by drawing dotted lines :

1. 

2. 

3. 

4. 

5. 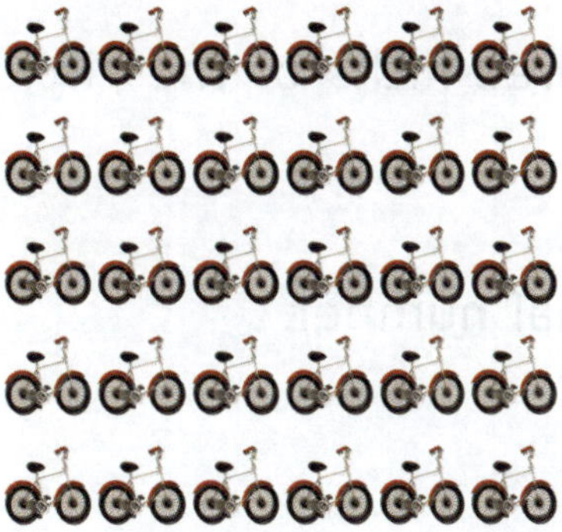

6. 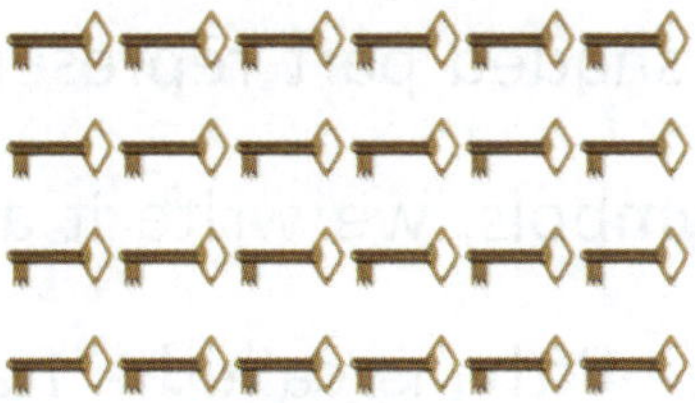

G In each of the following write the fraction representing the shaded portion:

1. 

______

2. 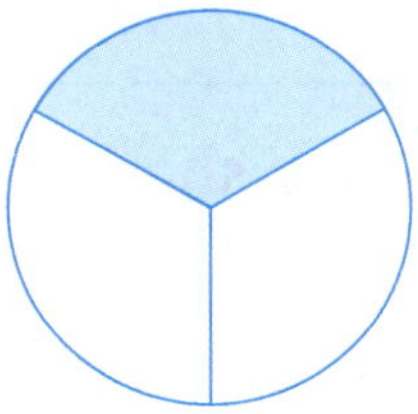

______

3. 

______

4. 

______

5. 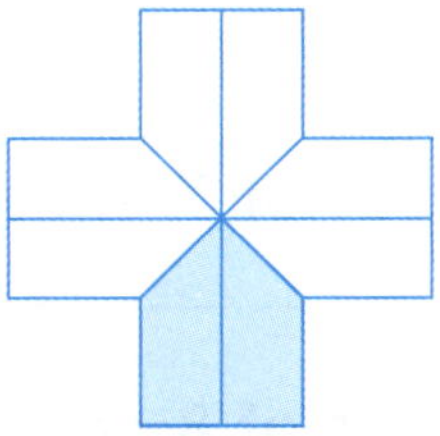

______

6. 

______

H In each of the following figures, shade as mentioned :

1.  $\frac{1}{4}$

2. 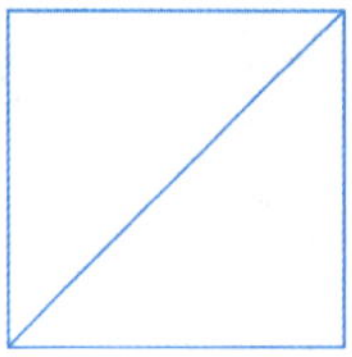 $\frac{1}{2}$

3. 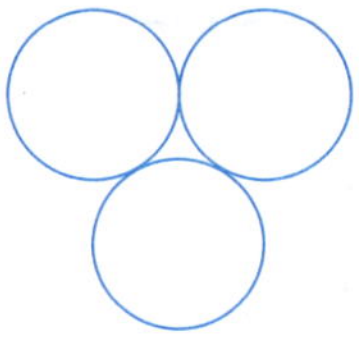 $\frac{1}{3}$

4.  $\frac{1}{3}$

5. 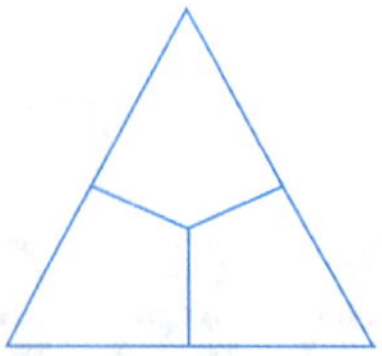 $\frac{1}{3}$

6. 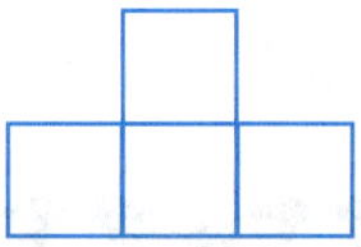 $\frac{1}{4}$

Explore and Learn

Fractional Parts

In this figure, a circle is divided into 5 equal parts and 3 parts are shaded.

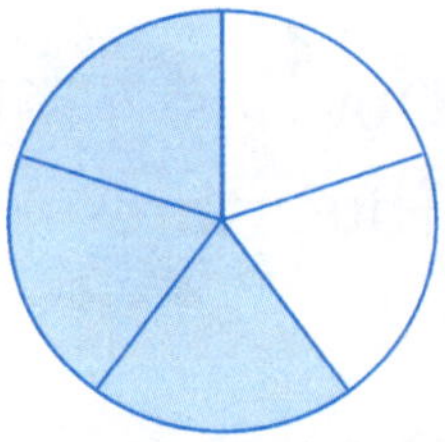

The shaded part represents three-fifths of the circle.

In symbols, we write it as $\frac{3}{5}$.

Three-fifths is called a fractional number.

$\frac{3}{5}$ is called a fraction.

The unshaded part represents two-fifths of the circle.

In symbols, we write it as $\frac{2}{5}$.

Figure	Parts shaded	Fraction	Fractional number
(a) 	2 parts out of 3 equal parts	$\frac{2}{3}$	two-thirds
(b) 	4 parts out of 5 equal parts	$\frac{4}{5}$	four-fifths
(c) 	5 parts out of 7 equal parts	$\frac{5}{7}$	five-sevenths
(d) 	6 parts out of 8 equal parts	$\frac{6}{8}$	six-eighths

Numerator and Denominator of a Fraction

A fraction is written with two numbers one over the other and separated by a line. The number above the line is called the '**numerator**' of the fraction and the number below the line is called the '**denominator**' of the fraction.

CODE-1z7A

For example, in fraction $\frac{4}{11}$, 4 is the numerator and 11 is the denominator. Also, in fraction $\frac{2}{7}$, 2 is the numerator and 7 is the denominator.

How many halves make a whole?

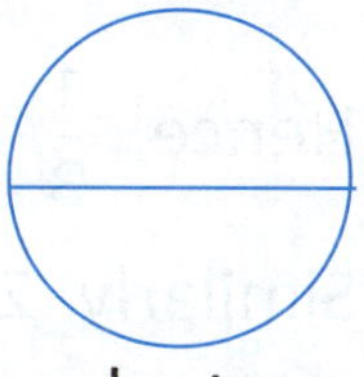

Draw a circle. Divide it into two equal parts. Each part represents $\frac{1}{2}$. Obviously, two-halves are there in a whole. Thus, two-halves make a whole.

How many thirds make a whole?

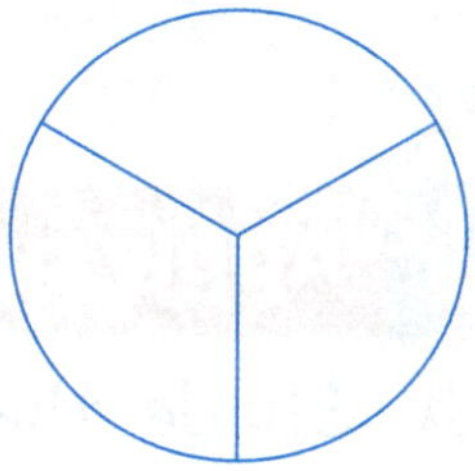

Draw a circle. Divide it into three equal parts.

Then each part represents $\frac{1}{3}$.

Obviously, three-thirds are there in a whole.

Thus, three-thirds make a whole.

How many fourths make a whole?

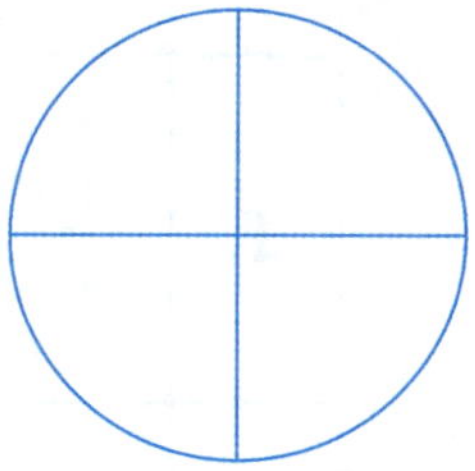

Draw a circle. Divide it into four equal parts.

Then, each part represents $\frac{1}{4}$.

Obviously, four-fourths are there in a whole.

Thus, four-fourths make a whole.

Parts of a Collection

CODE-Vmrp

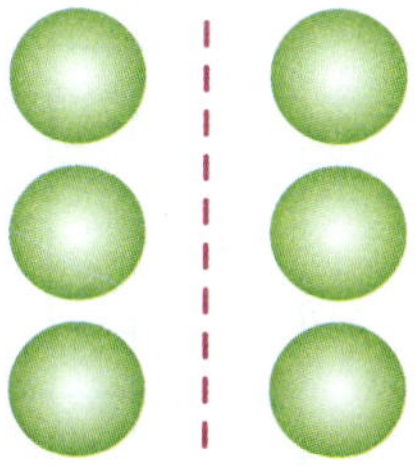

The figure alongside is a collection of 6 objects. Draw a dotted line to divide the collection into two equal parts. Each part represents $\frac{1}{2}$. Also, each part contains 3 objects.

Hence, $\frac{1}{2}$ of 6 = 3.

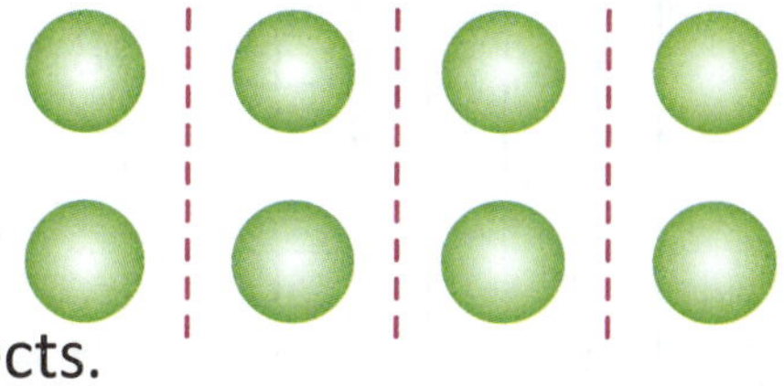

The figure alongside is a collection of 8 objects.

Draw dotted lines to divide the collection into 4 equal parts.

Then each part represents $\frac{1}{4}$. Also, each part contains 2 objects.

Hence, $\frac{1}{4}$ of 8 = 2.

The figure alongside contains 12 objects.

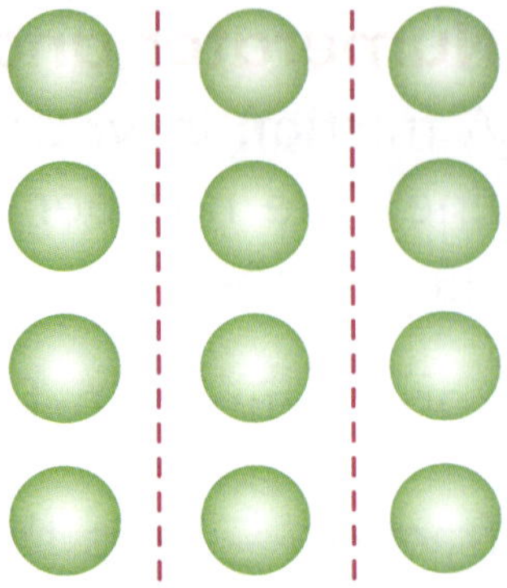

Draw dotted lines to divide the collection into 3 equal parts.

Then, each part represents $\frac{1}{3}$.

Also, each part contains 4 objects.

Hence, $\frac{1}{3}$ of 12 = 4.

Similarly, 2 parts of the collection represent $\frac{2}{3}$.

Also, 2 parts contain 8 objects.

Hence, $\frac{2}{3}$ of 12 = 8.

Exercise 3B

Apply and Learn

A Shade the figures and fill in the blanks :

	Figure	Shade	Fraction	Fractional number
1.	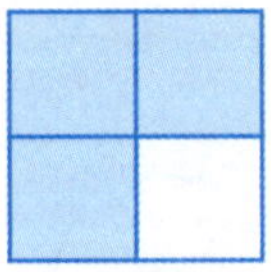	3 parts out of 4 equal parts	$\frac{3}{4}$	three-fourths
2.	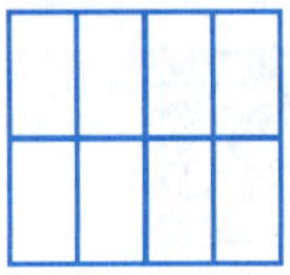	5 parts out of 8 equal parts	....	....
3.	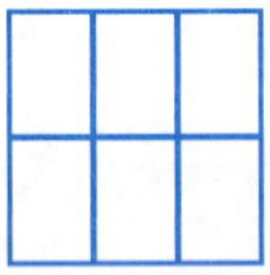	2 parts out of 6 equal parts	....	....
4.	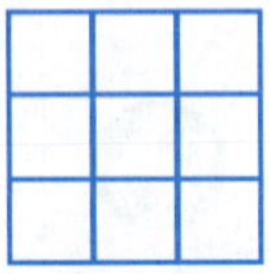	8 parts out of 9 equal parts	....	....
5.		7 parts out of 12 equal parts	....	....

B In each of the following, write the fraction and the fractional number corresponding to the unshaded part.

Figure	Fraction	Fractional number
1. 	....	....
2. 	....	....
3. 	....	....
4. 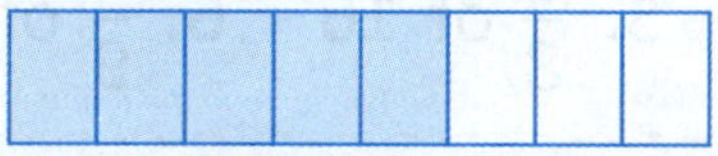	....	....
5. 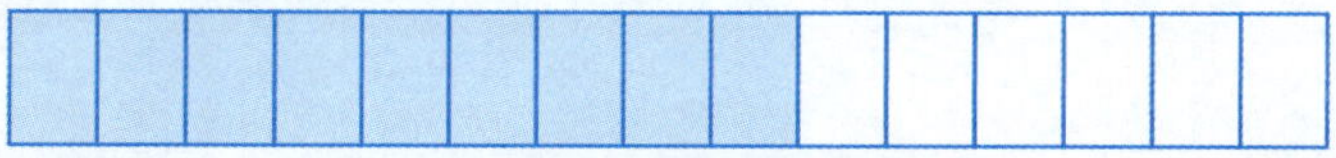	....	....

C Write the numerator and the denominator of the following fractions :

	Numerator	Denominator		Numerator	Denominator
1.	$\frac{3}{11}$ ________	________	2.	$\frac{15}{16}$ ________	________
3.	$\frac{7}{9}$ ________	________	4.	$\frac{2}{15}$ ________	________
5.	$\frac{5}{11}$ ________	________	6.	$\frac{13}{22}$ ________	________

D Write the fraction whose

1. numerator is 4 and denominator is 7. ________
2. numerator is 7 and denominator is 15. ________
3. numerator is 10 and denominator is 21. ________
4. numerator is 22 and denominator is 35. ________

E How many one-fifths are there in a whole?

F How many one-sixths are there in a whole?

G Divide each collection into suitable number of equal parts and fill in the blanks:

1.  $\frac{1}{3}$ of 6 = ...	2. 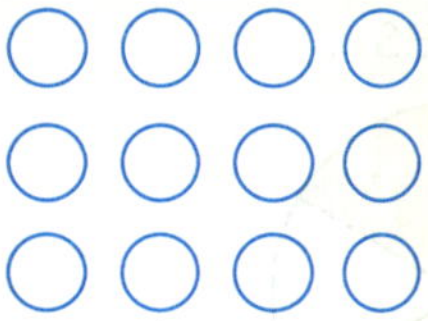 $\frac{1}{4}$ of 12 = ...	3. 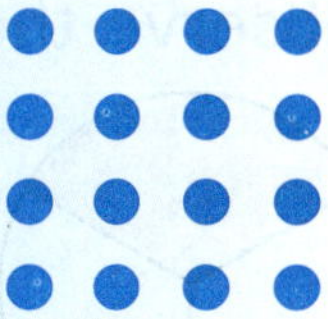 $\frac{1}{8}$ of 16 = ...

4.  $\frac{1}{5}$ of 20 = ...	**5.**  $\frac{2}{3}$ of 6 = ...	**6.** 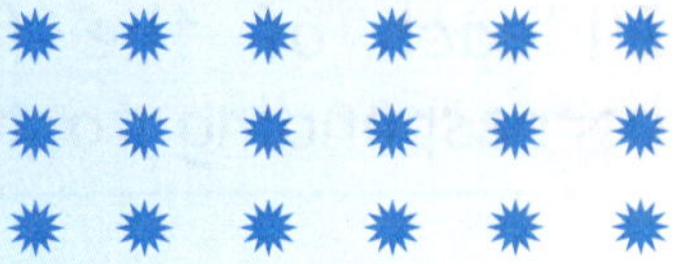 $\frac{5}{6}$ of 18 = ...

H Draw a collection of objects. Divide the collection into suitable number of equal parts and find :

1. $\frac{1}{4}$ of 16 **2.** $\frac{1}{3}$ of 9 **3.** $\frac{2}{5}$ of 15 **4.** $\frac{3}{7}$ of 14 **5.** $\frac{5}{8}$ of 16 **6.** $\frac{4}{9}$ of 18

Explore and Learn

Equivalent Fractions

CODE-n44X

Observe the following figures :

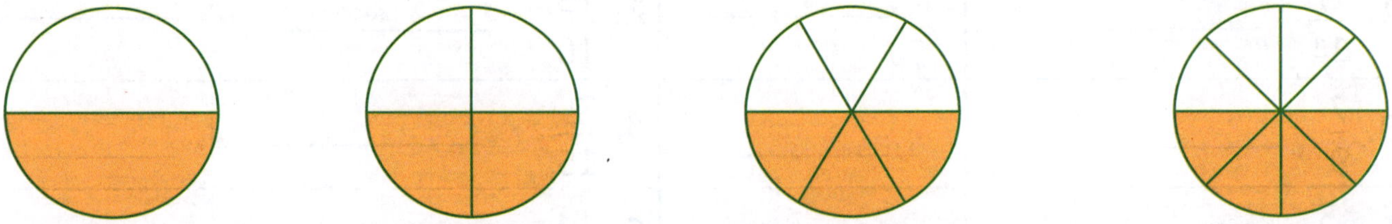

$\frac{1}{2}$ is shaded $\frac{2}{4}$ is shaded $\frac{3}{6}$ is shaded $\frac{4}{8}$ is shaded

What do we observe?

We see that the shaded regions in all the figures are the same.

So, the fractions represented by these shaded portions are equal.

Hence, $\frac{1}{2}, \frac{2}{4}, \frac{3}{6}, \frac{4}{8}$ are equivalent fractions.

Or $\frac{1}{2} = \frac{2}{4} = \frac{3}{6} = \frac{4}{8}$.

Also, $\frac{1}{2} = \frac{1\times2}{2\times2} = \frac{1\times3}{2\times3} = \frac{1\times4}{2\times4}$ and so on.

Again observe the following figures :

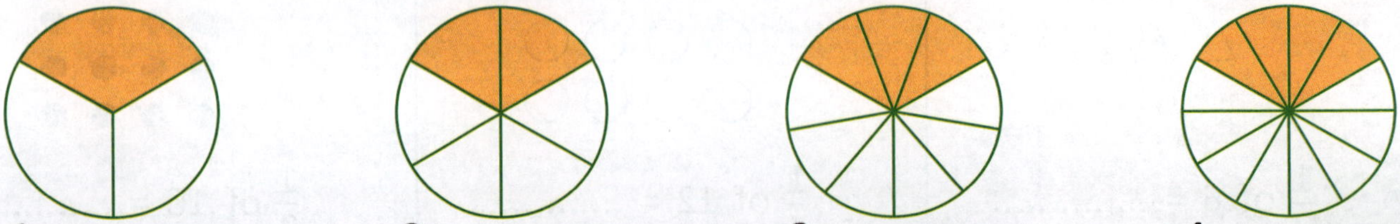

$\frac{1}{3}$ is shaded $\frac{2}{6}$ is shaded $\frac{3}{9}$ is shaded $\frac{4}{12}$ is shaded

We see that the shaded regions in all the circles are the same.
So, the fractions represented by these shaded portions are equal.

Hence, $\frac{1}{3}, \frac{2}{6}, \frac{3}{9}, \frac{4}{12}$ are equivalent fractions

Or $\frac{1}{3} = \frac{2}{6} = \frac{3}{9} = \frac{4}{12}$.

Also, $\frac{1}{3} = \frac{1\times 2}{3\times 2} = \frac{1\times 3}{3\times 3} = \frac{1\times 4}{3\times 4}$ and so on.

Similarly, we can conclude that $\frac{1}{5} = \frac{1\times 2}{5\times 2} = \frac{1\times 3}{5\times 3} = \frac{1\times 4}{5\times 4} = \frac{1\times 5}{5\times 5}$ and so on.

Or $\frac{1}{5} = \frac{2}{10} = \frac{3}{15} = \frac{4}{20} = \frac{5}{25}$.

Hence, we can say that,

When we multiply the numerator and the denominator of a fraction by the same non-zero number, we get its equivalent fraction.

Again observe the following equivalent fractions $\frac{2}{7}, \frac{4}{14}, \frac{6}{21}$

$$\frac{4}{14} = \frac{4\div 2}{14\div 2} = \frac{2}{7}, \quad \frac{6}{21} = \frac{6 \div 3}{21 \div 3} = \frac{2}{7}.$$

What do we observe?

We see that when the numerator and the denominator of a fraction are divided by the same non-zero number, we get its equivalent fraction.

Example 1 : Write next three equivalent fractions of $\frac{3}{4}$.

Solution : We have : $\frac{3\times 2}{4\times 2} = \frac{6}{8}, \quad \frac{3\times 3}{4\times 3} = \frac{9}{12}, \quad \frac{3\times 4}{4\times 4} = \frac{12}{16}$

So, $\frac{3}{4} = \frac{6}{8} = \frac{9}{12} = \frac{12}{16}$.

Hence, the equivalent fractions to $\frac{3}{4}$ are $\frac{6}{8}, \frac{9}{12}, \frac{12}{16}$.

Example 2 : Find an equivalent fraction of $\frac{2}{5}$ with numerator 8.

Solution : Let $\frac{2}{5} = \frac{8}{\ldots\ldots}$

To get 8 in the numerator, we multiply 2 by 4, and also 5 by 4.

So, $\frac{2}{5} = \frac{2 \times 4}{5 \times 4} = \frac{8}{20}$.

Hence, $\frac{2}{5}$ and $\frac{8}{20}$ are equivalent fractions.

Example 3 : Find an equivalent fraction of $\frac{3}{5}$ with denominator 15.

Solution : Let $\frac{3}{5} = \frac{\ldots\ldots}{15}$

To get 15 in the denominator, we multiply 5 by 3 and also 3 by 3.

So, $\frac{3}{5} = \frac{3 \times 3}{5 \times 3} = \frac{9}{15}$.

Hence, $\frac{3}{5}$ and $\frac{9}{15}$ are equivalent fractions.

An Important Property of Equivalent Fractions

CODE-mogk

Consider the equivalent fractions: $\frac{3}{5}$ and $\frac{12}{20}$

Now, multiplying the numerator of $\frac{3}{5}$ by the denominator of $\frac{12}{20}$, we get 3 × 20 = 60

Again, multiplying the denominator of $\frac{3}{5}$ by the numerator of $\frac{12}{20}$, we get

$$5 \times 12 = 60$$

We see that the two products are the same.

Hence, if two fractions are equivalent, the product of numerator of the first and denominator of the second is equal to the product of denominator of the first and numerator of the second.

Thus, the two fractions are equivalent if the cross products, are equal.

Numerator of first × Denominator of second = Denominator of first × Numerator of second.

Example 4 : Are $\frac{2}{3}$ and $\frac{10}{15}$ equivalent fractions?

Solution : $\frac{2}{3} \times \frac{10}{15}$

REMEMBER

The method used here is called cross-multiplication method.

$2 \times 15 = 30$, $3 \times 10 = 30$

Both the products are equal.

Hence, $\frac{2}{3}$ and $\frac{10}{15}$ are equivalent fractions.

Example 5 : Are $\frac{4}{5}$ and $\frac{16}{18}$ equivalent fractions?

Solution : $\frac{4}{5} \times \frac{16}{18}$

Here, $4 \times 18 = 72$, $5 \times 16 = 80$

Products are not the same.

Hence, $\frac{4}{5}$ and $\frac{16}{18}$ are not equivalent fractions.

Exercise 3C

Apply and Learn

A Write the next three equivalent fractions of each of the following :

1. $\frac{4}{5}$ 2. $\frac{1}{4}$ 3. $\frac{2}{3}$ 4. $\frac{5}{9}$ 5. $\frac{4}{10}$

B Fill in the missing numerators to make the statement true :

1. $\frac{3}{4} = \frac{\square}{20}$ 2. $\frac{4}{7} = \frac{\square}{14}$ 3. $\frac{\square}{9} = \frac{30}{54}$ 4. $\frac{\square}{8} = \frac{27}{72}$

C Fill in the missing denominators to make the statement true :

1. $\frac{8}{11} = \frac{16}{\square}$ 2. $\frac{3}{5} = \frac{24}{\square}$ 3. $\frac{2}{7} = \frac{6}{\square}$ 4. $\frac{4}{\square} = \frac{28}{63}$

D Find an equivalent fraction of $\frac{3}{4}$ with :

1. numerator 21 2. numerator 15 3. denominator 16
4. denominator 24 5. numerator 30 6. denominator 48

E Check whether the given fractions are equivalent :

1. $\frac{3}{15}, \frac{1}{5}$ 2. $\frac{7}{21}, \frac{2}{3}$ 3. $\frac{4}{9}, \frac{8}{18}$
4. $\frac{1}{5}, \frac{4}{19}$ 5. $\frac{2}{11}, \frac{6}{21}$ 6. $\frac{7}{14}, \frac{3}{6}$

Explore and Learn

CODE-btmL

Fractions in Lowest Terms

A fraction is said to be in its lowest terms (simplest form) when its numerator and denominator do not have any common factor except 1.

Observe the following :

Fraction	*Factors of the numerator	Factors of the denominator	Common factors	Whether the fraction is in its lowest terms or not?
$\frac{4}{10}$	**1**, **2**, 4	**1**, **2**, 5, 10	1, 2	No
$\frac{3}{12}$	**1**, **3**	**1**, 2, **3**, 4, 6, 12	1, 3	No
$\frac{5}{9}$	**1**, 5	**1**, 3, 9	1	Yes

To reduce a fraction to its lowest terms, we divide the numerator and the denominator by their common factors till only 1 is left as the common factor.

Example 1 : Express each of the following fractions to its lowest terms :

(a) $\frac{12}{18}$ (b) $\frac{30}{70}$

Solution : (a) We have, $12 = \boxed{2} \times 2 \times \boxed{3}$

$18 = \boxed{2} \times 3 \times \boxed{3}$

So, we can divide the numerator and the denominator by $2 \times 3 = 6$.

So, $\frac{12 \div 6}{18 \div 6} = \frac{2}{3}$.

Thus, the simplest form of $\frac{12}{18}$ is $\frac{2}{3}$.

(b) We have, $30 = 2 \times 3 \times \boxed{5}$

$70 = 2 \times \boxed{5} \times 7$

So, we can divide the numerator and the denominator by $2 \times 5 = 10$.

So, $\frac{30 \div 10}{70 \div 10} = \frac{3}{7}$. Thus, the simplest form of $\frac{30}{70}$ is $\frac{3}{7}$.

Example 2 : Reduce $\frac{60}{72}$ to its lowest terms.

Solution : We can divide the numerator and the denominator step by step, by their common factors.

*The topic "Factors of a Number" will be dealt in Chapter 8.

So, $\frac{60}{72} = \frac{60 \div 2}{72 \div 2} = \frac{30}{36} = \frac{30 \div 2}{36 \div 2} = \frac{15}{18} = \frac{15 \div 3}{18 \div 3} = \frac{5}{6}$.

Thus, $\frac{5}{6}$ is in its lowest terms.

Exercise 3D

Apply and Learn

A State whether the fraction is in its lowest terms or not :

1. $\frac{12}{20}$ **2.** $\frac{7}{8}$ **3.** $\frac{20}{29}$ **4.** $\frac{4}{6}$ **5.** $\frac{6}{7}$ **6.** $\frac{38}{57}$ **7.** $\frac{70}{95}$ **8.** $\frac{80}{81}$

B Encircle the fraction which is in its lowest terms :

1. $\frac{4}{5}, \frac{12}{15}, \frac{40}{50}, \frac{16}{20}$ **2.** $\frac{15}{36}, \frac{7}{56}, \frac{4}{57}, \frac{32}{36}$ **3.** $\frac{9}{42}, \frac{12}{56}, \frac{8}{45}, \frac{27}{135}$

C Reduce to the lowest terms :

1. $\frac{10}{20}$ **2.** $\frac{21}{28}$ **3.** $\frac{30}{42}$ **4.** $\frac{45}{60}$ **5.** $\frac{36}{48}$ **6.** $\frac{36}{54}$

Explore and Learn

Comparison of Fractions

CODE-7ZHL

1. Comparison of fractions with the same denominator

Observe the following figures.

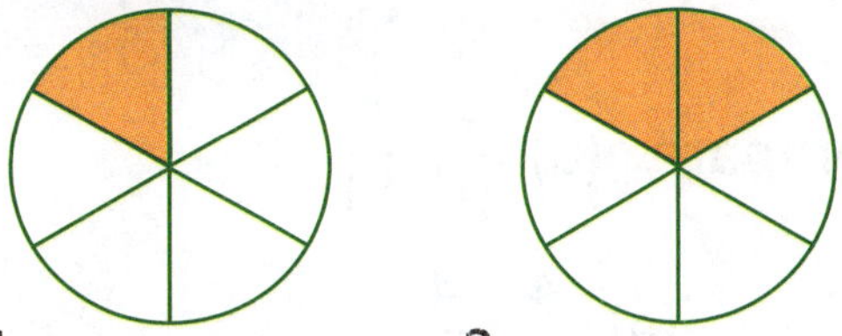

$\frac{1}{6}$ is shaded $\frac{2}{6}$ is shaded

In the first figure, 1 part out of 6 equal parts is shaded. In the second figure, 2 parts out of 6 equal parts are shaded. Clearly, shaded parts in the second circle are more than that in first circle.

Thus, $\frac{2}{6} > \frac{1}{6}$ or $\frac{1}{6} < \frac{2}{6}$.

Hence, among two fractions having the same denominator, the fraction with greater numerator is greater than the other.

Example 1 : Compare : (a) $\frac{2}{5}$ and $\frac{3}{5}$ (b) $\frac{7}{15}$ and $\frac{4}{15}$

Solution : We have :

(a) Consider $\frac{2}{5}, \frac{3}{5}$.

Since, 3 > 2, hence $\frac{3}{5} > \frac{2}{5}$ or $\frac{2}{5} < \frac{3}{5}$.

(b) Consider $\frac{7}{15}, \frac{4}{15}$.

Since, 7 > 4, hence $\frac{7}{15} > \frac{4}{15}$ or $\frac{4}{15} < \frac{7}{15}$.

2. Comparison of fractions with the same numerator

Take two strips of the same length.

 $\frac{3}{5}$ is shaded

 $\frac{3}{7}$ is shaded

First strip is divided into 5 equal parts and the second is divided into 7 equal parts. In first strip, out of 5 equal parts 3 parts are shaded and in second strip, out of 7 equal parts, 3 parts are shaded. Clearly, the shaded part in the first strip is more than that in the second strip.

Thus, $\frac{3}{5} > \frac{3}{7}$.

Hence, among two fractions having the same numerator, the fraction with smaller denominator is greater than the other.

Example 2 : Compare (a) $\frac{4}{9}, \frac{4}{11}$ (b) $\frac{11}{14}, \frac{11}{13}$

Solution :

(a) $\frac{4}{9}, \frac{4}{11}$

Since 9 < 11.

Hence $\frac{4}{9} > \frac{4}{11}$.

(b) $\frac{11}{14}, \frac{11}{13}$

Since 14 > 13

Hence $\frac{11}{14} < \frac{11}{13}$.

Comparison of Fractions with Unlike Numerators and Unlike Denominators

CODE-c1sx

To compare two fractions having unlike numerators and unlike denominators, we first convert them into the fractions having like (same) denominator. This can be done by multiplying the numerator and the denominator of each fraction by a suitable number. Then we compare the fractions as usual.

Example 3 : Compare $\frac{1}{5}$ and $\frac{3}{4}$.

Solution : $\frac{1}{5} = \frac{1 \times 4}{5 \times 4}$ [Multiplying the numerator and the denominator by 4]

$= \frac{4}{20}$

$\frac{3}{4} = \frac{3 \times 5}{4 \times 5}$ [Multiplying the numerator and the denominator by 5]

$= \frac{15}{20}$

Clearly, $\frac{4}{20} < \frac{15}{20}$ (Since 4 < 15).

Hence, $\frac{1}{5} < \frac{3}{4}$.

Another method : Two fractions can be compared by using the method of cross multiplication.

Example 4 : Compare (a) $\frac{3}{11}$ and $\frac{5}{7}$ (b) $\frac{4}{15}$ and $\frac{2}{13}$.

Solution : (a) Given fractions are $\frac{3}{11}$ and $\frac{5}{7}$.

$\frac{3}{11} \times \frac{5}{7}$ (Cross multiply)

Now 3 × 7 = 21 and 11 × 5 = 55.

Since 21 < 55, hence $\frac{3}{11} < \frac{5}{7}$.

(b) Given fractions are $\frac{4}{15}$ and $\frac{2}{13}$

$\frac{4}{15} \times \frac{2}{13}$ (Cross multiply)

Now 4 × 13 = 52 and 15 × 2 = 30.

Since, 52 > 30, hence, $\frac{4}{15} > \frac{2}{13}$.

CHALLENGE

Insert > or < in the blanks :

If $\frac{1}{2}$ ... $\frac{1}{3}$ and $\frac{1}{3}$ ... $\frac{1}{4}$,

then $\frac{1}{2}$ ... $\frac{1}{4}$.

Exercise 3E

Apply and Learn

A Fill in the blanks by putting > or < in each of the following to make the statement true :

1. $\frac{5}{11}$ ... $\frac{7}{11}$
2. $\frac{14}{15}$ ... $\frac{14}{17}$
3. $\frac{5}{8}$ ... $\frac{5}{16}$
4. $\frac{3}{20}$ ... $\frac{7}{20}$
5. $\frac{21}{22}$ ... $\frac{19}{22}$
6. $\frac{10}{21}$ ... $\frac{10}{13}$

B Which is greater in each of the following pairs of fractions?

1. $\frac{5}{7}, \frac{3}{5}$
2. $\frac{1}{8}, \frac{3}{7}$
3. $\frac{8}{14}, \frac{5}{21}$
4. $\frac{7}{15}, \frac{9}{10}$

C Which is smaller in each of the following pairs of fractions?

1. $\frac{5}{12}, \frac{3}{10}$
2. $\frac{3}{16}, \frac{21}{32}$
3. $\frac{18}{25}, \frac{2}{5}$
4. $\frac{2}{9}, \frac{1}{7}$

D Fill in the blanks by putting >, < or = in each of the following to make the statement true.

1. $\frac{2}{5}$ ... $\frac{4}{7}$
2. $\frac{6}{11}$ ... $\frac{6}{13}$
3. $\frac{11}{12}$ ... $\frac{5}{12}$

Explore and Learn

Addition of Fractions with the Same (Like) Denominator

CODE-vKtn

Observe the following figures :

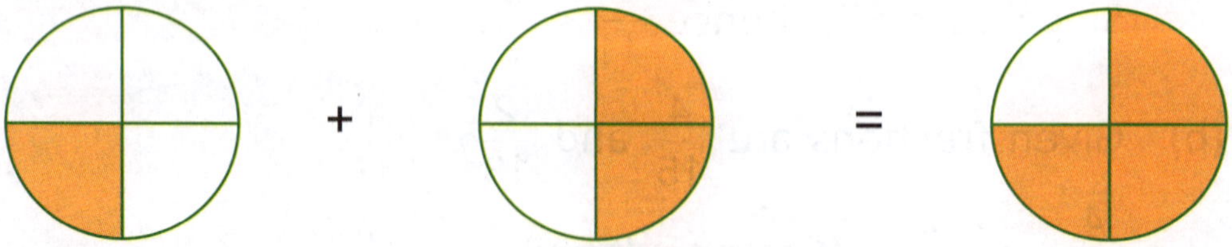

$\frac{1}{4}$ is shaded + $\frac{2}{4}$ is shaded = $\frac{3}{4}$ is shaded

What do we observe?

In the first figure, $\frac{1}{4}$ of the circle is shaded and in the second figure $\frac{2}{4}$ of the circle is shaded.

In all, we have $\frac{3}{4}$ of the circle is shaded.

Hence, $\frac{1}{4}+\frac{2}{4}=\frac{1+2}{4}=\frac{3}{4}$.

Thus, to add the fractions with the same denominator, we simply add their numerators and write the common denominator.

Sum of the fractions with like denominators $= \frac{\text{Sum of the numerators}}{\text{Common denominator}}$.

Example 1 : Find the sum of $\frac{4}{7}$ and $\frac{1}{7}$.

Solution : We have : $\frac{4}{7}+\frac{1}{7}=\frac{4+1}{7}=\frac{5}{7}$.

Example 2 : Find the sum of $\frac{3}{11}$, $\frac{4}{11}$ and $\frac{1}{11}$.

Solution : We have : $\frac{3}{11}+\frac{4}{11}+\frac{1}{11}=\frac{3+4+1}{11}=\frac{8}{11}$.

Exercise 3F

Apply and Learn

A Using the figures, fill in the blanks :

1. 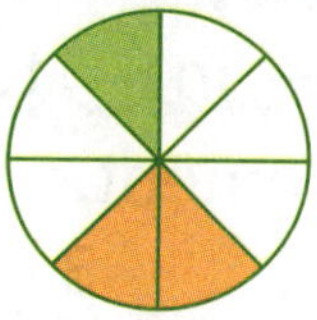 $\frac{1}{8} + \frac{2}{8} = \frac{\square + \square}{8} = \frac{\square}{8}$

2. 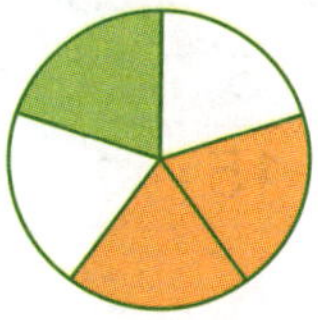 $\frac{1}{5} + \frac{2}{5} = \frac{\square + \square}{5} = \frac{\square}{5}$

3. 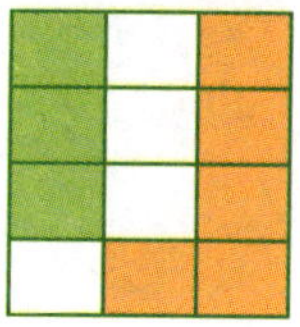 $\frac{3}{12} + \frac{5}{12} = \frac{\square + \square}{12} = \frac{\square}{12}$

4. 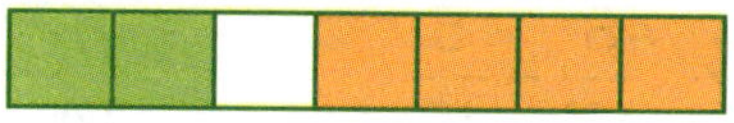 $\frac{2}{7} + \frac{4}{7} = \frac{\square + \square}{7} = \frac{\square}{7}$

5.  $\frac{1}{8}+\frac{2}{8}+\frac{2}{8}=\frac{\square+\square+\square}{8}=\frac{\square}{8}$

6. 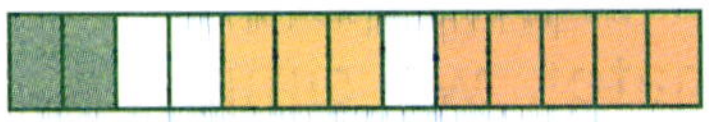 $\frac{2}{13}+\frac{3}{13}+\frac{5}{13}=\frac{\square+\square+\square}{13}=\frac{\square}{13}$

B Find the sum :

1. $\frac{1}{4}+\frac{2}{4}$
2. $\frac{4}{15}+\frac{6}{15}$
3. $\frac{13}{19}+\frac{2}{19}$
4. $\frac{5}{14}+\frac{6}{14}$
5. $\frac{1}{8}+\frac{3}{8}+\frac{2}{8}$
6. $\frac{7}{15}+\frac{2}{15}+\frac{4}{15}$
7. $\frac{7}{24}+\frac{5}{24}+\frac{6}{24}$
8. $\frac{9}{35}+\frac{2}{35}+\frac{11}{35}$

Explore and Learn

Subtraction of Fractions with the Same (Like) Denominator

CODE-XoL5

To subtract fractions with like denominator, we subtract smaller numerator from greater to obtain the numerator of the required fraction. The denominator of the required fraction is the common denominator of the given fractions.

Difference of two fractions with same (like) denominators $=\frac{\text{Difference of the numerators}}{\text{Common denominator}}$.

Example 1 : Subtract $\frac{2}{8}$ from $\frac{7}{8}$.

Solution : We have : $\frac{7}{8}-\frac{2}{8}=\frac{7-2}{8}=\frac{5}{8}$.

Example 2 : Subtract $\frac{4}{11}$ from $\frac{7}{11}$.

Solution : We have : $\frac{7}{11}-\frac{4}{11}=\frac{7-4}{11}=\frac{3}{11}$.

CHALLENGE

Write + or – in ◯ to make a true statement.

(a) $\frac{5}{8}$ ◯ $\frac{2}{8}$ ◯ $\frac{3}{8}=\frac{3}{4}$

(b) $\frac{9}{15}$ ◯ $\frac{5}{15}$ ◯ $\frac{4}{15}=\frac{2}{3}$

Exercise 3G

Apply and Learn

A Subtract :

1. $\frac{9}{13}-\frac{5}{13}$
2. $\frac{5}{17}-\frac{3}{17}$
3. $\frac{9}{22}-\frac{5}{22}$
4. $\frac{7}{12}-\frac{5}{12}$
5. $\frac{8}{17}-\frac{5}{17}$
6. $\frac{9}{14}-\frac{5}{14}$

B Fill in the blanks :

1. $\frac{8}{11} - \frac{6}{\square} = \frac{2}{11}$ 2. $\frac{12}{13} - \frac{\square}{13} = \frac{5}{13}$ 3. $\frac{5}{7} - \frac{\square}{7} = \frac{1}{7}$

4. $\frac{8}{21} - \frac{3}{\square} = \frac{5}{21}$ 5. $\frac{\square}{15} - \frac{3}{15} = \frac{4}{15}$ 6. $\frac{9}{16} - \frac{7}{\square} = \frac{2}{16}$

Explore and Learn

Types of Fractions

CODE-w1Bv

Like Fractions

Fractions with the same denominator are called like fractions.

For example, $\frac{1}{8}, \frac{2}{8}, \frac{3}{8}, \frac{5}{8}$ and $\frac{7}{8}$ are like fractions.

Unlike Fractions

Fractions with different denominators are called unlike fractions.

For example, $\frac{5}{7}, \frac{2}{9}, \frac{4}{11}, \frac{2}{5}$ and $\frac{1}{4}$ are unlike fractions.

Unit Fractions

Fractions having 1 as numerator are called unit fractions.

For example, $\frac{1}{7}, \frac{1}{8}, \frac{1}{11}, \frac{1}{15}$ and $\frac{1}{25}$ are unit fractions.

Proper and Improper Fractions

CODE-hSjk

Observe the following sets of fractions

$\frac{5}{11}, \frac{3}{7}, \frac{1}{9}, \frac{6}{13}, \frac{11}{15}$ ...(A) $\frac{11}{8}, \frac{7}{5}, \frac{23}{11}, \frac{15}{13}, \frac{14}{14}$ ...(B)

In what respect, are the two sets different?

In the first set, the numerator of each fraction is less than the denominator.

We call such type of fractions as **proper fractions**.

In the second set, the numerator of each fraction is either greater than or equal to the denominator. We call such type of fractions as **improper fractions**.

Clearly, a fraction whose numerator is less than the denominator is called a proper fraction and a fraction whose numerator is greater than or equal to the denominator is called an improper fraction.

Mixed Number (or Mixed Fraction)

Here a circle is divided into 4 equal parts. All the 4 parts are shaded. Thus, the shaded part represents $\frac{4}{4}$ or a whole or 1.

What do we get if we add a quarter more to $\frac{4}{4}$?

We get $\frac{4}{4} + \frac{1}{4} = \frac{4+1}{4} = \frac{5}{4}$. We also have $1 + \frac{1}{4} = \frac{5}{4}$.

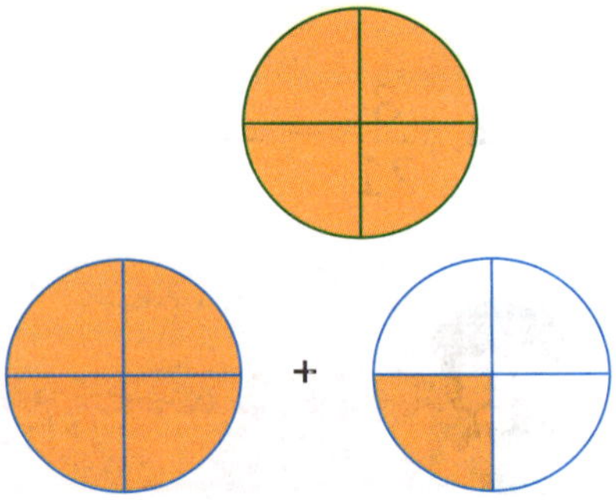

We write $1+\frac{1}{4}$ as $1\frac{1}{4}$.

Thus, $\frac{5}{4} = 1\frac{1}{4}$.

> When an improper fraction is written as a combination of a whole number and a proper fraction, it is called a mixed number or mixed fraction.

Thus, $2\frac{1}{5}$, $4\frac{1}{7}$, $5\frac{2}{3}$, $6\frac{1}{5}$, $7\frac{5}{7}$, etc, are mixed numbers.

Conversion of a Mixed Fraction into an Improper Fraction

Let us convert $5\frac{1}{7}$ into an improper fraction.

1. Multiply the whole number 5 by the denominator 7. $5 \times 7 = 35$
2. Add the numerator to it. $35 + 1$
3. This gives the numerator of the improper fraction. 36

   Denominator will remain the same. So, $5\frac{1}{7} = \frac{36}{7}$.

Conversion of an Improper Fraction into a Mixed Fraction

Let us convert $\frac{22}{5}$ into a mixed fraction.

$$\begin{array}{r|l} & 4 \\ 5 & 22 \\ & -20 \\ \hline & 2 \end{array}$$

Divide the numerator 22 by the denominator 5.

The quotient 4 gives the whole number. The remainder 2 is the numerator of the fraction.

The denominator of the fraction remains the same.

So, $\frac{22}{5} = 4\frac{2}{5}$

Look at another example.

Convert $\frac{41}{3}$ into a mixed fraction.

$$\begin{array}{r|l} & 13 \\ 3 & 41 \\ & -3 \\ \hline & 11 \\ & -9 \\ \hline & 2 \end{array}$$

So, $\frac{41}{3} = 13\frac{2}{3}$

Exercise 3H

Apply and Learn

A Which of the following is a set of like fractions?

1. $\frac{1}{7}, \frac{5}{7}, \frac{3}{7}, \frac{11}{7}$ 2. $\frac{1}{9}, \frac{2}{8}, \frac{4}{19}, \frac{7}{8}$ 3. $\frac{4}{11}, \frac{5}{8}, \frac{7}{9}, \frac{1}{6}$ 4. $\frac{2}{15}, \frac{4}{15}, \frac{11}{15}, \frac{7}{15}$

B Which of the following is a set of unlike fractions?

1. $\frac{1}{13}, \frac{13}{15}, \frac{15}{17}, \frac{17}{19}$ 2. $\frac{4}{11}, \frac{5}{11}, \frac{8}{11}, \frac{9}{11}$ 3. $\frac{5}{16}, \frac{1}{16}, \frac{7}{16}, \frac{11}{16}$ 4. $\frac{8}{9}, \frac{1}{7}, \frac{7}{8}, \frac{8}{11}$

C Which of the following are proper fractions?

1. $\frac{5}{8}$ 2. $\frac{6}{19}$ 3. $\frac{13}{7}$ 4. $\frac{23}{24}$ 5. $\frac{5}{9}$

D Which of the following are improper fractions?

1. $\frac{3}{14}$ 2. $\frac{15}{16}$ 3. $\frac{11}{14}$ 4. $\frac{15}{26}$ 5. $\frac{9}{16}$

E Which of the following are mixed numbers?

1. $1\frac{5}{4}$ 2. $3\frac{2}{3}$ 3. $\frac{3}{5}$ 4. $\frac{5}{3}$ 5. $3\frac{3}{5}$

6. $\frac{15}{8}$ 7. $5\frac{4}{9}$ 8. $2\frac{11}{15}$ 9. $4\frac{3}{7}$ 10. $\frac{25}{16}$

F Convert the following into improper fraction :

1. $3\frac{1}{3}$ 2. $6\frac{1}{2}$ 3. $7\frac{2}{3}$ 4. $8\frac{4}{9}$ 5. $9\frac{5}{7}$ 6. $12\frac{3}{8}$

G Convert the following into mixed fractions :

1. $\frac{10}{9}$ 2. $\frac{19}{5}$ 3. $\frac{21}{8}$ 4. $\frac{58}{9}$ 5. $\frac{65}{7}$ 6. $\frac{93}{5}$

Value Based Questions

Jatin is a needy boy. He never celebrates his birthday. But in the school, he is very helpful and all his friends and teachers love him. On his birthday, his friends thought of a plan. They gave a surprise visit to his house along with cake and other eatables. There were 20 children, but only 15 bottles of cold drinks.

1. What fraction of children would not be able to have a drink?
2. If the 15 bottles of cold drinks were shared equally among all 20 children, what fraction of a bottle of cold drink would each child have to drink?
3. The cake is divided equally into 25 equal parts. What fraction of cake does every child get?
4. By celebrating Jatin's birthday, which value is depicted by his friends?

Review and Refresh

A Change into equivalent fractions with numerator 18.

1. $\frac{2}{5}$ 2. $\frac{6}{7}$ 3. $\frac{9}{14}$ 4. $\frac{3}{8}$

B Change into equivalent fractions with denominator 32.

1. $\frac{3}{4}$ 2. $\frac{5}{8}$ 3. $\frac{1}{2}$ 4. $\frac{9}{16}$

C Fill in the circles with >, < or = to make true statements :

1. $\frac{3}{4}$ ◯ $\frac{2}{3}$ 2. $\frac{7}{8}$ ◯ $\frac{4}{5}$ 3. $\frac{5}{6}$ ◯ $\frac{15}{18}$

4. $\frac{10}{13}$ ◯ $\frac{10}{11}$ 5. $\frac{20}{32}$ ◯ $\frac{1}{2}$ 6. $\frac{7}{8}$ ◯ $\frac{7}{10}$

D Reduce the following fractions into their lowest terms :

1. $\frac{12}{18}$ 2. $\frac{20}{36}$ 3. $\frac{60}{84}$ 4. $\frac{80}{120}$ 5. $\frac{40}{56}$

E Add :

1. $\frac{2}{4}+\frac{3}{4}$ 2. $\frac{7}{10}+\frac{4}{10}$ 3. $\frac{1}{4}+\frac{1}{4}$ 4. $\frac{5}{14}+\frac{1}{14}+\frac{5}{14}$

5. $\frac{2}{18}+\frac{1}{18}+\frac{10}{18}$ 6. $\frac{3}{30}+\frac{7}{30}$ 7. $\frac{5}{14}+\frac{1}{14}+\frac{3}{14}$ 8. $\frac{8}{15}+\frac{1}{15}+\frac{2}{15}$

F Subtract :

1. $\frac{2}{10}-\frac{1}{10}$ 2. $\frac{4}{9}-\frac{1}{9}$ 3. $\frac{5}{12}-\frac{1}{12}$ 4. $\frac{5}{12}-\frac{4}{12}$

5. $\frac{9}{14}-\frac{4}{14}$ 6. $\frac{7}{12}-\frac{2}{12}$ 7. $\frac{5}{30}-\frac{4}{30}$ 8. $\frac{8}{34}-\frac{5}{34}$

Mental Maths

1. How many one-thirds make a whole? ____________

2. The numerator and the denominator of $\frac{5}{11}$ are ____________ and ____________ respectively.

3. Write the fractions whose numerator is 6 and denominator is 19. ____________

4. Find an equivalent fraction of $\frac{4}{9}$ with denominator 27. ____________

5. Is $\frac{22}{35}$ in its lowest terms? ____________

6. Which is greater : $\frac{7}{15}$ or $\frac{8}{15}$? ____________

7. Which is smaller : $\frac{7}{9}$ or $\frac{5}{9}$? ____________

8. $\frac{1}{7}+\frac{2}{7}+\frac{4}{7}=$ ____________ = ____________

9. Is $\frac{11}{11}$ an improper fraction? ____________

10. $\frac{4}{5}+\frac{2}{5}=$ ____________

Fun With Maths

1. Which fraction is the same even if you turn it upside down?

2. Anu said to Neha, Nishi and Homesh to make rectangle, circle and square shaped models and shade some part of each model.

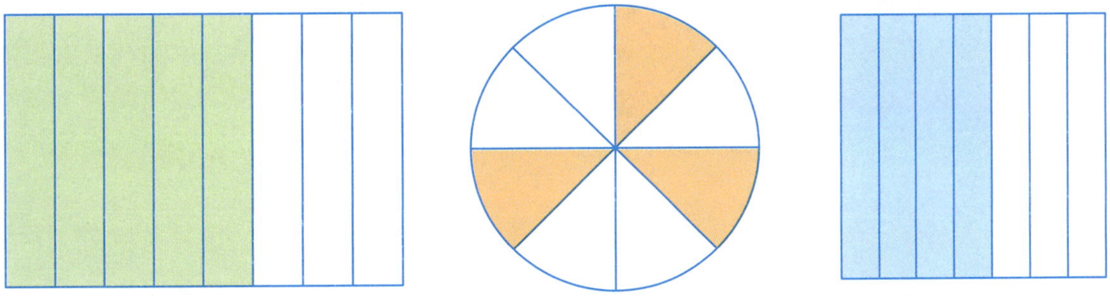

Neha's Model　　Nishi's Model　　Homesh's Model

Observe the above information and answer the following questions :

(i) The fraction for shaded part of the model made by Neha is :

(a) $\frac{5}{8}$ (b) $\frac{4}{7}$ (c) $\frac{1}{2}$ (d) $\frac{3}{8}$

(ii) The fraction for unshaded part of the model made by Nishi is :

(a) $\frac{5}{8}$ (b) $\frac{4}{7}$ (c) $\frac{1}{2}$ (d) $\frac{3}{8}$

(iii) The unshaded part of the model made by Homesh is :

(a) $\frac{5}{7}$ (b) $\frac{4}{7}$ (c) $\frac{1}{2}$ (d) $\frac{3}{7}$

(iv) The fraction equivalent to the fraction representing the shaded part of Homesh's model is : :

(a) $\frac{5}{8}$ (b) $\frac{4}{11}$ (c) $\frac{12}{21}$ (d) $\frac{3}{8}$

(v) The descending order of the shaded part of the model made by Neha, Nishi and Homesh is :

(a) $\frac{5}{8}, \frac{4}{7}, \frac{3}{8}$ (b) $\frac{4}{7}, \frac{5}{8}, \frac{3}{8}$ (c) $\frac{1}{2}, \frac{3}{7}, \frac{4}{8}$ (d) $\frac{3}{8}, \frac{5}{7}, \frac{4}{7}$

3. $\boxed{\frac{1}{12} + \frac{1}{12} + \frac{1}{12} + \frac{1}{12} + \frac{1}{12} + \frac{1}{12} + \frac{1}{12}} - \boxed{\frac{1}{2}} = ?$

(a) $\frac{1}{6}$ (b) $\frac{2}{12}$ (c) $\frac{1}{12}$ (d) $\frac{5}{12}$

To get worksheet on this chapter scan this QR code

CODE-HvyH

Maths Lab Activity

Objective : Understanding equivalent fractions by paper folding.

Materials Required : White sheets of paper, pencil colours.

Procedure/Demonstration : *Divide students in groups of 3.*

They will be given A-4 sheets or smaller sheets (but all the same size) and asked by the teacher to fold and create the following :

$\frac{1}{2}, \frac{2}{4}, \frac{4}{8}$

Each sheet will represent one of the above. All of them will be folded successively by the students. There will be some experimentation in this.

Once they have folded and unfolded, they will need to use colour to shade $\frac{1}{2}, \frac{1}{4}, \frac{1}{8}$.

$\frac{1}{2}$	$\frac{1}{2}$

$\frac{1}{4}$	$\frac{1}{4}$
$\frac{1}{4}$	$\frac{1}{4}$

$\frac{1}{8}$	$\frac{1}{8}$	$\frac{1}{8}$	$\frac{1}{8}$
$\frac{1}{8}$	$\frac{1}{8}$	$\frac{1}{8}$	$\frac{1}{8}$

Now, in each group, every bit of fraction will be cut out.

So each group will have 14 pieces.

Then on direction specified from the teacher, students will find how many of the smaller pieces fully cover. They will then paste those pieces together with fractions written on them on a separate sheet and present their findings in the following manner.

$\frac{1}{2}$	=	$\frac{1}{4}$	=	$\frac{1}{8}$ $\frac{1}{8}$
		$\frac{1}{4}$		$\frac{1}{8}$ $\frac{1}{8}$

So, $\frac{1}{2} = \frac{2}{4} = \frac{4}{8}$.

CHECK YOUR PACE

(Based on Chapters 1, 2, 3)

A Write the following numbers in words :

1. 40,257 **2.** 80,506 **3.** 70,001 **4.** 9,06,116 **5.** 6,10,053

B Write the following numbers in figures :

1. Twenty-one thousand four

2. Eighty-six thousand four hundred seven.

3. Seven lakh nine thousand eight.

4. Four lakh forty thousand three hundred fifty-four.

C Write the place value of :

1. 7 in 2,73,594 **2.** 4 in 36,840 **3.** 1 in 5,31,246 **4.** 9 in 9,42,653

D Write the expanded form of :

1. 40,736 **2.** 5,46,197 **3.** 9,83,216 **4.** 4,92,016 **5.** 7,05,293

E Find the smallest and the greatest number in each group :

1. 7,08,251, 7,80,521, 78,251, 87,351 **2.** 65,437, 2,80,156, 6,50,437, 5,67,237

3. 2,90,175, 2,09,175, 71,751, 2,00,751

F Write the Hindu-Arabic numeral for :

1. XIV **2.** XVIII **3.** XXI **4.** XXXVII

G Write the Roman numeral for :

1. 12 **2.** 19 **3.** 25 **4.** 34

H Which is greater?

1. 15 or XIV **2.** 28 or XXXI **3.** XXI or XXIV

I Find an equivalent fraction of :

1. $\frac{3}{5}$ with numerator 15 **2.** $\frac{16}{60}$ with denominator 15

J Compare :

1. $\frac{3}{5}$ and $\frac{1}{5}$ **2.** $\frac{8}{15}$ and $\frac{8}{11}$ **3.** $\frac{7}{9}$ and $\frac{11}{15}$ **4.** $\frac{2}{11}$ and $\frac{3}{10}$

K Add/subract :

1. $\frac{2}{15} + \frac{1}{15} + \frac{8}{15}$ **2.** $\frac{2}{8} + \frac{3}{8}$ **3.** $\frac{1}{15} + \frac{5}{15} + \frac{4}{15}$

4. $\frac{11}{16} - \frac{1}{12}$ **5.** $\frac{5}{12} - \frac{1}{12}$ **6.** $\frac{9}{14} - \frac{3}{14}$

L Convert into improper fractions :

1. $2\frac{1}{7}$ **2.** $4\frac{5}{8}$ **3.** $5\frac{2}{9}$

THEME 2 : NUMBER OPERATIONS

Addition

Learning Target

To understand addition of 4-digit numbers.

I Can

- **I can write** addition statement.
- **I can add** any 4-digit numbers.
- **I can explain** properties of addition.
- **I can solve** addition problems.

Let Us Recall

In Class 3, we have learnt about addition of numbers up to 3-digits.
Let us have a quick review of what we have read about addition of numbers.

Exercise 4A

A Add :

1. 583 + 201
2. 315 + 540
3. 587 + 148
4. 159 + 780
5. 520 + 164 + 305
6. 230 + 321 + 145

B Arrange in columns and add :

1. 321, 436 and 157
2. 430, 287 and 195
3. 215, 340 and 100
4. 136, 580 and 174

Here, we shall learn to add 4-digit numbers.

In an addition sum, the numbers that are added are called **addends** and the result of addition is called the **sum**.

	1	5	7	← Addends
+	1	3	2	← Addends
	2	8	9	← Sum

Explore and Learn

CODE-rtft

Addition without Carrying or (without Regrouping)

Example 1 : Add 4,032 and 1,746.

Solution :

Step 1. Arrange the numbers in columns.

	Th	H	T	O
	4	0	3	2
+	1	7	4	6

Step 2. Adding ones, we have

	Th	H	T	O
	4	0	3	2
+	1	7	4	6
				8

Step 3. Adding tens, we have

	Th	H	T	O
	4	0	3	2
+	1	7	4	6
			7	8

Step 4. Adding hundreds, we have

	Th	H	T	O
	4	0	3	2
+	1	7	4	6
		7	7	8

Step 5. Adding thousands, we have

	Th	H	T	O
	4	0	3	2
+	1	7	4	6
	5	7	7	8

Hence, 4,032 + 1,746 = 5,778.

(Five thousand, seven hundred seventy-eight).

Example 2 : Add 7,521; 1,025 and 1,352.

Solution :

Step 1. Arrange the numbers in columns.

	Th	H	T	O
	7	5	2	1
	1	0	2	5
+	1	3	5	2

Step 2. Adding ones, we have

	Th	H	T	O
	7	5	2	1
	1	0	2	5
+	1	3	5	2
				8

Step 3. Adding tens, we have

	Th	H	T	O
	7	5	2	1
	1	0	2	5
+	1	3	5	2
			9	8

Step 4. Adding hundreds, we have

	Th	H	T	O
	7	5	2	1
	1	0	2	5
+	1	3	5	2
		8	9	8

Step 5. Adding thousands, we have

	Th	H	T	O
	7	5	2	1
	1	0	2	5
+	1	3	5	2
	9	8	9	8

Hence, 7,521 + 1,025 + 1,352 = 9,898
(nine thousand eight hundred ninety-eight).

Exercise 4B

Apply and Learn

A Add :

1.

	Th	H	T	O
	7	0	5	4
+	2	8	3	1

2.

	Th	H	T	O
	2	5	7	2
+	4	3	2	5

3.

	Th	H	T	O
	2	3	0	9
+	6	4	7	0

4.

	Th	H	T	O
	1	8	3	1
+	7	0	4	7

5.

	Th	H	T	O
	5	3	7	2
+		4	2	0

6.

	Th	H	T	O
	1	5	3	9
+	2	0	1	0

7.

	Th	H	T	O
	2	5	1	7
+	4	3	2	1

8.

	Th	H	T	O
	6	5	4	6
	2	0	3	0
+	1	3	2	1

9.

	Th	H	T	O
	1	6	3	5
	2	1	4	0
+	5	2	1	4

10.

	Th	H	T	O
	2	5	0	1
	5	1	7	2
+	2	0	1	4

11.

	Th	H	T	O
	6	3	1	4
	1	2	4	0
+		4	1	3

12.

	Th	H	T	O
	1	3	6	1
	4	5	2	7
+	3	0	1	0

B Arrange in columns and add :

1. 6,344 and 2,305
2. 4,518; 2,402 and 2,140
3. 3,614; 2,143 and 2,312
4. 5,201; 1,534 and 2,142

C Fill in the ☐ with the correct digits :

1.

	3	0	5	
	5	6		0
+		2	0	2
	9		6	9

2.

	8	7	0	4
	0	1	4	
+	1		1	3
		8	7	9

Explore and Learn

Addition with Carrying (or with Regrouping)

CODE-4UxN

Example 1: Add 5,386 and 3,927.

Solution :

Step 1. Arrange the numbers in columns.

	Th	H	T	O
	5	3	8	6
+	3	9	2	7

Step 2. Adding ones, we have 6 ones + 7 ones = 13 ones = 1 ten + 3 ones. Carry over 1 to tens column and write 3 under ones column.

	Th	H	T	O
			①	
	5	3	8	6
+	3	9	2	7
				3

Step 3. Adding tens, we have

1 ten (carried) + 8 tens + 2 tens = 11 tens = 1 hundred + 1 ten.

Carry over 1 to hundreds column and write 1 under tens column.

	Th	H	T	O
		①	①	
	5	3	**8**	6
+	3	9	**2**	7
			1	3

Step 4. Adding hundreds, we have

1 hundred (carried) + 3 hundreds + 9 hundreds = 13 hundreds = 1 thousand + 3 hundreds.

Carry over 1 to thousands column and write 3 under hundreds column.

	Th	H	T	O
	①	①	①	
	5	**3**	8	6
+	3	**9**	2	7
		3	1	3

Step 5. Adding thousands, we have

1 thousand (carried)

+ 5 thousands + 3 thousands

= 9 thousands.

	Th	H	T	O
	①	①	①	①
	5	3	8	6
+	**3**	9	2	7
	9	3	1	3

Hence,

5,386 + 3,927 = 9,313

(Nine thousand three hundred thirteen).

Example 2 : Add 2,908, 6,123 and 254

Solution :

Step 1.

	Th	H	T	O
	2	9	0	8
+	6	1	2	3
		2	5	4

Step 2.

	Th	H	T	O
			①	
	2	9	0	**8**
+	6	1	2	**3**
		2	5	**4**
				5

Step 3.

	Th	H	T	O
			①	
	2	9	0	8
+	6	1	2	3
		2	5	4
			8	5

Step 4.

	Th	H	T	O
	①		①	
	2	9	0	8
+	6	1	2	3
		2	5	4
		2	8	5

Step 5.

	Th	H	T	O
	①		①	
	2	9	0	8
+	6	1	2	3
		2	5	4
	9	2	8	5

Hence,
2,908 + 6,123 + 254 = 9,285
(Nine thousand two hundred eighty-five).

Exercise 4C

Apply and Learn

A Find the sum :

1.

	Th	H	T	O
	5	2	4	0
+	4	6	9	8

2.

	Th	H	T	O
	3	7	2	4
+	2	6	9	8

3.

	Th	H	T	O
	5	4	0	5
+	2	8	9	7

4.

	Th	H	T	O
	4	3	7	4
+	4	8	6	2

5.

	Th	H	T	O
	6	1	8	4
	2	8	5	3
+		3	6	9

6.

	Th	H	T	O
	4	9	8	7
	3	5	4	6
+		3	0	5

7.

	Th	H	T	O
	3	6	9	4
	5	0	2	7
+		7	1	6

8.

	Th	H	T	O
	2	5	8	3
	1	6	1	4
+	5	7	6	2

B Arrange in columns and find the sum :

1. 6,359 + 1,415 + 935
2. 3,143 + 1,208 + 2,453
3. 4,321 + 2,075 + 1,982
4. 5,196 + 2,861 + 1,674

C Fill in the ☐ with the correct digits :

1.

	4		5	6
+		7	4	
	7	2		4

2.

	5	0		5
+	3		7	
		0	5	2

3.

		5	8
	5		4
+	6	4	7
1	6	5	

4.

	5	3	2	
		9	0	8
+	2	5		3
	9		2	1

D Answer the following questions :

1. Find the sum of the largest 3-digit number and the smallest 4-digit number.
2. Find the sum of the smallest 4-digit number and the largest 2-digit number.

3. Write the greatest and the smallest 4-digit numbers using the digits 2, 6, 3, 8 only once. Find the sum of the two numbers so obtained.
4. Write the greatest and the smallest 4-digit numbers using all of the digits 6, 0, 8, 2. Find the sum of the numbers so obtained.

Explore and Learn

CODE-MXJy

Properties of Addition

1. **Zero added to a number does not change the number.**

   8,789 + 0 = 8,789   5,879 + 0 = 5,879

2. **When we add two numbers in different order, the sum remains the same. This is called order property or commutative property of addition.**

   2,023 + 5,453 = 7,476   Also, 5,453 + 2,023 = 7,476

3. **When three or more numbers are grouped in different order, the sum remains the same.**

   5,436 + (7,203 + 9,375) = 22,014   Also, (5,436 + 7,203) + 9,375 = 22,014

   This is called grouping property or associative property of addition.

Exercise 4D

Apply and Learn

A What is one more than :

1. 8,271 ________ 2. 6,759 ________ 3. 8,643 ________
4. 2,456 ________ 5. 2,738 ________ 6. 2,434 ________

B What is 10 more than :

1. 2,359 ________ 2. 5,799 ________ 3. 8,399 ________
4. 2,321 ________ 5. 3,765 ________ 6. 9,634 ________

C What is 100 more than :

1. 3,721 ________ 2. 5,673 ________ 3. 7,132 ________
4. 7,375 ________ 5. 9,175 ________ 6. 4,695 ________

D What is 1000 more than :

1. 7,326 ________ 2. 5,217 ________ 3. 6,382 ________
4. 6,549 ________ 5. 8,939 ________ 6. 1,876 ________

E Fill in the blanks :

1. 2,817 + 5,775 = ________ + 2,817
2. 1,937 + 3,132 = 3,132 + ________
3. 5,754 + (2,699 + 3,042) = (5,754 + ________) + ________
4. (2,032 + 7,923) + 3142 = 2,032 + (________ + ________)

Explore and Learn

Word Problems

Example 1 : The population of town A is 2,301, the population of town B is 4,875, the population of town C is 1,835. What is the total population of the three towns?

Solution : Population of town A = 2,301

Population of town B = 4,875

Population of town C = 1,835

Total population of the three towns

= 2,301 + 4,875 + 1,835 = 9,011.

	(2)	(1)	(1)	
	2	3	0	1
	4	8	7	5
+	1	8	3	5
	9	0	1	1

Hence, the total population of the three towns = 9,011.

Example 2 : Which number is 528 more than 7,874?

Solution : The required number = 7,874 + 528 = 8,402.

Hence, the required number is 8,402.

(1)	(1)	(1)	
7	8	7	4
+	5	2	8
8	4	0	2

Exercise 4E

Apply and Learn

1. Monika had ₹2,183 in her bank account. She again deposited ₹1,345. What is the amount in Monika's bank account now?

2. In a public library, there are 536 books on Literature, 2,508 books on Mathematics and 1,253 books on other subjects. Find the total number of books in the library.

3. At a meeting addressed by a political leader, there were 2,649 men 3,259 women and 837 children. How many people were present in the meeting?

4. A cycle factory produced 2,851 cycles in year 2010, 3,670 cycles in 2011 and 2,895 in 2012. What was the production in these three years?

5. In an examination, 6,381 boys and 2,954 girls appeared. How many students in all appeared for the examination?

6. In an election, there were three candidates. The first candidate got 2,635 votes, the second candidate got 2,583 votes and the third candidate got 1,307 votes. In all how many votes were polled?

7. A number is 573 more than 8,734. Find the number.

8. A milk dairy produced 2,563 litres, 2,359 litres, and 2,681 litres of milk in three months. How much milk was produced at this dairy in these three months?

9. According to 2011 census, the population of three towns is 4,072, 1,598 and 1,272. Find the total population of the three towns. Express the answer in words as well.

10. A company produced 2,756; 1,751 and 3,058 pencils in three successive months. In all how many pencils were produced by the company in these three months?

Value Based Questions

Rekha has many books in her library. She reads the books daily. She has read 3,219 pages so far. She still needs to read 6,175 pages so as to complete reading all the books of her library.

1. How many pages are there in all the books of the library?
2. Do you think reading books is a good habit or simply waste of time?

Review and Refresh

A Arrange the following numbers in columns and add :

1. 4,256; 1,543 and 3,098

2. 3,894; 4,093 and 1,954

B Fill in the ☐ with the correct digits :

1.

	5		6	0
+	2	5		8
		9	9	

2.

	2		8	3
+		3		6
	8	1	0	

C Find the sum of the smallest 4-digit number and the smallest 3-digit number.

D Fill in the blanks :

1. 1,350 + ____________ = 8,754 + 1,350

2. 8,403 + ______________ = 8,403

3. 0 + _______________ = 9,351

4. 1754 + _____ = _____ + 8,234

Mental Maths

1. 2,615 + 6,038 = 8,653. Here addends are _______________ and _______________.

2. 5,914 + 6,890 = 6,890 + ____________________________

3. ________________________ + 1,529 = 1,529 + ________________________ = 1,529.

4. Find the sum of the greatest 3-digit number and the smallest 4-digit number. ____

5. What number should be added to the greatest 3-digit number to get the smallest 4-digit number? ________________________

6. Find the sum of the place-values of 5s in 25,610 and 526. ______________________

7. Find the number which is 1,000 more than 7,539. ______________________

Fun With Maths

1. Write numbers from 1 to 9 in the magic square so that the sum of numbers in each row, in each column and diagonally is 15.

6		
	5	
		4

2. There is an odd number of students in your class. There are more than 21 and less than 25 students. How many students are in your class?

Maths Lab Activity

Objective : Checking addition sums using digital root method.

Materials Required : Pencil and paper only.

Procedure/Demonstration : Take any number between 10 and 100. Add its two digits. Keep adding the digits until you get a single digit.

Let us take the number 85.

85 $\quad$ 8 + 5 = 13 $\quad$ 1 + 3 = 4

The single digit so obtained is the digital root of the original number. Here, the digital root of 85 is 4.

Now, try to find the digital roots of the following numbers: 26, 57, 68, 127, 468

In ancient times, when there were no calculators, digital roots were used to check for the mistakes.

Consider the sum 254 + 583 = 837.

Now find the digital roots of the three numbers : 254 → 2, 583 → 7, 837 → 9

Now add the digital roots and see if it is correct. 2 + 7 = 9

Since the sum of the digital roots is also correct, hence, the addition is correct.

Again, consider the sum 408 + 347 = 745

Now find the digital roots of the three numbers : 408 → 3, 347 → 5, 745 → 7

We see that 3 + 5 = 8

So, 3 + 5 is not equal to 7.

Since the sum of the digital roots is not correct, hence the addition is not correct.

Now, use the digital roots to check whether the following additions are correct or not.

1. 356 + 481 = 837 $\quad$ **2.** 472 + 705 = 1167

3. 641 + 573 = 1214 $\quad$ **4.** 895 + 724 = 1579

5. 438 + 297 = 755 $\quad$ **6.** 608 + 536 = 1144

To get worksheet on this chapter scan this QR code

CODE-WZve

THEME 2 : NUMBER OPERATIONS

Subtraction

Learning Target To understand subtraction of 4-digit numbers.

I Can

- **I can write** subtraction statement.
- **I can subtract** any 4-digit numbers.
- **I can explain** properties of subtraction.
- **I can solve** subtraction problems.

Let Us Recall

In Class 3, we have learnt about subtraction of numbers up to 3-digits.

In a subtraction problem, the larger number from which we subtract the other number (the smaller number) is called **minuend,** the number (the smaller number) which is subtracted is called **subtrahend** and the result of subtraction is called the **difference**.

Here, we shall learn subtraction of 4-digit numbers. Let us have a quick review of what we have learnt about subtraction.

	4	3	7	← Minuend
–	2	1	0	← Subtrahend
	2	2	7	← Difference

Exercise 5A

A Subtract :

1.

	3	7	8
–	1	0	6

2.

	5	9	1
–	3	6	0

3.

	2	8	9
–	1	3	4

4.

	4	0	0
–	3	2	1

5.

	2	5	3
–	1	0	5

6.

	6	0	0
–	3	7	2

B Find the difference between :

1. 725 and 700
2. 153 and 256
3. 781 and 651

C Subtract :

1. 431 from 935
2. 261 from 530
3. 524 from 702

D Answer the following questions :

1. What must be added to 243 to get 783?
2. The sum of two numbers is 838. If the greater of the two numbers is 528, find the smaller number.

Explore and Learn

Subtraction without Borrowing (or without Regrouping)

CODE-szXJ

Example 1 : Subtract 5,013 from 8,347.

Solution :

Step 1. Arrange the numbers in columns.

	Th	H	T	O
	8	3	4	7
–	5	0	1	3

Step 2. Subtracting ones, we have

	Th	H	T	O
	8	3	4	7
–	5	0	1	3
				4

Step 3. Subtracting tens, we have

	Th	H	T	O
	8	3	4	7
–	5	0	1	3
			3	4

Step 4. Subtracting hundreds, we have

	Th	H	T	O
	8	3	4	7
–	5	0	1	3
		3	3	4

Step 5. Subtracting thousands, we have

	Th	H	T	O
	8	3	4	7
–	5	0	1	3
	3	3	3	4

Hence, 8,347 – 5,013 = 3,334

(Three thousand, three hundred thirty-four).

CHALLENGE

If 40 * 15 * 5 = 20 and 25 * 5 * 8 = 12, then find the value of 32 * 10 * 13.

Exercise 5B

Apply and Learn

A Subtract :

1.

	Th	H	T	O
	8	3	6	5
–	7	2	1	0

2.

	Th	H	T	O
	1	6	2	4
–		3	1	3

3.

	Th	H	T	O
	9	5	6	9
–	5	2	1	5

4.

	Th	H	T	O
	5	6	4	9
–	2	4	3	4

5.

	Th	H	T	O
	1	5	6	4
–		3	5	1

6.

	Th	H	T	O
	5	7	3	6
–	3	7	2	0

7.

	Th	H	T	O
	2	8	1	6
–		6	1	4

8.

	Th	H	T	O
	7	1	0	5
–	4	0	0	2

9.

	Th	H	T	O
	5	2	1	4
–	4	0	1	2

B Arrange in columns and subtract :

1. 6,518 – 2,306 **2.** 8,364 – 5,241

3. 4,321 – 1,210 **4.** 8,379 – 6,054

5. 6,587 – 5,463 **6.** 4,321 – 2,101

REMEMBER

To find the difference of two numbers, we always subtract the smaller number from the greater number.

C Find the difference between :

1. 4,256 and 6,469 **2.** 5,876 and 2,305

3. 1,513 and 4,836 **4.** 6,315 and 2,103

D Fill in the ☐ with the correct digits :

1.

		5	7	
–	6		1	3
	2	3		3

2.

	9		6	3
–		6	3	
	4	2		3

Explore and Learn

Subtraction with Borrowing (or with Regrouping)

CODE-1uqF

Example 1 : Subtract 2,856 from 8,153.

Solution :

Step 1. Arrange the numbers in columns.

	Th	H	T	O
	8	1	5	3
–	2	8	5	6

Step 2. Subtract the ones. Here 3 < 6, so regroup 5 tens 3 ones as 4 tens and 13 ones.

	Th	H	T	O
			(4)	(13)
	8	1	~~5~~	~~3~~
–	2	8	5	6
				7

Step 3. Subtract the tens. Here, 4 < 5, so, regroup 1 hundred 4 tens as 0 hundreds and 14 tens.

	Th	H	T	O
			(14)	(13)
		0	~~4~~	
	8	~~1~~	~~5~~	~~3~~
–	2	8	5	6
			9	7

Step 4. Subtract the hundreds. Here, 0 < 8, so regroup 8 thousands 0 hundreds as 7 thousand and 10 hundreds.

	Th	H	T	O
	7	(10)	(14)	(13)
		~~0~~	~~4~~	
	~~8~~	~~1~~	~~5~~	~~3~~
–	2	8	5	6
		2	9	7

Step 5. Subtract the thousands.

	Th	H	T	O
	7	10	14	13
		~~0~~	~~4~~	
	~~8~~	~~1~~	~~5~~	~~3~~
–	2	8	5	6
	5	2	9	7

Hence, 8,153 – 2,856 = 5,297.
Five thousand two hundred ninety-seven).

Example 2 : Subtract: 9,000 – 6,124 .

Solution :

Step 1. Arrange the numbers in columns.

	Th	H	T	O
	9	0	0	0
–	6	1	2	4

Step 2. Regroup 9 thousands.

9 thousands = 8 thousands + 10 hundreds

10 hundreds = 9 hundreds + 10 tens

10 tens = 9 tens + 10 ones

	Th	H	T	O
	8	9	9	10
		~~10~~	~~10~~	
	~~9~~	~~0~~	~~0~~	~~0~~
–	6	1	2	4

Step 3. Subtract the ones.

	Th	H	T	O
	8	9	9	10
		~~10~~	~~10~~	
	~~9~~	~~0~~	~~0~~	~~0~~
–	6	1	2	4
				6

Step 4. Subtract the tens.

	Th	H	T	O
	8	9	9	10
		~~10~~	~~10~~	
	~~9~~	~~0~~	~~0~~	~~0~~
–	6	1	2	4
			7	6

Step 5. Subtract the hundreds.

	Th	H	T	O
	(8)	(9)	(9)	(10)
		~~10~~	~~10~~	
	~~9~~	~~0~~	~~0~~	~~0~~
−	6	1	2	4
		8	7	6

Step 6. Subtract the thousands.

	Th	H	T	O
	(8)	(9)	(9)	(10)
		~~10~~	~~10~~	
	~~9~~	~~0~~	~~0~~	~~0~~
−	6	1	2	4
	2	8	7	6

Hence, 9,000 − 6,124 = 2,876.

Exercise 5C

Apply and Learn

A Subtract :

1.

	Th	H	T	O
	5	3	2	6
−	1	7	5	8

2.

	Th	H	T	O
	6	4	3	6
−	2	9	4	5

3.

	Th	H	T	O
	4	1	5	8
−	1	3	7	4

4.

	Th	H	T	O
	4	5	2	9
−	2	7	3	6

5.

	Th	H	T	O
	7	4	0	5
−	4	5	3	8

6.

	Th	H	T	O
	6	3	0	0
−	4	5	7	1

7.

	Th	H	T	O
	7	0	0	1
−	5	2	6	4

8.

	Th	H	T	O
	8	3	0	0
−	6	5	7	1

9.

	Th	H	T	O
	5	0	0	0
−	2	1	7	2

B Arrange in columns and subtract :

1. 6,534 − 3,165
2. 1,471 − 1,204
3. 2,673 − 1,285
4. 7,000 − 5,321
5. 4,500 − 1,637
6. 8,031 − 3,825

C Find the difference between :

1. 8,653 and 3,430
2. 7,281 and 3,530
3. 6,197 and 4,200
4. 7,000 and 3,547
5. 6,400 and 8,291
6. 8,092 and 5,174

D Fill in the boxes :

1.

	6		2	8
–	2	7		5
		6	0	

2.

		4	3	
–	4		6	4
	2	4		3

3.

	8	6		7
–	4		2	
		3	9	4

4.

	5			2
–		7	3	8
	1	0	4	

Explore and Learn

Properties of Subtraction

CODE-7tet

1. **Zero subtracted from any number is the number itself.**

   9,562 – 0 = 9,562 5,786 – 0 = 5,786

2. **Any number subtracted from itself is zero.**

   2,563 – 2,563 = 0 8,127 – 8,127 = 0

3. **Order of numbers to be subtracted can not be changed, as the answer we get will be different.**

Exercise 5D

Apply and Learn

Fill in the blanks :

1. 115 – 0 = ______
2. 129 – 1 = ______
3. 491 – 10 = ______
4. 6,821 – 10 = ______
5. 4,863 – 1 = ______
6. 9,386 – 100 = ______
7. 4,532 – 4,532 = ______
8. 900 – 100 = ______
9. 80 – 80 = ______
10. 849 – 100 = ______
11. 2,657 – 1,000 = ______
12. 3,458 – 1,000 = ______
13. 796 – 0 = ______
14. 6,789 – 1,000 = ______
15. 100 – 10 = ______

Explore and Learn

Addition and Subtraction Together

CODE-49fq

Example 1 : Simplify : 7,530 + 1,817 – 5,173

Solution :

Step 1

	1			
	7	5	3	0
+	1	8	1	7
	9	3	4	7

Step 2

		2	14	
	9	~~3~~	~~4~~	7
–	5	1	7	3
	4	1	7	4

Hence, 7,530 + 1,817 – 5,173 = 4,174.

Example 2 : 3,856 – 2,385 + 6,389 – 987

Solution :

Step 1

		1	15	
	3	~~8~~	~~5~~	6
–	2	3	8	5
	1	4	7	1

Step 2

		1	1	
	1	4	7	1
+	6	3	8	9
	7	8	6	0

Step 3

	6	17	15	10
	~~7~~	~~8~~	~~6~~	~~0~~
–		9	8	7
	6	8	7	3

Hence, 3,856 – 2,385 + 6,389 – 987 = 6,873

Exercise 5E

Apply and Learn

Simplify :

1. 2,517 + 6,121 – 1,925
2. 6,312 – 2,610 + 5,001
3. 5,418 – 2,513 + 4,563
4. 6,391 – 4,543 + 1,001
5. 4,381 + 3,800 – 2,901
6. 8,401 – 6,361 + 1,032 – 1,519
7. 5,392 + 1,834 – 2,721 – 984
8. 2,001 + 5,123 – 6,123 + 1,850
9. Subtract the difference of 6,351 and 2,175 from their sum.

Explore and Learn

Word Prolems

Example 1 : A factory produced 3,263 mercury lamps in 2012. In 2013, it produced 4,450 mercury lamps. By how much did the factory's production increase?

Solution : Production in 2013 = 4,450

Production in 2012 = 3,263

Increase in production = 4,450 – 3,263

= 1,187.

Hence, the production increased by 1,187.

		(3)	(14)	(10)
			~~4~~	
	4	~~4~~	~~5~~	~~0~~
–	3	2	6	3
	1	1	8	7

Example 2 : What must be added to 4,213 to get 7,631?

Solution : The sum of two numbers = 7,631.

One number = 4,213

The other number = 7,631 – 4,213 = 3,418

Hence, the required number = 3,418.

			(2)	(11)
	7	6	~~3~~	~~1~~
–	4	2	1	3
	3	4	1	8

Exercise 5F

Apply and Learn

1. Last year, a cycle factory produced 8,319 cycles. This year the production came down by 5,761 cycles. What is the production this year?

2. In year 2010, a poultry farm produced 6,134 eggs. In 2011, it produced 1,785 eggs less than that in 2010. How many eggs were produced in 2011?

3. The population of a town is 9,123. If the number of males is 3,572, find the number of females in the town.

4. In an examination, 8,380 candidates appeared. Out of these, 4,090 candidates failed. How many candidates passed?

5. A factory produced 8,540 bulbs in year 2014. Out of them, 3,479 bulbs were found defective. How many bulbs were found good?

6. The sum of two numbers is 7,561. If one of them is 4,078, find the other.
7. What must be added to 3,172 to get 8,051?
8. What must be added to 2,176 to get 5,158?
9. By how much is 7,312 greater than 3,627?
10. The difference between two numbers is 4,527. If the greater number is 6,196, find the smaller number.

Value Based Questions

In a library there are 4,076 books on Literature, 2,536 books on Science and 2,452 books on Mathematics.

1. How many more Literature books are there in the library than that on Science?
2. Are books on Literature more than the books on Science and Mathematics together? If yes, by how many?
3. Do you think libraries are useful for us? Should a library have a 'Silence Please' board?

Review and Refresh

A Find the difference between :

1. 8,019 and 5,364 2. 5,786 and 6,354 3. 8,000 and 3,947 4. 2,754 and 8,027

B Fill in the ☐ with the correct digits :

1.

	8	7		9
−		1	2	
	5		9	4

2.

	6	0		8
−			6	
		4	0	9

C Answer the following questions :

1. Find the difference between the largest 4-digit number and the smallest 4-digit number.

2. Subtract the difference of 5,196 and 3,926 from their sum.
3. What number should be added to 8,164 to get 9,020?
4. By how much is 8,241 greater than 3,465?

Mental Maths

1. 6,542 – 2,260 = 4,282. Here, minuend and subtrahend are ____________ and ____________ respectively.
2. To find the difference between two numbers, we always subtract the ____________ number from the ____________ number.
3. 8,850 – 8,850 = ____________.
4. Find the difference of the place values of 4s in 4,416. ____________
5. What number should be subtracted from the smallest 4-digit number to get the largest 3-digit number? ____________
6. The difference between the smallest 3-digit number and the largest 2-digit number is ____________.
7. 2,875 – 1,000 = ____________
8. 4,329 – 2,000 = ____________
9. What should be subtracted from 5 thousands to get 6 hundreds? ____________
10. 2,500 – 500 + 3,000 = ____________

Fun With Maths

1. Write the numbers from 9 to 1 in descending order. Now, insert + and – signs between them so that the result becomes 100. One is done for you.

   98 + 7 + 6 – 5 – 4 – 3 + 2 – 1 = 100

   Achieve the above target in two more ways.
2. Look at the numbers shown below. Subtract 12 from the third number from the left.

   13   98   37   25   35

   Left   Right

   The answer is same as the number from the right is :

   (a) 1st   (b) 2nd   (c) 3rd   (d) 4th

To get worksheet on this chapter scan this QR code

CODE-85DV

THEME 2 : NUMBER OPERATIONS
Multiplication

Learning Target To understand multiplication

I Can

- **I can write** multiplication statement.
- **I can explain** properties of multiplication.
- **I can estimate** numbers.
- **I can estimate** the sum/difference/product.
- **I can solve** word problems on multiplication.

Multiplication Tables

Learn the table from 2 to 10.

2	×	1	=	2
2	×	2	=	4
2	×	3	=	6
2	×	4	=	8
2	×	5	=	10
2	×	6	=	12
2	×	7	=	14
2	×	8	=	16
2	×	9	=	18
10	×	10	=	20

3	×	1	=	3
3	×	2	=	6
3	×	3	=	9
3	×	4	=	12
3	×	5	=	15
3	×	6	=	18
3	×	7	=	21
3	×	8	=	24
3	×	9	=	27
3	×	10	=	30

4	×	1	=	4
4	×	2	=	8
4	×	3	=	12
4	×	4	=	16
4	×	5	=	20
4	×	6	=	24
4	×	7	=	28
4	×	8	=	32
4	×	9	=	36
4	×	10	=	40

5	×	1	=	5
5	×	2	=	10
5	×	3	=	15
5	×	4	=	20
5	×	5	=	25
5	×	6	=	30
5	×	7	=	35
5	×	8	=	40
5	×	9	=	45
5	×	10	=	50

6	×	1	=	6
6	×	2	=	12
6	×	3	=	18
6	×	4	=	24
6	×	5	=	30
6	×	6	=	36
6	×	7	=	42
6	×	8	=	48
6	×	9	=	54
6	×	10	=	60

7	×	1	=	7
7	×	2	=	14
7	×	3	=	21
7	×	4	=	28
7	×	5	=	35
7	×	6	=	42
7	×	7	=	49
7	×	8	=	56
7	×	9	=	63
7	×	10	=	70

8	×	1	=	8
8	×	2	=	16
8	×	3	=	24
8	×	4	=	32
8	×	5	=	40
8	×	6	=	48
8	×	7	=	56
8	×	8	=	64
8	×	9	=	72
8	×	10	=	80

9	×	1	=	9
9	×	2	=	18
9	×	3	=	27
9	×	4	=	36
9	×	5	=	45
9	×	6	=	54
9	×	7	=	63
9	×	8	=	72
9	×	9	=	81
9	×	10	=	90

10	×	1	=	10
10	×	2	=	20
10	×	3	=	30
10	×	4	=	40
10	×	5	=	50
10	×	6	=	60
10	×	7	=	70
10	×	8	=	80
10	×	9	=	90
10	×	10	=	100

Let Us Recall

In Class 3, we learnt how to multiply a number by 1-digit numbers.

Following terms are used in multiplication :

1. **Multiplicand :** The number to be multiplied is called the **multiplicand**.
2. **Multiplier :** The number by which we multiply is called the **multiplier**.
3. **Product :** The result we obtain after the multiplication is called the **product**.

Thus, in 12 × 4 = 48, 12 is multiplicand, 4 is multiplier and 48 is product.

Let us have a quick review of what we have read.

Exercise 6A

A Find the following products in your notebook :

1.

2	8
×	7

2.

6	3
×	5

3.

6	6
×	3

4.

3	5
×	3

5.

6	9
×	9

6.

8	0
×	5

7.

6	8
×	8

8.

5	3
×	8

B Find the product :

1. 27 × 2 = ________ **2.** 6 × 10 = ________ **3.** 25 × 8 = ________

4. 16 × 7 = ________ **5.** 14 × 9 = ________ **6.** 37 × 6 = ________

7. 75 × 6 = ________ **8.** 2 × 90 = ________ **9.** 54 × 5 = ________

Explore and Learn

Multiplication of a 3-digit Number by a 1-digit Number

CODE-npH1

Multiply 167 by 4.

Step 1. Align the digits

H	T	O
1	6	7
×		4

Step 2. Multiply ones. 7 ones × 4 = 28 ones = 2 tens 8 ones. Write 8 below ones place and carry 2 to the tens place.

H	T	O
	(2)	
1	6	7
×		4
		8

Step 3. Multiply tens. 6 tens × 4 = 24 tens. 24 tens + 2 tens (carried) = 26 tens = 2 hundreds 6 tens. Write 6 below tens place and carry over 2 to hundreds place.

H	T	O
(2)	(2)	
1	6	7
×		4
	6	8

Step 4. Multiply hundreds. 1 hundred × 4 = 4 hundreds. 4 hundreds + 2 hundreds (carried) = 6 hundreds. Write 6 in hundreds place.

H	T	O
(2)	(2)	
1	6	7
×		4
6	6	8

So, 167 × 4 = 668

Multiply 439 by 7.

Step 1

Th	H	T	O
	4	3	9
	×		7

Step 2

Th	H	T	O
		(6)	
	4	3	9
	×		7
			3

Step 3

Th	H	T	O
	(2)	(6)	
	4	3	9
	×		7
		7	3

Step 4

Th	H	T	O
	(2)	(6)	
	4	3	9
	×		7
3	0	7	3

So, 439 × 7 = 3,073

Multiplication of a 4-digit Number by a 1-digit Number

CODE-9qgo

Multiply 2,634 by 3.

Step 1. Align the digits

	Th	H	T	O
	2	6	3	4
×				3

Step 2. Multiply ones. 4 ones × 3 = 12 ones = 1 ten 2 ones. Write 2 in ones place and carry 1 to the tens place.

	Th	H	T	O
			①	
	2	6	3	4
×				3
				2

Step 3. Multiply tens. 3 tens × 3 = 9 tens. 9 tens + 1 ten (carried) = 10 tens = 1 hundred 0 tens.

Write 0 in tens place and carry 1 to the hundreds place.

	Th	H	T	O
		①	①	
	2	6	3	4
×				3
			0	2

Step 4. Multiply hundreds. 6 hundreds × 3 = 18 hundreds. 18 hundreds + 1 hundred (carried) = 19 hundreds = 1 thousand 9 hundreds. Write 9 in hundreds place and carry 1 to the thousands place.

	Th	H	T	O
	①	①	①	
	2	6	3	4
×				3
		9	0	2

Step 5. Multiply thousands. 2 thousands × 3 = 6 thousands. 6 thousands + 1 thousand (carried) = 7 thousands. Write 7 in thousands place.

	Th	H	T	O
	①	①	①	
	2	6	3	4
×				3
	7	9	0	2

So, 2,634 × 3 = 7,902.

Exercise 6B

Apply and Learn

A Multiply :

1.

2	3	5
×		3

2.

4	6	8
×		2

3.

1	6	9
×		4

4.

4	1	3
×		7

5.

8	3	8
×		8

6.

8	7	3
×		7

7.

6	6	8
×		6

8.

7	6	4
×		2

B Multiply :

1.

2	4	2	7
×			7

2.

2	0	1	2
×			4

3.

1	6	6	5
×			6

4.

1	2	3	3
×			7

5.

3	7	4	0
×			2

6.

2	4	0	8
×			3

7.

4	5	6	7
×			2

8.

3	0	6	8
×			3

Explore and Learn

CODE-ZNAH

Multiplication by 2-digit Numbers

Multiply 35 by 26.

Step 1 : Write 35 and 26 as shown.

	3	5
×	2	6

Step 2 : Multiply 35 by 6 and write the partial product as shown.

	3	5
×	2	6
2	1	0

Step 3 : Now, since 2 is at tens place, we have to multiply 35 by 20. Now, Multiply 35 by 20.

	3	5
×	2	6
2	1	0
7	0	0

Step 4 : Add the two partial products.

	3	5
×	2	6
2	1	0
7	0	0
9	1	0

	3	5	
×	2	6	⟵ 20 + 6
2	1	0	⟵ 35 × 6
7	0	0	⟵ 35 × 20
9	1	0	⟵ 35 × 26

Hence, 35 × 26 = 910.

The above procedure can be summarised as :

Multiply 536 by 21.

We multiply 536 by 1 and 536 by 20 respectively.

Finally add the results to get the required product.

		5	3	6	
		×	2	1	⟵ 20 + 1
		5	3	6	⟵ 536 × 1
1	0	7	2	0	⟵ 536 × 20
1	1	2	5	6	⟵ 536 × 21

So, 536 × 21 = 11,256

Exercise 6C

Apply and Learn

A Multiply each of the following :

1.

	2	8
×	1	2

2.

1	5	9
×	1	9

3.

2	7	9
×	3	6

4.

5	6	4
×	2	2

5.

9	5	0
×	2	3

6.

1	7	6
×	3	9

B Multiply :

1. 45 by 28 **2.** 98 by 53 **3.** 136 by 42 **4.** 216 by 63

Explore and Learn

Multiplication by a 3-digit Number

Example : Multiply 514 by 126

Solution :

126 = 100 + 20 + 6

We multiply 514 by 6, 20 and 100 respectively. Finally, we add the results to get the required product.

CODE-aS1r

		5	1	4	
	×	1	2	6	⟵ 100 + 20 + 6
	3	0	8	4	⟵ 514 × 6
1	0	2	8	0	⟵ 514 × 20
5	1	4	0	0	⟵ 514 × 100
6	4	7	6	4	⟵ 514 × 126

Observe the following examples.

		1	5	1	9	
		×	4	0	2	⟵ 400 + 0 + 2
		3	0	3	8	⟵ 1,519 × 2
	0	0	0	0	0	⟵ 1,519 × 0
6	0	7	6	0	0	⟵ 1,519 × 400
6	1	0	6	3	8	⟵ 1,519 × 402

		2	5	3	4	
		×	3	5	6	⟵ 300 + 50 + 6
	1	5	2	0	4	⟵ 2,534 × 6
1	2	6	7	0	0	⟵ 2,534 × 50
7	6	0	2	0	0	⟵ 2,534 × 300
9	0	2	1	0	4	⟵ 2,534 × 356

Exercise 6D

Apply and Learn

A Find the following products :

1.

	9	5	4
×	2	5	6

2.

	6	2	1
×	1	2	5

3.

3	2	5	6
×	2	5	8

4.

4	0	2	6
×	2	3	6

5.

1	9	2	4
×	2	1	0

6.

2	0	1	8
×	1	7	6

B Multiply :

1. 654 by 431 **2.** 501 by 123 **3.** 2,397 by 315 **4.** 1,245 by 319

Explore and Learn

Properties of Multiplication

1. Order Property : Observe the following :

	3	4	⟵ Multiplicand
×	2	6	⟵ Multiplier
2	0	4	
6	8	0	
8	8	4	⟵ Product

	2	6	⟵ Multiplicand
×	3	4	⟵ Multiplier
1	0	4	
7	8	0	
8	8	4	⟵ Product

What do we observe?

We see that the product in both the cases is the same.

Hence, the product does not change when the order of numbers is changed. This property is known as **order property of multiplication.**

2. Multiplicative Property of 1 : Observe the following :

$6 \times 1 = 6$, $98 \times 1 = 98$, $115 \times 1 = 115$

What do we observe?

We see that the product of a number and 1 is the number itself. This property is known as **multiplicative property of 1**.

3. Multiplicative Property of 0 : Observe the following :

$3 \times 0 = 0$, $24 \times 0 = 0$, $157 \times 0 = 0$

What do we observe?

We see that the product of any number and 0 is 0. This property is known as **multiplicative property of 0.**

Multiplication by Tens

To multiply a number by 10, 20, 30, ..., 90, multiply the number by 1, 2, 3, ..., 9 respectively and insert one zero on the right of the product.

Example 1 : Multiply 754 by 30.

Solution :

Step 1 : Multiply 754 by 3.

Step 2 : Insert one zero on the right of the product to get 22,620.

Hence, 754 × 30 = 22,620.

	7	5	4
		×	3
2	2	6	2

Example 2 : Multiply 1,369 by 90.

Solution :

Step 1 : Multiply 1,369 by 9.

Step 2 : Insert one zero on the right of the product to get 1,23,210.

Hence, 1,369 × 90 = 1,23,210.

	1	3	6	9
			×	9
1	2	3	2	1

Multiplication by Hundreds

CODE-sAjR

To multiply a number by 100, 200, 300, ... 900, we multiply the number by 1, 2, 3, ..., 9 respectively and insert two zeros on the right of the product.

Example 1 : Multiply 487 by 300.

Solution :

Step 1 : Multiply 487 by 3.

Step 2 : Insert two zeros on the right of the product to get 1,46,100.

Hence, 487 × 300 = 1,46,100.

	4	8	7
		×	3
1	4	6	1

Example 2 : Multiply 153 by 800.

Solution :

Step 1 : Multiply 153 by 8.

Step 2 : Insert two zeros on the right of the product to get 1,22,400.

Hence, 153 × 800 = 1,22,400.

	1	5	3
		×	8
1	2	2	4

Multiplication by Thousands

CODE-62oC

To multiply a number by 1,000, 2,000, 3,000, ..., 9,000, we multiply the number by 1, 2, 3, ..., 9 respectively and insert three zeros on the right of the product.

Example 1 : Multiply 231 by 4,000.

Solution :

Step 1 : Multiply 231 by 4.

Step 2 : Insert three zeros on the right of the product to get 9,24,000.

Hence, 231 × 4,000 = 9,24,000.

2	3	1
	×	4
9	2	4

Example 2 : Multiply 105 by 7,000.

Solution :

Step 1 : Multiply 105 by 7.

1	0	5
	×	7
7	3	5

Step 2 : Insert three zeros on the right of the product to get 7,35,000.

Hence, 105 × 7,000 = 7,35,000.

CHALLENGE

A 1-digit number is multiplied by 10. This 1-digit number is also multiplied by 100. The difference between the two products is 450. Identify the 1-digit number.

Exercise 6E

Apply and Learn

A Fill in the blanks :

1. 518 × 9 = 9 × ______
2. 624 × ______ = 38 × 624
3. 79,125 × ______ = 79,125
4. 4,875 × 69 = 69 × ______
5. ______ × 165 = 165
6. 19,150 × 0 = ______
7. 27,891 × ______ = 0
8. 71,240 × ______ = 71,240
9. ______ × 58,319 = 0
10. 27 × 43,194 = ______ × 27
11. 2,586 × ______ = 2,586
12. 57,130 × ______ = 1,576 × 57,130
13. 600 × 516 = 516 × ______
14. 2,893 × ______ = 0

B Find the following products :

1. 12,635 × 10
2. 8,685 × 20
3. 2,611 × 80
4. 11,653 × 60
5. 3,635 × 100
6. 8,781 × 200
7. 187 × 900
8. 1,410 × 300
9. 217 × 2,000
10. 83 × 7,000
11. 192 × 5,000
12. 74 × 8,000

Explore and Learn

Word Problems

Example 1 : A bag contains 125 kg rice. How much rice will 89 such bags have?

Solution : 1 bag contains = 125 kg.

89 bags contain = 125 × 89 kg.

Hence, 89 bags will contain 11,125 kg rice.

		1	2	5
		×	8	9
	1	1	2	5
1	0	0	0	0
1	1	1	2	5

Example 2 : A bus travels a distance of 285 km every day. What distance will it travel in a year?

Solution : Distance travelled by the bus in one day = 285 km

There are 365 days in a year.

Distance travelled by the bus in 365 days = 285 km × 365

			2	8	5
		×	3	6	5
		1	4	2	5
	1	7	1	0	0
	8	5	5	0	0
1	0	4	0	2	5

Hence, the bus will travel 1,04,025 km in a year.

Exercise 6F

Apply and Learn

1. The cost of a pack of *Ghee* is ₹ 308. Find the cost of 97 such packs.

2. There are 622 pages in a notebook. How many pages are there in 65 such notebooks?

3. A rack can hold 1,850 books. How many books can be kept in 46 such racks?
4. A transistor costs ₹ 1,642. Find the cost of 95 such transistors.
5. A farmer produced 735 quintals of rice. He sold it at the rate of ₹ 1525 per quintal. How much money did he get?

6. A computer operator can compose 8,314 words in a day. How many words will he compose in 4 months?

7. The cost of a doll is ₹ 314. What is the cost of 680 such dolls?

8. A carton can hold 15 dozens of oranges. How many oranges are there in 825 cartons?

9. A candle factory produce 814 candles in a day. How many candles will this factory produce in one year?

10. The capacity of a water tank is 7,325 litres. In a city, there are 125 such tanks. What is the water storage capacity of the city?

11. The weight of a bag containing wheat is 5 kg 850 g. Find the weight of 235 such bags.

12. The weight of a toy is 736 g. What is the weight of 250 such toys? Give your answer in kg.

REMEMBER

1 month = 30 days.
1 year = 365 days.
1 kg = 1,000 g.
1 dozen = 12.

Explore and Learn

Quick Multiplications

1. The product of a number ending in 5 with itself can be done mentally as follows.

Cross out 5 from the number to obtain the new number.

Multiply this new number by its successor.

Suffix the product by 25 to obtain the answer.

Let us find 75 × 75 using the method shown alongside.

Deleting 5 from 75 we obtain 7.

Successor of 7 is 8.

Multiplying 7 by 8, we get 56.

Suffixing 56 by 25, we get the answer as 5625.

		7	5
	×	7	5
5	6	2	5

7 × 8 = 56   5 × 5 = 25

8 is successor of 7.

So, 75 × 75 = 5625.

2. Let us multiply two numbers with sum of ones digits as 10 and remaining digits same.

For example :

	2	8
×	2	2
6	1	6

2 × 3 = 6   8 × 2 = 16

3 is successor of 2.

So, 28 × 22 = 616.

For example :

		1	0	9
	–	1	0	1
1	1	0	0	9

10 × 11 = 110   9 × 1 = 9 = 09

3 is successor of 2.

So, 109 × 101 = 11009

9 is written as 09 to give it a 2-digit representation.

Exercise 6G

Apply and Learn

Find the following products mentally :

1.

	3	5
×	3	5

2.

	6	5
×	6	5

3.

	8	5
×	8	5

4.

	9	9	5
×	9	9	5

5.

	7	9	5
×	7	9	5

6.

	7	1
×	7	9

7.

	9	8
×	9	2

8.

	1	9	3
×	1	9	7

9.

	4	9	9
×	4	9	1

10.

	9	9	2
×	9	9	8

Explore and Learn

Rounding Numbers

CODE-UMWz

In our daily life, we come across many situations where we do not state the exact number as the answer to the questions which require to tell us how many.

We present the number as the nearest multiple of ten, hundred or thousand.

This is called **rounding the numbers**.

For example : There are about 2,000 children in this school.

There were about 200 cars on the road at 4 : 30 p.m.

The bus will arrive in about 10 minutes.

Rounding Off to the Nearest 10

To round off to the nearest 10, look at the digit in the ones place.

If the digit is 1, 2, 3 or 4, we round off to the same ten and mark 0 in the ones place. If it is 5, 6, 7, 8 or 9 we round off to the next ten and mark 0 in the ones place.

33 is rounded off to 30. 27 is rounded off to 30.

125 is rounded off to 130. 282 is rounded off to 280.

Rounding a number to a smaller number is known as **rounding down**.

Rounding a number to a greater number is known as **rounding up**.

Rounding Off to the Nearest 100

Look at the digit in the tens place.

If the digit in the tens place is 0, 1, 2, 3 or 4, we round of to the same hundred with zeroes in tens and ones places.

528 is rounded off to 500. 640 is rounded off to 600. 749 is rounded off to 700.

If the digit in the tens place is 5, 6, 7, 8 or 9, we round off to the next hundred with zeroes in tens and ones places.

392 is rounded off to 400. 7,654 is rounded off to 7,700. 2350 is rounded off to 2400.

882 is rounded off to 900. 9,376 is rounded off to 9,400. 2499 is rounded off to 2500.

351 is rounded off to 400. 6,268 is rounded off to 6,300. 8372 is rounded off to 8400.

Rounding Off to the Nearest 1000

Look at the digit in the hundreds place.

If the digit in the hundreds place is 0, 1, 2, 3 or 4, we round off to the same thousand with zeroes in hundreds, tens and ones places.

4,125 is rounded off to 4,000. 9,356 is rounded off to 9,000.

3,240 is rounded off to 3,000. 7,481 is rounded off to 7,000.

If the digit in the hundred place is 5, 6, 7, 8 or 9, we round off to the next thousand with zeroes in hundreds, tens and ones places.

3,972 is rounded off to 4,000. 2,611 is rounded off to 3,000.

7,519 is rounded off to 8,000. 30,512 is rounded off to 31,000.

Exercise 6H

Apply and Learn

A Round off the following numbers to the nearest tens :

1. 51	**2.** 174	**3.** 397	**4.** 3,542	**5.** 29,834
6. 26	**7.** 469	**8.** 875	**9.** 9,283	**10.** 13,528

B Round off the following numbers to the nearest hundreds :

1. 158	**2.** 426	**3.** 6,861	**4.** 3,098	**5.** 38,472
6. 1,047	**7.** 816	**8.** 5,982	**9.** 4,351	**10.** 29,804

C Round off the following numbers to the nearest thousands :

1. 9,155	**2.** 7,983	**3.** 33,888	**4.** 15,742	**5.** 87,083
6. 8,396	**7.** 4,550	**8.** 6,237	**9.** 87,483	**10.** 46,637

Explore and Learn

CODE-Bxct

Estimation of Sum/Difference/Product

While adding two or more numbers, or subtracting them or multiplying them, we like to make the rough idea of their approximate sum or their difference or their product respectively.

Let us try to estimate the sum, difference or product of two or more numbers and see how close it is to their actual sum.

Example 1 : Estimate the sum (66 + 94) to the nearest tens and verify its closeness to actual sum.

Solution : On estimating to nearest tens, we have :

66 $\rightarrow$ 70

94 $\rightarrow$ 90

Estimated sum = 70 + 90 = 160.

Actual sum = 66 + 94 = 160.

Example 2 : Estimate the sum (4,760 + 7,245).

(a) to the nearest 100 (b) to the nearest 1,000.

Also, find the actual sum.

Solution : (a) Rounding off to nearest 100, we have

$4{,}760 \rightarrow 4{,}800.$ [As $6 > 5 \Rightarrow 60 \rightarrow 100 \Rightarrow 760 \rightarrow 800$]

$7{,}245 \rightarrow 7{,}200.$ [As $4 < 5 \Rightarrow 45 \rightarrow 0 \Rightarrow 245 \rightarrow 200$]

Thus, $4{,}760 + 7{,}245 \rightarrow 4{,}800 + 7{,}200 \rightarrow 12{,}000.$

(b) Rounding off the same numbers to nearest 1,000, we have

$4{,}760 \rightarrow 5{,}000.$ [As $7 > 5 \Rightarrow 760 \rightarrow 1{,}000 \Rightarrow 4{,}760 \rightarrow 5{,}000$]

$7{,}245 \rightarrow 7{,}000.$ [As $2 < 5 \Rightarrow 245 \rightarrow 00 \Rightarrow 7{,}245 \rightarrow 7{,}000$]

Thus, $4{,}760 + 7{,}245 \rightarrow 5{,}000 + 7{,}000 \rightarrow 12{,}000.$

Actual sum = 7,245 + 4,760 = 12,005

Example 3 : Estimate the difference 4,587 – 2,338.

(a) to the nearest tens

(b) to the nearest hundreds

(c) Which of them closer to the actual difference?

Solution : (a) Rounding off to nearest 10, we have

$4{,}587 \rightarrow 4{,}590.$ [As $7 > 5 \Rightarrow 7 \rightarrow 10$ and $87 \rightarrow 90$.]

and $2{,}338 \rightarrow 2{,}340.$ [As $8 > 5 \Rightarrow 8 \rightarrow 10$ and $38 \rightarrow 40$.]

Thus, $4{,}587 - 2{,}338 \rightarrow 4{,}590 - 2{,}340 = 2{,}250.$

(b) Rounding off to nearest 100, we have

$4{,}587 \rightarrow 4{,}600.$ [As $8 > 5 \rightarrow 87 \rightarrow 100$ or $587 \rightarrow 600$.]

and $2{,}338 \rightarrow 2{,}300.$ [As $3 < 5 \rightarrow 38 \rightarrow 00$ or $338 \rightarrow 300$.]

Thus, $4{,}587 - 2{,}338 \rightarrow 4{,}600 - 2{,}300 = 2{,}300$

(c) Actual difference = 4,587 – 2,338 = 2,249.

The first approximation (to the nearest 10) 2,250 is closer to the actual difference which is 2,249.

Example 4 : Estimate the product of 325 and 18.

Solution : $325 \rightarrow 300$ (Rounding off to hundred's place)

$18 \rightarrow 20$ (Rounding off to ten's place).

$325 \times 18 \rightarrow 300 \times 20$, i.e., 6,000.

Thus, estimated product is 6,000.

Exercise 61

Apply and Learn

A Estimate the following sums to the nearest tens :

1. 61 + 23 **2.** 65 + 32 **3.** 19 + 72 **4.** 36 + 63

Also, compare the sums with the actual sums.

B Estimate the following sums to the nearest hundreds :

1. 273 + 68 **2.** 623 + 128 **3.** 287 + 437

Also, compare the sums with the actual sums.

C Estimate the following sums to the nearest thousands :

1. 3,256 + 1,802 **2.** 6,708 + 2,376 **3.** 3,256 + 7,285

D Make an estimate of the following.

(a) to the nearest tens **(b)** to the nearest hundreds

1. 2,312 – 513 **2.** 9,072 – 3,825 **3.** 1,875 – 381

Compare your results with the actual difference .

E Estimate each of the following products by rounding off each number to the nearest tens :

1. 38 × 63 **2.** 52 × 43 **3.** 41 × 62 **4.** 63 × 52

Value Based Questions

Anushka gets ₹ 500 per month as her pocket money from her father and ₹ 200 per month from her mother. She saves ₹ 325 every month and puts it in a piggy bank.

1. In all how much money does Anushka get from her parents in 1 year?

2. How much money does she save in 1 year?

3. Do you think saving money is a good habit?

Review and Refresh

A Multiply :

1. 816 by 6 **2.** 36 by 72 **3.** 36 by 34

4. 605 by 527 **5.** 2,186 by 42 **6.** 5,219 by 152

B Find the following products :

1. 587 × 50 **2.** 4,937 × 200 **3.** 1,595 × 500 **4.** 254 × 3,000

C Fill in the blanks :

1. 16,853 × ____________ = 16,853 **2.** 61,926 × ____________ = 0

3. 4,532 × 157 = 157 × ____________ **4.** 1 × ____________ = 1,493

D Answer the following questions :

1. A farmer produced 87 quintals of wheat. He sold it at the rate of ₹1425 per quintal. How much money did he get?

2. A truck is carrying 4,325 cartons of mangoes. If a carton contains 120 mangoes, find the total number of mangoes in the truck.

Mental Maths

1. 631 × 28 = ____________ × 631.

2. ____________ × 1 = 2,845.

3. 1,936 × ____________ = ____________ × 1,936 = 0.

4. 1,592 × 126 = 1,592 × 100 + 1,592 × ____________ + ____________ × 6.

5. Find the product of the place-values of 6 in 6,965. ____________

6. Find the product of the greatest 2-digit number and the smallest 4-digit number. ____________

7. 65 × 600 = ____________

8. 219 × 1,000 = ____________

9. 7 × 8,000 = ____________

10. How many zeros are there in the product 25 × 4,000? ____________

Fun With Maths

1. What must you do to make the following statement true?

8| × 9 = 80|

2. By what number 25 be multiplied to get (a) 2525 (b) 252525?

3. A farmer has 40 wooden boxes of apples. Each box contains 25 red apples and 30 green apples.

Which of the following expressions can be used to find the total number of apples in all the wooden boxes?

(a) 40 + (25 × 30)

(b) 40 × (25 + 30)

(c) (40 + 25) × (40 + 30)

(d) (40 × 25) × (40 × 30)

To get worksheet on this chapter scan this QR code

CODE-ziC2

Maths Lab Activity

Objective : Multiplying a number by 11 using short cuts.

Materials Required : Paper and pencil only.

Procedure/Demonstration : *We can multiply any 2-digit number by 11 very quickly.*

Case 1. When the sum of the digits of the given number is less than 10.

Let us multiply 26 × 11.

Here, the sum of the digits of 26 is 2 + 6 = 8. This is less than 10.

Write down the ones digit (6) at the ones place of the product. Add the ones digit (6) and tens digit (2) and write the sum at the tens place of the product. Write down the tens digit at the hundreds place of the product.

Case 2. When the sum of the digits of the given number is more than 9.

Let us multiply 78 × 11.

Here, the sum of the digits of 78 is 7 + 8 = 15, which is greater than 10.

Write down the ones digit(8) at the ones place of the product.

Add the ones digit (8) and tens digit (7). Write 5 of 15 (8 + 7) in the tens place of the product and carry 1 to hundreds place.

Add the hundreds digit (7) and 1 (carried) to get 8. Write 8 at the hundreds place of the product.

Now, try the following multiplications :

	4	2
×	1	1

	2	7
×	1	1

	4	3
×	1	1

	5	6
×	1	1

	8	4
×	1	1

	9	7
×	1	1

CHECK YOUR PACE

(Based on Chapters 4, 5, 6)

A Add :

1. 3,276, and 4,381

2. 2,196, 6,183 and 146

3. 5,896, 3,216 and 27

4. 2,163, 5,173 and 830

B Subtract :

1. 4,218 – 1,063 **2.** 7,859 – 2,016 **3.** 6,003 – 2,519 **4.** 4,290 – 2,657

C Fill in the boxes :

1.

	7		2	6
+	1	7	4	
		3		2

2.

		3	0	4
–	4		3	7
	1	6		

D Simplify :

1. 4,259 – 2,635 + 1,827

2. 2,516 + 5,089

E Multiply :

1.

2	5	7
	×	4

2.

	8	3	2
		×	5

3.

1	2	5	7
		×	6

4.

	5	6	9	8
			×	3

5.

	8	5	5
	×	1	6

6.

	3	5	9
×	1	2	7

F Find the products :

1. 256 × 100 **2.** 439 × 1,000 **3.** 805 × 200

G Estimate the following sums to the nearest tens :

1. 432 + 147 **2.** 5,832 + 2,347 **3.** 458 – 273 **4.** 6,524 – 1,785

THEME 2 : NUMBER OPERATIONS

7 Division

Learning Target To understand division.

I Can

- **I can explain** dividend, divisor and quotient.
- **I can divide** 2-digit, 3-digit and 4-digit numbers by 1-digit number.
- **I can explain** properties of division.
- **I can solve** word problems on division.

Let Us Recall

In Class 3, we learnt how to divide a number by a 1-digit number. Let us have a quick review of what we read there.

Exercise 7A

Divide :

1. 44 ÷ 4	**2.** 54 ÷ 6	**3.** 48 ÷ 6
4. 63 ÷ 7	**5.** 64 ÷ 8	**6.** 35 ÷ 5
7. 72 ÷ 8	**8.** 28 ÷ 7	**9.** 90 ÷ 9

Explore and Learn

Terms Associated with Division

1. **Dividend :** The number to be divided is called the **dividend**.

2. **Divisor :** The number by which we divide the dividend is called the **divisor.**

3. **Quotient :** The number that we get after the division is called the **quotient.**

4. **Remainder :** The number which is left undivided is called the **remainder.**

5. In a division sum, we always have :

   Dividend = divisor × quotient + remainder.

```
            8  ← Quotient
Divisor → 7) 5 8  ← Dividend
           −5 6
           ----
              2  ← Remainder
```

REMEMBER

Remainder is always less than the divisor.

Here, we shall further practice with dividend up to 4-digit numbers to attain mastery over this operation.

Dividing a 2-digit Number by a 1-digit Number without Remainder

CODE-bX8e

Divide 63 by 3.

We proceed as follows :

Step 1. Arrange the 2 numbers as shown.

```
3)63
```

Step 2. Divide the 6 tens by 3.

We know, 3 × 2 = 6.

Write 2 in tens place of the quotient and 6 below 6.

Subtract 6 from 6 to get 0.

```
   2
3)63
 −6
  0
```

Step 3. Bring down 3 ones and divide it by 3.

We know, 3 × 1 = 3.

Write 1 in the ones place of the quotient and 3 below 3.

Subtract 3 from 3 to get 0.

Thus, 63 ÷ 3 = 21 and remainder = 0.

```
  21
3)63
 −6↓
  03
  −3
   0
```

Dividing a 2-digit Number by a 1-digit Number with Remainder

CODE-WGbg

Divide 95 by 4.

1. Start by looking at the first number in the dividend.
   Find a number in the table of 4 less than or equal to 9.
   4 × 1 = 4, 4 × 2 = 8, 4 × 3 = 12.
   So, 2 is the required number.
   4 × 2 = 8 , so write 8 below 9.

```
4)95
```

```
    2
4) 95
  −8
```

2. Subtract the number you got by multiplying the divisor, from the number in the dividend.

9 − 8 = 1

```
    2
4) 95
  - 8
   ---
    1
```

3. Bring down the next digit, from the number in the dividend.

```
    2
4) 95
  - 8↓
   ---
   15
```

4. Repeat the same process again.

4 × 1 = 4 ; 4 × 2 = 8 ; 4 × 3 = 12 ;

15 − 12 = 3.

So, quotient = 23, and remainder = 3.

```
   23
4) 95
  - 8↓
   ---
   15
  -12
   ---
    3
```

Now, let us find 62 ÷ 5.

So, 62 is dividend, 5 is divisor

12 is quotient, 2 is remainder

Check : Dividend = Quotient × Divisor + Remainder

= 12 × 5 + 2

= 60 + 2 = 62 = Dividend.

```
   12
5) 62
  - 5↓
   ---
   12
  -10
   ---
    2
```

Exercise 7B

Apply and Learn

A Find the quotient and the remainder, using long division method :

1. 24 ÷ 7 **2.** 30 ÷ 8 **3.** 36 ÷ 5 **4.** 50 ÷ 9 **5.** 42 ÷ 8

B Divide the following and check your answer using division algorithm.

1. 45 ÷ 7 **2.** 82 ÷ 9 **3.** 62 ÷ 8 **4.** 34 ÷ 4 **5.** 56 ÷ 6

C Divide the following :

1. 84 ÷ 4 **2.** 56 ÷ 7 **3.** 82 ÷ 2 **4.** 78 ÷ 6 **5.** 91 ÷ 7

6. 96 ÷ 8 **7.** 70 ÷ 5 **8.** 84 ÷ 7 **9.** 78 ÷ 3 **10.** 75 ÷ 5

D Divide and check your answer :

1. 89 ÷ 8 **2.** 45 ÷ 2 **3.** 97 ÷ 3 **4.** 69 ÷ 4 **5.** 88 ÷ 5

6. 52 ÷ 7 **7.** 65 ÷ 8 **8.** 61 ÷ 6 **9.** 83 ÷ 6 **10.** 92 ÷ 6

Explore and Learn

Dividing a 3-digit Number by a 1-digit Number without Remainder

Divide 669 by 3.

1. Start by looking at the first number in the dividend.

```
3)669
```

Find a number in the table of 3 less than or equal to 6.

3 × 1 = 3; 3 × 2 = 6.

So, 2 is the required number.

3 × 2 = 6, so write 6 below 6.

```
   2
3)669
 -6
```

2. Subtract, the number you got by multiplying the divisor, from the number in the dividend.

6 − 6 = 0

```
   2
3)669
 -6
  0
```

3. Bring down the next digit, from the number in the dividend.

```
   2
3)669
 -6
  06
```

4. Repeat the same process again.

6 − 6 = 0.

```
   22
3)669
 -6
  06
 - 6
  09
```

5. Bring down 9. Since, 9 > 3.

Since remainder is greater than divisor, therefore, we will repeat the process again.

Therefore,

669 ÷ 3 = 223.

```
   223
3)669
 -6
  06
 - 6
  09
 - 9
   0
```

Dividing a 3-digit Number by a 1-digit Number with Remainder

CODE-Ty7P

Let us divide 625 by 4.

```
   156
4)625
 -4
  22
 -20
   25
  -24
    1
```

So, Quotient = 156 and Remainder = 1.

Check : Quotient × Divisor + Remainder

= 156 × 4 + 1 = 624 + 1

= 625 = Dividend

Again **let us divide 426 by 4.**

```
    106
 4)426
  -4
   02
    0
   26
  -24
    2
```

So, quotient = 106 and remainder = 2.

Let us divide 259 by 6.

Here 2 < 6, so we divide 25 by 6 and 6 × 4 = 24.

So, we write the 4 just above 5.

Then proceed as usual.

So, 259 ÷ 6 gives quotient = 43 and remainder = 1.

```
    43
 6)259
  -24
    19
  - 18
     1
```

Exercise 7C

Apply and Learn

A Divide the following :

1. 936 ÷ 3	**2.** 464 ÷ 2	**3.** 550 ÷ 5	**4.** 484 ÷ 4	**5.** 585 ÷ 3
6. 840 ÷ 7	**7.** 636 ÷ 4	**8.** 755 ÷ 5	**9.** 616 ÷ 7	**10.** 348 ÷ 4

B Find the quotient and the remainder :

1. 315 ÷ 6	**2.** 386 ÷ 6	**3.** 258 ÷ 7	**4.** 353 ÷ 8	**5.** 179 ÷ 2
6. 408 ÷ 5	**7.** 540 ÷ 7	**8.** 419 ÷ 6	**9.** 270 ÷ 8	**10.** 372 ÷ 7

Explore and Learn

Division of 4-digit Numbers by a 1-digit Number

CODE-HfqH

Let us divide 4,272 by 6.

Step 1. Arrange the numbers as shown.

```
6)4272
```

Step 2. We begin from left, i.e., with thousands Divide 4 thousands by 6. Also, 6 × 1 = 6. But, 6 > 4. So, we take 6 × 0 = 0.

Write 0 in the thousands place of the quotient and 0 below 4. Subtract 0 from 4.

```
   0
6)4272
 -0
  4
```

Step 3. Bring down 2 and divide 42 by 6.
Also, 6 × 7 = 42. So, write 7 in the hundreds place of the quotient and 42 below 42. Subtract 42 from 42.

```
      0 7
6 ) 4 2 7 2
  – 0
  -----
    4 2
  – 4 2
  -----
      0
```

Step 4. Bring down 7 and divide it by 6. Also, 6 × 1 = 6. So, write 1 in the tens place of the quotient and 6 below 7. Subtract 6 from 7.

```
      0 7 1
6 ) 4 2 7 2
  – 0
  -------
    4 2
  – 4 2
  -------
      0 7
    –   6
  -------
        1
```

Step 5. Bring down 2 and divide 12 by 6. Also, 6 × 2 = 12. So, write 2 in the ones place of the quotient and 12 below 12. Subtract 12 from 12.

```
      0 7 1 2
6 ) 4 2 7 2
  – 0
  ---------
    4 2
  – 4 2
  ---------
      0 7
    –   6
  ---------
        1 2
      – 1 2
  ---------
          0
```

Thus, 4,272 ÷ 6 = 712 and remainder = 0

Let us divide 4,361 by 9.

Step 1.

```
9 ) 4 3 6 1
```

Step 2.

```
      0
9 ) 4 3 6 1
  – 0
  -------
    4
```

Step 3.

```
      0 4
9 ) 4 3 6 1
  – 0
  -------
    4 3
  – 3 6
  -------
      7
```

Step 4.

```
      0 4 8
9 ) 4 3 6 1
  – 0
  -------
    4 3
  – 3 6
  -------
      7 6
    – 7 2
  -------
        4
```

Step 5.

```
      0 4 8 4
9 ) 4 3 6 1
  – 0
  ---------
    4 3
  – 3 6
  ---------
      7 6
    – 7 2
  ---------
        4 1
      – 3 6
  ---------
          5
```

Thus, 4,361 ÷ 9 = 484 and remainder = 5.

Check : We can verify our solution as below :

	4	8	4	⟵ Quotient
	×		9	⟵ Divisor
4	3	5	6	
	+		5	⟵ Remainder
4	3	6	1	⟵ Dividend

Hence, our answer is correct.

CHALLENGE

All the missing numbers are the same. Find the missing numbers.

$$3 \overline{) \, 2\square\square7} = \square\square\square$$

Solve in your notebook.

Now, we have read division, so to check whether a number is even or odd, we use the concept of division. In fact, all even numbers are divisible by 2.

All those numbers which when divided by 2 give 0 as remainder, are even numbers.

Let us check which of the following are even and which are odd.

204, 649 and 5390

Let us divide these numbers by 2.

```
     102              324              2695
 2 ) 204          2 ) 649          2 ) 5390
    −2               −6               −4
    ---              ---              ---
     04               04               13
    −04              −4               −12
    ---              ---              ---
      0               09                19
                     −8               −18
                     ---              ---
                       1                10
                                       −10
                                       ---
                                         0
```

We see that on dividing 204 and 5,390 by 2, we get the remainder as 0. It means these numbers are divisible by 2. Hence, these numbers are even numbers.

On the other hand, if we divide 649 by 2, we get the remainder as 1. It means it is not divisible by 2. Hence, it is an odd number.

Exercise 7D

Apply and Learn

A Divide and find the quotient :

1. 1,352 ÷ 8 **2.** 2,742 ÷ 6 **3.** 5,448 ÷ 8 **4.** 5,600 ÷ 7

5. 4,160 ÷ 8 **6.** 4,716 ÷ 9 **7.** 5,820 ÷ 4 **8.** 3,150 ÷ 5

B Find the quotient and the remainder. Also, check your answer.

1. 3,561 ÷ 2
2. 8,303 ÷ 5
3. 1,954 ÷ 7
4. 3,510 ÷ 4
5. 3,512 ÷ 6
6. 4,001 ÷ 7

C Divide by 2 and state whether the following numbers are even or odd.

1. 47
2. 105
3. 862
4. 2570

Explore and Learn

CODE-ZoeZ

Division by 10 and 100

Divide 75 by 10

$$\begin{array}{r|l} & 7 \\ \hline 10 & 75 \\ & -70 \\ \hline & 5 \end{array}$$

Quotient → 7 | 5 ← Remainder

7 5 ÷ 10

Divide 405 by 10

$$\begin{array}{r|l} & 40 \\ \hline 10 & 405 \\ & -40 \\ \hline & 05 \\ & -0 \\ \hline & 5 \end{array}$$

Quotient → 40 | 5 ← Remainder

4 0 5 ÷ 10

Divide 1528 by 10

$$\begin{array}{r|l} & 152 \\ \hline 10 & 1528 \\ & -10 \\ \hline & 52 \\ & -50 \\ \hline & 28 \\ & -20 \\ \hline & 8 \end{array}$$

Quotient → 152 | 8 ← Remainder

1 5 2 8 ÷ 10

Divide 16000 by 10

$$\begin{array}{r|l} & 1600 \\ \hline 10 & 16000 \\ & -10 \\ \hline & 60 \\ & -60 \\ \hline & 00 \\ & -0 \\ \hline & 00 \\ & -0 \\ \hline & 0 \end{array}$$

Quotient → 1600 | 0 ← Remainder

1 6 0 0 0 ÷ 10

What do we observe?

We see that when a number (dividend) is divided by 10, the quotient is obtained by removing the ones digit from the number (dividend) and the digit at ones place is the remainder.

Divide 452 by 100

```
        4
100 ) 4 5 2
    – 4 0 0
    -------
        5 2
```

Thus, we can say :

Quotient → 4 | 52 ← Remainder

4 52 ÷ 100

Divide 8357 by 100

```
         8 3
100 ) 8 3 5 7
    – 8 0 0
    ---------
        3 5 7
      – 3 0 0
    ---------
          5 7
```

Quotient → 83 | 57 ← Remainder

83 57 ÷ 100

What do we observe?

We see that when a number (dividend) is divided by 100, the quotient is obtained by removing the last two digits on the extreme right of the number (dividend). The number formed by these last two digits is the remainder.

Properties of Division

CODE-VM7J

1. When the divisor is 1, quotient is the same as the dividend.
   8 ÷ 1 = 8, 15 ÷ 1 = 15, 40 ÷ 1 = 40
2. When the divisor and dividend are the same non-zero numbers, then the quotient is 1.
   9 ÷ 9 = 1, 16 ÷ 16 = 1, 52 ÷ 52 = 1
3. When the dividend is 0, the quotient is 0.
   0 ÷ 5 = 0, 0 ÷ 7 = 0, 0 ÷ 21 = 0
4. The divisor can never be 0. Or division by 0 is meaningless.

Exercise 7E

Apply and Learn

A Find the quotient and the remainder :

1. 91 ÷ 10
2. 167 ÷ 10
3. 5,428 ÷ 10
4. 7,918 ÷ 10
5. 8,732 ÷ 100
6. 4,035 ÷ 100
7. 3,500 ÷ 100
8. 8,501 ÷ 100

B Fill in the blanks :

1. 9 ÷ 1 = ________
2. 6 ÷ 6 = ________
3. 0 ÷ 10 = ________
4. 15 ÷ 15 = ________
5. 10 ÷ ________ = 10
6. 12 ÷ ________ = 1
7. 21 ÷ 1 = ________
8. ________ ÷ 12 = 0
9. ________ ÷ 16 = 1

Explore and Learn

Word Problems

Example 1: The cost of 6 kg sugar is ₹78. Find the cost of 1 kg sugar.

Solution : Cost of 6 kg sugar = ₹78.

Cost of 1 kg sugar = ₹78 ÷ 6.

Hence, the cost of 1 kg sugar is ₹13.

```
    13
6 ) 78
   -6
   ---
    18
   -18
   ---
     0
```

Example 2 : A milk container can store 8 litres of milk. How many containers are required to store 3,408 litres of milk?

Solution : Capacity of one container = 8 litres of milk.

Required number of containers = 3,408 ÷ 8.

Hence, 426 containers are required.

```
     426
8 ) 3408
   -32
   ----
     20
    -16
   ----
      48
     -48
   ----
       0
```

Example 3: 1,506 roses are there in 6 crates. How many roses are there in 1 crate? How many roses can be packed in 19 such crates?

Solution : Number of roses = 1,506.

Number of crates = 6.

Each crate contains 1,506 ÷ 6 roses

Thus, each crate contains 251 roses.

Now, number of roses in 1 crate = 251.

Number of crates = 19.

Total number of roses = 251 × 19.

Thus, 4,769 roses can be packed into 19 crates.

	2	5	1
	×	1	9
2	2	5	9
2	5	1	0
4	7	6	9

```
     251
6 ) 1506
   -12
   ----
     30
    -30
   ----
       6
      -6
   ----
       0
```

Exercise 7F

Apply and Learn

1. The cost of 4 chocolates is ₹52. What is the cost of one chocolate?

2. Manish has ₹84. The cost of one pencil box is ₹14. How many pencil boxes can Manish buy for ₹84?

3. The weight of 8 boxes is 144 kg. What is the weight of one box?
4. There are 280 students. They are divided equally into 4 sections. How many students are there in each section?
5. The cost of one pen is ₹ 8. How many pens can be bought for ₹648?
6. Rakesh distributed ₹ 875 among 7 children equally. How many rupees did each child get?
7. The total number of seats in a train is 675 and there are 9 compartments. All the compartments have the same number of seats. How many seats are there in each compartment?

8. A candle factory produces 1,792 candles in a week. Find the number of candles produced in 18 days.

9. There are 10 notebooks of the same kind. If the total number of pages is 1,450, find the number of pages in each notebook.
10. 9,800 books are made into bundles, each containing 8 books. How many bundles are made?
11. The cost of 8 kg of sugar is ₹ 280. Find the cost of 1 kg of sugar. Also, find the cost of 15 kg of sugar.

12. A bus covers 192 km in 6 hours. Find the distance covered by it in 11 hours.

Value Based Questions

The students of class 4 donated ₹ 4,200 for flood victims. Each student contributed the same amount and there are 100 students in the class.

1. How much money was donated by each student?
2. By donating money for the flood victims which value is depicted by the students?

Review and Refresh

A Write the dividend, the divisor and the quotient in each of the following:

1. 45 ÷ 5 = 9 **2.** 21 ÷ 7 = 3 **3.** 152 ÷ 8 = 19

B Divide and find the quotient and the remainder :

1. 960 ÷ 8 **2.** 1,792 ÷ 7 **3.** 3,975 ÷ 5 **4.** 2,640 ÷ 3
5. 2,520 ÷ 6 **6.** 3,655 ÷ 7 **7.** 3,608 ÷ 8 **8.** 5,954 ÷ 7

C In each of the following, find the quotient and the remainder :

1. 35 ÷ 10 **2.** 185 ÷ 10 **3.** 1,703 ÷ 100 **4.** 6,815 ÷ 100
5. 4,103 ÷ 100 **6.** 5,010 ÷ 100 **7.** 3,102 ÷ 100 **8.** 9,358 ÷ 10

D Fill in the blanks :

1. 105 ÷ 1 = ________ **2.** ________ ÷ 1 = 9,762
3. ________ ÷ 2,314 = 1 **4.** 0 ÷ 521 = ________

E Answer the following questions :

1. I want to distribute ₹3,600 among 8 persons. How many rupees will each person get?
2. A cyclist covers 126 km in 6 hours. What distance will he cover in 5 hours?
3. In a division, divisor = 100, quotient = 25 and remainder = 75, find the dividend.

Mental Maths

1. 8 × 6 = 48 gives the division facts ________ and ________
2. In a division, remainder is always ________ than the divisor.
3. 5000 ÷ 5 = ________
4. 4218 ÷ 10 gives quotient = ________ and remainder = ________
5. 6308 ÷ 100 gives quotient = ________ and remainder = ________
6. ________ ÷ 1 = 5926.
7. 2895 ÷ ________ = 1
8. ________ ÷ 62 = 0
9. 4444 ÷ 4 = ________
10. Can we divide 0 by a number? ________

Fun With Maths

1. Can you make eight 8s equal to 1,000, using – and ÷ signs?

2. The teacher encouraged some children to use their own strategies to solve the problem on the following criteria.

- Division as equal sharing.
- Division as equal grouping.
- Division as repeated subtraction.

Madhav is making sweets on the occasion of Diwali. He has made a tray of some ladoos and packed them in small boxes as shown in the image below.

Observe the above information and answer the following questions:

(i) How many total ladoos are there in a tray as shown in the above picture?

(a) 40 (b) 80 (c) 100 (d) 120

(ii) If 4 ladoos are packed in each box, then how many boxes are needed?

(a) 20 (b) 15 (c) 30 (d) 40

(iii) Which strategy did Madhav use in the above question?

(a) Division as equal sharing (b) Division as equal grouping

(c) Division as repeated subtraction (d) Division of terms

(iv) There are a total of 516 ladoos in 6 boxes. There are an equal number of ladoos in each box. Exactly how many ladoos are there in each box?

(a) 96 (b) 86 (c) 81 (d) 68

3. If  ÷ 8 = ,  × 2 = 18, then, the value of  +  is:

(a) 72 (b) 81 (c) 9 (d) 48

To get worksheet on this chapter scan this QR code

CODE-uc8R

Maths Lab Activity

Objective : Dividing a 2-digit or a 3-digit number by 9 using short cut method.

Materials Required : Pen and paper only.

Procedure/Demonstration : We can divide any 2 or 3-digit number by 9 quickly.

Case I : Dividing a 2-digit number by 9.

Type 1 : When the sum of the digits is less than 9.

In this case, the tens digit of the dividend gives quotient and the sum of the two digits gives remainder.

Let us divide 62 by 9.

Quotient = 6

$62 \div 9$

Remainder = 6 + 2 = 8

Type 2 : When the sum of the digits is greater than or equal to 9 but less than 18.

In this case, 1 more than the tens digit of the dividend gives quotient. To get the remainder, subtract 9 from the sum of the digits of the dividend.

$75 \div 9$ gives quotient $= 7 + 1 = 8$ and remainder $= 12 - 9 = 3$

$63 \div 9$ gives quotient $= 6 + 1 = 7$ and remainder $= 9 - 9 = 0$

Case II : Dividing a 3-digit number by 9.

Type 1 : When the sum of the digits is less than 9.

In this case, the quotient is obtained by adding the number formed by hundreds and tens digits to the hundreds digit. The sum of the three digits gives the remainder.

$213 \div 9$, gives quotient $= 21 + 2 = 23$ and remainder $= 2 + 1 + 3 = 6$

Type 2 : When the sum of the digits is greater than or equal to 9 but less than 18.

Here, we first add the number formed by hundreds and tens digits to the hundreds digit. 1 more than this sum is the quotient. To get the remainder, subtract 9 from the sum of the digits.

$537 \div 9$ gives quotient $= 53 + 5 + 1 = 59$ and

remainder $= (5 + 3 + 7) - 9 = 15 - 9 = 6$

Now try the following divisions :

1. $56 \div 9$ **2.** $60 \div 9$ **3.** $71 \div 9$ **4.** $80 \div 9$

5. $36 \div 9$ **6.** $58 \div 9$ **7.** $83 \div 9$ **8.** $95 \div 9$

9. $150 \div 9$ **10.** $231 \div 9$ **11.** $602 \div 9$ **12.** $710 \div 9$

13. $254 \div 9$ **14.** $603 \div 9$ **15.** $575 \div 9$ **16.** $943 \div 9$

THEME 3 : PLAYING WITH NUMBERS

Multiples and Factors

Learning Target

To understand multiples and factors.

I Can

- **I can explain** multiples and factors.
- **I can find** multiples and factors of any number.
- **I can explain** properties of factors and multiples.
- **I can identify** prime and composite numbers.
- **I can express** any number as product of its prime factors.
- **I can apply** the divisibility tests.
- **I can find** H.C.F. and L.C.M. of two or more numbers.

Explore and Learn

CODE-X2zu

Multiples

Observe the following :

$3 \times 1 = 3$	$3 \times 4 = 12$
$3 \times 2 = 6$	$3 \times 5 = 15$
$3 \times 3 = 9$	$3 \times 6 = 18$

Here, 3 is multiplied by 1, 2, 3, 4, 5 and 6 consecutively to get the products 3, 6, 9, 12, 15 and 18, respectively. We call 3, 6, 9, 12, 15 and 18 multiples of 3.

Similarly, multiples of 4 are 4, 8, 12, 16, 20, ...

Multiples of 5 are 5, 10, 15, 20, ...

Multiples of 8 are 8, 16, 24, 32, ...

REMEMBER

The dots indicate that there is no end to the process.

Again, (a) $5 \times 6 = 30$ means 30 is a multiple of 5.

Is 30 a multiple of 6?

Yes, 30 is also a multiple of 6, since $6 \times 5 = 30$.

Thus, 30 is a multiple of 5 as well as 6.

(b) $8 \times 4 = 32$ means 32 is a multiple of 8. Also, 32 is a multiple of 4. Thus, 32 is a multiple of 8 as well as 4.

(c) $5 \times 4 \times 3 = 60$

Is 60 a multiple of 5?

Yes, 60 is a multiple of 5, since $5 \times 12 = 60$.

Is 60 a multiple of 4?

Yes, 60 is a multiple of 4, since $4 \times 15 = 60$.

Is 60 a multiple of 3?

Yes, 60 is a multiple of 3, since $3 \times 20 = 60$.

Thus, 60 is a multiple of 5, 4 and 3.

What do we conclude?

We see that when two or more numbers are multiplied together, we obtain a product which is a multiple of each of the numbers multiplied.

Is 25 a multiple of 4?

There is no number that you can multiply by 4 to get 25. So 25 is not a multiple of 4.

Example 1 : Find first four multiples of 6.

Solution : We know, $6 \times 1 = 6$, $6 \times 2 = 12$, $6 \times 3 = 18$, $6 \times 4 = 24$

Hence, the first 4 multiples of 6 are 6, 12, 18 and 24.

Example 2 : Write the first 6 multiples of 15.

Solution : We know, $15 \times 1 = 15$, $15 \times 2 = 30$

$15 \times 3 = 45$, $15 \times 4 = 60$

$15 \times 5 = 75$, $15 \times 6 = 90$

Hence, the first 6 multiples of 15 are 15, 30, 45, 60, 75 and 90.

REMEMBER

Multiples of a number are infinite.

Example 3 : Is 108 a multiple of 9?

Solution : Here, 9 divides 108 exactly.

Thus, 108 is a multiple of 9.

```
     1 2
   ------
9 ) 1 0 8
   -9
   ------
     1 8
    -1 8
   ------
       0
```

Example 4 : Is 116 a multiple of 8?

Solution : Here, 8 does not divide 116 exactly.

Thus, 116 is not a multiple of 8.

$$\begin{array}{r|l} & \ \ 14 \\ 8 & 116 \\ & -8 \\ \hline & \ \ 36 \\ & -32 \\ \hline & \quad 4 \end{array}$$

Example 5 : Find the 8th multiple of 12.

Solution : 8th multiple of 12 = 12 × 8 = 96.

CODE-mPFY

Properties of Multiples

Observe the following : 12 × 1 = 12, 18 × 1 = 18, 25 × 1 = 25

12 × 1 = 12 implies 12 is a multiple of 12 and 12 is a multiple of 1.

18 × 1 = 18 implies 18 is a multiple of 18 and 18 is a multiple of 1.

25 × 1 = 25 implies 25 is a multiple of 25 and 25 is a multiple of 1.

What do we conclude?

We conclude,

(a) Every number is a multiple of itself.

(b) Every number is a multiple of 1.

Again, observe the following :

Multiples of 5 are 5, 10, 15, 20, ...

Multiples of 12 are 12, 24, 36, 48, ...

Multiples of 18 are 18, 36, 54, 72, ...

What do we observe?

We see that every multiple of 5 is either greater than or equal to 5.

Similarly, every multiple of 12 is either greater than or equal to 12.

Every multiple of 18 is either greater than or equal to 18.

Hence, we can say that

Every multiple of a number is either greater than or equal to the number.

Exercise 8A

Apply and Learn

A Tick (✓) the true statement and cross (✗) the false statement. The first is done for you:

1. 36 is a multiple of 9. (✓)

2. 49 is a multiple of 7. ( )

3. 95 is a multiple of 12. ( )
4. 103 is a multiple of 1. ( )
5. 120 is a multiple of 14. ( )
6. 6 is the least non-zero multiple of 6. ( )
7. 60 is the greatest multiple of 6. ( )
8. There is no end to multiples of a number. ( )
9. Fifth multiple of 9 is 45. ( )
10. 1 is the multiple of 5. ( )

B Write the next four multiples :

1. 12, 24, 36, ____, ____, ____, ____
2. 9, 18, 27, ____, ____, ____, ____
3. 14, 28, 42, ____, ____, ____, ____
4. 11, 22, 33, ____, ____, ____, ____
5. 19, 38, 57, ____, ____, ____, ____
6. 25, 50, 75, ____, ____, ____, ____

C Answer the following questions :

1. Is 72 a multiple of 9?
2. Is 144 a multiple of 16?
3. Is 168 a multiple of 21?
4. Is 169 a multiple of 14?
5. Is 220 a multiple of 25?
6. Find the first five multiples of 8.
7. Find first three multiples of 14.
8. Find the first four multiples of 6.
9. Find the tenth multiple of 9.
10. Find the fourth multiple of 15.

D Fill in the blanks :

1. 12 × 8 = 96 means 96 is a multiple of ______ and ______.
2. 12 × 13 = 156 means 156 is a multiple of ______ and ______.
3. 15 × 18 = 270 means 270 is a multiple of ______ and ______.
4. 13 × 14 = 182 means ______ is a multiple of 13 and 14.
5. 15 × 16 = 240 means ______ is a multiple of 15 and 16.

Explore and Learn

Factors

CODE-9VZk

Observe the following : 5 × 7 = 35 implies 35 is a multiple of 5 and 7.

We also call 5 and 7 as factors of 35.

8 × 9 = 72 implies 72 is a multiple of 8 and 9.

We also call 8 and 9 as factors of 72.

15 × 6 = 90 implies 90 is a multiple of 15 and 6.

We also call 15 and 6 as factors of 90.

$5 \times 7 = 35$

7 and 5 are factors of 35 ← → 35 is a multiple of 7 and 5

$12 \times 9 = 108$

12 and 9 are factors of 108 ← → 108 is a multiple of 12 and 9

$8 \times 7 \times 4 = 224$

8, 7 and 4 are factors of 108 ← → 224 is a multiple of 8, 7 and 4

Thus, we can say that when two or more numbers are multiplied, then each number is a factor of the product and the product is a multiple of each one of the numbers.

Observe the following :

8 × 6 = 48 implies 8 and 6 are factors of 48.

Also corresponding to the multiplication fact 8 × 6 = 48, we have two division facts

48 ÷ 8 = 6 and 48 ÷ 6 = 8

Here 8 divides 48 exactly and 6 divides 48 exactly.

Hence, a number is a factor of the other if the first divides second exactly. Or a number is a factor of the other if the second is divisible by the first.

Example 1 : Is 8 a factor of 112?

Solution :

```
     1 4
8 ) 1 1 2
   - 8
    ----
     3 2
   - 3 2
    ----
       0
```

Here, 8 divides 112 exactly, so 8 is a factor of 112.

REMEMBER

If M is divisible by F:
- F is a factor of M
- M is a multiple of F.

Example 2 : Is 8 a factor of 1,625?

Solution :

```
      2 0 3
8 ) 1 6 2 5
  - 1 6
   --------
        2 5
      - 2 4
   --------
          1
```

Here, 8 does not divide 1,625 exactly, so 8 is not a factor of 1,625.

Example 3 : Find all the factors of 18.

Solution :

18 = 1 × 18

18 = 2 × 9

18 = 3 × 6

Hence, all the factors of 18 are 1, 2, 3, 6, 9 and 18.

Example 4 : Find all the factors of 45.

Solution :

45 = 1 × 45

45 = 3 × 15

45 = 5 × 9

Hence, all the factors of 45 are 1, 3, 5, 9, 15 and 45.

Properties of Factors

CODE-oJFv

Observe the following :

25 ÷ 1 = 25 30 ÷ 1 = 30 105 ÷ 1 = 105

1 divides every number exactly or every number is divisible by 1.

Hence, we can say that

1 is a factor of every number.

Again observe the following :

7 ÷ 7 = 1, 18 ÷ 18 = 1 115 ÷ 115 = 1

Every non-zero number divides itself exactly or every non-zero number is divisible by itself.

Hence, we can say that

Every non-zero number is a factor of itself.

Again, observe the following :

All the factors of 25 are 1, 5, 25

All the factors of 36 are 1, 2, 3, 4, 6, 9, 12, 18, 36.

The smallest factor of 25 is 1.

The largest factor of 25 is 25.

The smallest factor of 36 is 1.

The largest factor of 36 is 36.

Hence, we can say that

The factor of a non-zero number is either less than or equal to the number.

Exercise 8B

Apply and Learn

A Tick (✓) the true statement and cross (✗) the false statement :

1. 5 is a factor of 35. ( )

2. 3 is a factor of 63. ( )

3. 10 is a factor of 100. ( )

4. 18 is a factor of 55. ( )

5. 6 is a factor of 72. ( )

6. 2 is a factor of 32. ( )

7. 48 is the largest factor of 48. ( )

8. 1 is a factor of every number. ( )

9. All the factors of 15 are 3, 5, 15. ( )

10. Every non-zero number is a factor of itself. ( )

B Answer the following questions :

1. Is 8 a factor of 760?

2. Is 12 a factor of 3900?

3. Is 14 a factor of 1752?

4. Is 25 a factor of 8100?

5. Is 17 a factor of 8918?

6. Find all the factors of 35.

7. Find all the factors of 54.

8. Find all the factors of 78.

9. Find all the factors of 144.

10. Find the smallest and the largest factor of 125.

11. Find the smallest and the largest factor of 120.

C Fill in the blanks :

1. 7 × 8 = 56 implies that 56 is a ____________ of 7 and 8. Also, 7 and 8 are ____________ of 56.

2. 9 × 11 = 99 implies that 99 is a ____________ of 9 and 11. Also, 9 and 11 are ____________ of 99.

3. 12 × 13 = 156 implies that 13 and 12 are ____________ of 156 and 156 is a ____________ of 12 and 13.

Explore and Learn

Even Numbers

A number which is a multiple of 2 is called an **even number**.

Thus, 2, 4, 6, 8, 10, 12, ... are even numbers.

Odd Numbers

A number which is not a multiple of 2 is called an **odd number**.

Thus, 1, 3, 5, 7, 9, 11, ... are odd numbers.

In the following table, bold numbers are even numbers and remaining numbers are odd numbers.

1	**2**	3	**4**	5	**6**	7	**8**	9	**10**
11	**12**	13	**14**	15	**16**	17	**18**	19	**20**
21	**22**	23	**24**	25	**26**	27	**28**	29	**30**
31	**32**	33	**34**	35	**36**	37	**38**	39	**40**
41	**42**	43	**44**	45	**46**	47	**48**	49	**50**
51	**52**	53	**54**	55	**56**	57	**58**	59	**60**
61	**62**	63	**64**	65	**66**	67	**68**	69	**70**
71	**72**	73	**74**	75	**76**	77	**78**	79	**80**
81	**82**	83	**84**	85	**86**	87	**88**	89	**90**
91	**92**	93	**94**	95	**96**	97	**98**	99	**100**

Prime Numbers

CODE-7v4B

Observe the following :

All the factors of 2 are 1 and 2.

All the factors of 3 are 1 and 3.

All the factors of 4 are 1, 2 and 4.

All the factors of 5 are 1 and 5.

All the factors of 6 are 1, 2, 3 and 6.

We see that 2, 3 and 5 have only two factors namely 1 and the number itself. We call these numbers as prime numbers.

Hence, the numbers having exactly two different factors, namely 1 and itself, are known as **prime numbers**.

2, 3, 5, 7, 11, 13, 17, 19, ... are prime numbers.

Composite Numbers

CODE-5beK

Observe the following :

All the factors of 4 are 1, 2, 4.

All the factors of 6 are 1, 2, 3, 6.

All the factors of 8 are 1, 2, 4, 8.

All the factors of 9 are 1, 3, 9.

REMEMBER

(a) 1 is neither prime nor composite.

(b) 2 is the smallest even prime number.

We see that 4, 6, 8 and 9 have more than two factors.
We call these numbers as composite numbers.

Hence, the numbers having more than two different factors are known as **composite numbers**.

To find Prime Numbers between 1 and 100

CODE-mM9F

Prepare a table of numbers from 1 to 100.

Since, 1 is not a prime number, cross it out.

Since, $2 = 1 \times 2$. So, 2 is a prime number. Encircle 2. Cross out the multiples of 2 as these are composite numbers.

Similarly, $3 = 1 \times 3$. So, 3 is a prime number. Encircle 3. Cross out the multiples of 3 as these are composite numbers.

Similarly, $5 = 1 \times 5$. So, 5 is a prime number. Encircle 5. Cross out the multiples of 5 as these are composite numbers.

Similarly, $7 = 1 \times 7$. So, 7 is a prime number. Encircle 7. Cross out the multiples of 7 as these are composite numbers.

Now, encircle each one of the remaining numbers.

All the encircled numbers are the prime numbers.

There are 25 prime numbers between 1 and 100.

~~1~~	**(2)**	**(3)**	~~4~~	**(5)**	~~6~~	**(7)**	~~8~~	~~9~~	~~10~~
(11)	~~12~~	**(13)**	~~14~~	~~15~~	~~16~~	**(17)**	~~18~~	**(19)**	~~20~~
~~21~~	~~22~~	**(23)**	~~24~~	~~25~~	~~26~~	~~27~~	~~28~~	**(29)**	~~30~~
(31)	~~32~~	~~33~~	~~34~~	~~35~~	~~36~~	**(37)**	~~38~~	~~39~~	~~40~~
(41)	~~42~~	**(43)**	~~44~~	~~45~~	~~46~~	**(47)**	~~48~~	~~49~~	~~50~~
~~51~~	~~52~~	**(53)**	~~54~~	~~55~~	~~56~~	~~57~~	~~58~~	**(59)**	~~60~~
(61)	~~62~~	~~63~~	~~64~~	~~65~~	~~66~~	**(67)**	~~68~~	~~69~~	~~70~~
(71)	~~72~~	**(73)**	~~74~~	~~75~~	~~76~~	~~77~~	~~78~~	**(79)**	~~80~~
~~81~~	~~82~~	**(83)**	~~84~~	~~85~~	~~86~~	~~87~~	~~88~~	**(89)**	~~90~~
~~91~~	~~92~~	~~93~~	~~94~~	~~95~~	~~96~~	**(97)**	~~98~~	~~99~~	~~100~~

Example : In the following, identify prime numbers and composite numbers.

12 15 19 23 27 51 69 83

Solution : 12 = 1 × 12, 12 = 2 × 6, 12 = 3 × 4,

All the factors of 12 are 1, 2, 3, 4, 6 and 12.

15 = 1 × 15, 15 = 3 × 5.

All the factors of 15 are 1, 3, 5 and 15

19 = 1 × 19

All the factors of 19 are 1 and 19

23 = 1 × 23

All the factors of 23 are 1 and 23

27 = 1 × 27, 27 = 3 × 9

All the factors of 27 are 1, 3, 9 and 27

51 = 1 × 51, 51 = 3 × 17

All the factors of 51 are 1, 3, 17 and 51

69 = 1 × 69, 69 = 3 × 23

All the factors of 69 are 1, 3, 23 and 69.

83 = 1 × 83

All the factors of 83 are 1 and 83.

REMEMBER

1 has exactly one factor, 1 itself.

CHALLENGE

The product is 63. The sum of the two factors is 16. Their difference is 2. What are the factors?

From the above, we see that the numbers having only two factors are 19, 23 and 83 Therefore, these numbers are prime numbers.

The remaining numbers namely 12, 15, 27, 51 and 69 are composite numbers.

CODE-b8kH

Tests for Divisibility

For finding factors of composite numbers, we have been actually dividing the number by smaller numbers like 2, 3, 5, 7, etc., to check whether the given composite number is exactly divisible by another number or not.

When we shall be dealing with large numbers, the process of actual division may become time consuming. To save time, we need to know some techniques which could help us to check whether a number can divide the other number, without actually doing the division. This is going to help us in breaking a number into factors. There are some divisibility tests which will enable us not to waste our time in working out long divisions actually.

Divisibility by 2

A number is divisible by 2, if the digit at the one's place is 0, 2, 4, 6 or 8.

For example : 328, 146, 8054, 92860, 572 are all divisible by 2.

Divisibility by 3

Observe the table of 3 carefully. We find the multiples in the following table :

	Sum of digits of the multiples of 3		**Sum of digits of the multiples of 3**
3 × 1 = 3	3	3 × 6 = 18	1 + 8 = 9
3 × 2 = 6	6	3 × 7 = 21	2 + 1 = 3
3 × 3 = 9	9	3 × 8 = 24	2 + 4 = 6
3 × 4 = 12	1 + 2 = 3	3 × 9 = 27	2 + 7 = 9
3 × 5 = 15	1 + 5 = 6	3 × 10 = 30	3 + 0 = 3

Sum of the digits in the multiples is always divisible by 3. Therefore, we can say that

If the sum of the digits of a number is divisible by 3, the number will be divisible by 3.

Let us check a large number for its divisibility by 3.

Take the numbers 8,90,124 and 5,94,124

Sum of digits : 8 + 9 + 0 + 1 + 2 + 4 = 24. 5 + 9 + 4 + 1 + 2 + 4 = 25

24 is exactly divisible by 3. 25 is not divisible by 3

∴ The number 8,90,124 is divisible by 3. ∴ 5,94,124 is not divisible by 3.

Divisibility by 4

We know that 100 ÷ 4 = 25, i.e., 100 is divisible by 4. All the multiples of 100, i.e., 100, 200, 300, ..., 900 will also be divisible by 4.

Now let us check the divisibility of a number like 452.

We break 452 as 400 + 52 (sum of hundreds and ones).

As 400 is divisible by 4, so we are left to check the divisibility of only 52 by 4.

Because 52 ÷ 4 gives quotient = 13, remainder = 0, we can say that 52 is divisible by 4.

∴ 452 which is 400 + 52 will also be divisible by 4.

This leads us to say that :

A number is divisible by 4, if the number formed by its last two digits is divisible by 4.

To verify this rule, let us apply this rule to a number which is not divisible by 4. We take the number 214, which is not divisible by 4.

We see that the number formed by its last two digits is 14, which is not divisible by 4.

∴ 214 will not be divisible by 4.

Divisibility by 5

Let us observe some multiples of 5.

5, 10, 15, 20, ..., are all multiples of 5.

All of them end with the digits 0 or 5, i.e., they have either 0 or 5 at their unit's place. So,

A number is divisible by 5, if its unit's digit is either 0 or 5.

For example, 395, 840, 9,835, 7680 are all divisible by 5.

Divisibility by 9

Let us write the multiples of 9. They are 9, 18, 27, 36, 45, ...

If we add the digits of each multiple of 9, we notice that their sum is always 9 or 18 or a multiple of 9, when we take larger multiples of 9.

So, we can write the rule :

Multiples of 9	Sum of digits of the multiples of 9
9	0 + 9 = 9
18	1 + 8 = 9
27	2 + 7 = 9
36	3 + 6 = 9
45	4 + 5 = 9
54	5 + 4 = 9
63	6 + 3 = 9
72	7 + 2 = 9
81	8 + 1 = 9
90	9 + 0 = 9
99	9 + 9 = 18, 1 + 8 = 9
108	1 + 0 + 8 = 9

A number will be divisible by 9, if the sum of the digits of the given number is divisible by 9.

For example, let us take the number 7,28,316.

Sum of its digits is 7 + 2 + 8 + 3 + 1 + 6 = 27.

Since 27 is divisible by 9, we say that 7,28,316 is divisible by 9.

Divisibility by 10

A number which has 0 at one's place is divisible by 10.

For example, 20, 50, 170, 2,490 all are divisible by 10.

Prime Factorization

Expressing a number as the product of its factors is called **factorization.**

For example, 24 = 2 × 12.

Here, 24 is factorised.

There are many other forms of factorization of 24. Such as

24 = 2 × 2 × 6

= 2 × 2 × 2 × 3

In 24 = 2 × 2 × 2 × 3, we see that each factor of 24 is a prime number. It is called prime factorization.

When a number is expressed as a product of prime numbers, we call it **prime factorization**.

or

A factorization in which every factor is prime, is called the **prime factorization** of the number.

Prime factorization of 30 and 48 are given below :

30 = 2 × 3 × 5

48 = 2 × 2 × 2 × 2 × 3

To make the prime factorization of a number, we divide the given number by the prime numbers 2, 3, 5, 7 and 11 etc., in this order repeatedly so long as the quotient is divisible by that number.

Example 1 : Express 420 as the product of prime numbers.

Solution :

2	420	⟵ Dividing by 2
2	210	⟵ Dividing by 2
3	105	⟵ Dividing by 3
5	35	⟵ Dividing by 5
7	7	⟵ Dividing by 7
	1	

Hence, 420 = 2 × 2 × 3 × 5 × 7.

This process can be shown diagramatically, known as **factor tree**.

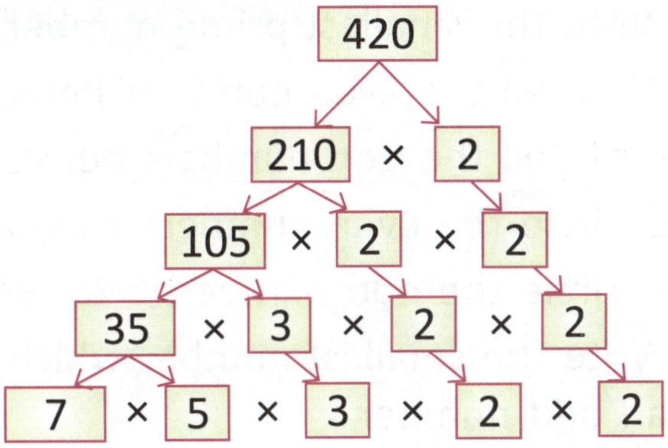

Example 2 : Draw a factor tree to show the prime factorization of 42, 96 and 108.

Solution :

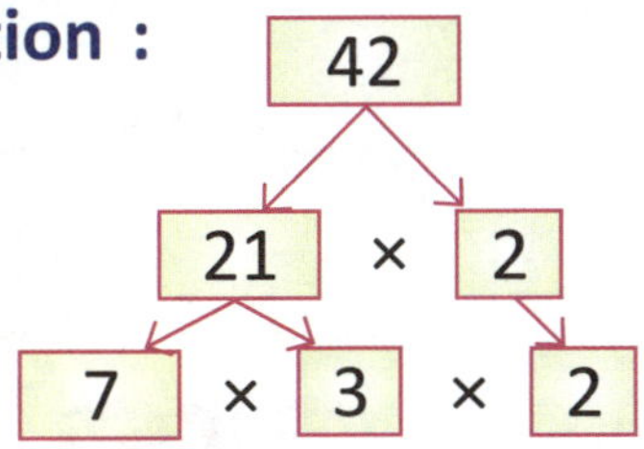

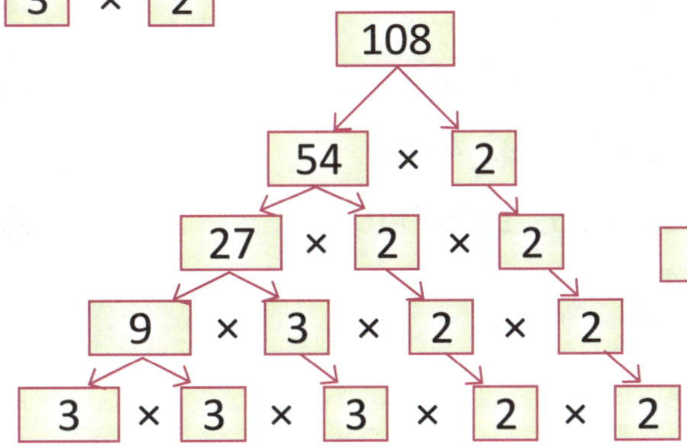

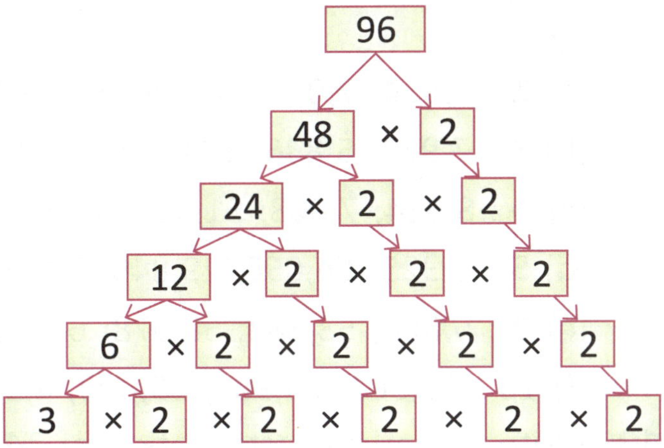

Exercise 8C

Apply and Learn

1. Write down all the prime numbers between 10 and 20.
2. List all the prime numbers between 5 and 35.
3. Write down all the prime numbers between 25 and 50.

4. Write down all the prime numbers between 40 and 75.
5. Write down all the prime numbers between 60 and 100.
6. Write down all the composite numbers less than 20.
7. Write down all the composite numbers between 51 and 70.
8. Encircle the prime numbers : 14, 19, 37, 45, 61, 69, 77, 81, 99.
9. Encircle the composite numbers : 21, 31, 39, 49, 51, 53, 63, 91, 97.
10. Write the number which is prime as well as an even number.
11. Write the smallest prime number.
12. Write all the even numbers between 35 and 55.
13. Write all the odd numbers between 40 and 70.
14. Encircle the even numbers : 13, 21, 58, 76, 91, 104, 116, 309.
15. Encircle the odd numbers : 25, 34, 53, 69, 96, 103, 115, 203.
16. Write the smallest number which when added to an even number makes the sum an odd number.
17. Is 1 a prime number?
18. Using the tests of divisibility, check whether the following numbers are divisible by :

    (a) **2** : 7,854; 2,065; 18,976; 65,180; 5,90,007

    (b) **3** : 7,962; 5,836; 17,094; 26,236; 1,79,622

    (c) **4** : 8,534; 7,008; 51,936; 18,547; 2,56,068

    (d) **5** : 8,325; 64,058; 29,840; 53,263; 8,74,265

    (e) **9** : 5,886; 53,883; 58,978; 6,28,527; 5,93,470

    (f) **10** : 25,301; 63,980; 25,000; 4,32,705; 1,83,040

19. Write the prime factorization of 24.
20. Write the prime factorization of 72.
21. Write the prime factorization of 96.

22. Express each of the following as the product of prime numbers :

(a) 120 (b) 150 (c) 210

23. Draw a factor tree to show the prime factorisation of :

(a) 30 (b) 40 (c) 64 (d) 72 (e) 98 (f) 120

Explore and Learn

Common Factors

Observe the following :

(a) All the factors of 15 are 1, 3, 5 and 15.
All the factors of 20 are 1, 2, 4, 5, 10 and 20.
Thus, common factors of 15 and 20 are 1 and 5.

(b) All the factors of 32 are 1, 2, 4, 8, 16, 32.
All the factors of 48 are 1, 2, 3, 4, 6, 8, 12, 16, 24, 48.
Thus, common factors of 32 and 48 are 1, 2, 4, 8, 16.

CODE-XUdR

Highest Common Factor (H.C.F.)

In the example (a) given above, common factors of 15 and 20 are 1 and 5. Out of these two common factors, 5 is the highest (greatest) common factor. Therefore, we call 5 as the highest common factor of 15 and 20.

Again in example (b), common factors of 32 and 48 are 1, 2, 4, 8 and 16. Out of these, 16 is the highest (greatest) common factor. Therefore, 16 is the highest common factor of 32 and 48.

Hence, the H.C.F. (highest common factor) of two or more than two numbers is the highest (greatest) among all their common factors.

Highest common factor (H.C.F.) is also called **greatest common divisor (G.C.D.)**.

Example 1 : Find all the common factors of :

(a) 24 and 40 (b) 20 and 64

Solution : (a) $24 = 1 \times 24$, $24 = 2 \times 12$, $24 = 3 \times 8$, $24 = 4 \times 6$

Therefore, all the factors of 24 are 1, 2, 3, 4, 6, 8, 12 and 24.

Also, $40 = 1 \times 40$, $40 = 2 \times 20$, $40 = 4 \times 10$, $40 = 5 \times 8$.

Therefore, all the factors of 40 are 1, 2, 4, 5, 8, 10, 20 and 40.

Thus, common factors of 24 and 40 are 1, 2, 4 and 8.

(b) $20 = 1 \times 20$, $20 = 2 \times 10$, $20 = 4 \times 5$

Therefore, all the factors of 20 are 1, 2, 4, 5, 10 and 20.

Also, $64 = 1 \times 64$, $64 = 2 \times 32$, $64 = 4 \times 16$, $64 = 8 \times 8$.

Therefore, all the factors of 64 are 1, 2, 4, 8, 16, 32 and 64.

Thus, common factors of 20 and 64 are 1, 2 and 4.

Example 2 : Find the H.C.F. of 25 and 45.

Solution : $25 = 1 \times 25$, $25 = 5 \times 5$

All the factors of 25 are 1, 5 and 25.

Also, $45 = 1 \times 45$, $45 = 3 \times 15$, $45 = 5 \times 9$.

All the factors of 45 are 1, 3, 5, 9, 15 and 45.

Common factors of 25 and 45 are 1 and 5.

Thus, H.C.F. of 25 and 45 is 5.

REMEMBER

H.C.F. of two consecutive even numbers is 2.

Example 3 : Find the H.C.F. of 18, 45 and 63.

Solution : $18 = 1 \times 18$, $18 = 2 \times 9$, $18 = 3 \times 6$

All the factors of 18 are 1, 2, 3, 6, 9 and 18.

Also, $45 = 1 \times 45$, $45 = 3 \times 15$, $45 = 5 \times 9$.

All the factors of 45 are 1, 3, 5, 9, 15 and 45.

Also, $63 = 1 \times 63$, $63 = 3 \times 21$, $63 = 7 \times 9$.

All the factors of 63 are 1, 3, 7, 9, 21 and 63.

Common factors of 18, 45 and 63 are 1, 3 and 9.

Thus, H.C.F. of 18, 45 and 63 is 9.

Example 4 : Find the H.C.F. of 15 and 28.

Solution : $15 = 1 \times 15$, $15 = 3 \times 5$.

All the factors of 15 are 1, 3, 5 and 15.

Also, $28 = 28 \times 1$, $28 = 2 \times 14$, $28 = 4 \times 7$

All the factors of 28 are 1, 2, 4, 7, 14 and 28.

Common factor of 15 and 28 is 1.

Thus, H.C.F. of 15 and 28 is 1.

REMEMBER

Two numbers are said to be co-prime, if their H.C.F. is 1.

CODE-67Ao

H.C.F. by Long Division Method

To find the HCF of two or three given numbers, divide the greater number by the smaller one. Then divide the divisor by the remainder. Go on repeating the process of dividing the preceding divisor by the remainder, till zero remainder is obtained. The last divisor is the HCF of the given numbers.

Properties of H.C.F.

(a) The H.C.F. of two or more numbers cannot be greater than any one of them.

(b) If a number is a factor of another number, then their H.C.F. is the smaller number.

Example 5 : Find the H.C.F. of 20 and 36.

Solution : We have :

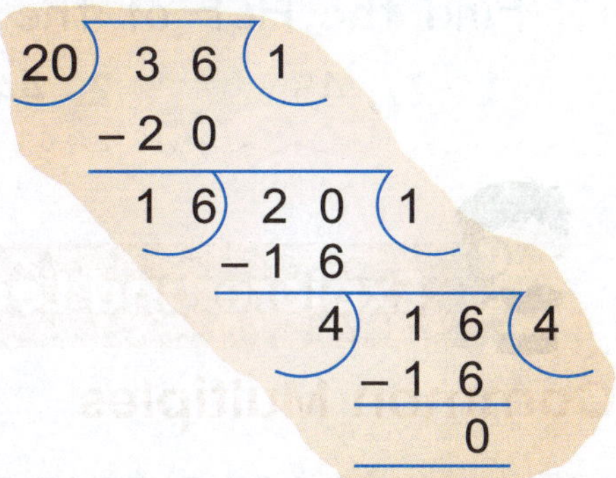

Here, the last divisor is 4.

Hence, the H.C.F. of 20 and 36 is 4.

Example 6 : Find the H.C.F. of 42 and 78.

Solution : We have :

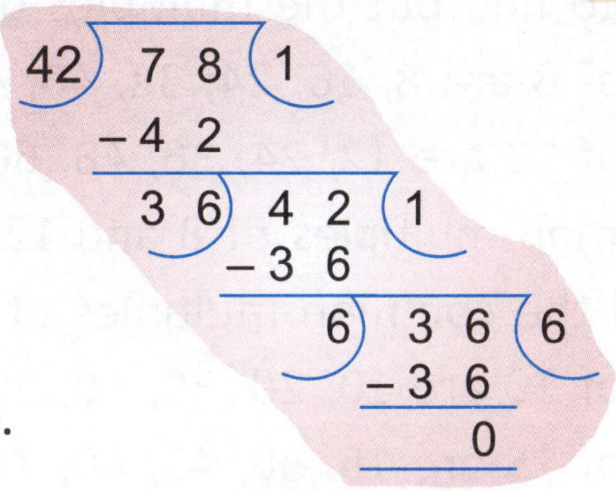

Here, the last divisor is 6.

Hence, the H.C.F. of 42 and 78 is 6.

Example 7 : Find the H.C.F. of 20, 35 and 50.

Solution : First we find the H.C.F. of any two numbers (say 20 and 35).

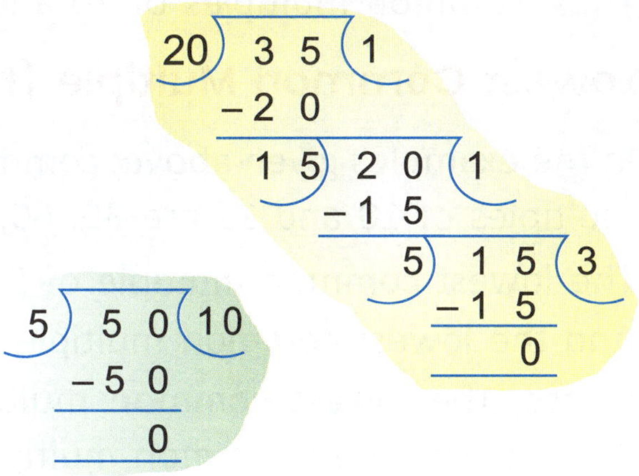

Since, the last divisor is 5, So, 5 is the HCF of 20 and 35.

Now, we find the HCF of 5 and 50.

Hence, H.C.F. of 20, 35 and 50 is 5.

Exercise 8D

Apply and Learn

A Find all the common factors of :

1. 12 and 15 **2.** 10 and 28 **3.** 18 and 45

4. 21 and 49 **5.** 20 and 50 **6.** 16 and 40

B Find the H.C.F. of :

1. 8 and 40 **2.** 15 and 35 **3.** 18 and 45

4. 16, 48 and 80 **5.** 12, 30 and 54 **6.** 30, 75 and 90

C Find the HCF of the following numbers by long division method :

1. 27, 45 **2.** 44, 110 **3.** 81, 117 **4.** 18, 24, 27 **5.** 18, 45, 36

Explore and Learn

Common Multiples

Let us try to find out the multiples of 8 and 12.

Multiples of 8 are 8, 16, 24, 32, 40, 48, ...

Multiples of 12 are 12, 24, 36, 48, 60, 72, ...

Thus, common multiples of 8 and 12 are 24, 48, ...

Again, find the common multiples of 10 and 15.

Multiples of 10 are 10, 20, 30, 40, 50, 60, ...

Multiples of 15 are 15, 30, 45, 60, 75, ...

Thus, common multiples of 10 and 15 are 30, 60, ...

CODE-iwyj

Lowest Common Multiple (L.C.M.)

In the examples given above, common multiples of 8 and 12 are 24, 48, ... and common multiples of 10 and 15 are 30, 60, ...

The lowest common multiple of 8 and 12 is 24.

And the lowest common multiple of 10 and 15 is 30.

Hence, the lowest common multiple (L.C.M.) of two or more numbers is the least (smallest) of their common multiples.

Example 1 : Find the first two common multiples of : (a) 4 and 10 (b) 5, 6 and 15.

Solution : (a) Multiples of 4 are 4, 8, 12, 16, 20, 24, 28, 32, 36, 40, ...

Multiples of 10 are 10, 20, 30, 40, ...

Thus, the first two common multiples of 4 and 10 are 20 and 40.

(b) Multiples of 5 are 5, 10, 15, 20, 25, 30, 35, 40, 45, 60, 65, ...

Multiples of 6 are 6, 12, 18, 24, 30, 36, 42, 48, 54, 60, ...

Multiples of 15 are 15, 30, 45, 60, 75, ...

Thus, the first two common multiples of 5, 6 and 15 are 30 and 60.

Example 2 : Find the L.C.M. of 12 and 18.

Solution : Multiples of 12 are 12, 24, 36, 48, 60, 72, ...
Multiples of 18 are 18, 36, 54, 72, 90, ...
Thus, common multiples of 12 and 18 are 36, 72, ...
Therefore, L.C.M. of 12 and 18 is 36.

CODE-nXYm

L.C.M. by Long Division Method

We proceed as below :

1. Arrange the given numbers in a line, in any order.
2. Divide by a number which exactly divides at least two of the given numbers and carry forward the numbers which are not divisible.
3. Repeat the process till none of the two given numbers are divisible by the same number.
4. The product of all the divisors and the numbers left undivided is the required LCM.

Properties of L.C.M.

(a) The L.C.M. of two co-prime numbers is their product.
(b) If one number is the multiple of the other, then their L.C.M. is the greater number.
(c) The L.C.M. of two or more numbers cannot be less than any one of them.

Example 3 : Find the LCM of 24 and 30 by division method.

Solution : LCM of 24 and 30
$= 2 \times 2 \times 2 \times 3 \times 5 = 120.$

2	24	30
2	12	15
2	6	15
3	3	15
	1	5

Example 4 : Find the LCM of 18, 36 and 42 by long division method.

Solution : LCM of 18, 36 and 42
$= 2 \times 3 \times 3 \times 2 \times 7 = 252.$

2	18	36	42
3	9	18	21
3	3	6	7
2	1	2	7
	1	1	7

Exercise 8E

Apply and Learn

A Find :

1. the first two common multiples of 6 and 15.
2. the first three common multiples of 4 and 10.

3. the first two common multiples of 12 and 18.
4. the first five common multiples of 2, 4 and 6.

B Find the L.C.M. of the following numbers :

1. 6 and 10	2. 5 and 8	3. 10 and 12
4. 26 and 15	5. 8, 10 and 20	6. 6, 8 and 18

C Find the LCM by long division method :

1. 18, 30	2. 13, 39	3. 12, 15,	4. 38, 72
5. 88, 99	6. 15, 35, 45	7. 6, 8, 45	8. 48, 72, 80

Review and Refresh

1. Is 56 a multiple of 6?
2. Is 105 a multiple of 105?
3. Is 819 is a multiple of 1?
4. Find the first four multiples of 15.
5. Find the tenth multiple of 21.
6. 1 is a multiple of every non-zero number. Is it true?
7. Is 7 a factor of 126?
8. Is 14 a factor of 1,722?
9. Find all the factors of 100.
10. Write the smallest and the largest factor of 180.
11. The factor of a non-zero number is either greater than or equal to the number. Is it true?
12. Which of the following numbers are divisible by 9?
    23,076; 41,102; 52,056; 1,70,766
13. List all the prime numbers between 16 and 39.
14. List all the composite numbers between 45 and 60.
15. What is the number which is prime as well as an even number?
16. Find the prime factors of 96.
17. Find the prime factors of 105.
18. Draw a factor tree to find the prime factorization of 63.

Mental Maths

1. Is 2,000 a multiple of 10? ____________________
2. HCF of two co-prime numbers is ____________________.
3. 15 × 8 = 120. Here 15 and 8 are ____________________ of 120 and 120 is a ____________________ of 15 and 8.
4. Every multiple of a number is greater than the number. Is it true? ____________
5. All the factors of 25 are ____________________
6. The largest factor of a number is ____________________
7. The smallest multiple of a number is ____________________
8. A prime number has exactly ____________________ factors.
9. Which even number is prime? ____________________
10. Which number has exactly 1 factor? ____________________

Fun With Maths

1. If two successive odd numbers are prime, they are known as twin primes. e.g., (3, 5) is a pair of twin primes. From 1 to 100, write all such pairs.

2. You fill 7 pages of an album. Each page has 4 photos and at the end you have 2 photos left. How many photos did you have to start?

3. Ashok explains how to find multiples of numbers to class 4 students through an example. This is based on the following information.
   - The cat is trying to catch the mouse.
   - Mouse is now on the 14th step and it can jump 2 steps at a time.
   - The cat is on the 3rd step. She can jump 3 steps at a time.

- If the mouse reaches 28 the step, it can hide in the hole.

Observe the above information and answer the following questions :

(i) The steps on which the mouse jumps :

(a) 14, 16, 18, 20, 22, 24, 26 (b) 16, 18, 20, 22, 24, 26, 28

(c) 18, 20, 22, 24, 26, 28, 30 (d) 16, 18, 20, 23, 25, 27, 28

(ii) The steps on which the cat jumps :

(a) 4, 6, 8, 10, 12, 14, 26,28 (b) 16, 18, 20, 22, 24, 26, 28

(c) 3, 6, 9, 12, 15, 18, 21, 24, 27 (d) 6, 9, 12, 15, 18, 21, 24, 27

(iii) The steps on which both the cat and the mouse jump

(a) 18, 24 (b) 16, 18, 20, 22, 24, 26, 28

(c) 18, 24, 26, 28 (d) 6, 9, 12, 15, 18, 21, 24, 27

(iv) If the cat starts from the 5th step and jumps five steps at a time and the mouse starts from the 8th step and jumps four steps at a time, which common step will be followed during the jump by both?

(a) 16 (b) 18 (c) 20 (d) 24

To get worksheet on this chapter scan this QR code

CODE-U1FF

Maths Lab Activity

Objective : Finding factors of small numbers by activity method.

Materials Required : Squared paper (graph paper)

Procedure/Demonstration : Let us find all the factors of 20.

1. We know that 1 is a factor of every number. On a squared sheet, draw a rectangle whose vertical side is 1 cm and total number of squares enclosed by it is 20.

   We see that the horizontal side of this rectangle is 20 cm.

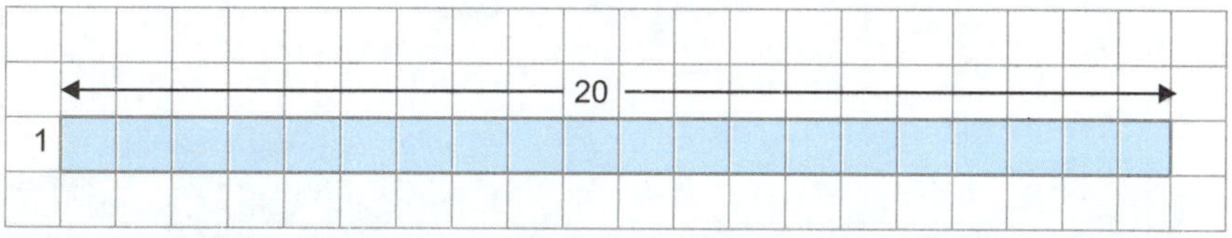

   So, 1 and 20 (length and breadth of this rectangle) are factors of 20.

2. Now on the same squared paper, draw a rectangle whose vertical side is 2 cm and total number of squares enclosed by it is 20. We see that the horizontal side of this rectangle comes out to be 10 cm. So, 2 and 10 (length and breadth of this rectangle) are factors of 20.

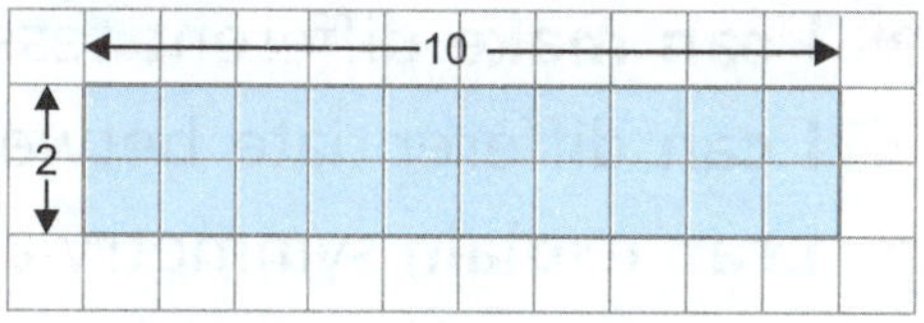

3. Next on the same squared paper, draw a rectangle whose vertical side is 3 cm and total number of squares enclosed by it is 20. Here we will not able to form such a rectangle. It means 3 is not a factor of 20.

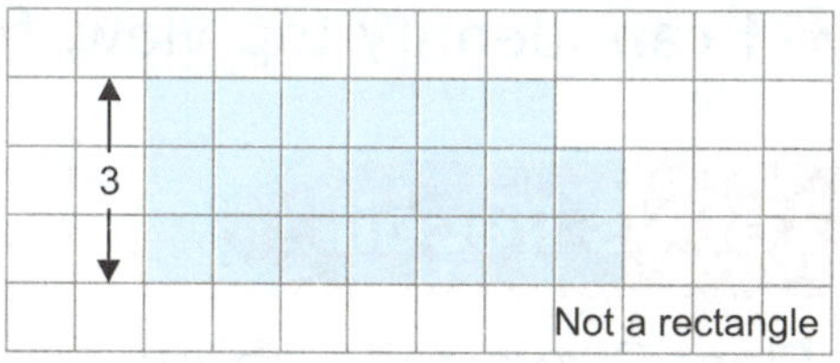

4. Now, repeat the above process by taking the vertical side 4 cm. Here, the horizontal side of this rectangle comes out to be 5 cm. So, 4 and 5 are factors of 20.

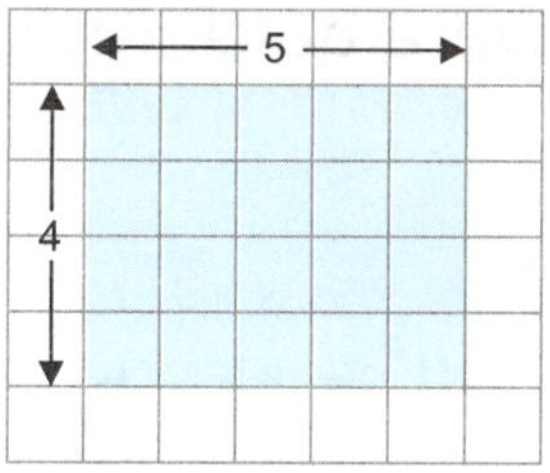

5. Next repeat the above process by taking vertical side as 5 cm. Here, the horizontal side comes out to be 4 cm. So, 5 and 4 are factors of 20, which we have already found in Step 4. So, we stop here.

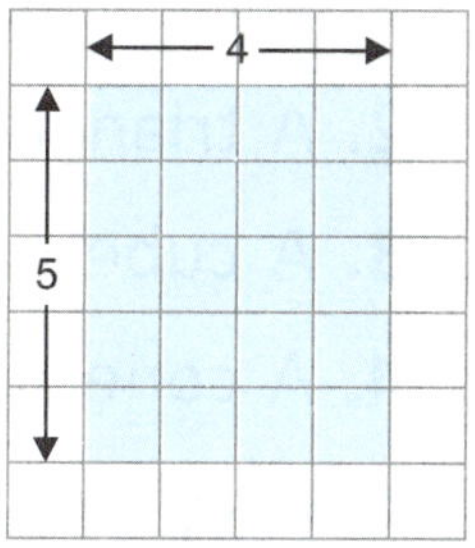

   Thus all the factors of 20 are :

   1, 20, 2, 10, 4, 5 or 1, 2, 4, 5, 10, 20

9

THEME 4 : GEOMETRY

Geometrical Shapes

Learning Target

Understanding Geometrical Shapes.

I Can

- **I can explain** different 2-D and 3-D shapes and their features.
- **I can make** a 7-piece tangram and create different images using its pieces.
- **I can make** different tessellations.
- **I can** differentiate between parallel and perpendicular lines.
- **I can explain** symmetry and find number of lines of symmetry of different images.
- **I can explain** reflection.
- **I can** identify top view, front view and side view of an object.

Let Us Recall

In Class 3, we read about some basic plane shapes and solid shapes. Let us have a quick review what we read.

Exercise 9A

A Fill in the blanks :

1. A rectangle has ______________ sides and ______________ vertices.

2. A triangle has ______________ sides and ______________ vertices.

3. A cube has ______________ faces and ______________ vertices.

4. A cone has ______________ faces.

5. A cylinder has ______________ flat faces.

6. A cuboid has ______________ sides.

B Answer the following questions :

1. Name any four objects which look like a cuboid.

____

2. Name any four objects which look like a cylinder.

____

3. Name any four objects which look like a cone.

____

4. Name any four objects which look like a sphere.

____

C Write the shape of the following objects :

1. Carrot __________
2. Cricket ball __________
3. Cotton thread reel __________
4. Football __________
5. Book __________
6. Tubelight __________
7. Sugar cube __________
8. Road roller __________
9. Fire extinguisher __________
10. Tree trunk __________
11. Shoe box __________
12. Apple __________

D Fill in the blanks :

1. A cube has __________ edges.
2. A cylinder has __________ flat faces.
3. A cuboid has 6 __________ .
4. A sphere has __________ vertices.
5. A cylinder has __________ curved edges.

Explore and Learn

CODE-DcLN

Tangram

The tangram is a Chinese puzzle. Tangram pieces can be used to make many shapes of people, animals, things, etc.

Here is a set of 7-piece tangram.

Trace the figure and cut the pieces.

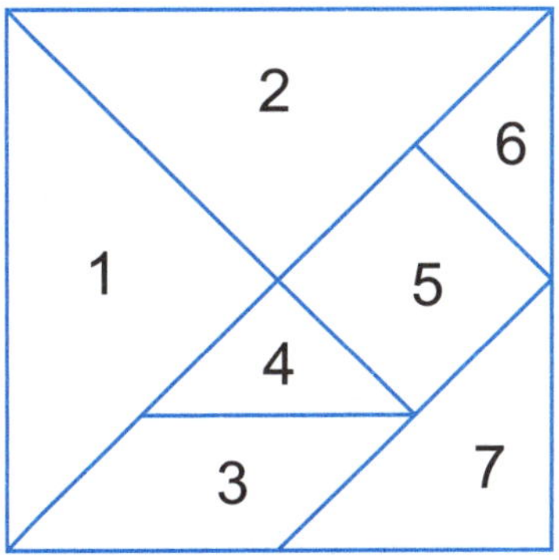

Tangram Puzzle

Using these pieces, we can make shapes like boat, candle, person, rocket, house, etc.

Boat

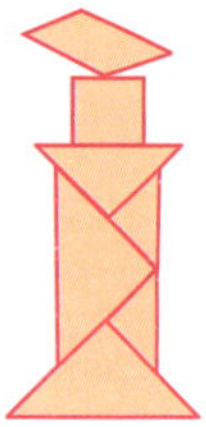
Candle

Person

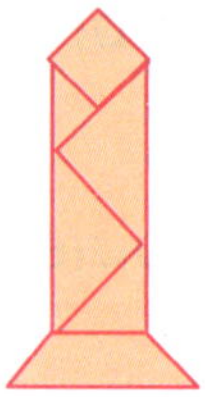
Rocket

House

We can also make shapes of animals like rabbit, dog, horse, swan, cat and fish using the seven pieces of above tangram puzzle.

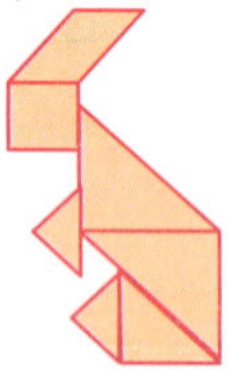
Rabbit

Dog

Horse

Swan

Cat

Fish

Tessellation

CODE-YLoJ

To cover a surface with a pattern of flat shapes so that there are no overlaps or gaps is called **tessellation** or **tiling**.

Observe the following tessellations which have been made using one shape.

Rectangles

Triangles

Squares

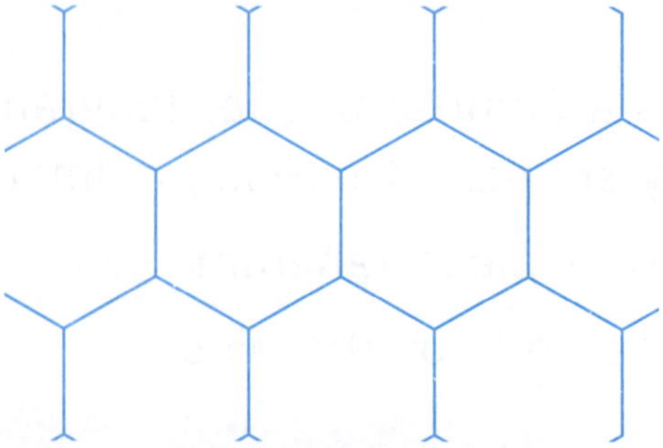
Hexagons

However in each of the following tessellations, more than one shape have been used.

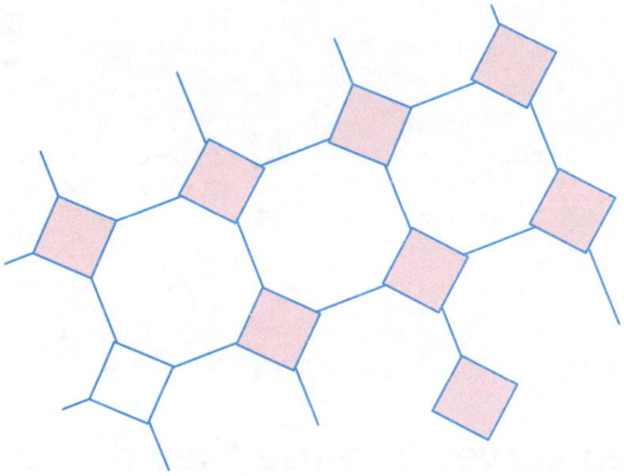

Octagons and Squares

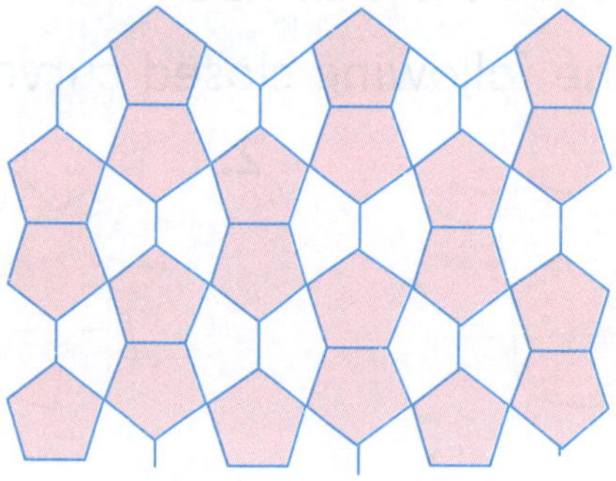

Different Pentagons

Exercise 9B

Apply and Learn

1. How many triangles are there in a 7-piece tangram?
2. How many squares are there in a 7-piece tangram?
3. Make a triangle using any (a) 2 pieces (b) 4 pieces of the 7-piece tangram.
4. Use any 4 pieces of the 7-piece tangram to make a rectangle.
5. Make the digits 1 to 8 using these tangram pieces.
6. Make some tessellation (tiling) patterns using (a) a triangle (b) a square.

Explore and Learn

CODE-Pq8N

Open and Closed Curves

The figures which have the same starting and the end points are called closed curves.

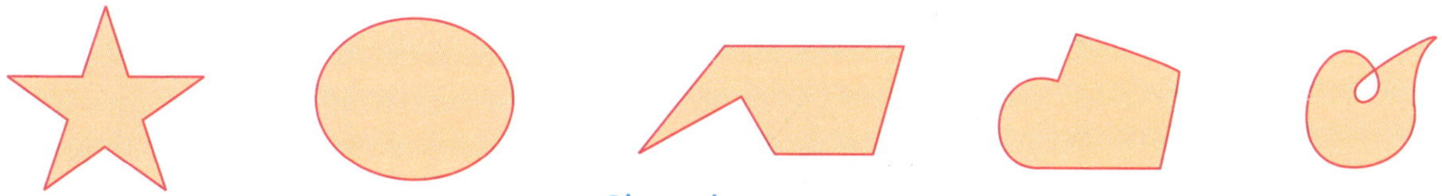

Closed curves

In the following figures we can see the starting point and the end point are not same. Such figures are known as open curves.

Open curves

CODE-Nupw

Simple Closed Curves

Observe the following closed curves :

1. 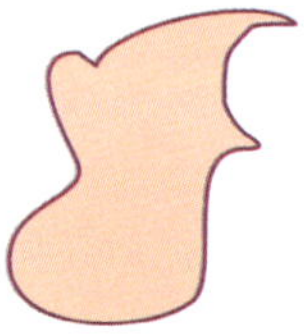

2. 

3. 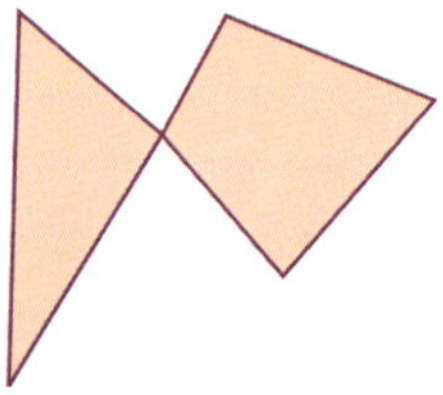

4. 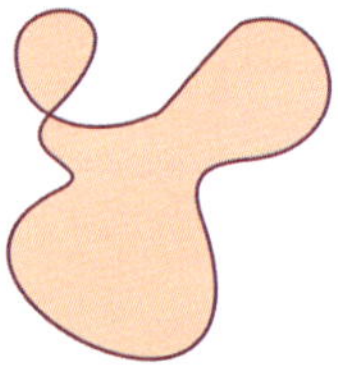

In the above closed curves, 1 and 2 are simple closed curves because they do not cross themselves as in the case of 3 and 4.

A closed curve which does not cross itself is called a simple closed curve.

Each of the following curves is a simple closed curve.

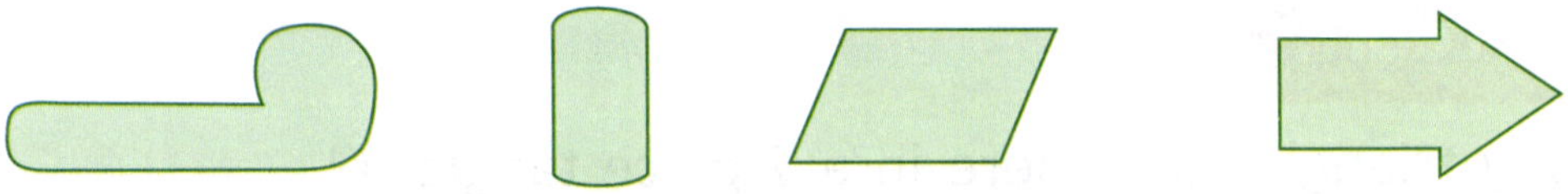

CODE-s7Lf

Polygons

Now, observe the following simple closed curves :

1. 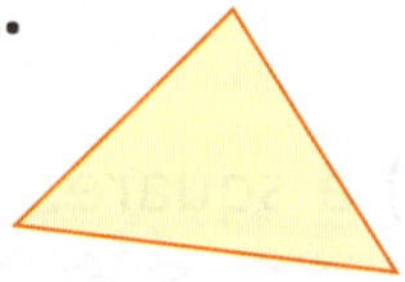

2. 

3. 

4. 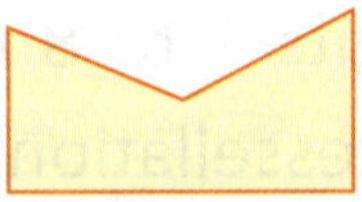

5. 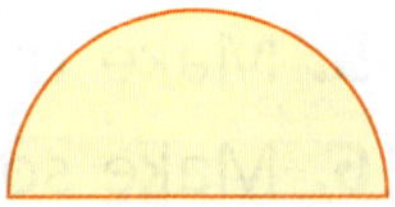

Curves 1, 3 and 4 are made of line segments only, while curves 2 and 5 are made of line segments and curves.

Curves 1, 3 and 4 are called polygons.

A simple closed curve made of line segments only is called a polygon.

All the following figures are polygons :

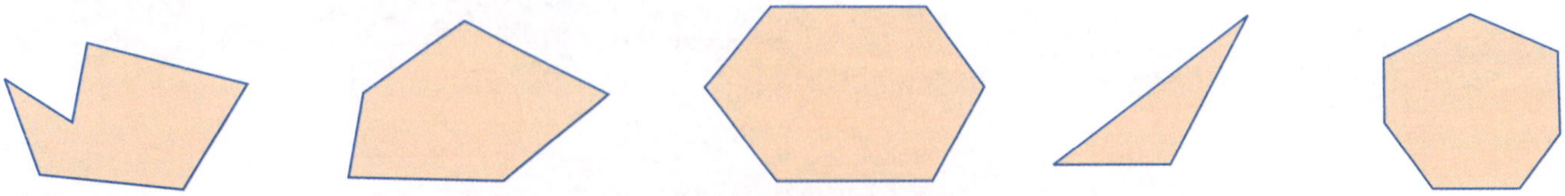

A polygon having three line segments is called a triangle.

The three line segments forming the triangle are its sides.

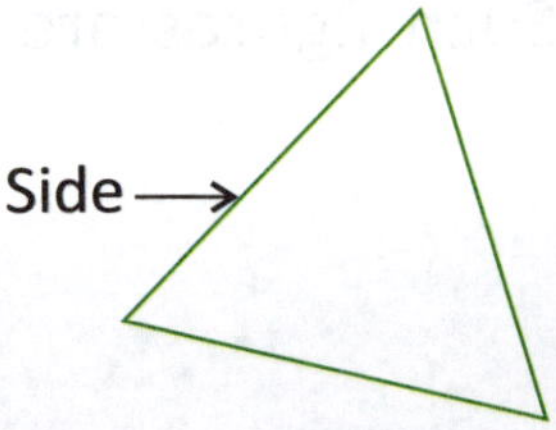

A polygon having four line segments is called a quadrilateral.

The four line segments forming the quadrilateral are its sides.

Each shape shown below is a quadrilateral.

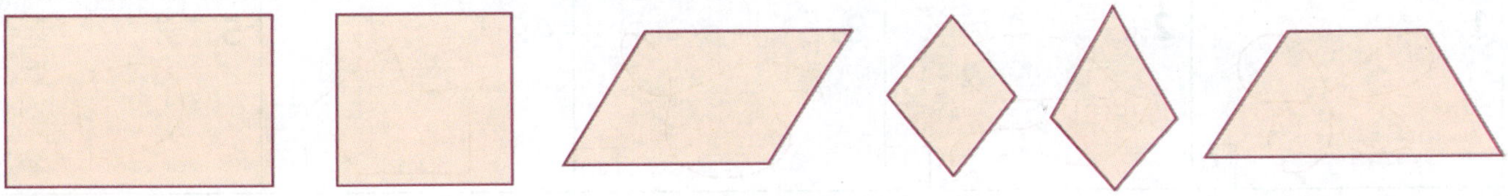

Rectangle

Rectangle is a quadrilateral whose opposite sides are equal.

Square

Square is a quadrilateral whose all the four sides are equal.

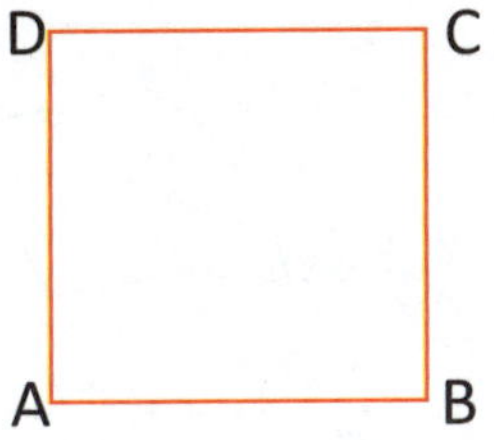

Take a sheet of paper. Do you know what is its shape? Obviously, it is rectangular. Fold the sheet in such a way that the horizontal side AB falls along the vertical side BC as shown in the figure.

Now, fold the paper along AE and cut out the piece ACDE. Unfold the paper. What do you get? The resulting paper is a squared sheet of paper.

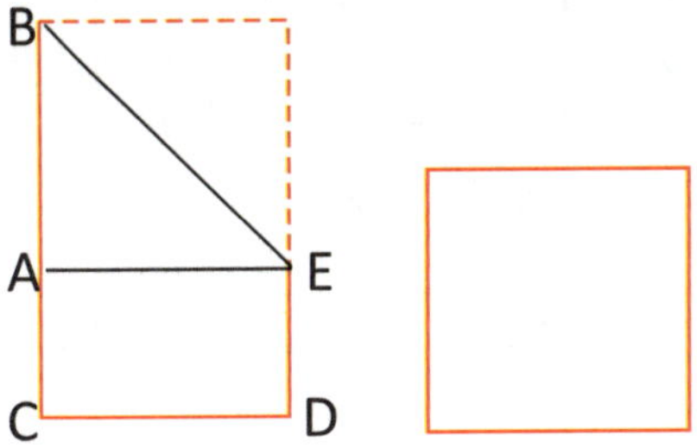

Exercise 9C

Apply and Learn

A Tick (✓) the open figures and cross (✗) the closed figures :

B Tick (✓) the simple closed curves :

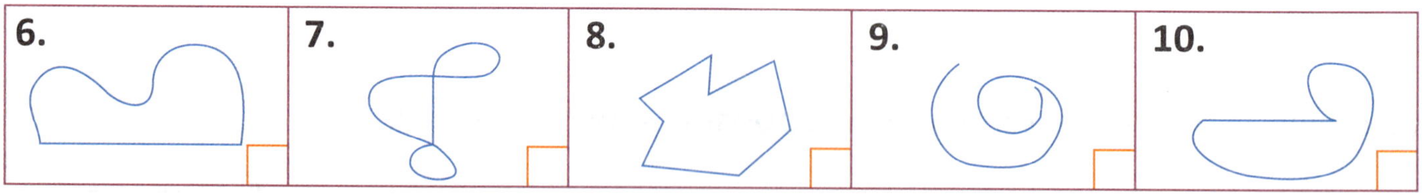

C Tick (✓) the curves which are polygons :

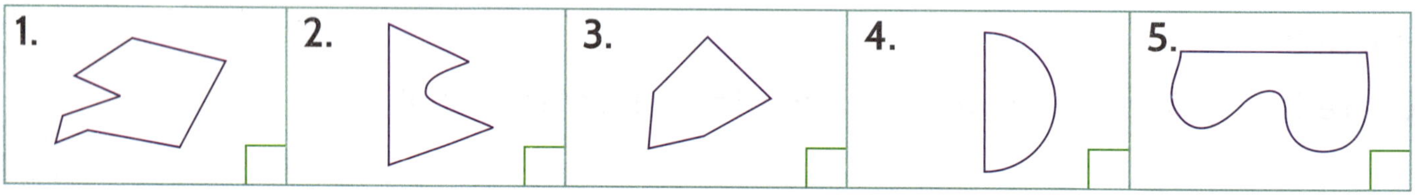

D Tick (✓) the polygons which are triangles :

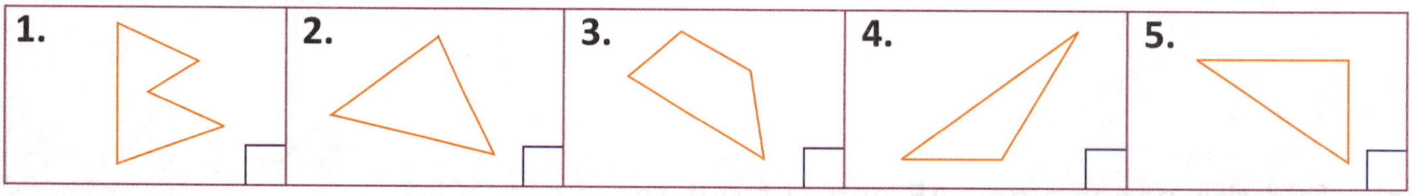

E Tick (✓) the polygons which are quadrilaterals :

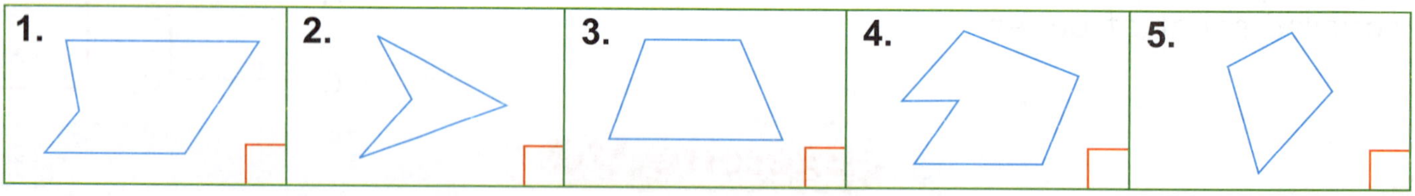

F Draw a rough sketch of a :

1. triangle **2.** rectangle **3.** square

4. Quadrilateral which is not a square or a rectangle.

5. A polygon having 6 sides

G Fill in the blanks :

1. A polygon made of three line segments is called a ____________.

2. A polygon made of four line segments is called a ____________.

3. All the sides of a ____________ are equal.

4. ____________ sides of a rectangle are equal.

5. A closed curve which does not cross itself is called a ____________ curve.

6. A simple closed curve made of line segments only is called a ____________.

Explore and Learn

CODE-ssTE

Basic Geometrical Concepts

Plane : Look at the table shown here. Its top is a flat surface. If we consider its extension in all the directions endlessly, the flat surface so formed becomes an example of a plane. It has no boundary. Thus, a flat surface which extends endlessly in all the directions is called a **plane**.

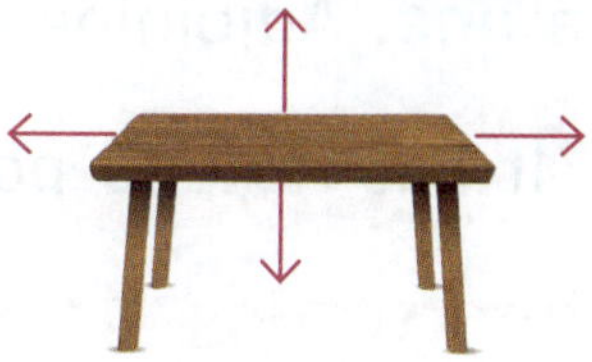

In fact, we can not draw a plane on a paper. We can just represent a part of it on a paper. Thus, the surface of a book, blackboard, roof of a building, etc, are parts of a plane.

Book

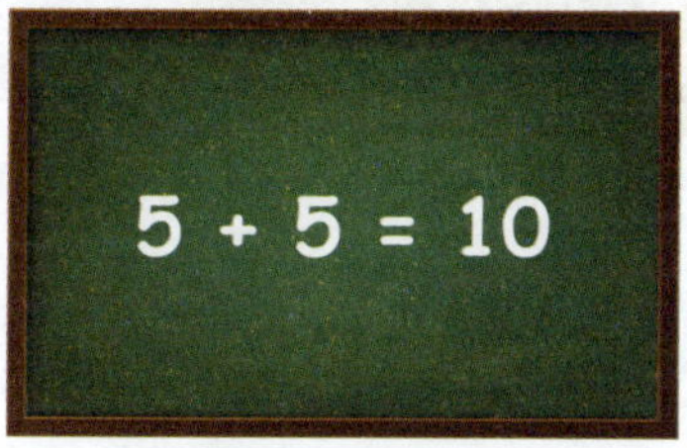

Blackboard

Roof

Point : A small dot made by a sharp pencil on a piece of paper represents a point.

A point has no length, no breadth and no thickness.

It has only position. A point is named by a single capital letter such as A, B, C, etc. In the figure, A is a point.

Line Segment : Mark any two points A and B on a paper and join A to B. The straight path from A to B is called the **line segment AB**.

A line segment has a fixed length.

Line segment AB is denoted as $\overline{AB}$.

The points A and B are called end points of $\overline{AB}$.

The distance between the points A and B is called the **length of $\overline{AB}$.**

Line segment AB is same as line segment BA.

Ray : A line segment extended endlessly in one direction only is called **a ray**. In figure, AB is a ray whose end point is A.

It has one end point.

It is denoted by $\overrightarrow{AB}$. Point A is also called the initial point of $\overrightarrow{AB}$. A ray has no definite length.

Note that while naming a ray we start with the initial point, that is ray AB ($\overrightarrow{AB}$) is different from ray BA ($\overrightarrow{BA}$)

Line : A line segment extended endlessly in both directions is called a **line**. Adjoining figure shows a line AB. It is denoted by $\overleftrightarrow{AB}$.

It has no end points.

Intersecting Lines : In figure, two lines AB and CD meet at a point O. Such lines are called **intersecting lines** and the point where they meet is called their **point of intersection**. Thus, in adjoining figure, AB and CD are intersecting lines and O is their point of intersection.

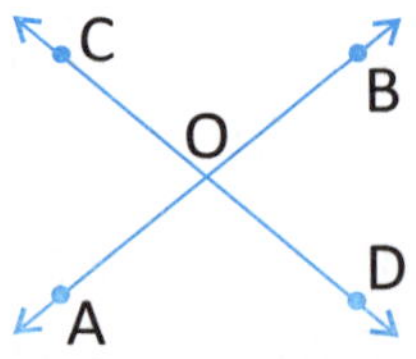

Exercise 9D

Apply and Learn

A Classify the following as point, line, line segment and ray:

1. 2. 3. 4. 5. 6.

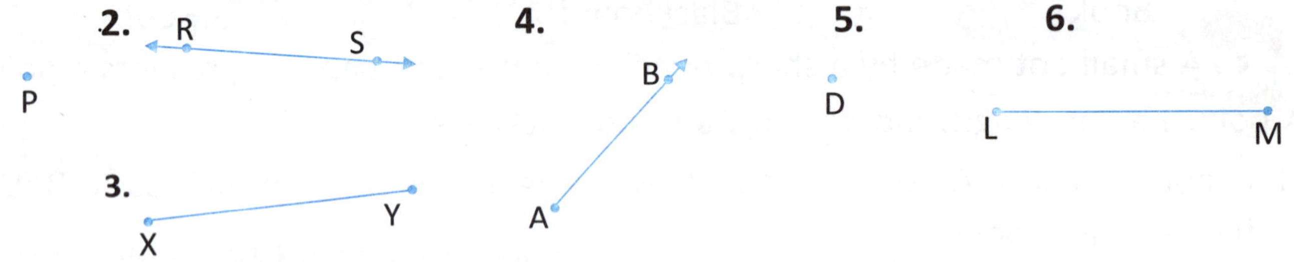

B Name the points marked between A and B.

C Name all the line segments in the following figure :

D Name the line segments in each of the following figures :

1.

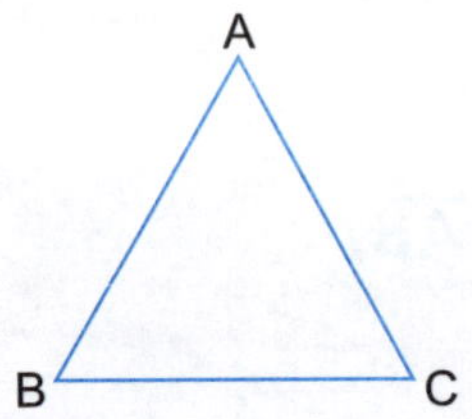

2.

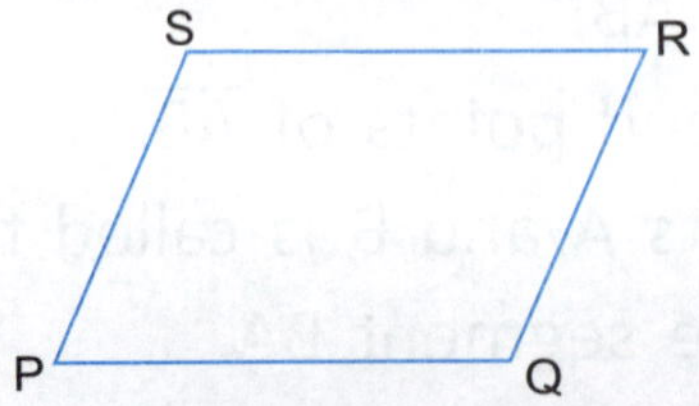

3.

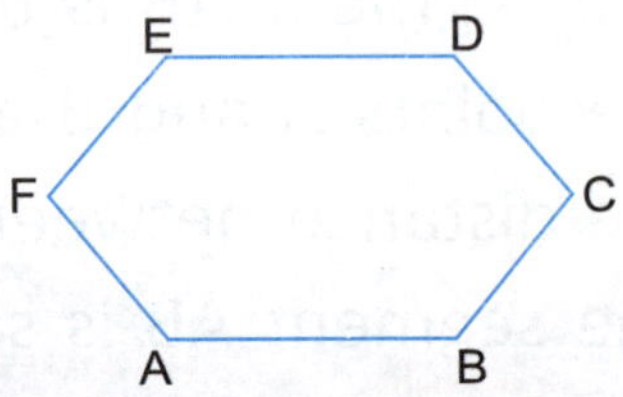

4. 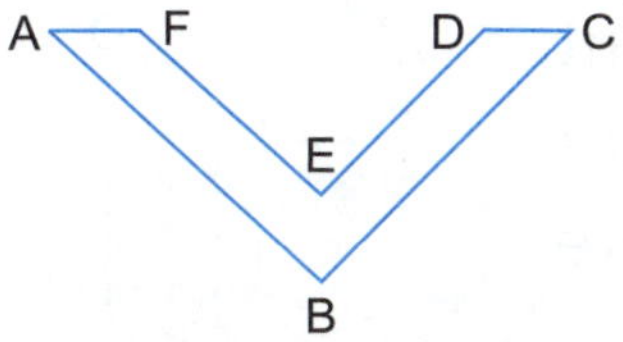

5. 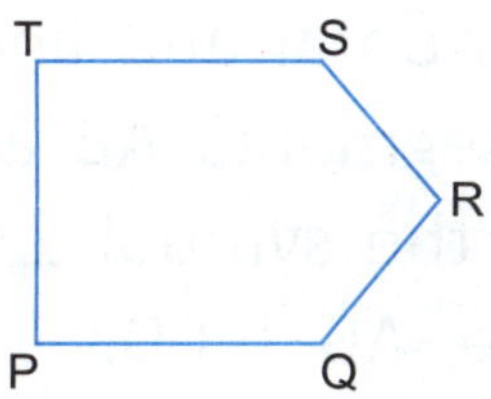

6. 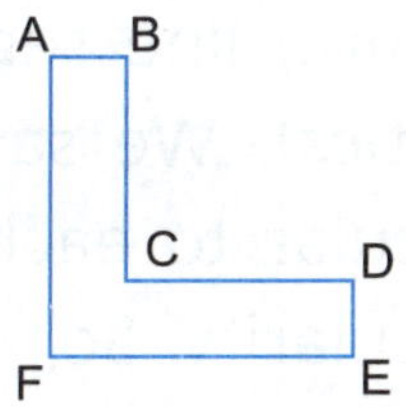

E In the figure, name the following :

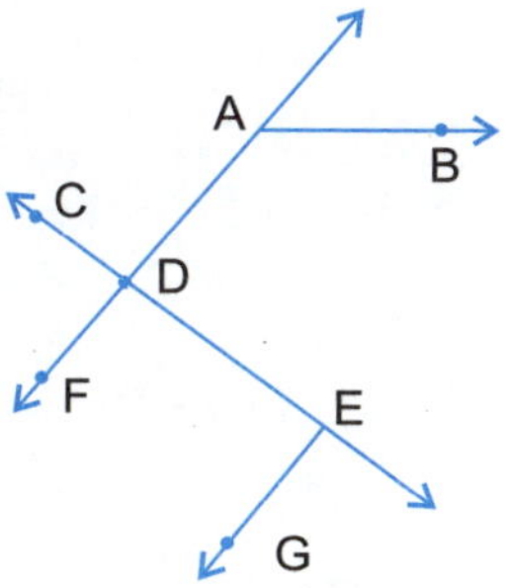

1. 4 line segments
2. 4 rays
3. 2 lines
4. Pair of intersecting lines

F In the figure, name :

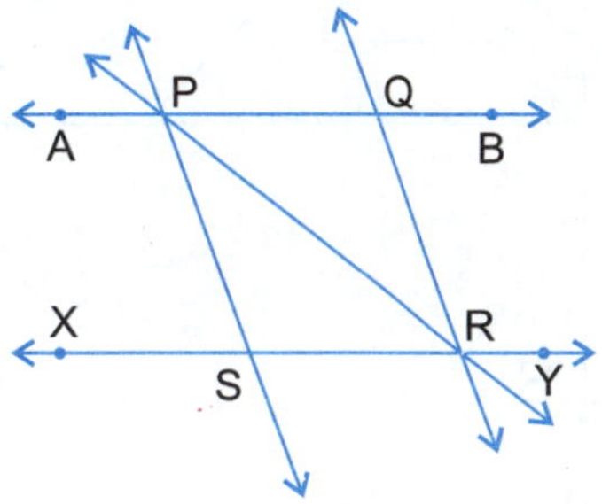

1. 2 pairs of intersecting lines
2. 4 line of segments
3. 4 rays

G State true or false :

1. A point has no length no breadth and no thickness. ________
2. A line has two end points. ________
3. A line segment has no definite length. ________
4. A ray has no definite length. ________
5. Ray AB is different from ray BA. ________

Explore and Learn

CODE-ATbx

Perpendicular Lines

We say that the electric pole is perpendicular to the ground, the wall is perpendicular to the floor of the room, when you stand erect, you are perpendicular to the floor.

In the figure, line segment AB is horizontal and line segment CD is vertical. We say that the line segments AB and CD are perpendicular to each other. We use the symbol ⊥ to denote perpendicularity. So, we have in figure, AB ⊥ CD.

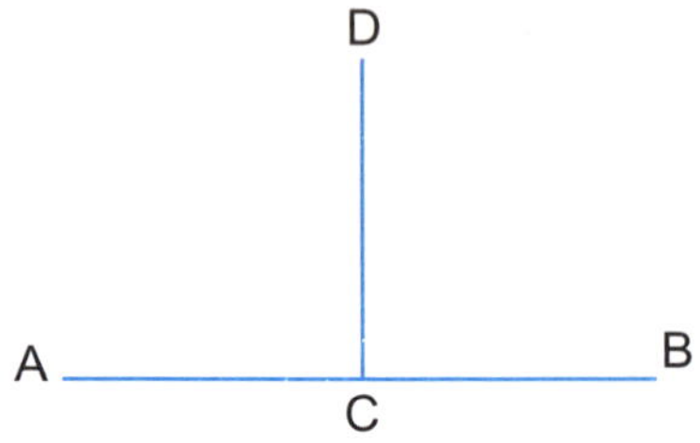

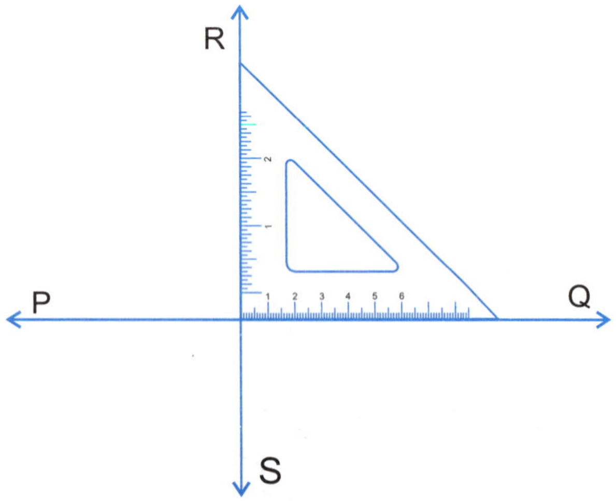

(i)

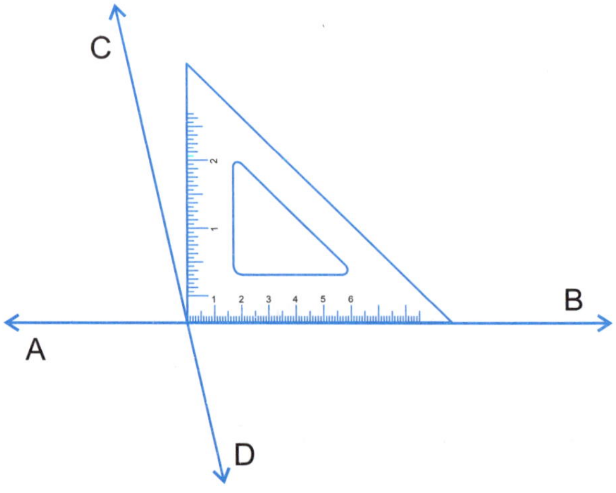

(ii)

To know whether two lines are perpendicular, we use the set squares. The set square has two edges which are perpendicular to each other.

Put the vertex (where the two smaller edges meet) of the set square at the point of intersection of the two lines as shown in the figure (i). If the lines fall along the edges of the set square, it means the lines are perpendicular.

In figure (ii), since the lines do not fall along the edges of the set square, so, these are not perpendicular lines.

Given a Segment AB and a Point P on It. To Draw Segment PQ Perpendicular to AB

First place set square (I) as shown in figure, with its edge coinciding with AB and hold it tightly without disturbing it from its position. Now, place the second set square as shown in the figure. The vertex (where the two smaller edges meet) of the set square coincides with P in this position. Now hold the set square (II) tightly and draw the segment PQ along the edge of the set square. Lift the set squares. Now PQ ⊥ AB.

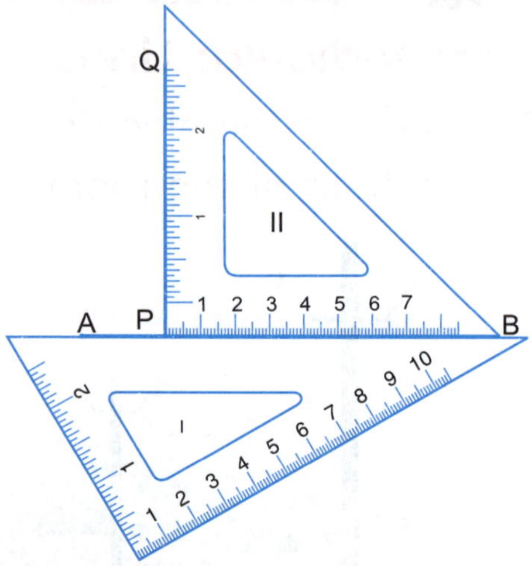

CODE-tCBs

Parallel Lines

Parallel lines do not meet even if they are extended indefinitely on either side. There can be more than two lines parallel to each other.

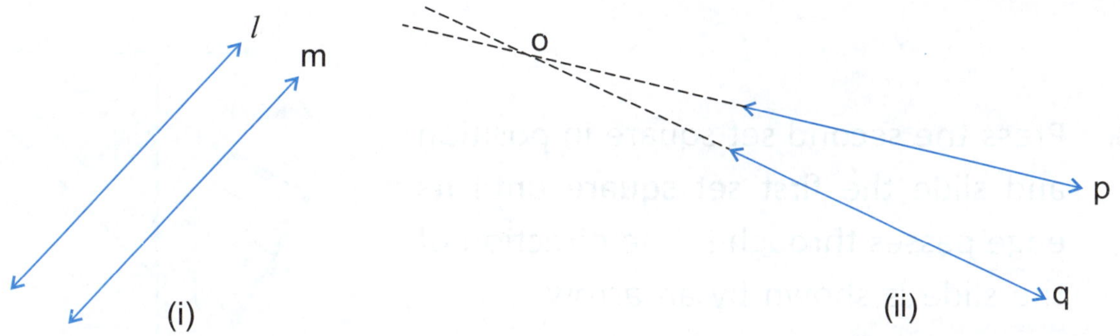

In figure (i), *l* is parallel to *m*. We also write it as $l \parallel m$. In figure (ii), the lines *p* and *q* do not intersect. But on extending these lines, they meet at a point O. So, these are not parallel lines.

From our daily life, we can say that the two rails of a railway line, the two edges of a ruler, etc., are examples of 'parallel lines'.

Railway line

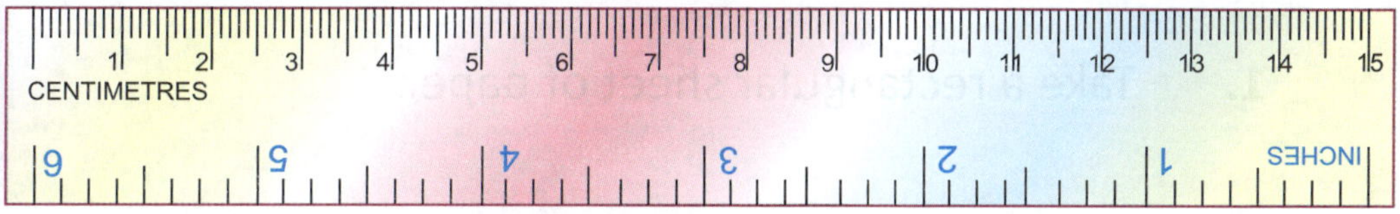

Ruler

Drawing Parallel Lines with Set Squares

CODE-AvmL

Example : Draw a line segment through P which is parallel to $\overleftrightarrow{AB}$.

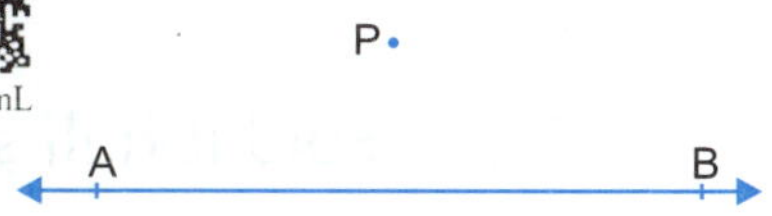

Procedure :

Step 1. Place one edge of the two smaller edges of any set-square along $\overleftrightarrow{AB}$.

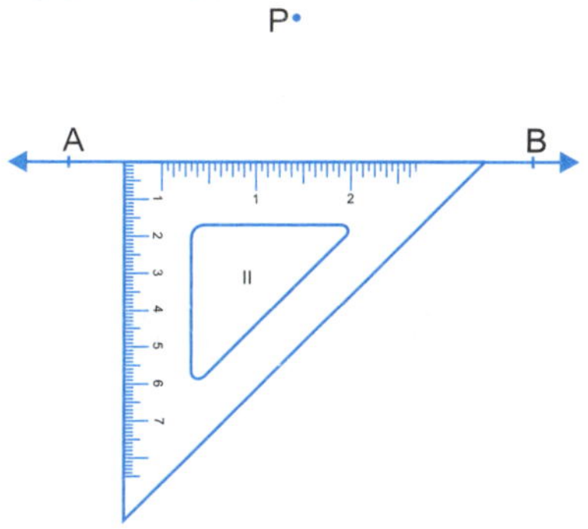

Step 2. Place the longest edge of the other set square along the free side of the first set square.

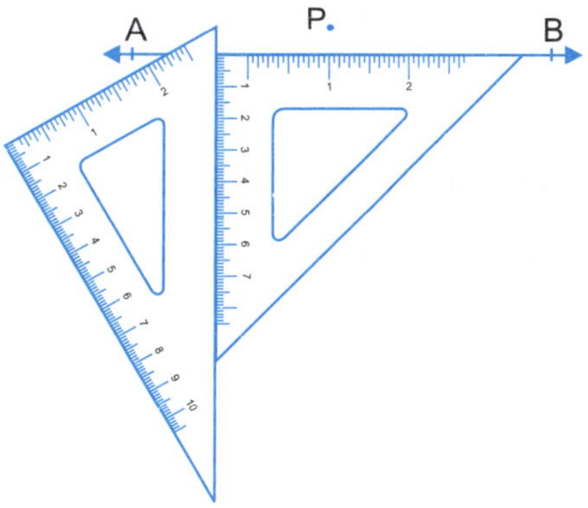

Step 3. Press the second set square in position and slide the first set square until its edge passes through P. The direction of the slide is shown by an arrow.

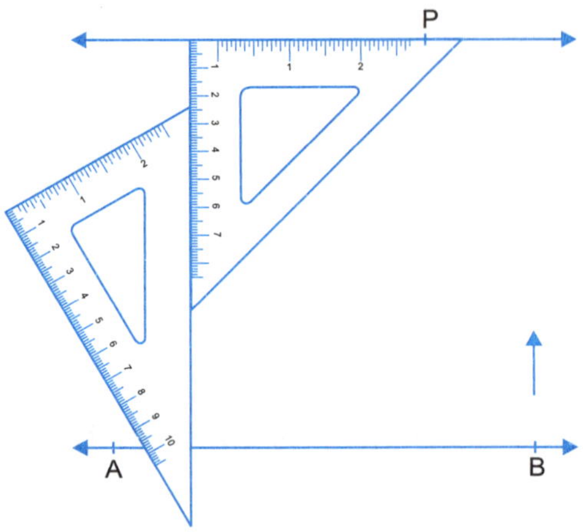

Step 4. Draw the line through P with the help of the edge passing through P. While drawing this line, the first set square must be pressed in position.

Activity

1. Take a rectangular sheet of paper.

2. Fold it half such that one part covers the other part completely.

3. Fold it again in the same manner.

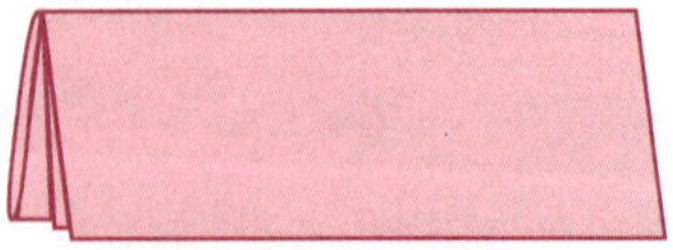

4. Now unfold it to get three creases. These creases are parallel to each other.

Exercise 9E

Apply and Learn

A State whether the segments are perpendicular to each other or not. Write 'yes' or 'no'.

1. 

2. 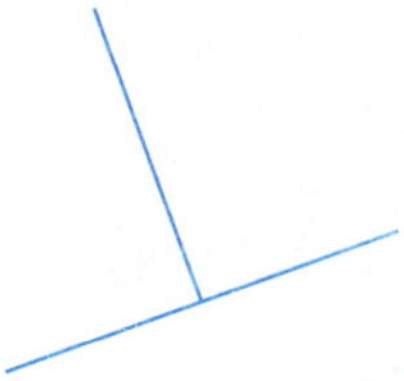

3. 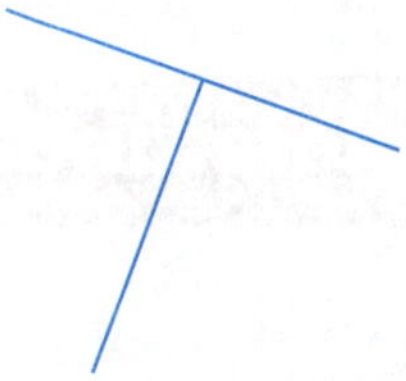

4. 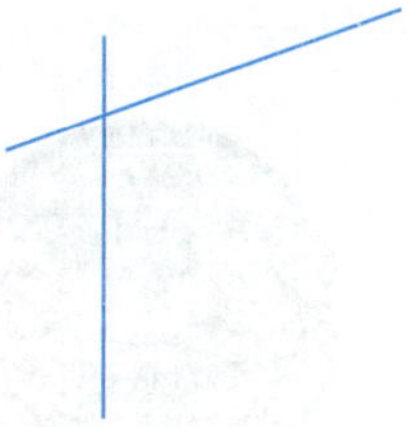

5. 

6. 

B Draw the following :

1. Draw a line segment CD = 6.3 cm. Mark a point E on it. Draw a line segment EF perpendicular to CD using set squares.
2. Draw a line segment AB of suitable length. Mark a point P above it. Draw PQ perpendicular to AB using set squares.
3. Draw a line segment AB. Mark a point C above it. Draw a line segment through C parallel to AB.
4. Draw a line segment EF. Mark a point G below it. Draw a line segment through G parallel to EF.
5. Draw a vertical line segment AB. Mark a point H on its right side. Draw a line segment through H parallel to AB.
6. Draw a vertical line segment CD. Mark a point L on its left side. Draw a line segment through L parallel to CD

C Give three example from your environment for each of the following :

1. a pair of perpendicular lines
2. a pair of parallel lines

D. Write T for true statement and F for false statement :

1. Two rays can be parallel.
2. Perpendicular lines never meet in a point.
3. Parallel lines meet in a point.
4. Opposite edges of a table are parallel.
5. Wall of a building is perpendicular to the ground.

Explore and Learn

Circle

We have read about circles in previous class.

Observe the following shapes :

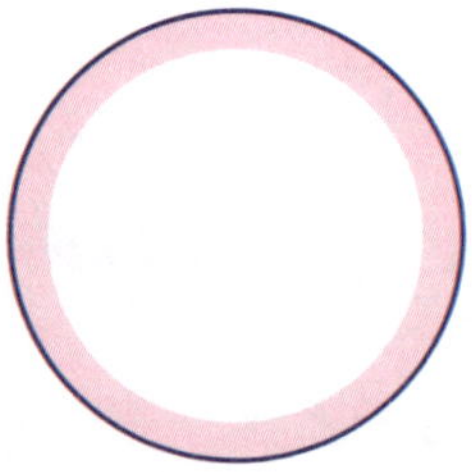

All the above shapes give us an idea of a circle

CODE-6ZqN

Drawing a Circle

We can draw a circle by moving a pencil around the edge of a bangle, a 1-rupee coin, a cylindrical water bottle, etc.

We can also draw a circle using a compass. To do so, we proceed as follows :

1. Fix a pencil in the pencil holding arm of the compass.
2. Put the metal tip of the compass on the paper.
3. Open the compass as needed.
4. Move the compass around, keeping the metal tip fixed, to get a circle.

   The mark made by the metal tip of the compass is the centre of the circle.

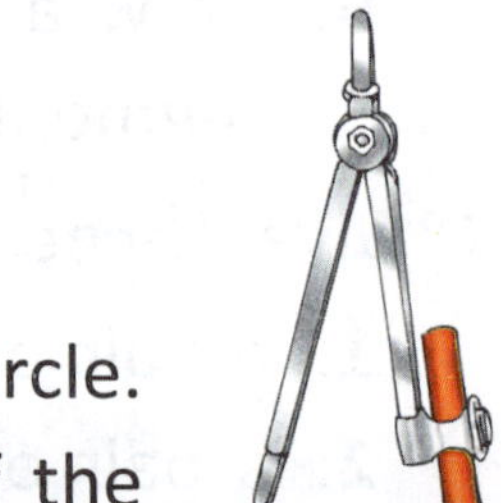

Terms Related to a Circle

Centre : The point O inside the circle is the centre of the circle.

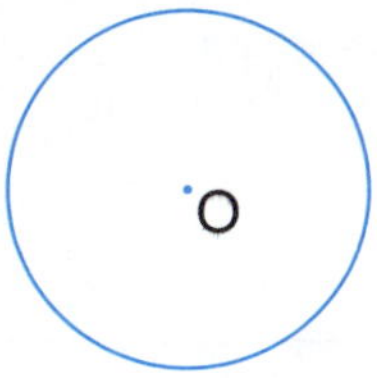

Radius : A line segment drawn from the centre to any point on the circle is called a radius of the circle.

In the figure, the line segment OA is a radius of the circle. Line segment OB is also a radius of the circle. The plural of radius is radii.

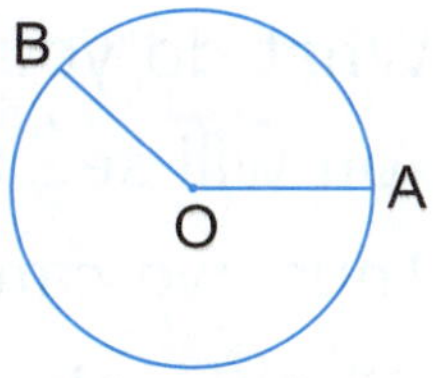

Diameter : The line segment drawn through the centre that joins two points on the circle is called a diameter of the circle. In the figure, line segment PQ is a diameter of the circle.

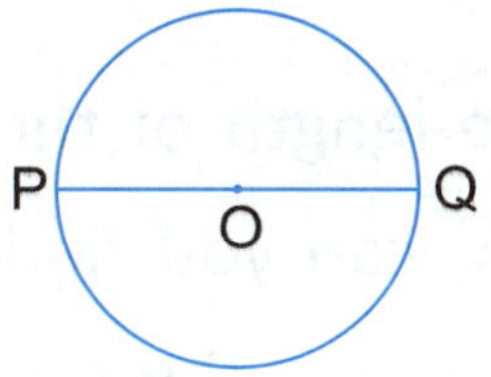

Chord : A line segment that joins two points on a circle is called a chord of the circle. In the figure, line segment DE and LM are chords of the circle.

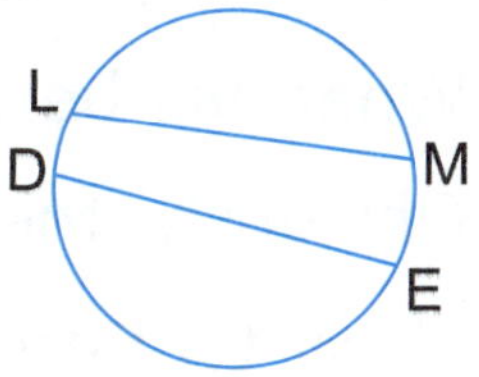

Circumference : The length of a circle (distance around) is called the circumference of the circle.

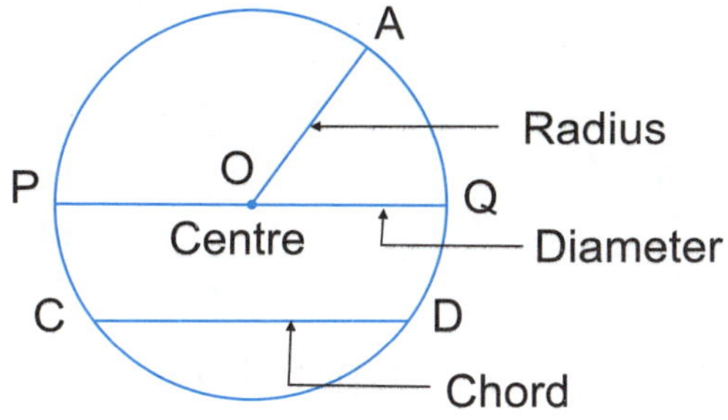

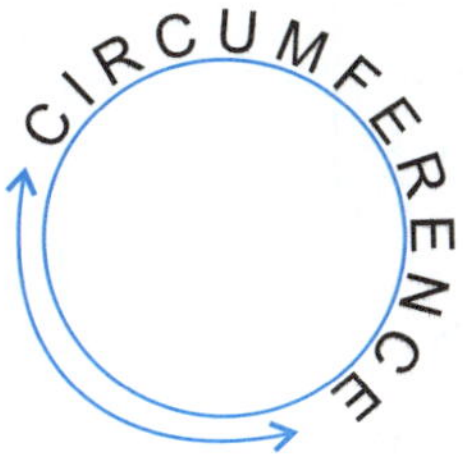

REMEMBER

Diameter is the longest chord of a circle.

Relationship Between Radius and Diameter of a Circle

Measure the radius and diameter of each circle and fill in the blanks :

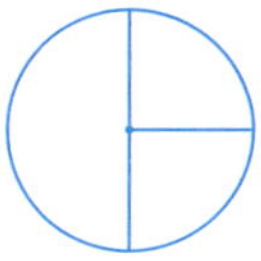	Radius = ____________ mm Diameter = ____________ mm
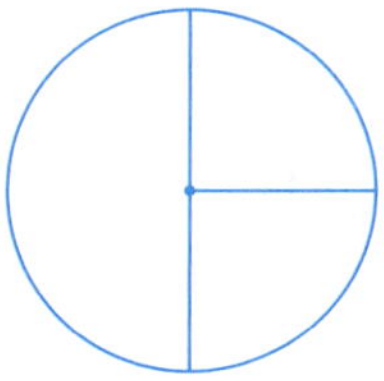	Radius = ____________ mm Diameter = ____________ mm

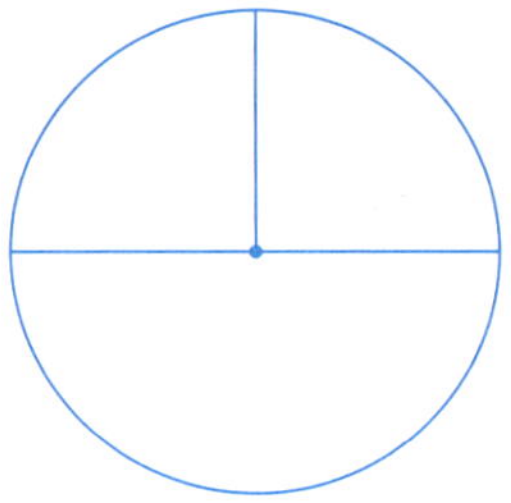

Radius = ______ mm

Diameter = ______ mm

What do you observe?

You will see that for each circle, the diameter is twice the length of the radius.

Thus, we can say that :

> The length of the diameter of a circle is twice the length of its radius.
>
> OR
>
> The length of the radius of a circle is half the length of its diameter.

Now, can you find the radius of a circle whose diameter is 10 cm?

Obviously, the radius of the circle is 10 cm ÷ 2 = 5 cm.

What will be the length of the diameter of a circle whose radius is 3 cm?

Obviously, the diameter of the circle is 3 cm × 2 = 6 cm.

How to Find the Centre of a Given Circle?

CODE-gatB

Let us try to find the centre of a given circle.

Trace the given circle on a tracing paper | Fold the tracing paper | Fold the tracing paper once more | Open it out

The point at which the two folding lines (creases) meet is the centre of the circle.

Exercise 9F

Apply and Learn

A Answer the following questions :

1. Draw three circles using three different circular objects.

2. Draw three circles of different radii using a compass.

3. Lable the circle.

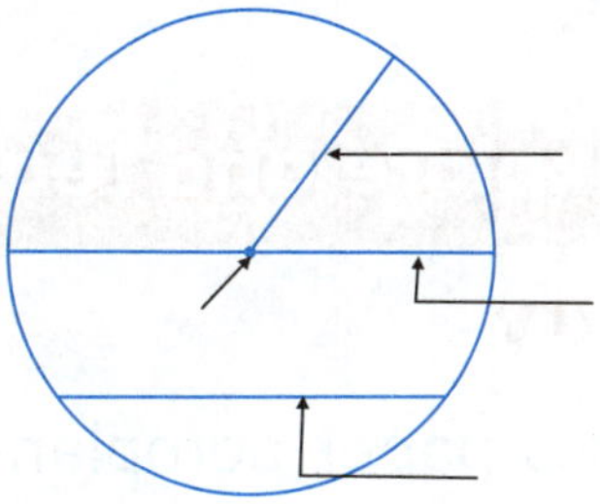

4. Name the parts of the given circle :

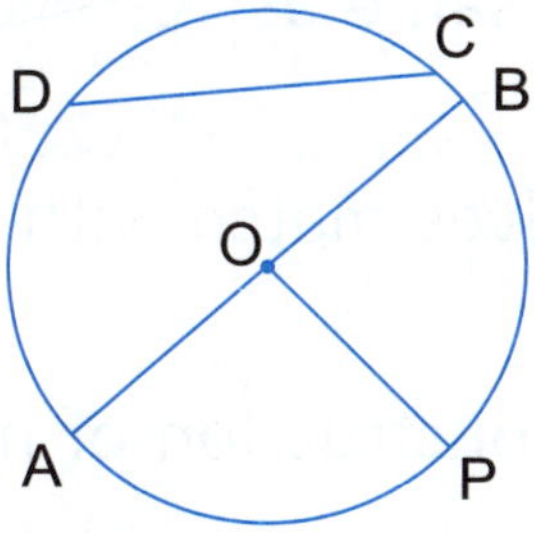

Centre ______________

Radii __________, __________, __________

Diameter ______________

Chords ______________

B Find the radius of the circle whose diameter is :

1. 8 cm **2.** 12 cm **3.** 14 cm **4.** 4 cm

C Find the diameter of the circle whose radius is :

1. 5 cm **2.** 8 cm **3.** 9 cm **4.** 3 cm

D Using tracing paper, find the centre of the following circles :

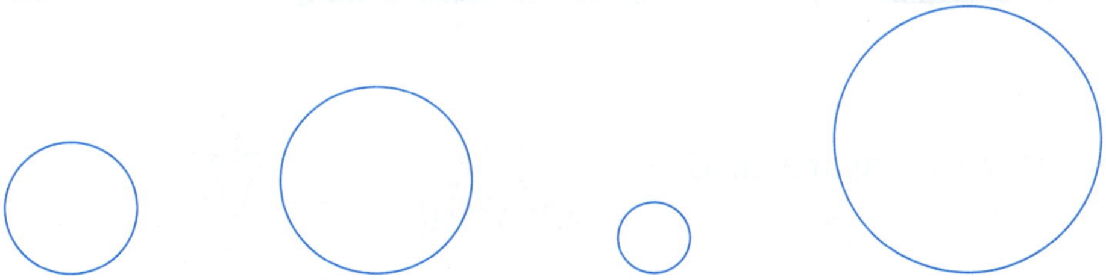

E Complete the following table :

Radius	3 cm	______ cm	______ m	5 m	15 mm
Diameter	______ cm	20 cm	6 m	______ m	______ mm

F Fill in the blanks :

1. A diameter of a circle passes through the ____________ of the circle.
2. The distance around a circle is called its ____________.
3. The length of the radius of a circle is ____________ the length of its diameter.
4. Diameter is also a ____________ of the circle.
5. The line segment that joins two points on a circle is called a __________ of the circle.

Explore and Learn

Symmetry

CODE-mCrj

Look at this paper aeroplane.

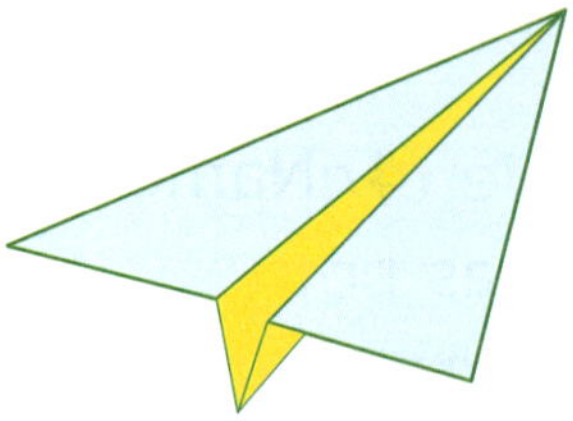

In the paper aeroplane, one half of the aeroplane is exactly same as the other half.

Flat shapes that can be folded in such a way that the two halves match with each other are called symmetrical shapes.

The concept of symmetry has been beautifully used in the construction of monuments like Taj Mahal, Humayu's Tomb, Char Minar, etc.

We can see symmetry in nature also.

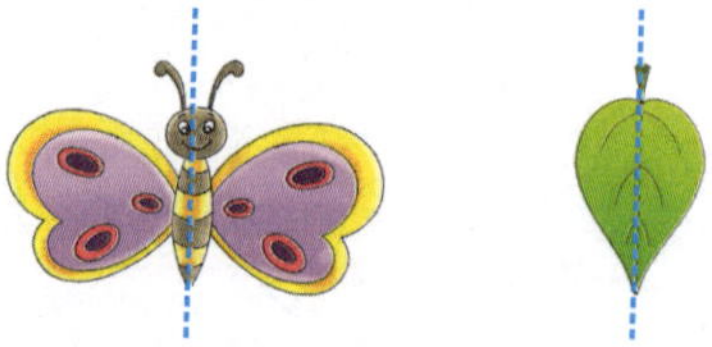

The dotted line which divides the figure into two equal parts is called its line of Symmetry.

Line of symmetry can be drawn vertically as well as horizontally depending upon the shape of the object.

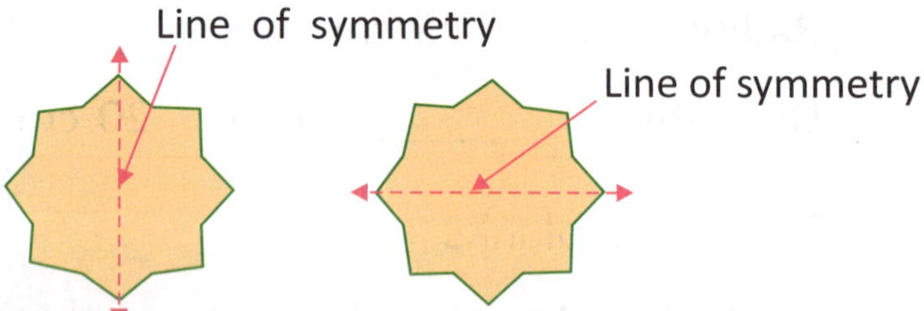

Observe the following letters of English alphabet :

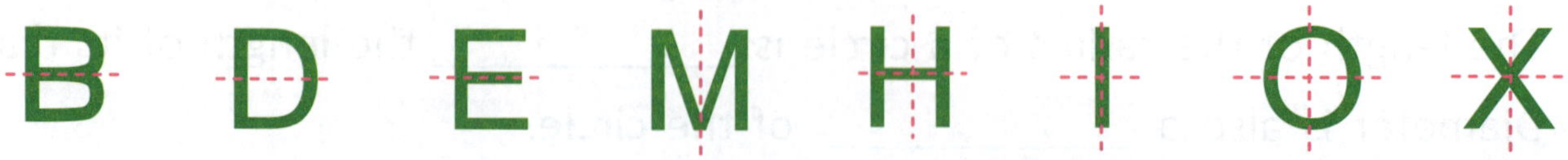

We see that the letters B, D, E, M has only one line of symmetry whereas the letters H, I, O and X have two lines of symmetry. We can also see that letters F, G, L, etc. have no line of symmetry.

Some figures may have more than two lines of symmetry.

We can complete this image by drawing the other half of it as both the halves are the same. We call such halves as mirror halves.

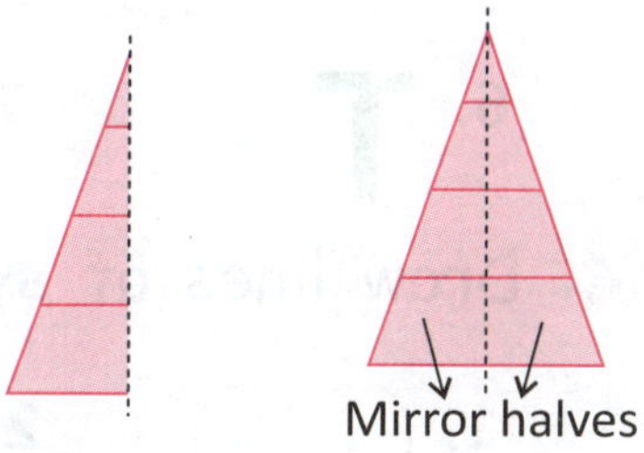

Reflection

CODE-CzSC

Take the alphabet P. Place a mirror in front of it.

We can see the reflection of P as shown.

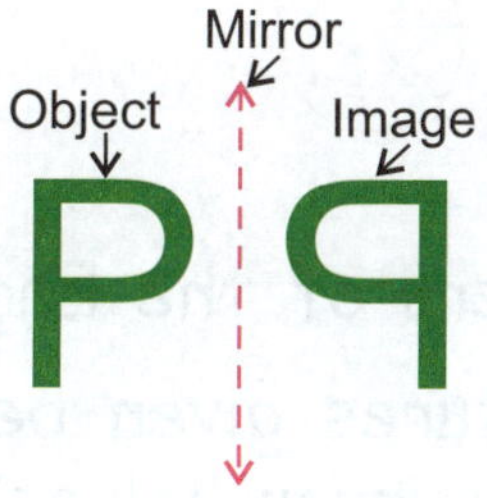

Take a pencil and place it in front of the mirror.
We can see its reflection in the mirror.

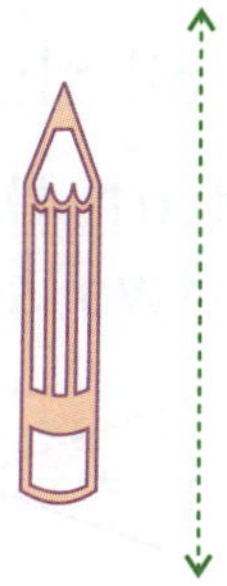

If we see the image of this figure, we can see the arrow is pointing towards the right in the figure, whereas the reflection of the arrow is pointing towards the left.

The right side of the image will appear as the left and left side of the image will appear as the right side in the mirror.

The mirror image of an object is exactly the same as the object; only, it is in the opposite direction.

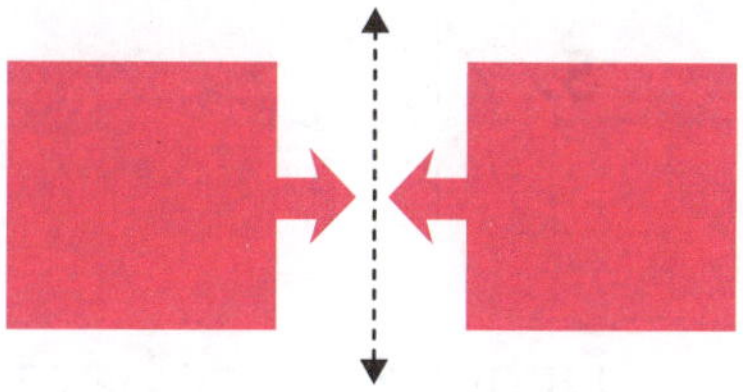

Exercise 9G

Apply and Learn

A Draw all possible lines of symmetry in the following figures :

1. 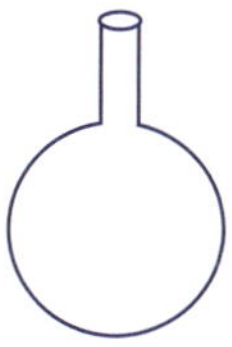

2. 

3. 

4. 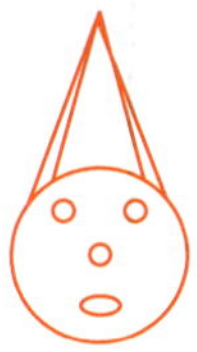

5. 

6. 

7. 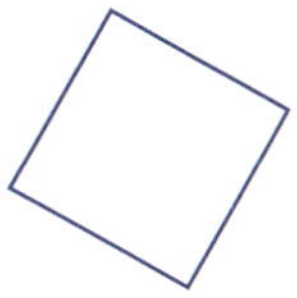

8. 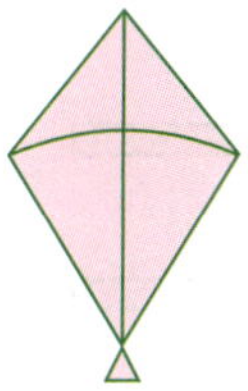

B Draw all possible lines of symmetry in the following letters :

1. C 2. M 3. N 4. R 5. S

6. T 7. U 8. V 9. W 10. Y

C Draw lines of symmetry for the following figures :

1. 
2. 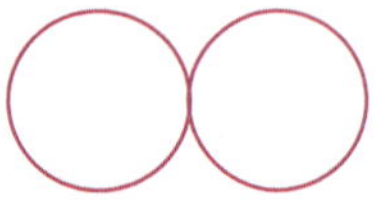
3. 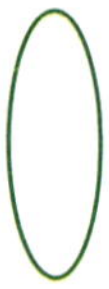
4. 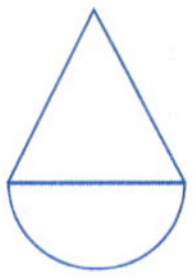
5. 
6. 

D List all the letters of the English alphabet which have no line of symmetry.

E Look at the pictures given below. Does the dotted line divide each picture into two similar mirror halves?

1. 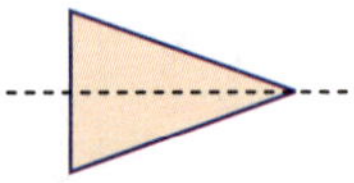
2. 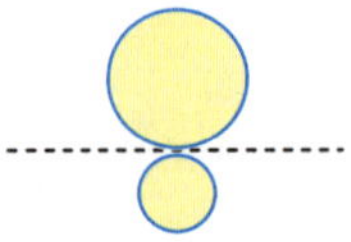
3. 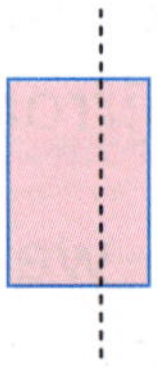
4. 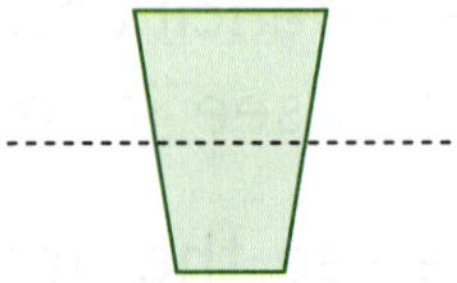
5. 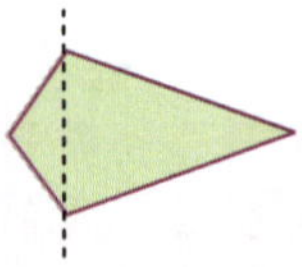
6. 
7. 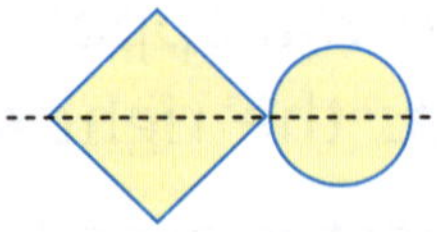
8. 

F Draw the reflections of the following :

T B D K E

G Draw the lines of symmetry of the following shapes :

1. 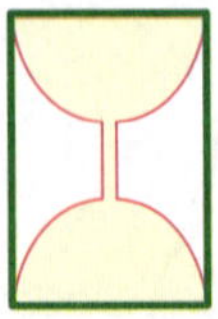
2. 
3. 
4. E
5. A
6. 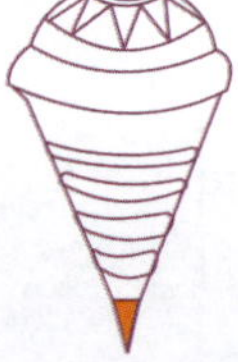

Explore and Learn

Views of an Object

CODE-gYTG

Look at the rectangle shown here.

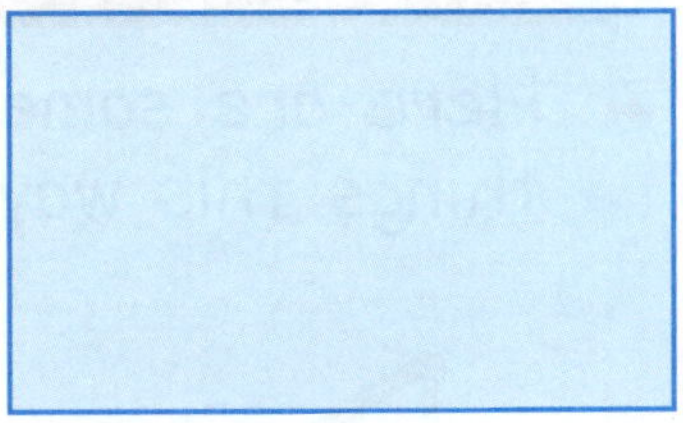

It will look like a rectangle when you view it from the top, from side or from the front. All plane figures have one view.

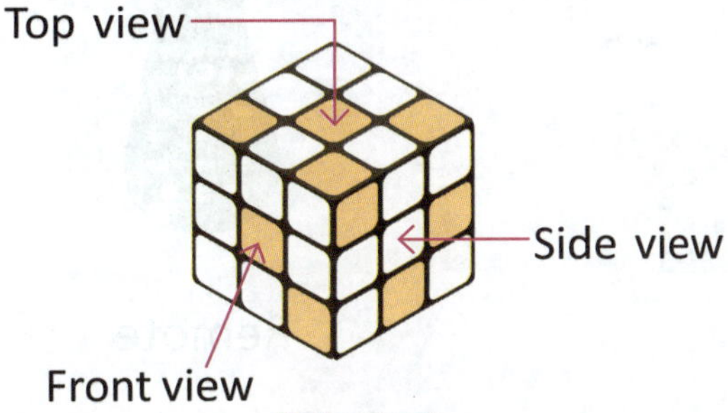

Now look at this cube.

It will look like :

 when you view it from the top.

 when you view it from the side.

 when you view it from the front.

All solid figures have three different views :

Top view of a Mobile Phone

Front view of a Mobile Phone

Side view of a Mobile Phone

Observe the solid shape given alongside.

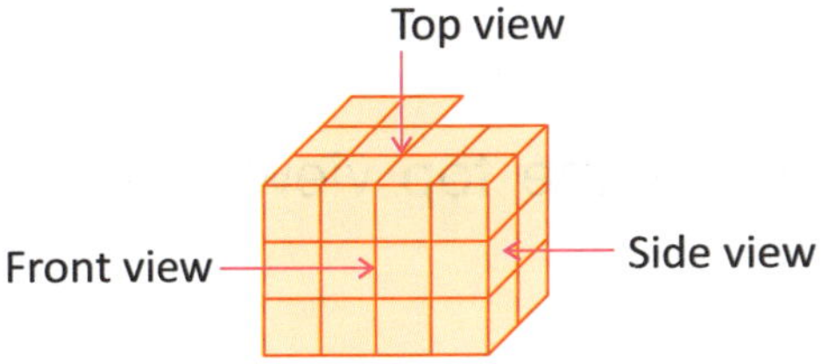

Its three views are given below :

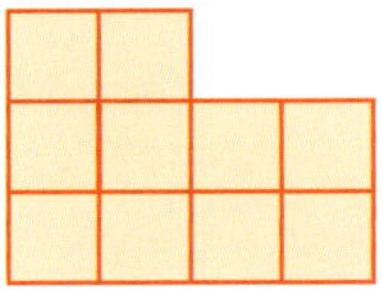

Top view

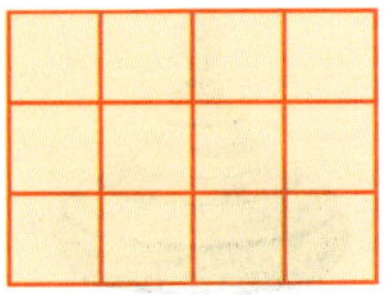

Front view

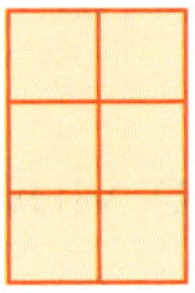

Side View

Exercise 9H

Apply and Learn

A Here are some pictures. Find out from where you have to look to see the things this way (like top views, side views and front views) :

Staircase

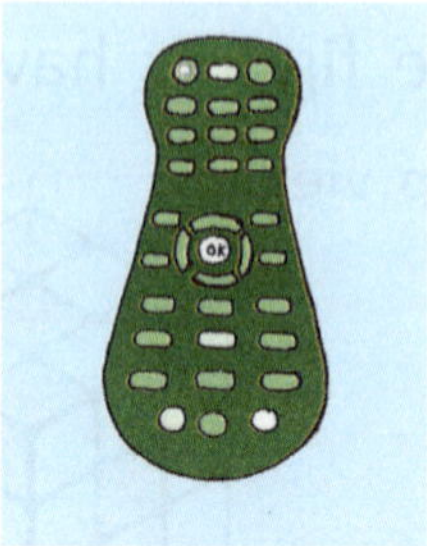

Remote

Table

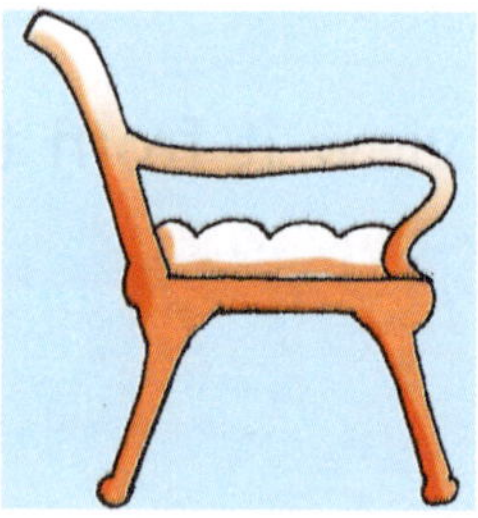

Chair

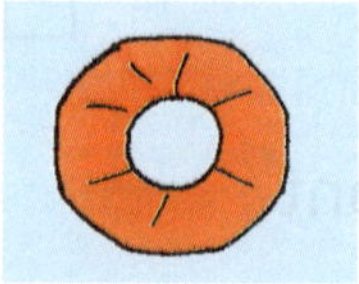

Pencil

Car

B Draw top views, side views and front views of few things which you use in your daily life :

C 1. Draw side view of the solid 

2. Draw the front view of the envelope 

3. Draw the top view of the container 

4. Draw the top view of the top. 

D The three views of the solids are given. Match the solids to their views :

Top view | Front view | Side view

1. 

(a) 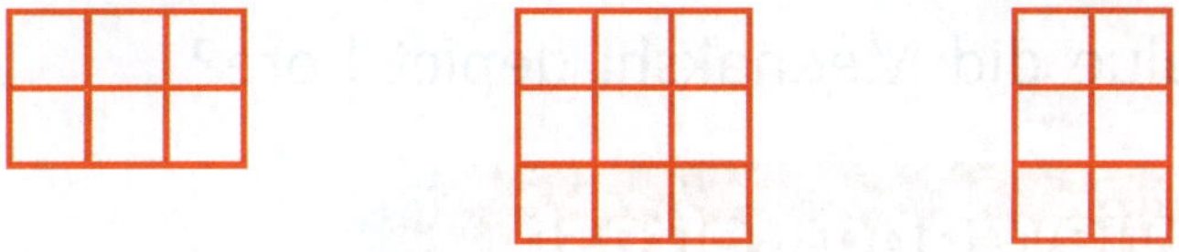

2. 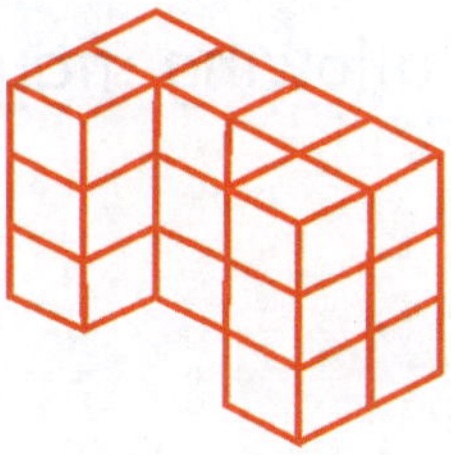

(b) 

3. 

(c) 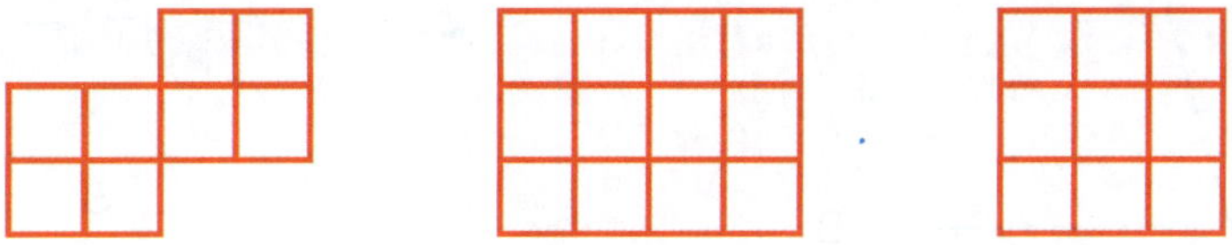

4. 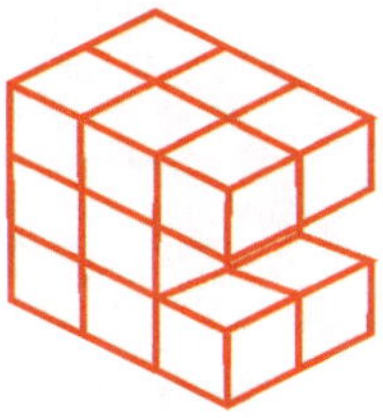

(d) 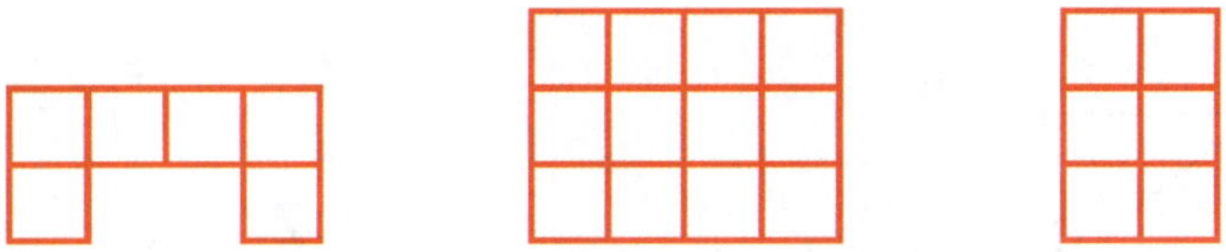

5. 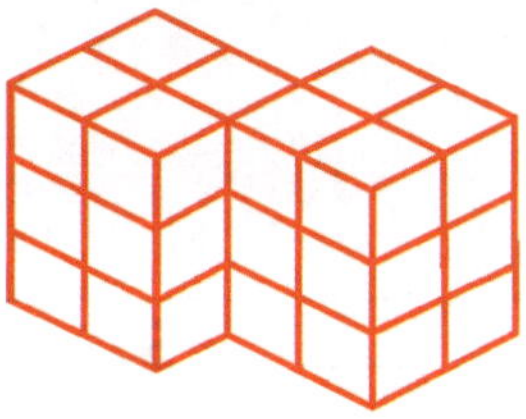

(e) 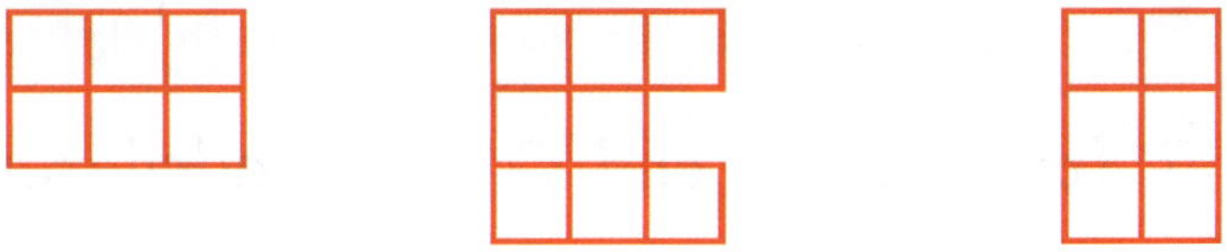

Value Based Questions

One day, Meenakshi visited some monuments with her parents. There she observed that most of the buildings are symmetrical. While Meenakshi was enjoying with her parents, she noticed that some guys are defacing the walls of the monument by writing on them. She went to the guys and asked them not to do so.

1. Did you ever visit any monument?

2. Can you name some famous buildings or monuments which are symmetrical?
3. What value is missing in the guys who were defacing the walls of the monument?
4. What value did Meenakshi depict here?

Review and Refresh

A Using the tangram pieces, make the letters C, F and H.

B How many line segments are there in each of the following figures? Name them :

1. 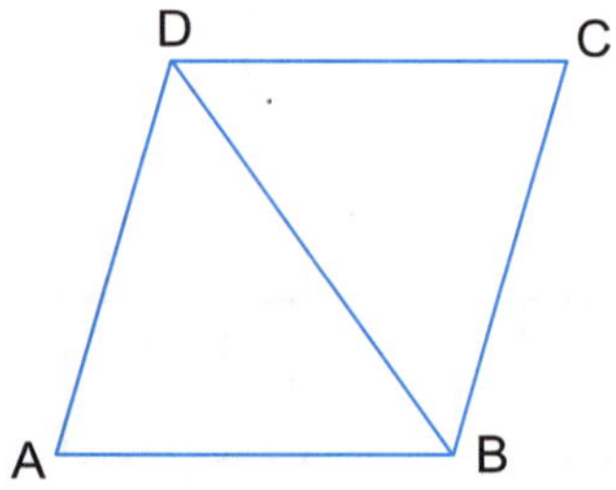

2. 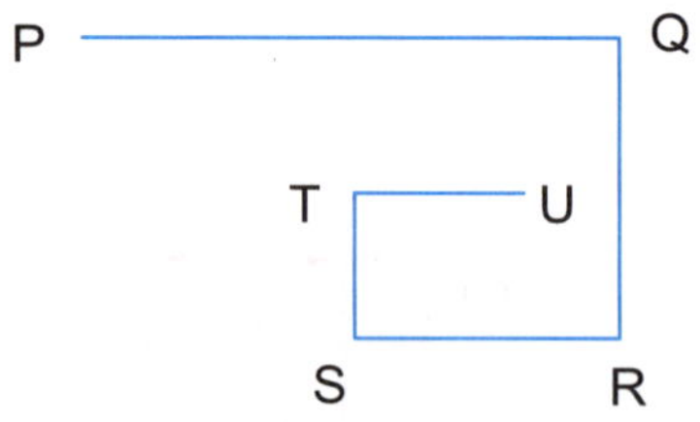

C Identify and name the line segments and rays in the following figures :

1. 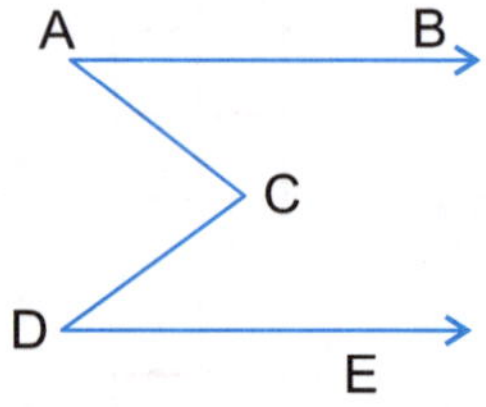

2. 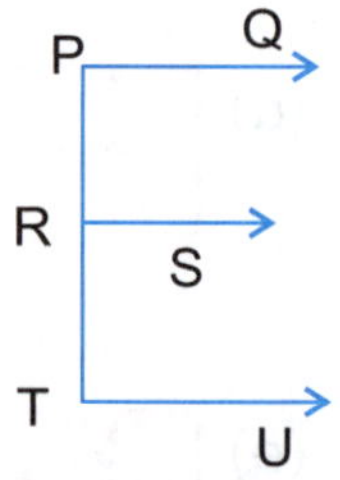

D Write T for triangle and Q for quadrilaterals :

1.  ☐	**2.** 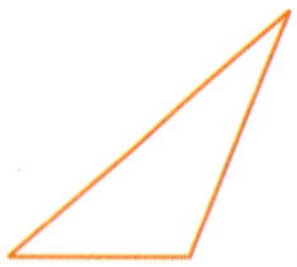 ☐	**3.**  ☐	**4.** 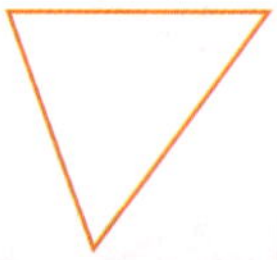 ☐	**5.**  ☐

E Draw three circles of different radii using a compass in your notebook.

F Complete the following table regarding circles :

Radius	5 cm	______ cm	______ cm	7 cm	25 cm
Diameter	______ cm	16 cm	18 cm	______ cm	______ cm

G Draw all possible lines of symmetry of the following figures :

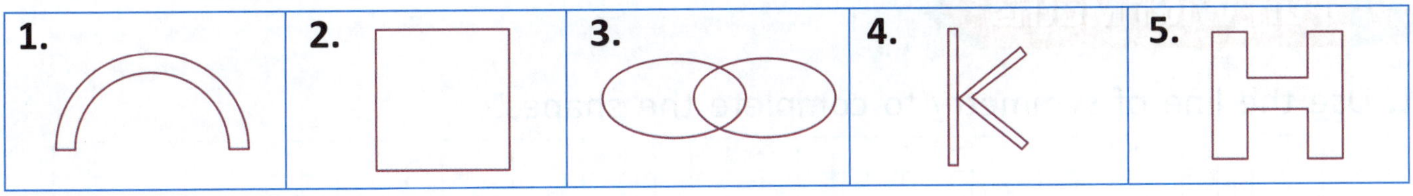

H Write T for true and F for false statements :

1. A line segment has two end points. ______
2. A ray has a fixed length. ______
3. We can always draw a plane on a sheet of paper. ______
4. Parallel lines never intersect. ______
5. Radius is also a chord of the circle. ______
6. Radius of a circle is half the diameter. ______
7. Every chord passes through the centre of the circle. ______
8. All the quadrilaterals are squares. ______
9. The letter A has only one line of symmetry. ______

Mental Maths

1. Is circle a polygon? ______
2. Is triangle a simple closed figure? ______
3. Are all the quadrilaterals rectangles? ______
4. Is ray AB different from ray BA? ______
5. Are all the chords of a circle equal in length? ______
6. Diameter is the longest chord of a circle. Is it true? ______
7. Radius is also a chord of the circle. Is it true? ______
8. Radius is double the diameter. Is it true? ______
9. We cannot have a polygon having only two line segments. Is It true? ______
10. The letter M has no line of symmetry. Is it true? ______

Fun With Maths

1. Use the line of symmetry to complete the shapes.

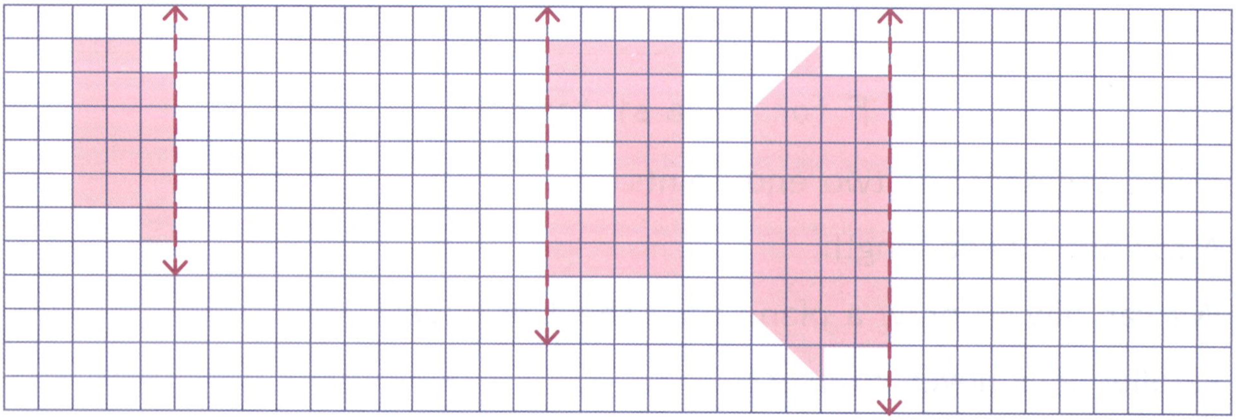

2. Puneet explained the students about how to draw a circle using compass and ruler in the class. He discussed about its components also. Now, he draws a circle on a whiteboard and its components as shown alongside.

Observe the above information and answer the following questions:

(i) Centre of the circle is :

(a) A (b) O (c) C (d) D

(ii) What are the radii of the circle?

(a) OA, OB, OC (b) OA, OC, OD (c) OB, OC, OD (d) AB, OA, AD

(iii) Which is the diameter of the given circle?

(a) AB (b) CD (c) OA (d) DE

(iv) A chord in the circle is :

(a) AE (b) CD (c) OA (d) DE

(v) The radius of a circle whose diameter is 4 cm will be :

(a) 1 cm (b) 2 cm (c) 3 cm (d) 4 cm

3. Ankit triced to draw the line of symmetry of some geometrical shapes. Which of the following figures correctly shows a line of symmetry?

(a) 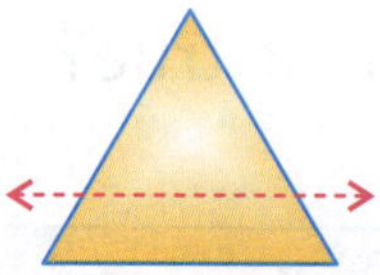 (b) 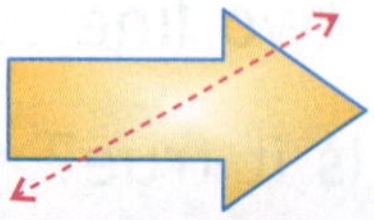 (c) 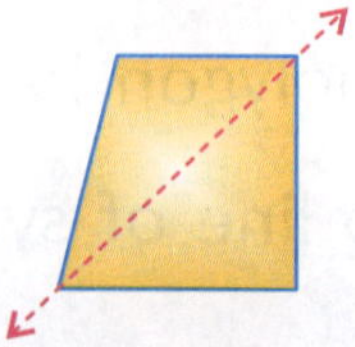 (d) 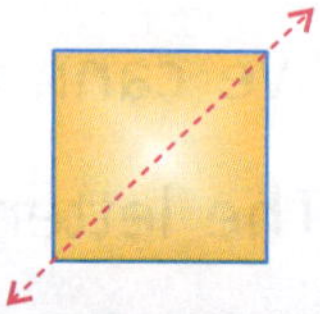

Maths Lab Activity

Objective : Making beautiful designs by drawing circles.

Materials Required : White sheets of paper, pencil colours, geometry box.

Procedure/Demonstration :

1. Using a compass, draw a circle of any convenient radius and mark its centre.

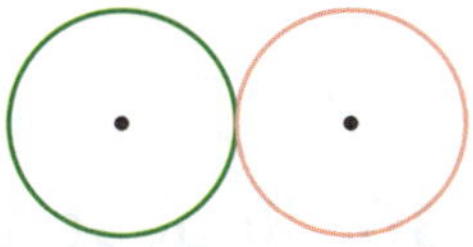

2. Draw another circle of the same radius (opening), so that it touches the previous circle. Mark its centre.

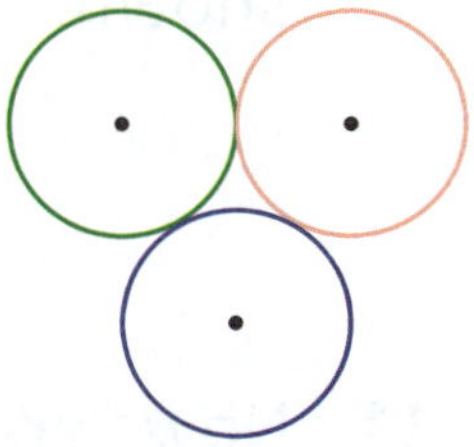

3. Now, without disturbing the opening of the compass, draw a circle such that it touches both the circles drawn above. Mark its centre.

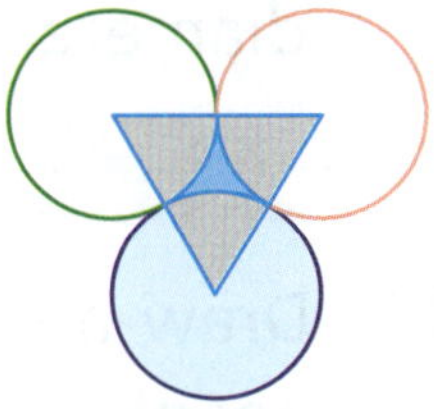

4. Join the centres of the circles drawn above and colour the design to make it beautiful.

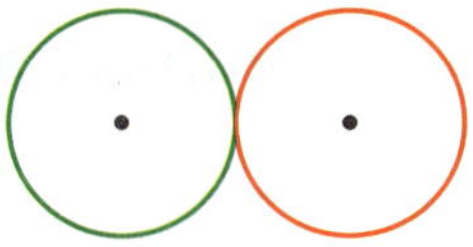

5. Draw two circles of the same radius so that they touch each other. Mark their centres.
6. With the same radius, draw a circle such that it touches one of the circles drawn above. Mark its centre.

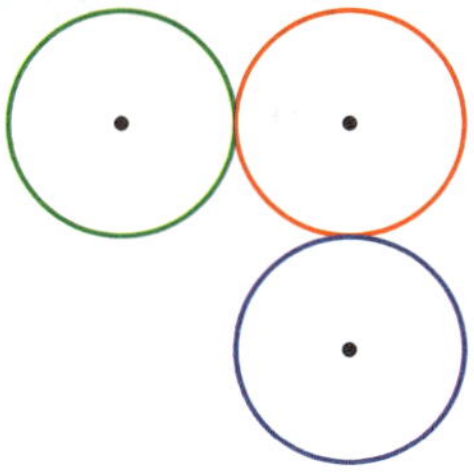

7. With the same opening (radius), draw another circle, which touches two of the three circles drawn above. Mark its centre. Join the centres of the circles as shown and colour the design.

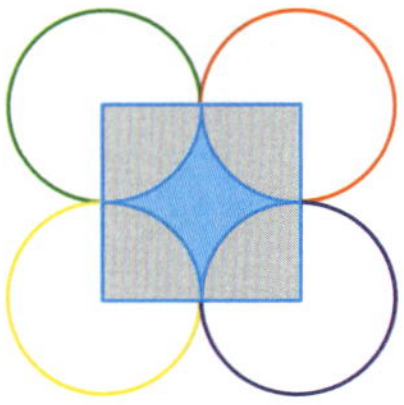

8. Draw, a circle of any convenient radius and draw its one diameter.

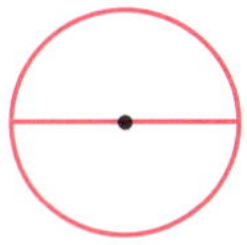

9. Now, draw a circle of smaller radius, whose centre lies on the diameter. Also, this circle touches the previous circle and passes through its centre.

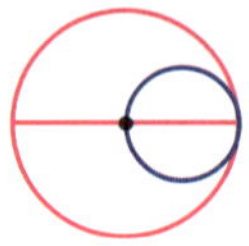

10. Repeat the above step to draw another circle as shown.

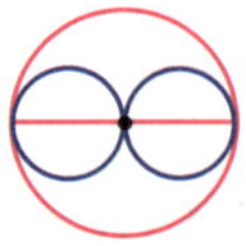

11. Now, erase the half portion of each circle and the diameter as shown. Colour the beautiful design.

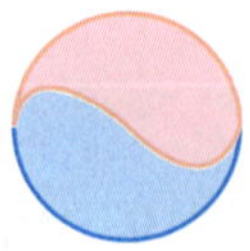

12. Draw a circle of any convenient radius.
Keeping the opening same, put the metal end of the compass at any point of the circle and draw a circle.

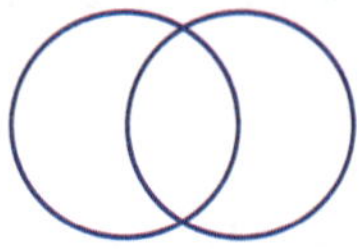

13. Now, keeping the opening same, put the metal end of the compass at one of the points where the two circles meet and draw a circle.

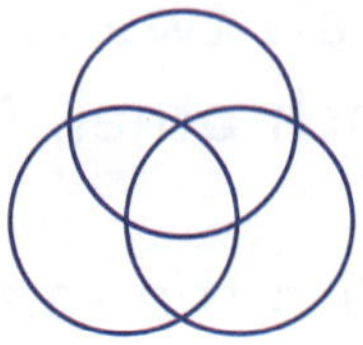

14. Continue the above steps to get a beautiful design as shown. Colour the design as per your choice.

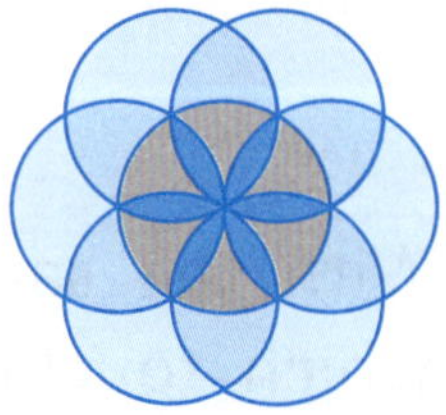

To get worksheet on this chapter scan this QR code

CODE-RWUr

CHECK YOUR PACE

(Based on Chapters 7, 8, 9)

A Divide and check your answer:

1. 72 ÷ 5 **2.** 89 ÷ 9 **3.** 415 ÷ 7 **4.** 708 ÷ 8

5. 1248 ÷ 6 **6.** 4319 ÷ 7 **7.** 8517 ÷ 9 **8.** 6519 ÷ 4

B Without actually dividing, find the quotient and the remainder.

1. 592 ÷ 10 **2.** 706 ÷ 10 **3.** 8320 ÷ 10

4. 432 ÷ 100 **5.** 801 ÷ 100 **6.** 7219 ÷ 100

C Write :

1. first 4 multiples of 12. **2.** eighth multiple of 7. **3.** tenth multiple of 15.

D Write :

1. the smallest factor of 15 **2.** the greatest factor of 24

3. the smallest multiple of 20

E List all prime numbers between 30 and 50.

F Find the prime factors of 98.

G Find the HCF of 15 and 48

H Find the LCM of 18 and 27

I Identify and name the line segments and rays in the following figure :

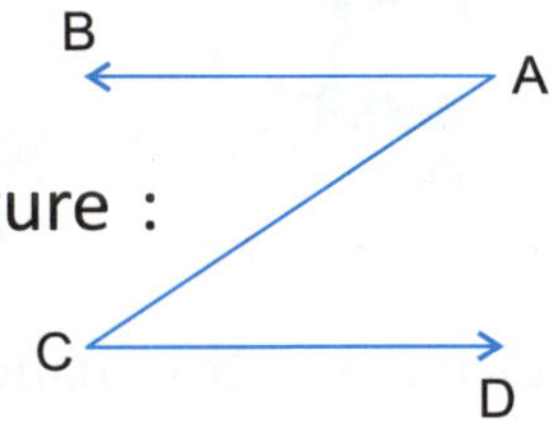

J Find the radius of the cirlce whose diameter is :

1. 14 cm **2.** 18 cm **3.** 24 cm

K Find the diameter of the cirlce whose radius is :

1. 4 cm **2.** 8 cm **3.** 10 cm

L Fill in the blanks :

1. A diameter of a circle passes through the ____________ of the cirlce.

2. The distance around a cirlce is called its ____________

3. The radius of a circle is ____________ its diameter.

4. Diameter is the ____________ chord of the circle.

5. All radius of a circle are ____________.

6. The simplest polygon is a ____________.

7. A ____________ has fixed length.

8. Top of a table represents a part of a ____________.

9. ____________ lines never intersect.

10. A ____________ has one end point.

10

THEME 4 : GEOMETRY

Perimeter and Area

Learning Target

Understanding Perimeter and Area

I Can

- **I can** find the perimeter of a shape.
- **I can** describe the area of a shape.
- **I can** compare the area and perimeter of a shape.
- **I can** find the area and perimeter of a shape.

Explore and Learn

CODE-uu2J

Perimeter

Observe the following figures :

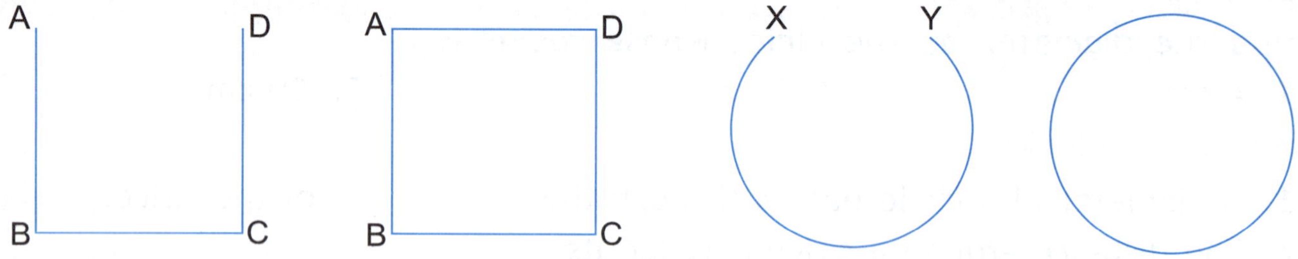

Fig. 1 Fig. 2 Fig. 3 Fig. 4

Figures 2 and 4 are closed figures as they start and end at the same point.

Some of the closed figures that can be drawn are shown below :

A farmer wishes to fence his field using barbed wire. To do so he wants to know, how many metres of barbed wire he should buy. Can you help him?

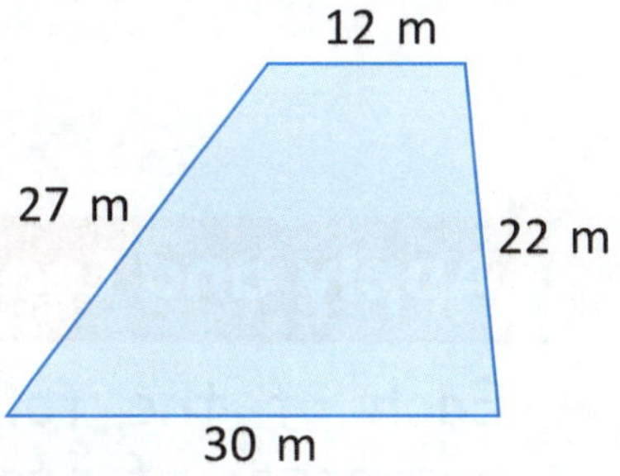

Obviously, to know the length of the wire needed to fence the field, he should add the lengths of the four sides of the field.

30 m + 22 m + 12 m + 27 m = 91 m

Thus, the farmer should buy 91 m of barbed wire to fence his field.

We see that the distance around the field gives the length of the barbed wire.

Such a distance around a figure is called the perimeter of the figure.

Perimeter of a closed figure is the length of its boundary.

The unit of perimeter is the same as the unit of the sides of the given polygon. For example, if the sides of a polygon are given in centimetres, then the perimeter of the polygon will also be in centimetres.

To Find the Perimeter of a Triangle

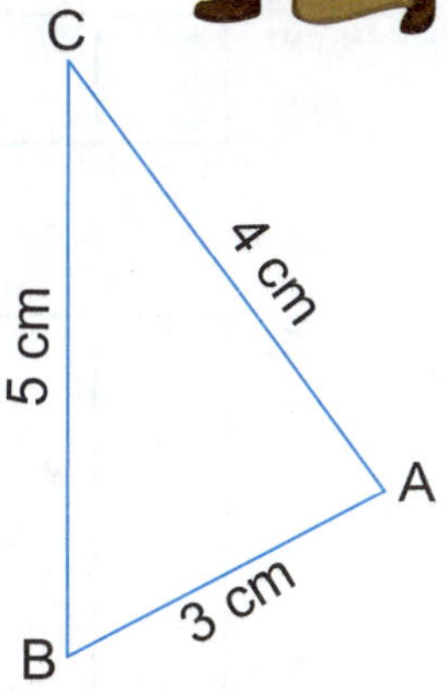

As we know a triangle has three sides. To find the perimeter of a triangle, we measure the three sides of the triangle and add them together.

In this figure, AB = 3 cm, BC = 5 cm and AC = 4 cm.

Thus, perimeter of the triangle = 3 cm + 4 cm + 5 cm

= 12 cm.

To Find the Perimeter of a Square or a Rectangle

A rectangle or a square has four sides.

To find the perimeter of a rectangle or a square, we measure all the four sides of the figure and add them together.

REMEMBER

Unit of perimeter is same as that of length.

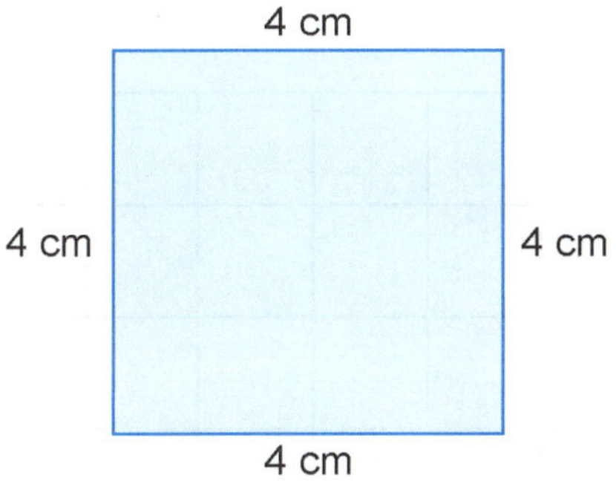

Fig (a)

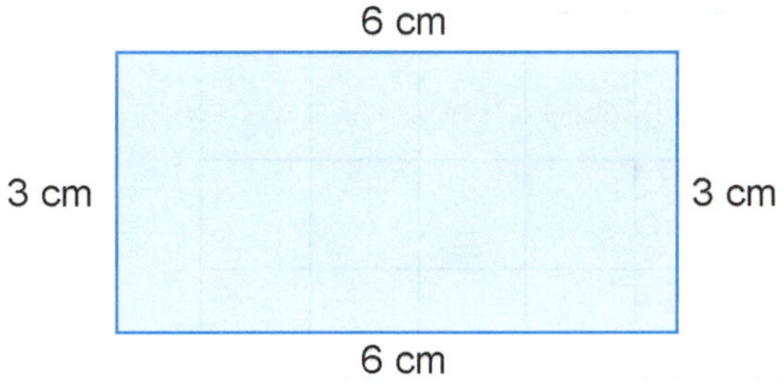

Fig (b)

Perimeter of the square in figure (a) = 4 cm + 4 cm + 4 cm + 4 cm = 16 cm

Perimeter of the rectangle in figure (b) = 6 cm + 3 cm + 6 cm + 3 cm = 18 cm

Exercise 10A

Apply and Learn

A Each of the following figures is drawn on 1 cm square graphs. Find the perimeter of each shaded figure :

1.

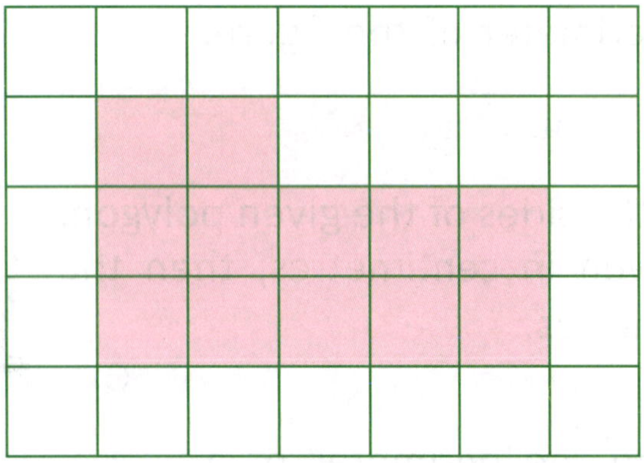

2.

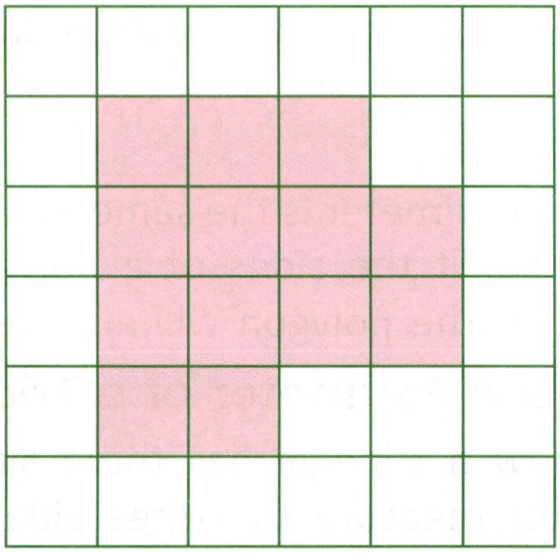

3.

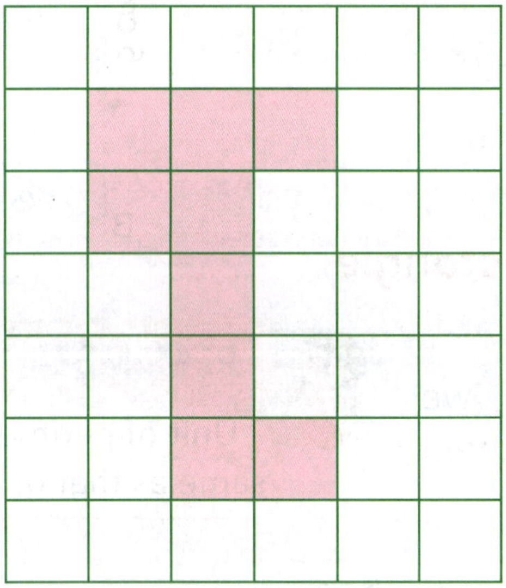

4.

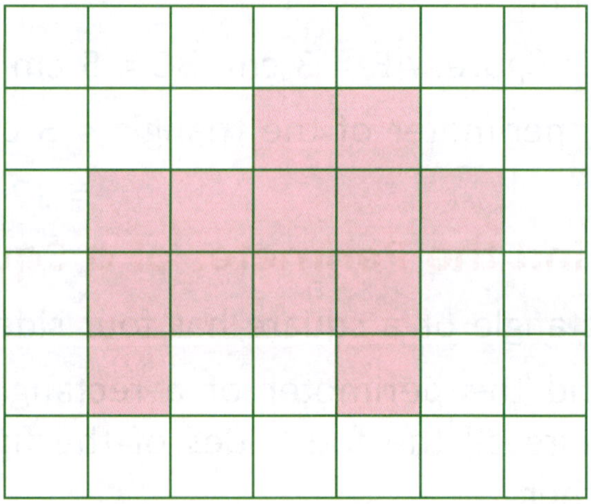

5.

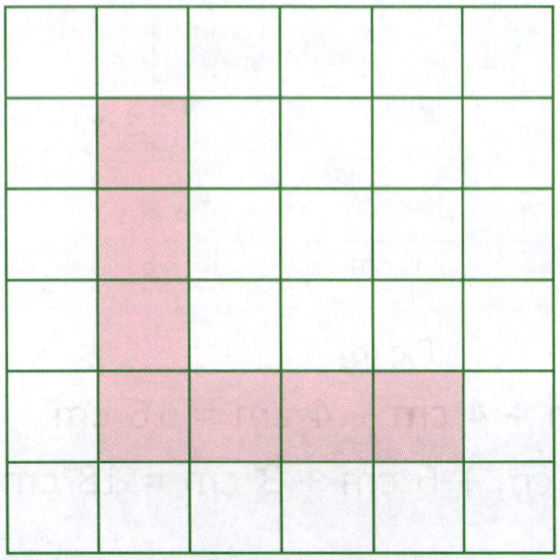

6.

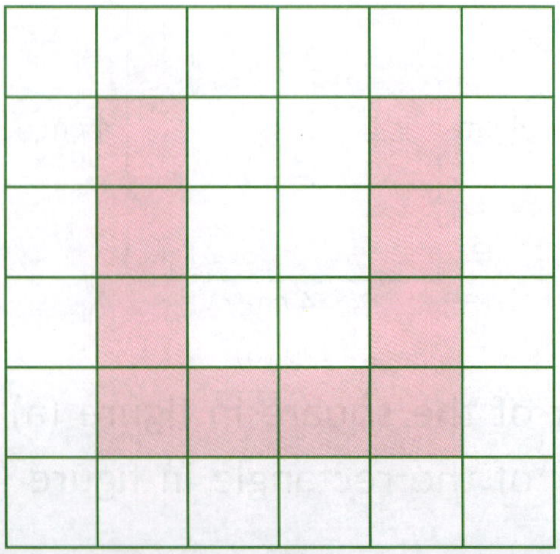

B Find the perimeter of each of the following figures :

1.

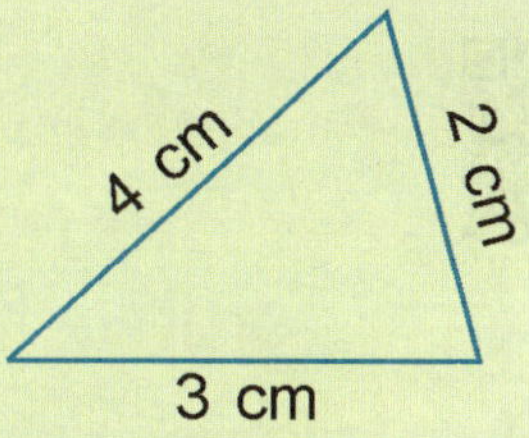

Perimeter of the triangle is ________ cm

2.

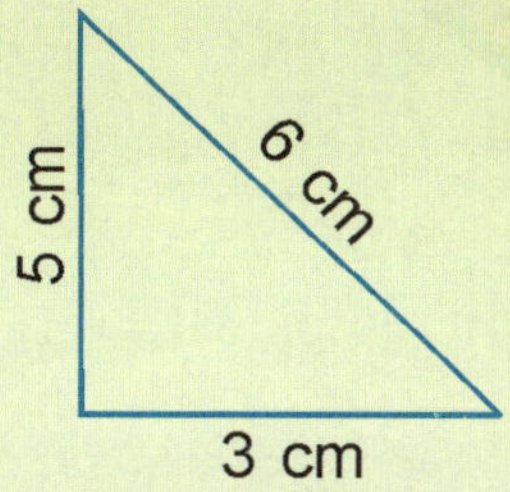

Perimeter of the triangle is ________ cm

3.

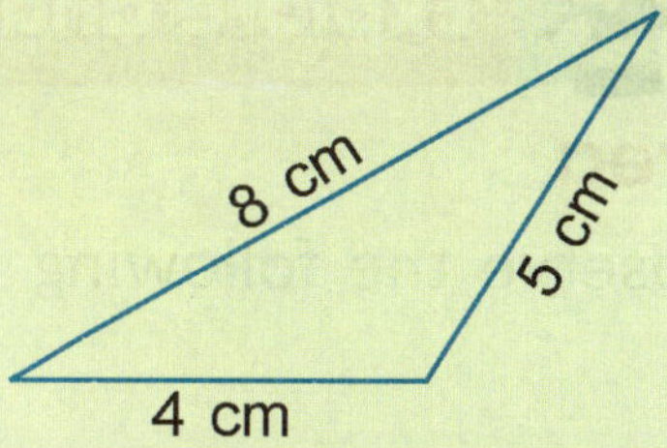

Perimeter of the triangle is ________ cm

4.

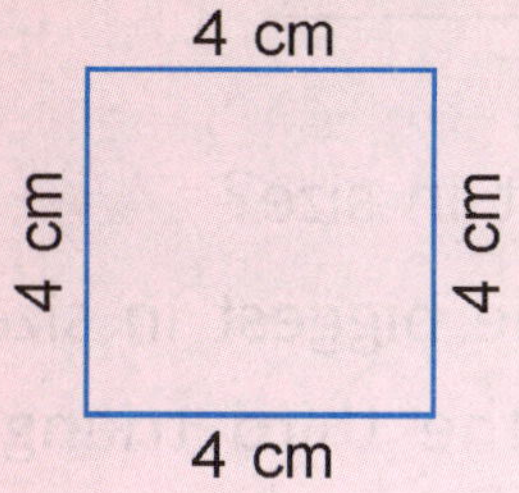

Perimeter of the square is ________ cm

5.

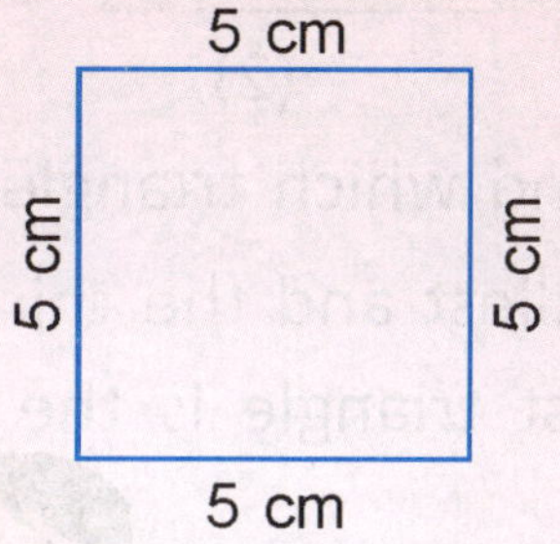

Perimeter of the square is ________ cm

6.

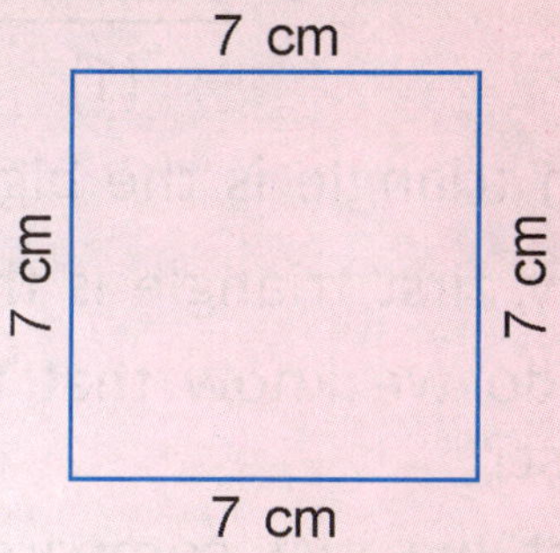

Perimeter of the square is ________ cm

7.

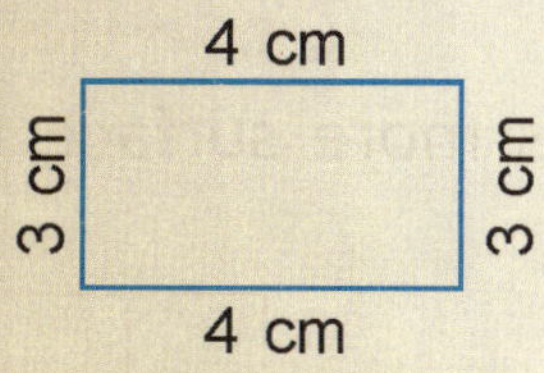

Perimeter of the rectangle is ________ cm

8.

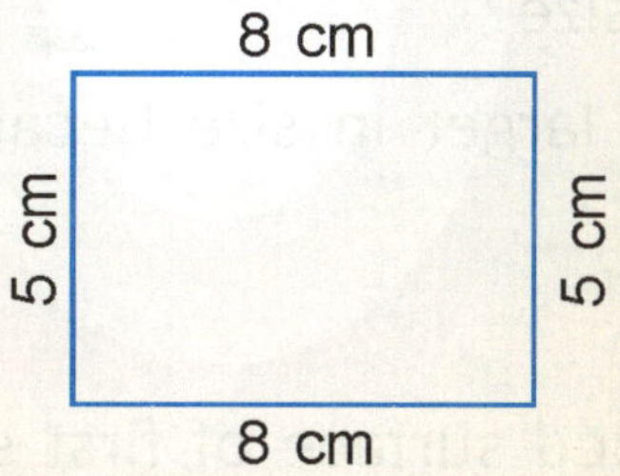

Perimeter of the rectangle is ________ cm

9.

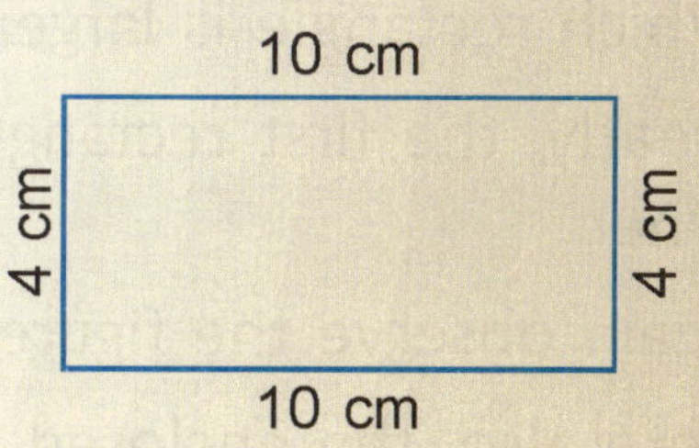

Perimeter of the rectangle is ________ cm

10.

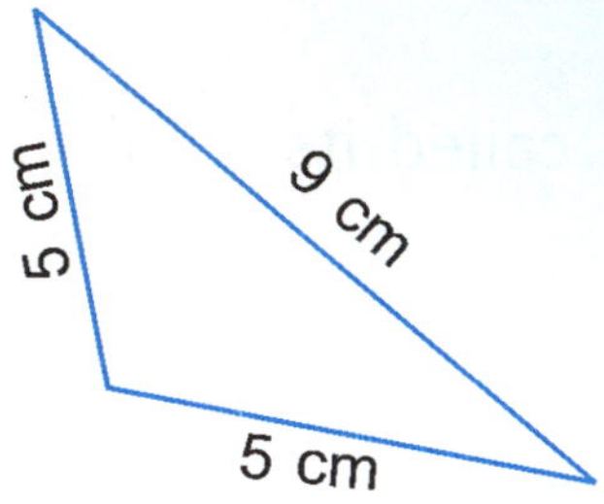

Perimeter of the triangle is ________ cm

11.

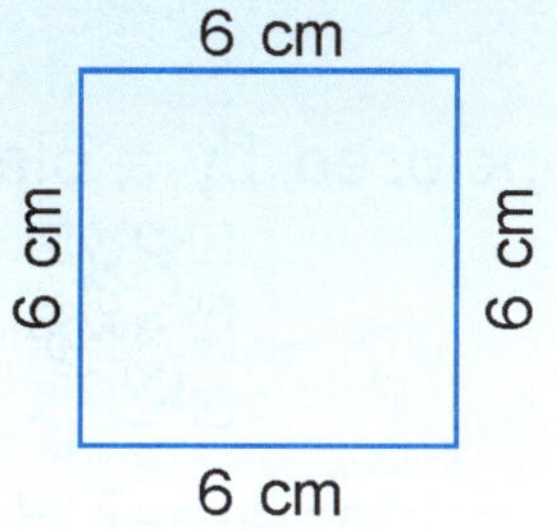

Perimeter of the triangle is ________ cm

12.

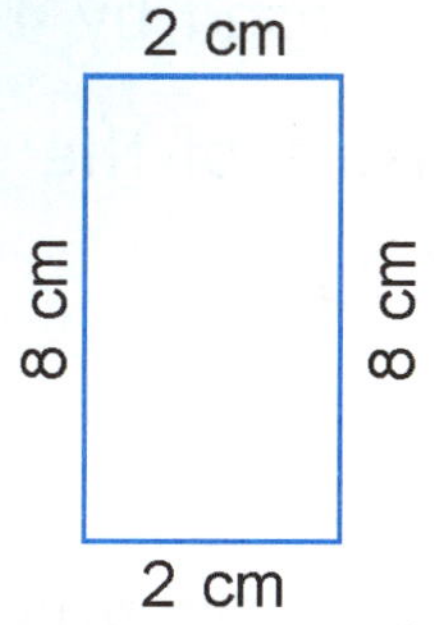

Perimeter of the triangle is ________ cm

Explore and Learn

Area

Observe the following figures :

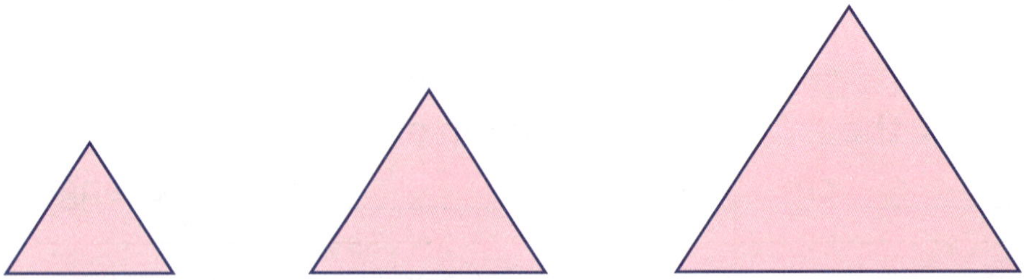

(1) (2) (3)

Which triangle is the biggest and which triangle is the smallest in size?

Clearly, first triangle is the smallest and the third triangle is the biggest in size.

How do we know that the first triangle is the smallest and the third triangle is the biggest?

In fact we just compared the surface of paper enclosed by each figure.

Again observe the figures :

Which rectangle is larger in size?

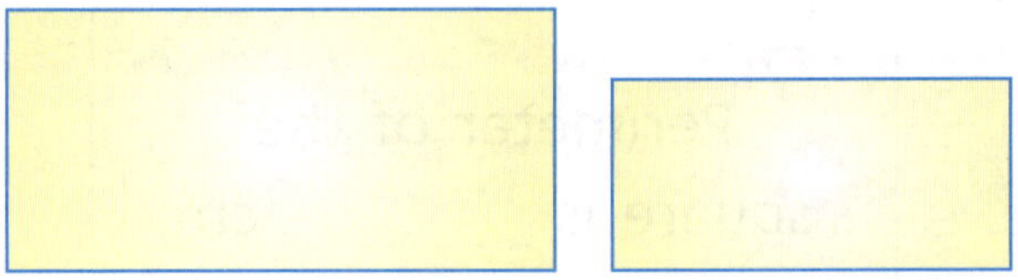

1. **2.**

Clearly, the first rectangle is larger in size because it encloses more surface than the other.

Again observe the figures :

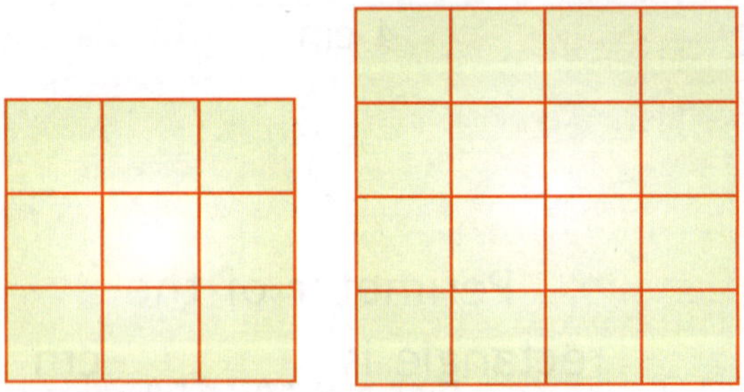

1. **2.**

Here also, the enclosed shaded surface of first square is less than the shaded region of the second. Hence, first figure is smaller in size.

From these examples, it is clear that when we talk about size of a plane figure, we consider the surface enclosed by it.

The measure of the surface enclosed by a plane figure is called its area.

Units of Area

Observe the figures :

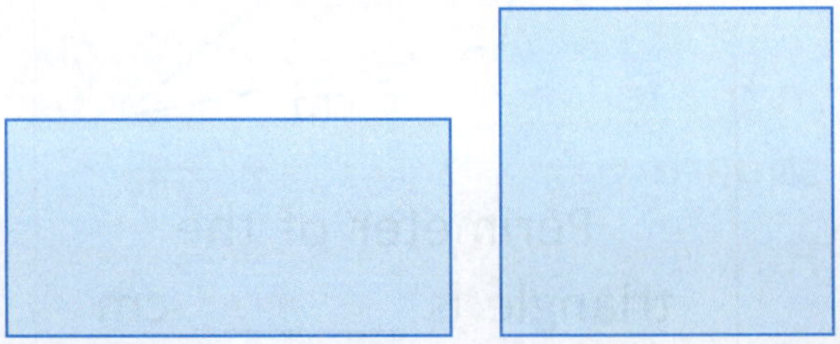

1. **2.**

Can you tell which figure has greater area? Here, it is difficult to say which figure has greater or smaller area by mere observation. To decide which figure has the greater area, perform the following activity.

Cover both the figures with the pieces of erasers.

We can see that 8 pieces of the eraser cover the first figure completely, and 9 pieces of the eraser cover the second figure completely. We say that the area of the first figure is equal to the area of 8 erasers and area of the second figure is equal to the area of 9 erasers.

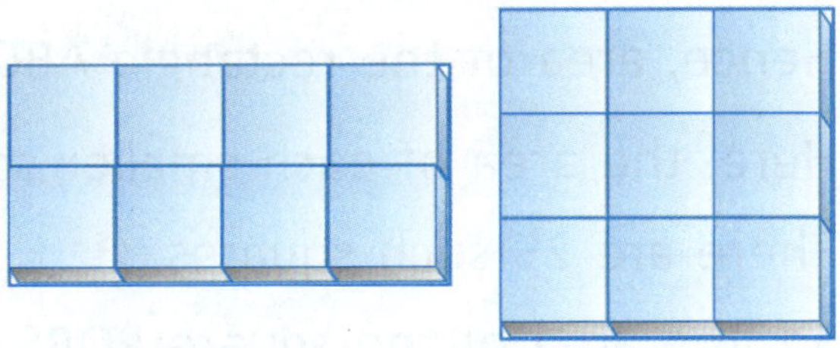

1. 2.

Thus, second figure has greater area.

Here the top face (or bottom) of the eraser has been taken as the unit for measuring the area of the figures.

In the above activity if we use bigger erasers, will we get the same answer? No, in this case the answer will be different. So to get the same answer every time, we need a standard unit for measuring the area.

To measure weight (mass), we use 1 g or 1 kg as the standard units.

To measure capacity, we use 1 ml or 1 l as the standard units.

To measure length, we use 1 mm, 1 cm or 1 m as the standard units.

Similarly, to measure area, square of side 1 mm, 1 cm or 1 m is taken as the standard unit.

The area of a square of side 1 mm is expressed as 1 square mm or sq mm.

The area of a square of side 1 cm is expressed as 1 square cm or 1 sq cm.

The area of a square of side 1 m is expressed as 1 square m or 1 sq m.

Bigger areas are measured in square kilometres (sq km). 1 sq km is the area of the square whose side is 1 km.

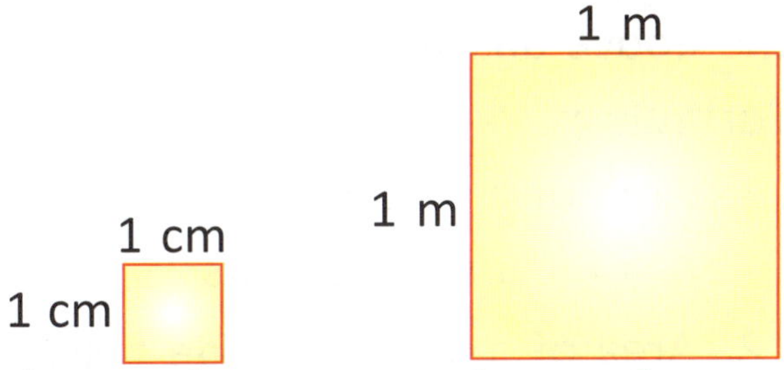

Area = 1 sq cm Area = 1 sq m

In the following figure, the area of each smaller square is 1 sq cm.

How many squares are there in all?

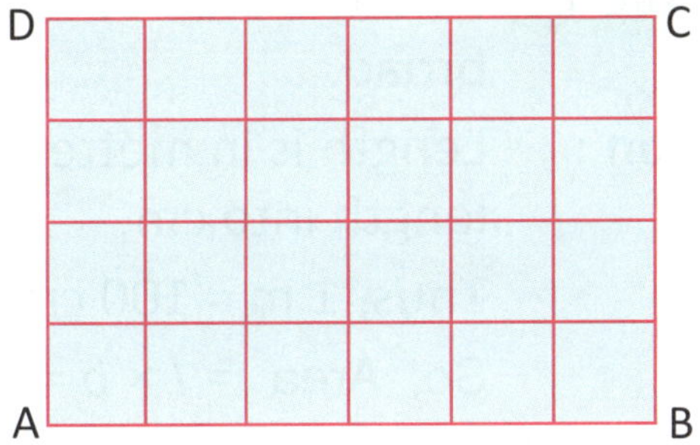

There are 24 squares.

Hence, area of the rectangle ABCD is 24 sq cm.

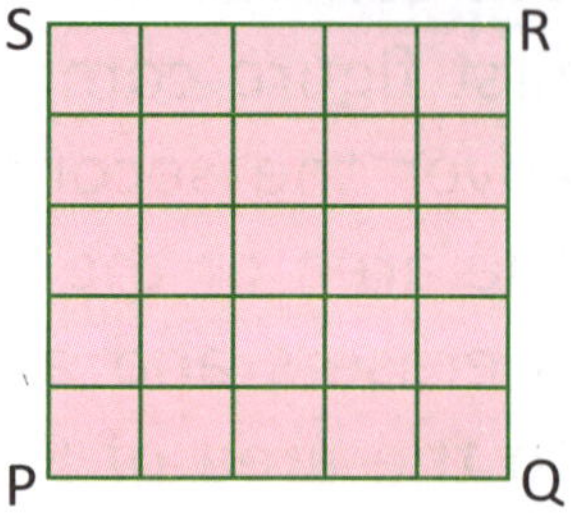

Here, the area of each smaller square is 1 sq mm.

There are 25 such squares.

So, the area of the square PQRS is 25 sq mm.

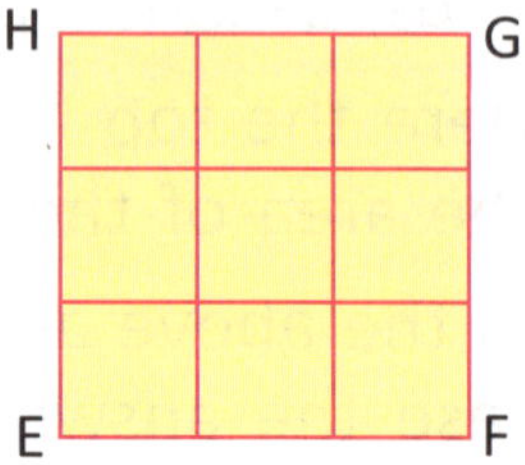

Here, the area of each smaller square is 1 sq cm.

There are 9 such squares.

So, the area of the square EFGH is 9 sq cm.

CODE-KiM1

Area of a Rectangle and a Square

If we wish to find the area of a rectangle, we express the length and breadth in terms of the same unit, say, centimetres. The product of length and breadth gives the area in square centimetres. This means that any other figure of the same area can be fully covered by the same number of 1 cm squares.

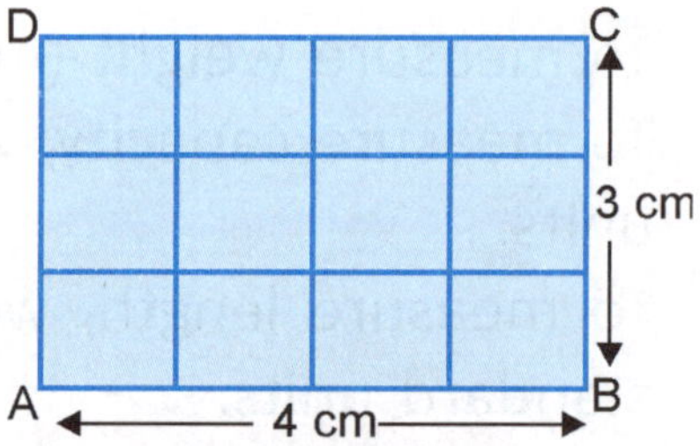

ABCD is a rectangle.

Also, AB = 4 cm, BC = 3 cm

So, Area = length × breadth

Area = 4 × 3 = 12 sq cm.

REMEMBER

Area is expressed in square units of length.

By actually counting the squares, we can easily verify the above answer.

REMEMBER

While calculating area, both length and breadth should be expressed in the same units.

Formula :

1. Area of a rectangle = length × breadth

   A = $l \times b$ square units.

2. Area of a square = side × side

Example 1 : Find the area of a rectangular cardboard 1 m long and 25 cm broad.

Solution : Length is in metres but the breadth is in cm. So, we change length into cm.

Thus, 1 m = 100 cm

So, Area $= l \times b = 100 \times 25$ sq cm = 2,500 sq cm.

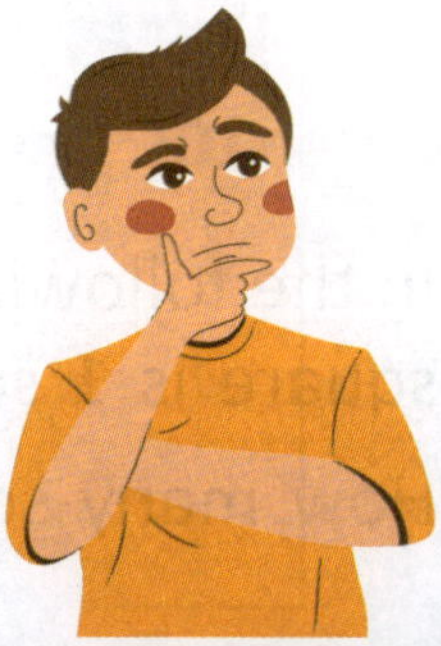

Example 2 : Find the area of a square with side 7 cm.

Solution : Area = side × side = 7 × 7 sq cm = 49 sq cm.

Example 3 : Length of a rectangular park is 3 times its breadth. If the length of the park is 90 metres, then find the area of the park.

Solution :

Length of rectangular park = 90 m

So, the breadth = 90 m ÷ 3 = 30 m.

Area of the rectangle = length × breadth

= 90 m × 30 m = 2700 sq m.

Exercise 10B

Apply and Learn

A By mere observation, state which has greater area?

1. 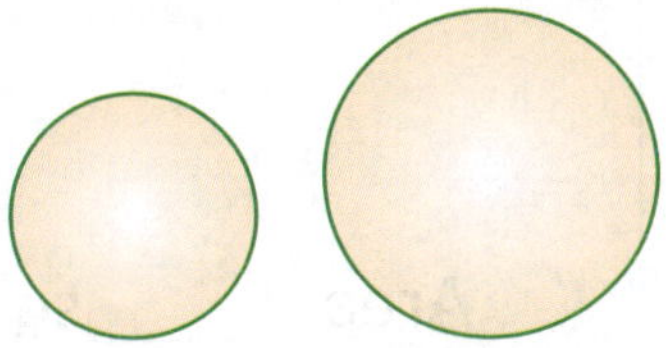 (a) (b)	**2.** 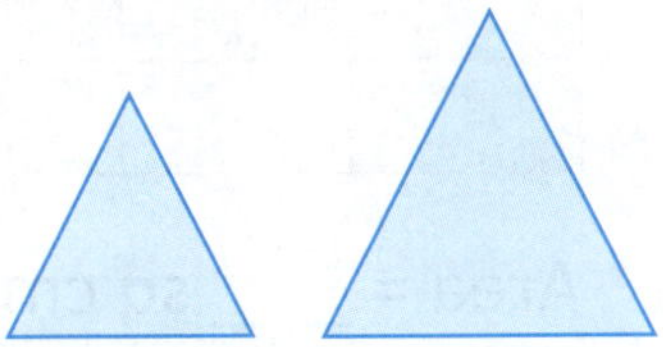 (a) (b)	**3.** 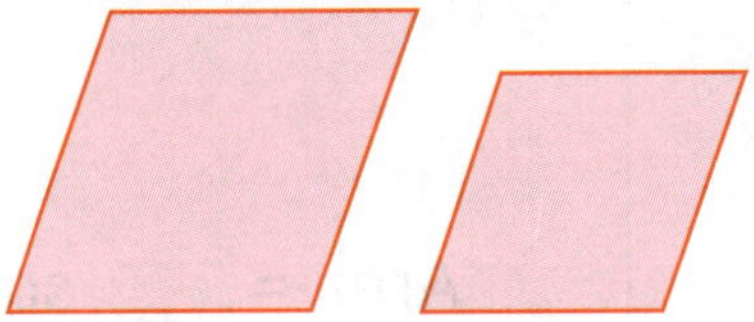 (a) (b)
4. 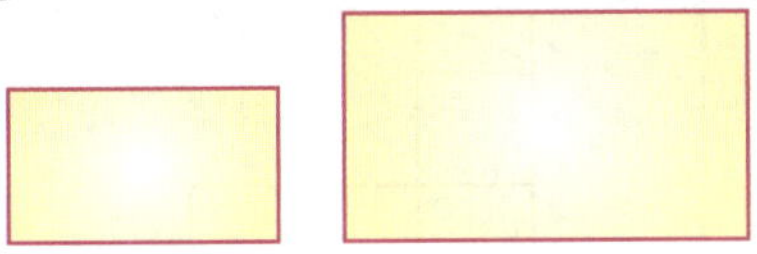 (a) (b)	**5.** 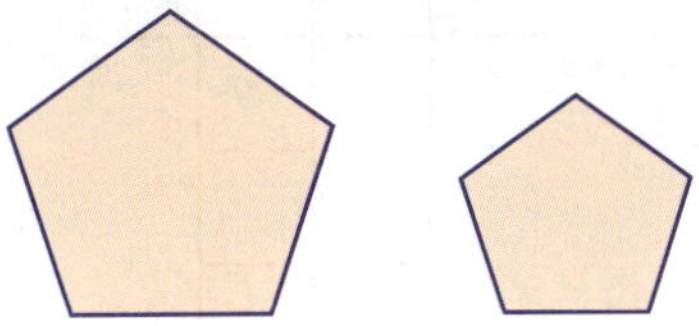 (a) (b)	**6.** 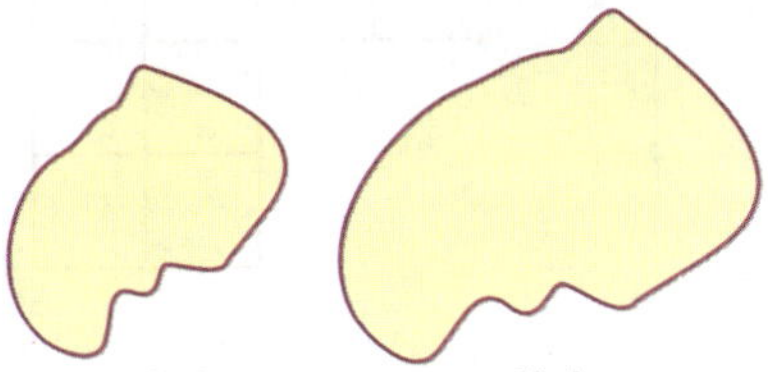 (a) (b)
7. 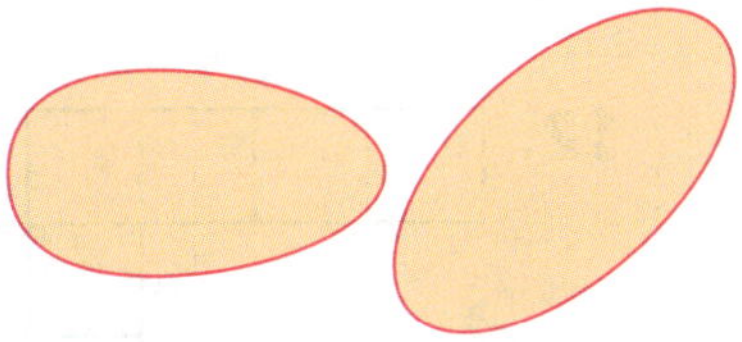 (a) (b)	**8.** 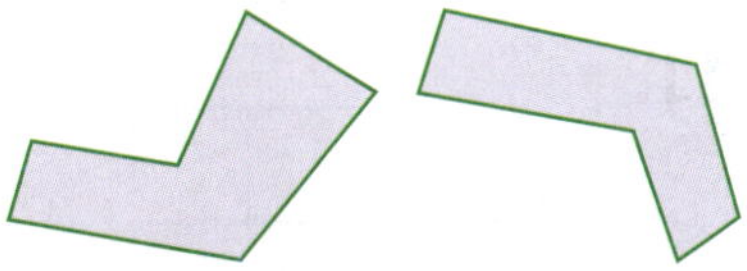 (a) (b)	**9.** 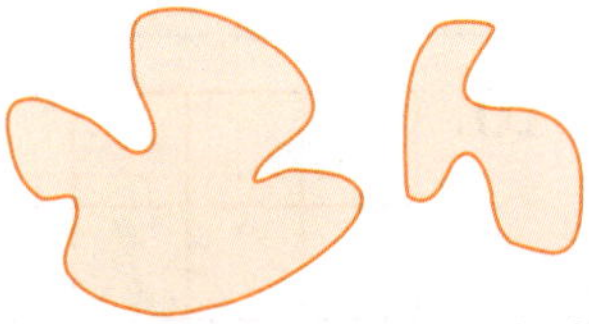 (a) (b)
10. 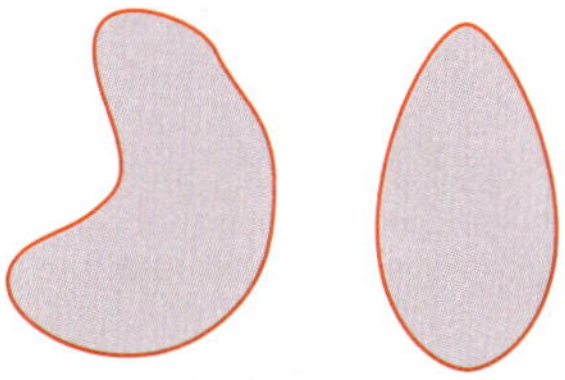 (a) (b)	**11.** 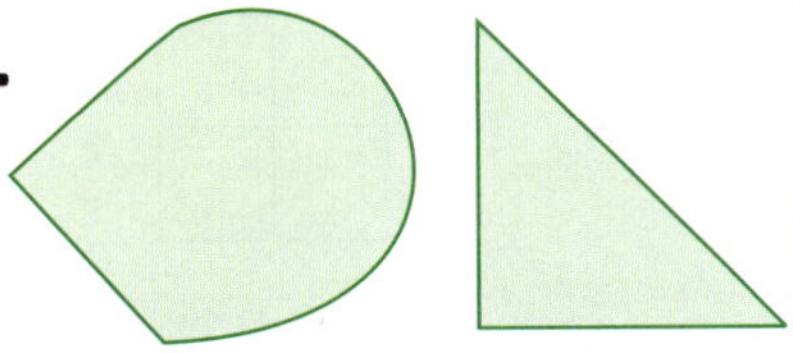 (a) (b)	**12.** 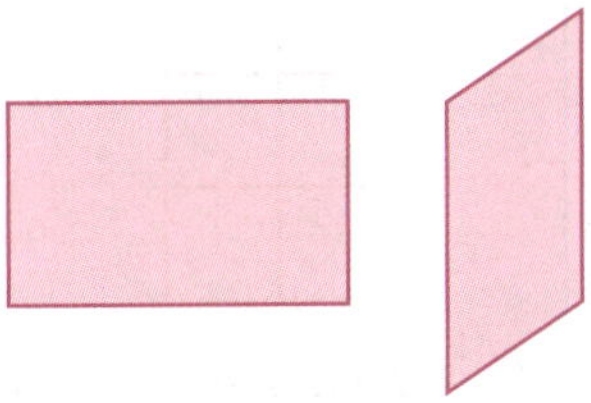 (a) (b)

B In the following figures, assume that each small square is 1 sq cm. Count the squares and find the area:

1.
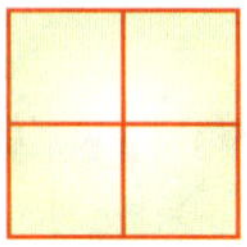
Area = ____ sq cm

2.
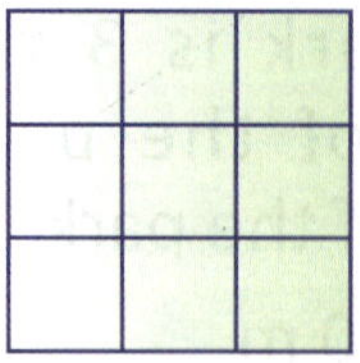
Area = ____ sq cm

3.
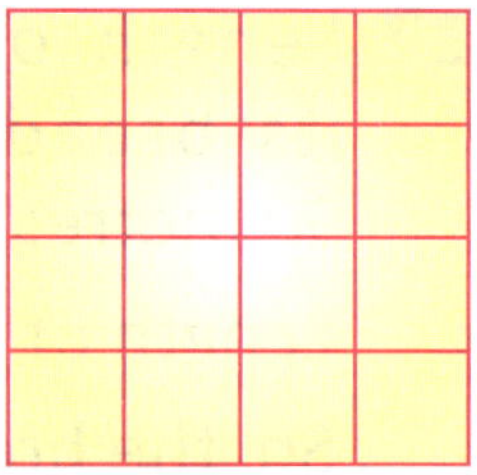
Area = ____ sq cm

4.

Area = ____ sq cm

5.
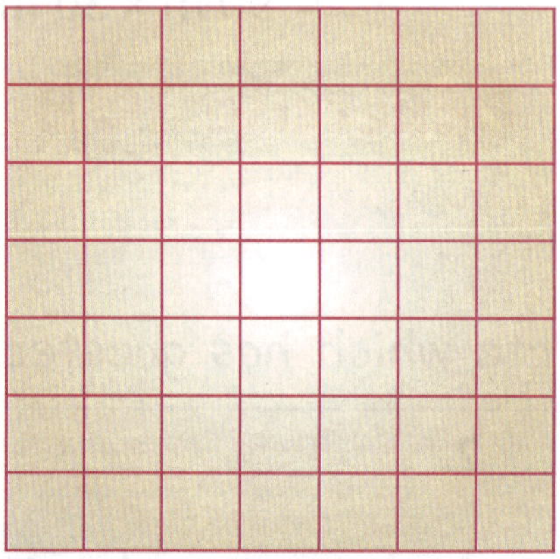
Area = ____ sq cm

6.
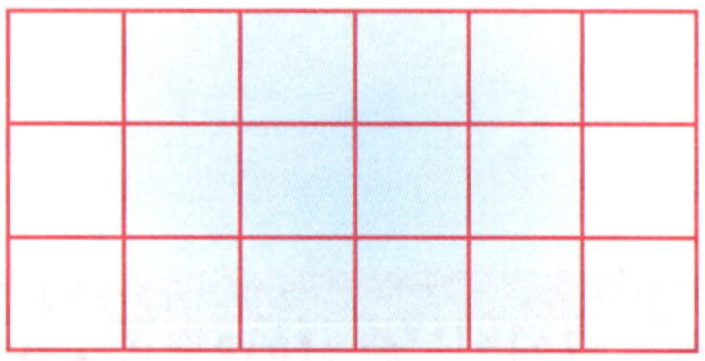
Area = ____ sq cm

7.
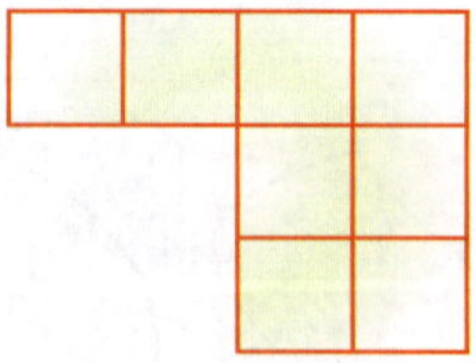
Area = ____ sq cm

8.
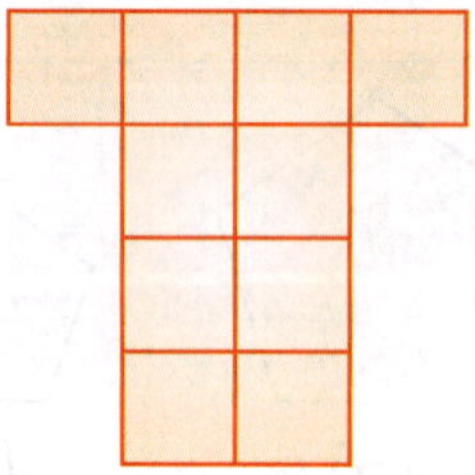
Area = ____ sq cm

9.
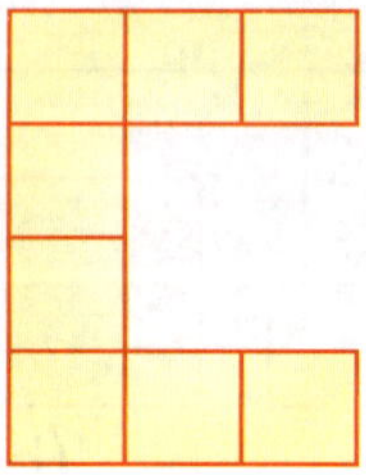
Area = ____ sq cm

10.
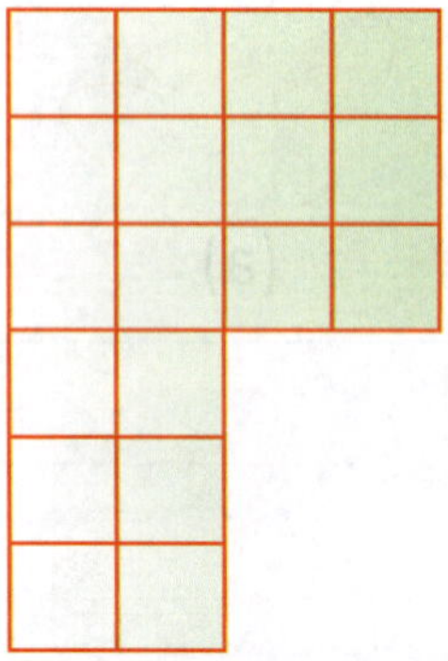
Area = ____ sq cm

11.

Area = ____ sq cm

12.
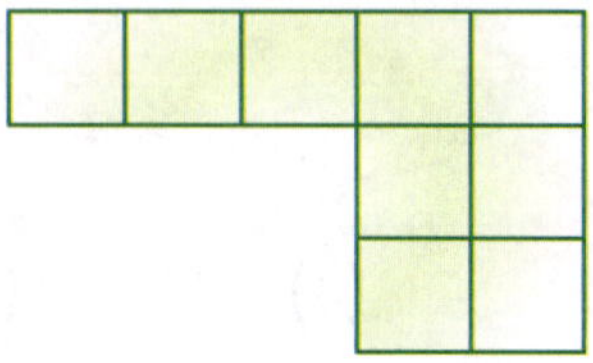
Area = ____ sq cm

C Find the area of the following squares :

1. 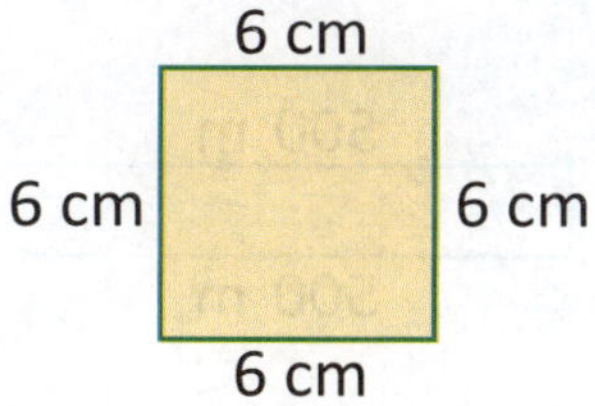

2. 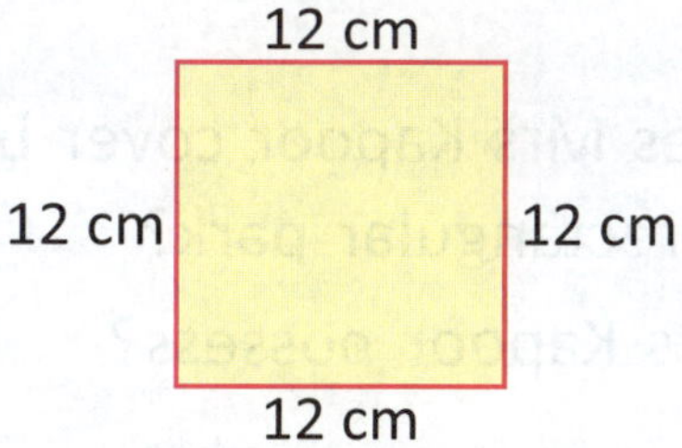

3. 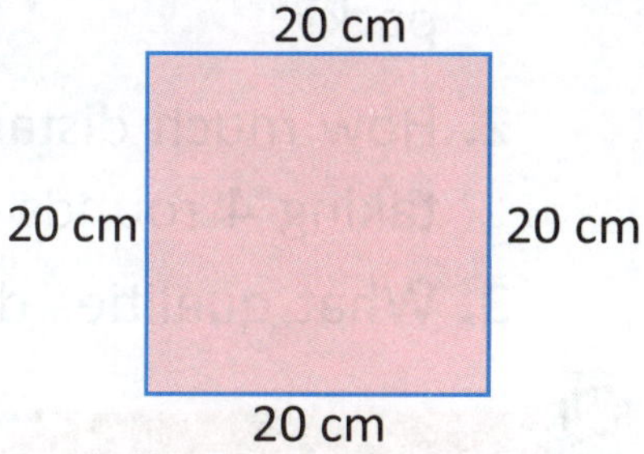

D Find the area of the following rectangles :

1. 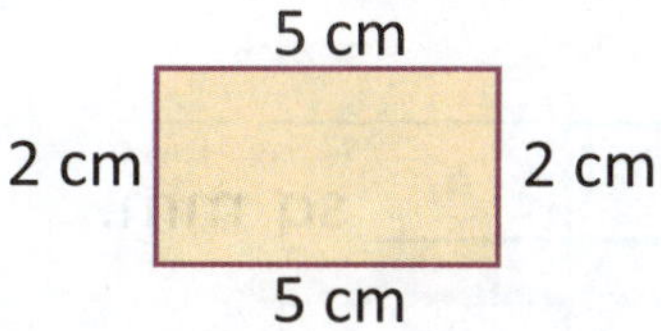

2. 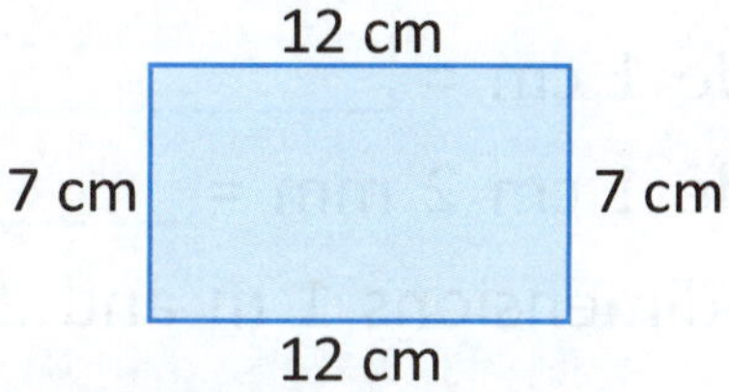

3. 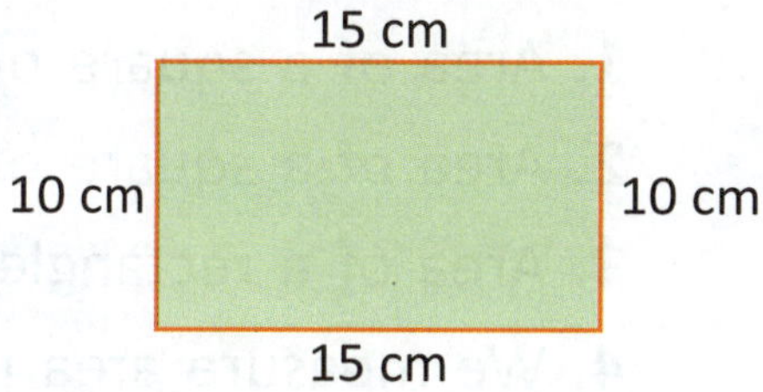

E Find the area of the rectangle, whose :

1. length = 100 m, breadth = 50 m
2. length = 8 cm, breadth = 6 cm
3. length = 2 m, breadth = 85 cm
4. length = 2 m 20 cm, breadth = 95 cm
5. length = 3 m 16 cm, breadth = 1 m 90 cm

F Find the area of the square, whose :

1. side = 20 cm
2. side = 7 cm
3. side = 112 m
4. side = 18 m
5. side = 92 dm
6. side = 256 dm

G Find the perimeter of :

1. the triangle whose sides are 8 cm, 9 cm, and 12 cm.
2. the rectangle whose sides are 10 cm and 7 cm.
3. the square whose side is 14 cm.

Value Based Questions

Mrs Kapoor is a health conscious lady. She jogs daily in the morning to keep herself physically fit. She takes 3 rounds of a square park whose side is 300 m.

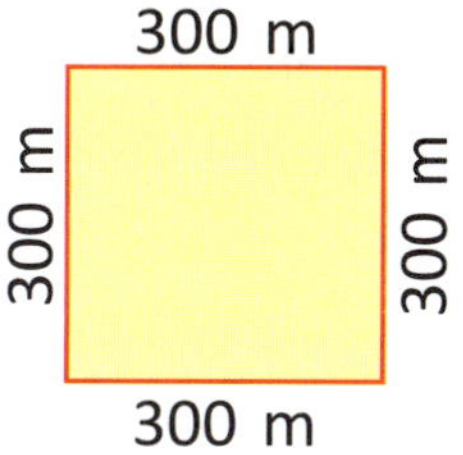

Sometimes she takes 4 rounds of a rectangular park of dimensions 500 m by 100 m.

1. How much distance does Mrs Kapoor cover by taking 3 rounds of the square park?
2. How much distance does Mrs Kapoor cover by taking 4 rounds of the rectangular park?

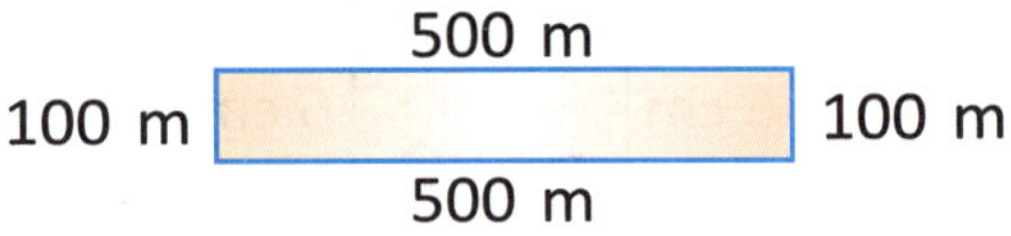

3. What qualities does Mrs Kapoor possess?

Mental Maths

1. Area of a square of side 1 cm = ______________
2. Area of a square of side 1 cm 2 mm = ______________ sq mm.
3. Area of a rectangle of dimensions 1 m and 2 m is ______________ sq m.
4. We measure area in the ______________ units of length.
5. Area of a rectangle = ______________ × ______________
6. Area of a square = ______________
7. Find the area of the rectangle whose length and breadth are 8 cm and 6 cm respectively. ______________
8. Find the area of a square whose perimeter is 4 cm. ______________

Fun With Maths

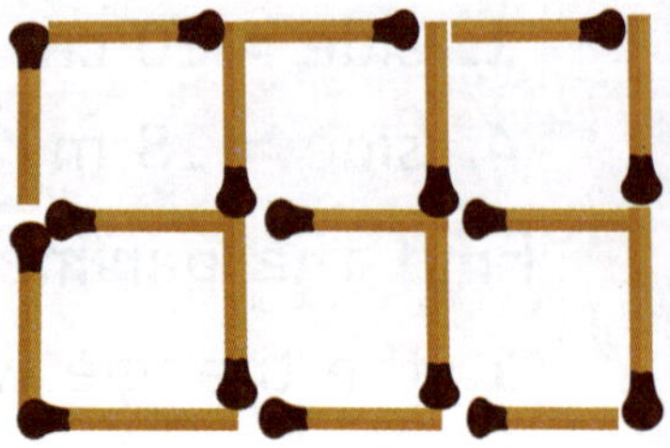

1. Here the grid is made up of 17 matchsticks.
   Its area is 6 sq units.
   Remove exactly 5 matchsticks, so that the area of the grid becomes 3 sq cm.

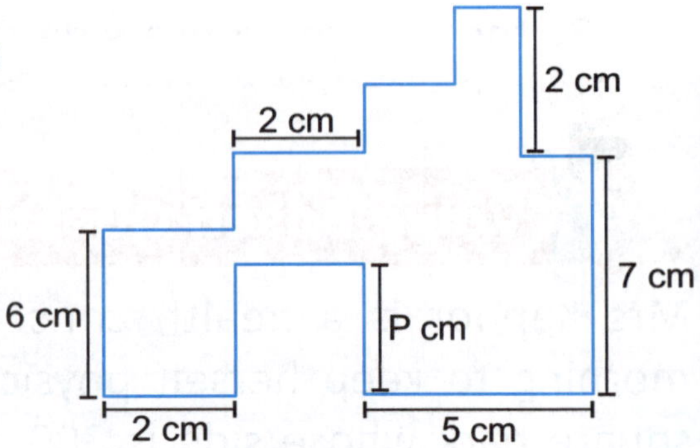

2. The value of P, if the perimeter of the figure given alongside is 46 cm, is :
   (a) 6 cm (b) 5 cm
   (c) 8 cm (d) 10 cm

To get worksheet on this chapter scan this QR code

CODE-PbA6

Maths Lab Activity

Objective : Making different shapes of desired area.

Materials Required : Squared paper (graph paper).

Procedure/Demonstration :

Take a 1 cm graph paper as shown below. Here, the area of each square is 1 sq. cm. On this graph paper, draw by shading 3 different shapes, each of whose area is 10 sq. cm.

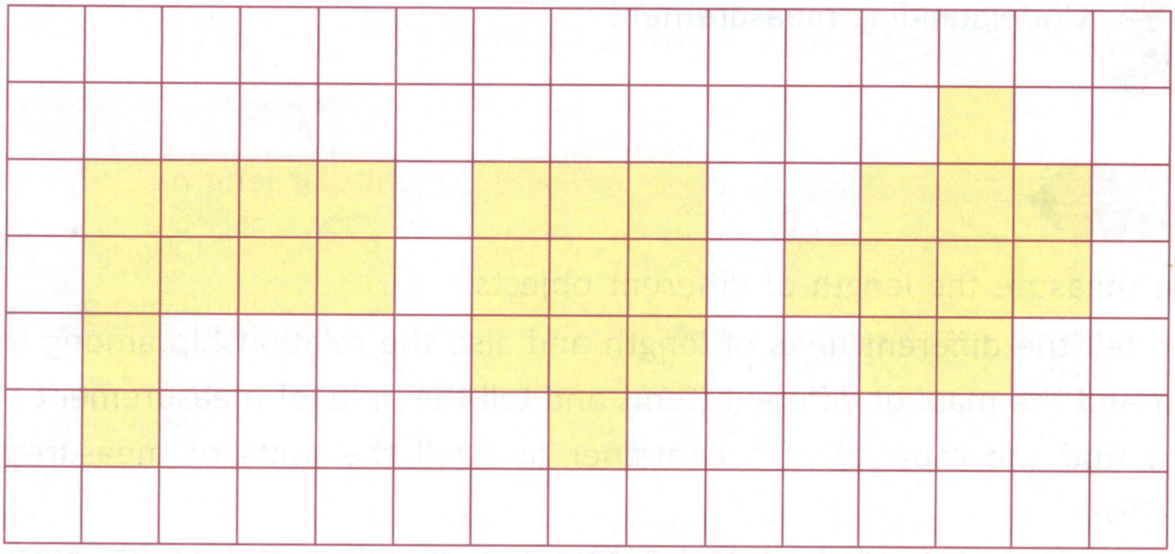

Now, draw

(a) 4 different shapes each of area 8 sq cm.

(b) 4 different shapes each of area 12 sq cm.

(c) 4 different shapes each of area 6 sq cm.

THEME 5 : MEASUREMENT

Measurement of Length, Mass and Capacity

Learning Target

Understanding measurement

I Can

- **I can measure** the length of different objects.
- **I can tell** the different units of length and also the relationship among them.
- **I can find** the mass of different items and tell the units of measurement of mass.
- **I can find** the capacity of a container and tell the units of measurement of capacity.
- **I can perform** the addition and subtraction of different lengths, masses and capacities.
- **I can solve** the word problems on length, mass and capacity.

Let Us Recall

In Class 3, we read about measurement of length, mass (or weight) and capacity. Let us have a quick review of what we read in Class 3.

Exercise 11A

A Convert the following lengths into centimetres :

1. 5 m **2.** 16 m **3.** 8 m 20 cm **4.** 45 m 50 cm

B Convert the following lengths into metres and centimetres :

1. 205 cm **2.** 816 cm **3.** 1,625 cm **4.** 3,405 cm

C Observe and fill in the blanks :

1. 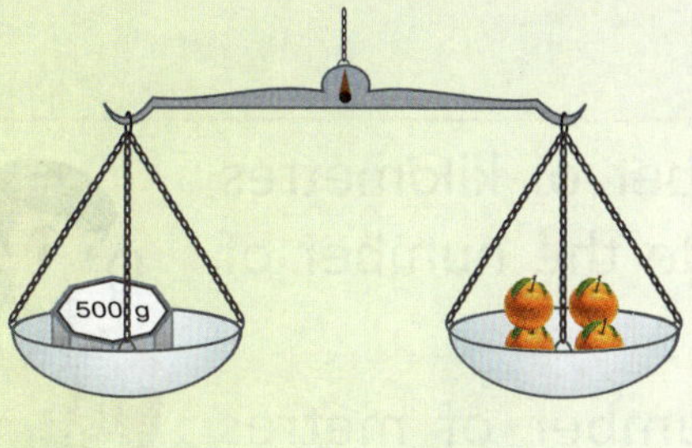 Weight of oranges is __________ g.	**2.**  Weight of the strawberries is __________ kg.	**3.** 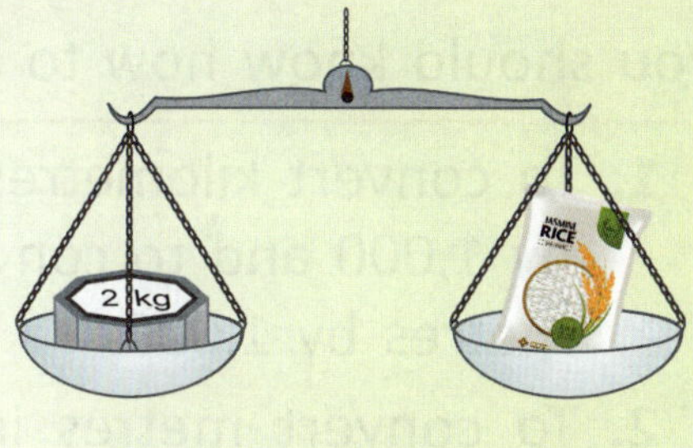 Weight of bag is __________ kg.

D How much more is to be added to 500 g to make it equal to 1 kg?

E How many 200 ml cups are needed to half fill a 2 *l* bottle?

F A 1 *l* bottle is half full. How many millilitres are there in the bottle?

Explore and Learn

Measurement of Length

CODE-iN2d

We know that the standard unit of length is **metre.** There are three units smaller than the metre. They are decimetre, centimetre, and millimetre. Kilometre is a bigger unit of length.

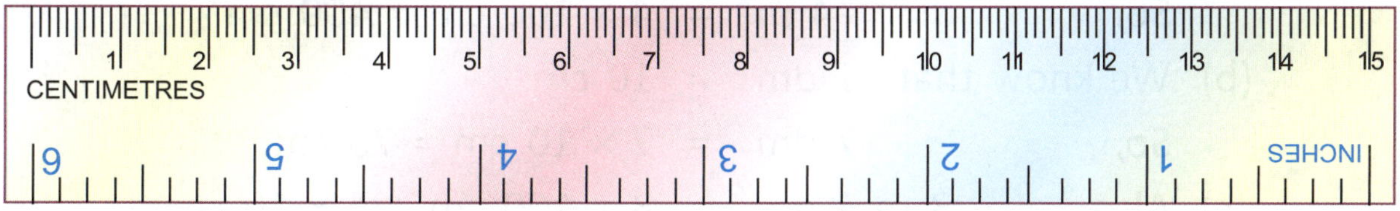

Scale

1 kilometre = 1,000 metres.	In symbols, 1 km = 1,000 m.
1 metre = 10 decimetres.	In symbols, 1 m = 10 dm.
1 metre = 100 centimetres.	In symbols, 1 m = 100 cm.
1 metre = 1,000 millimetres.	In symbols, 1 m = 1,000 mm.

We have different units of measurement because they are suitable for measuring different lengths.

The length of the school playground should be measured in terms of metres. The decimetre and centimetre units are far too small for this purpose. The length and breadth of a chart in the classroom can be measured in decimetres.

The length of a pencil, notebook, paper, comb, etc., can be measured in terms of centimetres.

You should know how to change one unit to the other.

1. To convert kilometres into metres, multiply the number of kilometres by 1,000 and to convert metres into kilometres, divide the number of metres by 1,000.

2. To convert metres into decimetres, multiply the number of metres by 10 and to convert decimetres into metres, divide the number of decimetres by 10.

3. To convert metres into centimetres, multiply the number of metres by 100 and to convert centimetres into metres, divide the number of centimetres by 100.

4. To convert metres into millimetres, multiply the number of metres by 1,000 and to convert millimetres into metres, divide the number of millimetres by 1,000.

5. To convert decimetres into centimetres, multiply the number of decimetres by 10 and to convert centimetres into decimetres, divide the number of centimetres by 10.

Example 1 : Change to centimetres :

(a) 4 m (b) 7 dm (c) 3 m 4 dm

(d) 2 m 5 dm 6 cm (e) 8 dm 3 cm

Solution : (a) We know that 1 m = 100 cm.

So, 4 m = 4 × 100 cm = 400 cm.

(b) We know that 1 dm = 10 cm.

So, 7 dm = 7 × 10 cm = 70 cm.

(c) Also, 3 m 4 dm = 3 × 100 cm + 4 × 10 cm

= 300 cm + 40 cm = 340 cm

(d) 2 m 5 dm 6 cm = 2 × 100 cm + 5 × 10 cm + 6 cm

= 200 cm + 50 cm + 6 cm = 256 cm

(e) 8 dm 3 cm = 8 × 10 cm + 3 cm

= 80 cm + 3 cm = 83 cm

Example 2 : Express as millimetres :

(a) 15 cm (b) 26 cm 5 mm

Solution : (a) We know that 1 cm = 10 mm.

So, 15 cm = 15 × 10 = 150 mm.

(b) We know that 1 cm = 10 mm.

So, 26 cm 5 mm= 26 × 10 mm + 5 mm.

= 260 mm + 5 mm = 265 mm.

Example 3 : Express as metres :

(a) 18 km (b) 62 km 305 m

Solution : (a) We know that 1 km = 1,000 m.

So,18 km = 18 × 1,000 m = 18,000 m

(b) We know that 1 km = 1,000 m.

So, 62 km 305 m = 62 × 1,000 m + 305 m

= 62,000 m + 305 m = 62,305 m

Example 4 : Express as km and m :

(a) 1,408 m (b) 12,576 m

Solution : We know that 1,000 m = 1 km

So, 1 m $= \frac{1}{1,000}$ km.

(a) 1,408 m $= 1,000$ m + 408 m

$= \frac{1,000}{1,000}$ km + 408 m.

= 1 km 408 m

(b) 12,576 m = 12,000 m + 576 m

$= \frac{12,000}{1,000}$ km + 576 m = 12 km 576 m.

Example 5 : Express as m and cm :

(a) 512 cm (b) 4,015 cm

Solution : We know that 100 cm = 1 m

So, 1 cm $= \frac{1}{100}$ m.

(a) 512 cm = 500 cm + 12 cm

$= \frac{500}{100}$ m + 12 cm.

= 5 m 12 cm.

(b) 4,015 cm = 4,000 cm + 15 cm

$= \frac{4,000}{100}$ m + 15 cm.

= 40 m 15 cm

Example 6 : Express as cm and mm :

(a) 75 mm (b) 109 mm

Solution : We know that 10 mm = 1 cm

So, 1 mm = $\frac{1}{10}$ cm.

(a) 75 mm = 70 mm + 5 mm

= $\frac{70}{10}$ cm + 5 mm.

= 7 cm 5 mm

(b) 109 mm = 100 mm + 9 mm

= $\frac{100}{10}$ cm + 9 mm.

= 10 cm 9 mm.

Exercise 11B

Apply and Learn

A Express as centimetres :

1. 5 m **2.** 12 m **3.** 92 m **4.** 152 m
5. 8 dm **6.** 16 dm **7.** 4 m 7 dm **8.** 5 m 40 cm
9. 16 m 65 cm **10.** 96 m 5 cm **11.** 3 m 2 dm 9 cm **12.** 6 dm 2 cm

B Express as metres :

1. 475 cm **2.** 1,750 cm **3.** 2,465 cm **4.** 3,986 cm
5. 73 dm **6.** 110 dm **7.** 172 dm **8.** 205 dm
9. 483 dm **10.** 519 dm **11.** 15 dm 5 cm **12.** 25 dm 40 cm

C Express as millimetres :

1. 8 cm **2.** 19 cm **3.** 54 cm **4.** 73 cm
5. 9 cm 2 mm **6.** 63 cm 9 mm **7.** 72 cm 5 mm **8.** 97 cm 8 mm

D Express as metres :

1. 7 km **2.** 12 km **3.** 12 km 50 m **4.** 26 km 212 m
5. 108 km 208 m **6.** 216 km 80 m **7.** 493 km 196 m **8.** 500 km 50 m

E Express as kilometres and metres :

1. 1,580 m **2.** 8,560 m **3.** 7,003 m **4.** 9,567 m

F Express as metres and centimetres :

1. 95 cm **2.** 275 cm **3.** 618 cm **4.** 803 cm

G Express as centimetres and millimetres :

1. 16 mm **2.** 37 mm **3.** 52 mm **4.** 83 mm

Explore and Learn

CODE-uaTG

Addition and Subtraction in Length

Example 1 : Add 5 m 56 cm and 7 m 75 cm.

Solution : 12 m 131 cm = 12 m + 100 cm + 31 cm

= 12 m + 1 m + 31 cm

= 13 m 31 cm. [Since 100 cm = 1 m]

	5 m	56 cm
+	7 m	75 cm
	12 m	131 cm

Example 2 : Add 8 km 506 m and 6 km 724 m

Solution : 14 km 1230 m = 14 km + 1,000 m + 230 m

= 14 km + 1 km + 230 m

= 15 km 230 m. [Since 1,000 m = 1 km]

	8 km	506 m
+	6 km	724 m
	14 km	1230 cm

Example 3 : Subtract 7 km 850 m from 16 km 110 m.

Solution : Here 110 m < 850 m.

So, regroup 16 km as 15 km + 1000 m.

1,000 m + 110 m = 1,110 m.

Now 1,110 m – 850 m = 260 m

Write 260 in the metres column.

Finally 15 km – 7 km = 8 km.

Write 8 in the km column.

	(15)	(1110)
	~~16~~ km	~~110~~ m
–	7 km	850 m
	8 km	260 m

Example 4 : Subtract 12 m 65 cm from 44 m 40 cm.

Solution : Here 40 cm < 65 cm.

So, regroup 44 m as 43 m + 100 cm.

Thus 100 cm + 40 cm = 140 cm

Now 140 cm – 65 cm = 75 cm

Write 75 in the cm column.

Finally 43 m – 12 m = 31 m.

Write 31 in the m column.

	(43)	(140)
	~~44~~ m	~~40~~ cm
–	12 km	65 cm
	31 km	75 cm

Exercise 11C

Apply and Learn

A Add :

1. 12 cm 6 mm + 25 cm 9 mm
2. 26 cm 3 mm + 39 cm 8 mm
3. 7 m 62 cm + 12 m 45 cm
4. 12 m 47 cm + 25 m 93 cm
5. 78 km 126 m + 93 km 508 m
6. 116 km 76 m + 94 km 782 m

B Subtract :

1. 93 cm 7 mm – 42 cm 8 mm
2. 86 cm 2 mm – 57 cm 5 mm
3. 86 m 46 cm – 49 m 80 cm
4. 125 m 12 cm – 68 m 56 cm
5. 17 km 104 m – 6 km 856 m
6. 37 km 832 m – 15 km 948 m

Explore and Learn

CODE-pHvp

Measurement of Mass

Mass is the quantity of matter contained in a body. Quite often people refer to the word 'mass' by the word 'weight'.

The standard unit of mass is **gram**. Lighter objects are weighed in grams. Heavy objects are weighed in kilograms.

Also, 1 kilogram= 1,000 grams. In symbols, 1 kg = 1,000 g.

Example 1 : Express as grams :

(a) 5 kg (b) 12 kg (c) 8 kg 360 g

Solution : We know that 1 kg = 1,000 g. So,

(a) 5 kg = 5 × 1,000 g = 5,000 g.

(b) 12 kg = 12 × 1,000 g = 12,000 g.

(c) 8 kg 360 g = 8 kg + 360 g = 8 × 1,000 g + 360 g

= 8,000 g + 360 g = 8,360 g.

Example 2 : Express as kg and g.

(a) 1,080 g (b) 2,304 g (c) 25,360 g

Solution : (a) 1,080 g = 1,000 g + 80 g

= 1 kg + 80 g [Since 1,000 g = 1 kg]

= 1 kg 80 g.

(b) 2,304 g = 2,000 g + 304 g

= 2 kg + 304 g [Since 1,000 g = 1 kg]

= 2 kg 304 g.

(c) 25,360 g = 25,000 g + 360 g

= 25 kg + 360 g [Since 1,000 g = 1 kg]

= 25 kg 360 g.

Exercise 11D

Apply and Learn

A Express as grams :

1. 48 kg **2.** 63 kg **3.** 84 kg **4.** 191 kg

5. 7 kg 50 g **6.** 16 kg 325 g **7.** 42 kg 980 g **8.** 75 kg 105 g

B Express as kg and g :

1. 2,456 g **2.** 3,208 g **3.** 7,562 g **4.** 8,005 g

5. 16,892 g **6.** 18,196 g **7.** 25,008 g **8.** 32,451 g

Explore and Learn

CODE-pKN2

Addition and Subtraction in Mass

Example 1. Add 5 kg 735 g and 8 kg 406 g

Solution : 13 kg 1141 g = 13 kg + 1,000 g + 141 g

= 13 kg + 1 kg + 141 g

= 14 kg 141 g.

	5 kg	735 g
+	8 kg	406 g
	13 kg	1141 g

Example 2 : Subtract 8 kg 635 g from 15 kg 240 g

Solution : Here 240 g < 635 g. So regroup 15 kg as 14 kg + 1,000 g.

Thus, 1,000 g + 240 g = 1,240 g.

Also, 1,240 g – 635 g = 605 g.

Finally, 14 kg – 8 kg = 6 kg.

	14	1240
	~~15~~ kg	~~240~~ g
–	8 kg	635 g
	6 kg	605 kg

Example 3 : Mamta's bag weighed 3 kg 750 g and Sushma's bag weighed 2 kg 440 g. Find the weight of both the bags together.

Solution : Weight of Mamta's bag = 3 kg 750 g

Weight of Sushma's bag = 2 kg 440 g

Weight of both the bags = 3 kg 750 g + 2 kg 440 g

Now, 5 kg 1,190 g = 5 kg + 1,000 g + 190 g

= 5 kg + 1 kg + 190 g = 6 kg 190 g

Hence, weight of both the bags = 6 kg 190 g.

	3 kg	750 g
+	2 kg	440 g
	5 kg	1190 g

Example 4 : A man bought 50 kg of rice for his family for a month. Out of this the quantity of rice that got spent was 32 kg 750 g. What quantity of rice was left?

Solution : Quantity of rice bought = 50 kg 0 g.

Quantity of rice consumed = 32 kg 750 g

Hence, quantity of rice left = 17 kg 250 g.

	49	1000
	~~50~~ kg	~~0~~ g
–	32 kg	750 g
	17 kg	250 kg

Exercise 11E

Apply and Learn

A Add :

1. 2 kg 405 g + 7 kg 215 g
2. 5 kg 635 g + 8 kg 450 g
3. 34 kg 105 g + 47 kg 796 g
4. 73 kg 290 g + 56 kg 405 g

B Subtract :

1. 7 kg 465 g – 3 kg 240 g
2. 8 kg 630 g – 5 kg 950 g
3. 32 kg 205 g – 17 kg 645 g
4. 100 kg 465 g – 52 kg 760 g

C Answer the following questions :

1. Deepak purchased 5 kg 270 g of potatoes and 2 kg 450 g of onions. How much weight of vegetables did he purchase?

2. Kartik's doll weighs 2 kg 890 g and Manohar's doll weighs 3 kg 890 g. What is the weight of both the dolls?

3. A family consumed 18 kg 570 g of wheat and 15 kg 490 g of rice in a month. In all how much cereals did the family consume in that month?

4. The weight of a watermelon is 3 kg 425 g. The weight of a pineapple is 2 kg 530 g. By how much is the watermelon heavier?

5. There were 8 kg 250 g of apples in a carton. 5 kg 825 g of apples were removed. What will be the weight of the apples left in the carton?

6. Sanjay bought 100 kg of wheat for his family for a month. Out of this, the quantity of wheat consumed was 76 kg 450 g. What quantity of wheat was left?

Explore and Learn

CODE-5yFC

Measurement of Capacity

We measure the capacity of a container in litres. Litre is the standard unit of capacity. Small quantities of liquids are measured in millilitres.

Also, 1 litre = 1,000 millilitres

In symbols, 1 *l* = 1,000 ml.

Example 1 : Express as ml :

(a) 4 *l* (b) 18 *l* (c) 9 *l* 405 ml

Solution : We know that 1 *l* = 1,000 ml

(a) 4 *l* = 4 × 1,000 ml = 4,000 ml.

(b) 18 *l* = 18 × 1,000 ml = 18,000 ml.

(c) 9 *l* 405 ml = 9 *l* + 405 ml = 9 × 1,000 ml + 405 ml

= 9,000 ml + 405 ml = 9,405 ml.

Example 2 : Express as *l* and ml :

(a) 1,678 ml (b) 4,360 ml (c) 15,047 ml

Solution : (a) 1,678 ml = 1,000 ml + 678 ml = 1 *l* + 678 ml = 1 *l* 678 ml.

(b) 4,360 ml = 4,000 ml + 360 ml
= 4 l + 360 ml = 4 l 360 ml.

(c) 15,047 ml = 15,000 ml + 47 ml
= 15 l + 47 ml (∵ 1000 ml = 1 l)
= 15 l 47 ml.

Exercise 11F

Apply and Learn

A Express as ml :

1. 2 l **2.** 9 l **3.** 24 l **4.** 56 l
5. 75 l **6.** 83 l **7.** 103 l **8.** 857 l
9. 5 l 210 ml **10.** 10 l 90 ml **11.** 29 l 785 ml **12.** 44 l 109 ml

B Express as l and ml :

1. 1,309 ml **2.** 18,596 ml **3.** 2,645 ml **4.** 8,345 ml
5. 56,210 ml **6.** 83,218 ml **7.** 90,003 ml **8.** 96,352 ml

Explore and Learn

Addition and Subtraction in Capacity

CODE-5qac

Example 1 : Add 12 l 240 ml and 15 l 926 ml

Solution : We have : 12 l 240 ml + 15 l 926 ml = 27 l 1166 ml

	12 l	240 ml
+	15 l	926 ml
	27 l	1166 ml

27 l 1166 ml = 27 l + 1,000 ml + 166 ml
= 27 l + 1 l + 166 ml
= 28 l 166 ml. [Since 1,000 ml = 1l]

Example 2 : Subtract 18 l 465 ml from 50 l.

Solution : Here, 0 ml < 465 ml.
So, regroup 50 l as
49 l + 1,000 ml.
Also, 1,000 ml + 0 ml = 1,000 ml
So, 1,000 ml – 465 ml = 535 ml.
Finally, 49 l – 18 l = 31 l.

	49	1000
	~~50~~ l	~~0~~ ml
–	18 l	465 ml
	31 l	535 ml

Example 3 : A tank contained 90 *l* 750 ml of water. 40 *l* 630 ml more water was poured into it. Find the quantity of water in the tank.

Solution : Quantity of water in the tank = 90 *l* 750 ml

Quantity of water poured into it = 40 *l* 630 ml

Total quantity of water in the tank

= 90 *l* 750 ml + 40 *l* 630 ml

	90 *l*	750 ml
+	40 *l*	630 ml
	130 *l*	1380 ml

130 *l* 1380 ml = 130 *l* + 1,000 ml + 380 ml

= 130 *l* + 1 *l* + 380 ml = 131 *l* 380 ml

Hence, total quantity of water in the tank = 131 *l* 380 ml.

Example 4 : A bucket contains 20 *l* 525 ml of water. Another bucket contains 9 *l* 850 ml of water. How much more water does the first bucket contain?

Solution : Quantity of water in the first bucket = 20 *l* 525 ml

Quantity of water in the second bucket = 9 *l* 850 ml

	(19)	(1525)
	~~20~~ *l*	~~525~~ ml
−	9 *l*	850 ml
Difference of the capacities =	10 *l*	675 ml

Hence, the first bucket contains 10 *l* 675 ml of water more than the second.

Exercise 11G

Apply and Learn

A Add :

1. 5 *l* 750 ml + 8 *l* 125 ml
2. 9 *l* 360 ml + 12 *l* 850 ml
3. 62 *l* 275 ml + 39 *l* 890 ml
4. 82 *l* 144 ml + 65 *l* 678 ml

B Subtract :

1. 6 *l* 50 ml − 2 *l* 425 ml
2. 8 *l* 425 ml − 3 *l* 720 ml
3. 12 *l* 125 ml − 7 *l* 925 ml
4. 18 *l* 636 ml − 12 *l* 950 ml
5. 50 *l* − 10 *l* 250 ml
6. 63 *l* 156 ml − 34 *l* 475 ml

C Answer the following questions :

1. Shikha bought 2 *l* 750 ml milk and Sarika bought 4 *l* 900 ml milk. How much quantity of milk did they both buy together?

2. A bottle contains 6 l 450 ml of juice. Another bottle contains 5 l 875 ml of juice. Both are emptied into an empty vessel. How much juice would be there in the vessel?

3. Mr Gupta filled 21 l 730 ml of petrol in his car in the first week of August. In the last week of August, he again filled 15 l 850 ml of petrol. How much petrol did he fill in his car in the two weeks?

4. A bucket contained 40 l of water. 16 l 750 ml of water is taken out. How much water is left in the bucket?
5. Urmila bought 6 l 250 ml of milk. Her friend Maya bought 4 l 725 ml of milk. How much more milk did Urmila buy?
6. A jar contains 30 l of juice. 6 l 875 ml of juice was taken away from it. What quantity of juice would be there in the jar?

Value Based Questions

Niharika is a student of IV class. Once she bought a bottle containing mango juice of 4 l from her school canteen. She decided to drink it with her friends. All of her friends including Niharika consumed 3 l 200 ml of mango juice.

1. What quantity of juice will be left in the bottle?
2. Do you also share food items among your friends?
3. Why is it so important to share food items with others? What kind of satisfaction do you get by doing so?

Review and Refresh

A Express as centimetres :

1. 7 m 2. 9 dm 3. 4 m 3 dm 6 cm 4. 7 m 8 dm 2 cm

B Express as metres and centimetres :

1. 325 cm 2. 1,540 cm 3. 1,507 cm

C Express as metres :

1. 5 km 2. 45 km 3. 87 km 4. 15 km 40 m
5. 25 km 215 m 6. 95 km 261 m 7. 100 km 10 m 8. 216 km 126 m

D Express as kg and g :

1. 5,627 g 2. 7,015 g 3. 4,007 g 4. 2,010 g

E Express as *l* and ml :

1. 4,278 ml 2. 3,096 ml 3. 2,008 ml 4. 6,397 ml

F Add :

1. 4 m 65 cm + 5 m 75 cm
2. 4 m 75 cm + 6 m 25 cm
3. 6 km 275 m + 7 km 845 m
4. 5 km 475 m + 6 km 675 m
5. 8 kg 840 g + 7 kg 85 g
6. 4 kg 384 g + 3 kg 15 g
7. 6 *l* 685 ml + 5 *l* 765 ml
8. 12 *l* 240 ml + 15 *l* 926 ml

G Subtract :

1. 8 km 225 m – 4 km 575 m
2. 9 km 125 m – 4 km 475 m
3. 9 m 25 cm – 4 m 75 cm
4. 8 m 50 cm – 3 m 75 cm
5. 7 kg 100 g – 3 kg 425 g
6. 12 kg 105 g – 5 kg 840 g
7. 65 *l* 156 ml – 35 *l* 476 ml
8. 60 *l* – 15 *l* 250 ml

Mental Maths

1. 22 cm 8 mm = ____________ mm.
2. 36 km = ____________ m = ____________ cm.
3. 42 km 107 m = ____________ m.
4. 15,000 m = ____________ km.
5. 75 mm = ____________ cm ____________ mm.
6. 6,327 m = ____________ km ____________ m.
7. 4 m 72 cm = ____________ cm.

8. 12 kg 108 g = ____________ g.

9. 26,750 ml = ____________ l ____________ ml

10. 12,705 ml = ____________ l ____________ ml.

Fun With Maths

1. Which is heavier : 1 kg cotton or 1 kg pebbles?

2. A pen is 180 mm long. A pen box is $22\frac{1}{2}$ cm long. Will the pen be able to fill inside the pen box?

3. Ruchi used a balance to measure the weight of certain items. It has been displayed alongside.

What is the weight of each box?

(a) 40 g (b) 60 g (c) 240 g (d) 100 g

4. Consider the balance used for weighing certain items for sale.

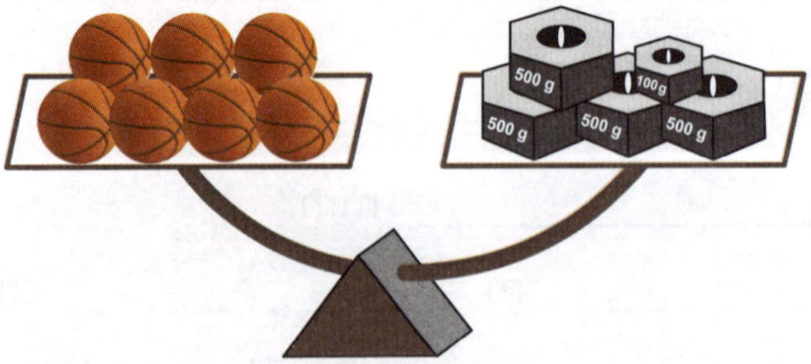

The weight of each of the 7 identical balls is :

(a) 450 grams (b) 500 grams (c) 300 grams (d) 700 grams

Maths Lab Activity

Objective : To verify that 1 m = 100 cm.

Materials Required : Ribbon of length exactly 1 m and other pieces of ribbon cut into different lengths like 10 cm, 20 cm, 30 cm, 40 cm, 50 cm, 60 cm.

Procedure/Demonstration :

1. Students selects 5 to 6 pieces of ribbons randomly.
2. They arrange the ribbon pieces in csuch a way so as to form 1 m and verify it with the 1 m ribbon.

   For example, 30 cm + 50 cm + 20 cm = 100 cm

   We know, 100 cm = 1 m.
3. Students keep on exchanging the ribbon pieces with their friends and form at least 5 combinations that make a metre.
4. They record their observations.

To get worksheet on this chapter scan this QR code

CODE-twAC

12

THEME 5 : MEASUREMENT

Time

Learning Target

Understanding time

I Can

- **I can read** and write time.
- **I can describe** time before and after the hour in different ways.
- **I can convert** time in to hours, minutes and seconds.
- **I can interpret** a calendar.

Let Us Recall

In the previous classes, we learnt to read time from a clock. We also learned the relation between hours and minutes. Let us review what we learnt earlier.

We learnt that : **1 hour = 60 minutes, 1 day = 24 hours**

Exercise 12A

A Write down the time shown by each of the following clocks :

1. 

2. 

3. 

4. 

5. 

6. 

7. 

8. 

B *Answer the following questions :*

1. How many minutes are there in 1 hour? ____________
2. How many days are there in a leap year? ____________
3. Which month comes just after May? ____________
4. Which month is the 9th month of the year? ____________
5. Which month comes in between July and September? ____________
6. How much time does the hour hand take to complete 1 round of the dial? ____
7. How much time does the minute hand take to go from one number to the next number? ____________

Explore and Learn

The faces of some clocks are marked in Roman numerals as shown in the following examples. We read the time in the same manner as we have read earlier.

Example 1 : Write down the time shown by each of the following clocks.

(a) 

(b) 

(c) 

(d)

(e)

(f)

Solution :

(a) The time is 4:35 or 25 minutes to 5.

(b) The time is 1:30 or half-past 1.

(c) The time is 3:45 or 15 minutes to 4.

(d) The time is 6:55 or 5 minutes to 7.

(e) The time is 8:10 or 10 minutes past 8.

(f) The time is 10:40 or 20 minutes to 11.

Exercise 12B

Apply and Learn

A Write the time shown by each of the following clocks :

1.

2.

3.

4.

5.

6.

7.

8.

9. 

10. 

11. 

12. 

B Draw hands of the clocks to show the time :

1. 1 : 40

2. 2 : 15

3. 6 : 50

4. 10 : 05

5. 12 : 25

6. 4 : 45

7. 12 : 50

8. 9 : 20

9. 7 : 10

10. 5 : 15

11. 2 : 35

12. 11 : 40

Explore and Learn

Use of a.m. and p.m.

CODE-VRyK

So far, we have learnt to read time. Now, we shall learn to use a.m. and p.m.

When we say time is 4 o'clock, it may be 4 o'clock in the early morning or 4 o'clock in the evening.

To avoid this, we use a.m. and p.m. notations. a.m. stands for ante meridiem and p.m. stands for post meridiem.

The time between 12 midnight and 12 noon is denoted as a.m. The time between 12 noon and 12 midnight is denoted as p.m.

REMEMBER

We do not attach a.m. or p.m. to 12:00. We write 12:00 at midnight as 12 midnight and 12:00 at noon as 12 noon.

Thus, 4 o'clock, in the morning is denoted by 4 a.m. and 4 o'clock in the evening is denoted by 4 p.m.

Example 1 : Write the time using a.m. or p.m.

(a) 6:30 in the evening
(b) 7:15 in the morning
(c) 4:08 in the morning
(d) 45 minutes after midnight.
(e) 1:45 after midnight.
(f) 1 hour after 12 noon

Solution : (a) 6:30 p.m. (b) 7:15 a.m. (c) 4:08 a.m.
(d) 12:45 a.m. (e) 1:45 a.m. (f) 1:00 p.m.

Example 2 : What time will it be

(a) 2 hours after 8 a.m.?
(b) 4 hours after 10 p.m.?
(c) 5 hours before 12 noon.?
(d) 4 hours before 2 a.m.?

Solution :

(a) 2 hours after 8 a.m. will be 10 a.m.

(b) 2 hours after 10 p.m. will be 12 midnight.
2 hours after 12 midnight will be 2 a.m.
Thus, 4 hours after 10 p.m. will be 2 a.m.

(c) 5 hours before 12 noon will be 7 a.m.

(d) 2 hours before 2 a.m. will be 12 midnight.
2 hours before 12 midnight will be 10 p.m.
Thus, 4 hours before 2 a.m. will be 10 p.m.

Exercise 12C

Apply and Learn

A Write a.m. or p.m. in the given blank spaces to make the sentences correct:

1. Divya goes to school at 7:30 ________.

2. Manoj takes his dinner at 9:00 ________.

3. You take your lunch at 1:00 __________.
4. Kavita goes to bed at 10:00 __________.
5. Shilpa cleans her teeth at 6:30 __________.
6. Dolly does her homework at 8:00 __________.
7. Piyush comes back from school at 2:00 __________.
8. Deepika plays at 4:00 __________.

B Write the time using a.m. or p.m. :

1. 5 : 45 in the evening
2. 6 : 40 in the morning
3. 12 : 05 in the night
4. 10 minutes after midnight
5. 2 : 40 in the morning
6. 9 : 35 in the evening
7. 8 : 15 in the morning
8. 4 : 10 in the evening
9. 11 : 30 in the night
10. 12 : 10 in the afternoon
11. 1 : 10 in the night
12. 5 : 35 in the morning
13. 11 : 50 in the morning
14. 11 : 50 in the night

C What time will it be :

1. 2 hours after 7:35 a.m.?
2. 1 hour before 12 midnight?
3. 3 hours after 11:10 p.m.?
4. 4 hours before 3:00 a.m.?
5. 2 hours after 10:00 p.m.?
6. 3 hours before 3:00 p.m.?
7. 5 hours after 8:10 p.m.?
8. 1 hour after 11:50 a.m.?
9. 2 hours before 1:30 p.m.?
10. 3 hours before 10:00 a.m.?

Explore and Learn

CODE-HFQ1

Conversion of Time

We know that time between sunrise and sunset is called daytime, whereas time between sunset and sunrise is called the night time. The total duration of the day-time and the night-time makes a day.

1 minute = 60 seconds, 1 hour = 60 minutes.

1 day = 24 hours, 1 week = 7 days, 1 year = 12 months

We multiply to convert larger units into smaller units.

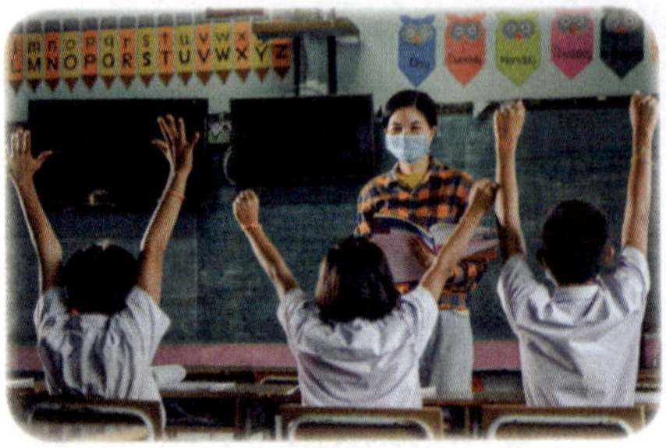

(a) Convert 8 minutes into seconds.

Since, 1 minute = 60 seconds.

So, 8 minutes = 8 × 60 seconds = 480 seconds.

(b) Convert 6 hours into minutes.

Since, 1 hour = 60 minutes

So, 6 hours = 6 × 60 minutes = 360 minutes.

(c) Convert 4 hours 35 minutes into minutes.

Since, 1 hour = 60 minutes

So, 4 hours = 4 × 60 minutes = 240 minutes.

Therefore, 4 hours 35 minutes

= 240 minutes + 35 minutes = 275 minutes.

(d) Convert 3 days 23 hours into hours.

Since, 1 day = 24 hours.

So, 3 days = 24 × 3 hours = 72 hours

Therefore, 3 days 23 hours = 3 days + 23 hours

= 72 hours + 23 hours = 95 hours.

(e) Convert 2 weeks into hours.

Since, 1 week = 7 days.

Therefore, 2 weeks = 2 × 7 days = 14 days

= 14 × 24 hours = 336 hours.

(f) Convert 6 years 8 months into months.

Since, 1 year = 12 months.

So, 6 years 8 months = 6 × 12 months + 8 months

= 72 months + 8 months = 80 months.

(g) Convert 5 months 16 days into days.

Since, 1 month = 30 days

So, 5 months 16 days = 5 × 30 days + 16 days

= 150 days + 16 days = 166 days.

We divide to convert smaller units into larger units.

(a) Convert 240 seconds into minutes.

Since, 60 seconds = 1 minute

So, 240 seconds = 240 ÷ 60 = 4 minutes

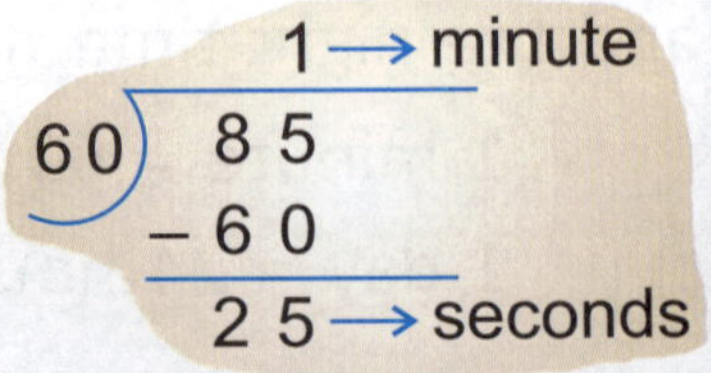

(b) Convert 85 seconds into minutes and seconds.

Since, 60 seconds = 1 minute

So, 85 seconds = 85 ÷ 60 = 1 minute 25 seconds

(c) Convert 120 minutes into hours.

Since, 60 minutes = 1 hour

So, 120 minutes = 120 ÷ 60 = 2 hours

(d) Convert 145 minutes into hours and minutes.

Since, 60 minutes = 1 hour

So, 145 minutes = 145 ÷ 60

= 2 hours 25 minutes.

```
     2 → hours
60 ) 1 4 5
   - 1 2 0
     -----
       2 5 → minutes
```

REMEMBER

While converting smaller units into larger units, if a remainder is there, then retain it as the smaller unit.

(e) Convert 42 days into weeks.

Since, 7 days = 1 week

So, 42 days = 42 ÷ 7 = 6 weeks

(f) Convert 92 days into weeks and days.

Since, 7 days = 1 week

So, 92 days = 92 ÷ 7

= 13 weeks 1 day

```
    1 3 → weeks
7 ) 9 2
  - 7
    ---
    2 2
  - 2 1
    ---
      1 → day
```

(g) Convert 120 hours into days.

Since, 24 hours = 1 day

So, 120 hours = 120 ÷ 24 = 5 days

(h) Convert 225 hours into days and hours.

Since, 24 hours = 1 day

So, 225 hours = 225 ÷ 24 = 9 days 9 hours

```
        9 → days
24 ) 2 2 5
   - 2 1 6
     -----
         9 → hours
```

(i) Convert 60 months into years.

Since, 12 months = 1 year

So, 60 months = 60 ÷ 12 = 5 years

(j) Convert 94 months into years and months.

Since, 12 months = 1 year

So, 94 months = 94 ÷ 12 = 7 years 10 months

```
       7 → years
12 ) 9 4
   - 8 4
     ---
     1 0 → months
```

(k) Convert 60 days into months.

Since, 30 days = 1 month

So, 60 days = 60 ÷ 30 = 2 months

(l) Convert 142 days into months and days.

Since, 30 days = 1 months

So, 142 days = 142 ÷ 30

= 4 months 22 days

$$\begin{array}{r|l} 30 & 142 \\ & -120 \\ \hline & 22 \end{array}$$

Quotient 4 → month; remainder 22 → days

Exercise 12D

Apply and Learn

A Convert the following into seconds :

1. 12 minutes **2.** 15 minutes **3.** 23 minutes **4.** 32 minutes

B Convert the following into minutes :

1. 8 hours **2.** 12 hours 30 minutes

3. 30 hours 12 minutes **4.** 45 hours

C Convert the following into hours :

1. 2 days 20 hours **2.** 3 days 15 hours **3.** 4 days 12 hours

D Convert the following into hours:

1. 3 weeks **2.** 5 weeks **3.** 4 weeks

E Convert the following into months :

1. 5 years **2.** 6 years **3.** 10 years 8 months

F Convert the following into days :

1. 8 months **2.** 6 months **3.** 10 months 12 days.

G Convert the following into minutes and seconds :

1. 720 seconds **2.** 3,000 seconds **3.** 400 seconds

4. 750 seconds **5.** 1620 seconds **6.** 1840 seconds

H Convert the following into days and hours :

1. 600 hours **2.** 1,080 hours **3.** 910 hours

4. 1,000 hours **5.** 1,150 hours **6.** 1,205 hours

I Convert the following into weeks and days :

1. 10 days **2.** 364 days **3.** 30 days

4. 85 days **5.** 98 days **6.** 100 days

J Convert the following into months and days :

1. 121 days	**2.** 380 days	**3.** 10 weeks
4. 16 weeks	**5.** 52 weeks	**6.** 70 weeks

K Convert the following into years and months :

1. 128 months	**2.** 360 months	**3.** 400 months
4. 540 months	**5.** 950 months	**6.** 1000 months

Explore and Learn

Time Duration

CODE-ekV7

Vineeta left for school at 6 : 10 a.m.

She reached the school at 6 : 55 a.m.

What was the duration of her journey?

Duration = 55 minutes – 10 minutes = 45 minutes.

A train started a journey at 10 : 20 a.m.

and completed it at 1 : 15 p.m.

Find the duration of the journey.

10 : 20 —40 minutes→ 11 : 00 —2 hours→ 1 : 00 —15 minutes→ 1 : 15

So, duration of journey = 2 hours and (40 + 15) minutes

= 2 hours 55 minutes.

A volleyball match started at 8 : 50 a.m.

It was finished at 10 : 25 a.m.

How many hours and minutes does the match last?

8 : 50 —10 minutes→ 9 : 00 —1 hour→ 10 : 00 —25 minutes→ 10 : 25

So, duration of the match = 1 hour and (10 + 25) minutes

= 1 hour 35 minutes.

Exercise 12E

Apply and Learn

A How many minutes have passed from clock I to clock II?

1.

Clock I Clock II

2.

Clock I Clock II

3.

Clock I Clock II

B Answer the following questions :

1. Ragini started her dance practice at 5 : 40 p.m. and stopped it at 7 : 10 p.m. How long did she practice?

2. Soumya started his yoga exercise at 5 : 55 a.m. It was over at 6 : 40 a.m. How long did the yoga exercise last?

3. A ferry boat started to sail at 11 : 30 a.m. It completed the journey at 3 : 10 p.m. How long did it sail?

4. A boxing match started at 11 : 40 p.m. It ended at 1 : 35 a.m. How long did the boxing match last?

5. Shilpa started playing volleyball at 4 : 45 p.m. She played for 1 hour 15 minutes. When did she stop playing?

6. Richard's pet cat Brownie fell in a well at 11 : 45 a.m. He took 50 minutes to bring it out. At what time was the cat out of well?

7. Manvar started dreaming at 11 : 50 p.m. His dream lasted for 40 minutes. When did his dream end?

Explore and Learn

CODE-2mHW

Interpreting a Calendar

While interpreting a calendar (calculating days), sometimes we include the last day in our calculations and sometimes we do not.

Example 1 : How many days are there from 16th March to 12th April?

Solution : Days left out in March = 31 – 15 = 16

Days in April = 12

Total number of days = 16 + 12 = 28

So, there are 28 days from 16th March to 12th April.

Example 2 : Maya joined an office on 26th July. She worked for 21 days only. On what date Maya left the office?

Solution : Days in July = 31 – 25 = 6

Days in August = 21 – 6 = 15.

So, Maya left the office on 15th August.

Example 3 : What date is 26 days after 18th February? Take February to have 28 days.

Solution : Days in February = 28 – 18 = 10

Days in March = 26 – 10 = 16.

So, the date 26 days after 18th February is 16th March.

Exercise 12F

1. How many days are there from 8th August to 9th September?
2. How many days are there from 24th January to 19th February?
3. How many days are there from 7th July to 18th September?
4. What date is 18 days after 10th October?
5. What date is 25 days after 16th April?
6. What date is 23 days before 8th June?
7. Kartik's father left for Ambala on 8th January. He returned home on 12th February. For how many days did he remain out of home?
8. A fair started on 8th February and ended on 10th March. How long did the fair last? Take February to have 28 days.

9. Kavita's school was closed from 15 December onwards for 28 days. On what date did the school reopen?
10. Salman's half-yearly exams begin on 18th October. He starts his revision 35 days earlier. When did he start his revision?

Value Based Questions

Sachin and Kabeer are classmates. They study in 4th class. Their first period starts at 8 o'clock in the morning and their last (eighth) period ends at 2 o'clock in the afternoon. After 4th period, there is a lunch period of 40 minutes. The duration of each period is 40 minutes. One day, Sachin forgot his lunch box at home. In the lunch period, when Kabeer came to know this, he shared his lunch box with Sachin.

1. At what time does the second period start?
2. At what time does the lunch period end?
3. At what time does the last (eighth) period start?
4. Here, which value is depicted by Kabeer?

Review and Refresh

A Write the time shown by each of the following clocks :

1. 

2. 

3. 

4. 

5. 

6. 

7. 

8. 

B Write the time using a.m. or p.m.

1. 6 : 30 in the morning.
2. 8 : 10 in the morning.
3. 1 : 45 in the afternoon.
4. 20 minutes after midnight.

C Convert the following into minutes and seconds :

1. 61 seconds
2. 185 seconds
3. 280 seconds
4. 435 seconds

D Convert the following into hours and minutes :

1. 75 minutes
2. 125 minutes
3. 200 minutes
4. 247 minutes

E Convert the following into days and hours :

1. 150 hours
2. 730 hours
3. 245 hours
4. 540 hours

F Convert the following into years and months :

1. 72 months
2. 50 months
3. 100 months
4. 60 months

Mental Maths

1. 1 day = ______________ hours.
2. 1 : 30 after midnight = 1: 30 ______________
3. You usually go to bed at 9 : 30 ______________
4. There are ______________ days from 12th March to 5th April.
5. You usually take your breakfast at ______________ a.m.
6. 1640 hours = ______________ p.m.
7. The minute hand is at 8 and the hour hand is between 3 and 4. The time is ______________
8. In how many minutes, does the seconds' hand complete one round of the dial? ______________
9. If it is 12 o'clock in the day, we say the time is 12 ______________
10. Express the time 7 hours after 6 : 30 in the morning as a.m. or p.m. ______________

To get worksheet on this chapter scan this QR code

CODE-5QPQ

Maths Lab Activity

Objective : To enable the children to read time from the face of a clock.

Materials Required : Pencil and paper only.

Procedure/Demonstration : Make each pair of clocks given below show the same time.

Choose any three times on the clocks above and write what you could be doing at that time of a day.

1. ______________________________

2. ______________________________

3. ______________________________

CHECK YOUR PACE

(Based on Chapters 10, 11, 12)

A Find the perimeter of the following figures :

1.

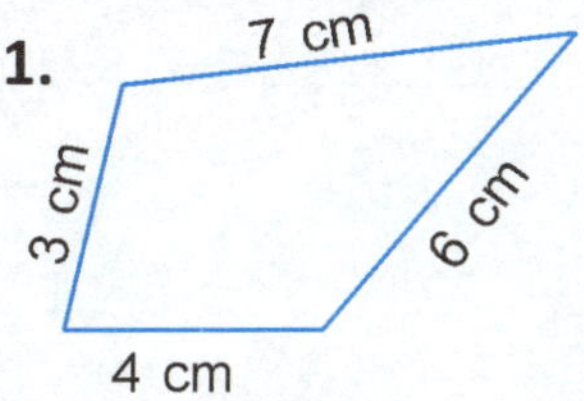

2.

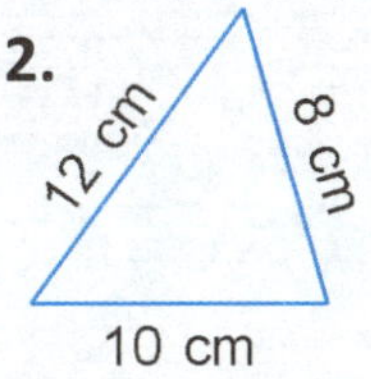

3.

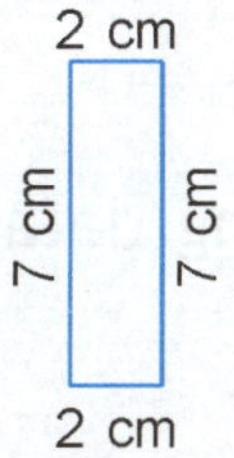

4.

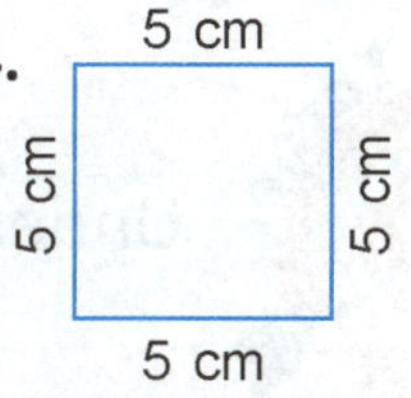

B Each small square stands for 1 sq cm. Find the areas of the following figures :

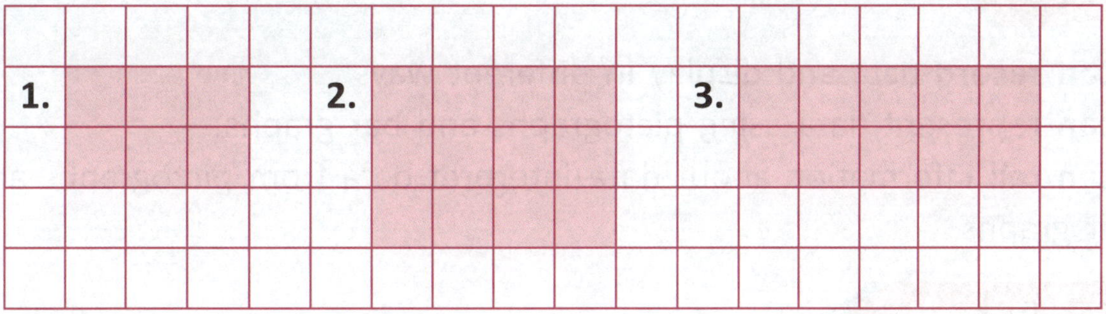

C Find the area of :

1. the rectangle with dimensions 8 cm and 7 cm. **2.** the square with side 10 cm.

D Express as km and m :

1. 15,250 m **2.** 56,081 m **3.** 8,007 m **4.** 1,26,700 m

E Express as kg and g :

1. 2,875 g **2.** 4,083 g **3.** 26,270 g **4.** 15,080 g

F Express as *l* and ml :

1. 8,035 ml **2.** 21,572 ml **3.** 81,080 ml **4.** 2,16,576 ml

G Add/Subtract :

1. 8 km 150 m + 16 km 780 m **2.** 26 kg 85 g + 54 kg 116 g

3. 115 *l* 40 ml – 58 *l* 65 ml **4.** 96 km 75 m – 48 km 80 m

H What time it will be :

1. 4 hours after 9:30 a.m. **2.** 3 hours after 11:10 p.m.

3. 1 hour before 12:05 p.m. **4.** 2 hours before 1:40 a.m.

I Convert :

1. 8 hours into minutes. **2.** 12 years 6 months into months.

3. 40 minutes 15 seconds into seconds. **4.** 136 minutes into hours and minutes.

5. 210 hours into days and hours. **6.** 186 days into months and days.

THEME 6 : DATA HANDLING

Data Handling

Learning Target Understanding data

I Can

- **I can record** data and display in different ways.
- **I can represent** data using pictographs and bar graphs.
- **I can tell** information about data/interpret data from pictographs and bar graphs.

Let Us Recall

Exercise 13A

A Following pictograph shows the number of candles brought by some children of class 4 for a Festival.

Name of Student	Number of Candles brought
Shubham	
Neha	
Anshu	
Ridhima	
Daksh	

Look at the pictograph and answer the following questions :

1. How many candles are brought by Anshu? ____________
2. How many candles are brought by Daksh? ______________
3. Name the two students who have brought the same number of candles? ____________, __________

4. Who has brought the maximum number of candles and how many? ____________, ____________

5. What is the total number of candles brought by children? ____________

B The pictograph given below shows preference of the students for winter activities:

Winter Activities	Number of Students (one ☺ represents 10 students)
Skiing	☺ ☺ ☺
Ice Skating	☺ ☺ ☺ ☺ ☺ ☺
Sleighing	☺ ☺ ☺ ☺ ☺ ☺ ☺ ☺ ☺ ☺
Hockey	☺ ☺ ☺ ☺

Answer the following questions :

1. Which is the most popular winter activity? ____________.
2. How many students like skiing? ____________.
3. Which is more popular activity : hockey or ice skating? ____________.

Explore and Learn

CODE-dzKW

Drawing Pictographs

For providing transport facility, a school conducted a class-wise survey of students coming from different places. The class teacher of class IV collected data of her class and presented it in the form of a table as given below :

Distance from home to school	1 km	2 km	3 km	4 km	5 km
Number of students	5	8	10	7	4

If we want to present this data in the form of a pictograph, we can easily do so in the following way.

☺ = 1 student

Distance from home to school	Number of students
1 km	☺ ☺ ☺ ☺ ☺
2 km	☺ ☺ ☺ ☺ ☺ ☺ ☺ ☺

3 km	
4 km	
5 km	

From the above pictograph, we can also answer the following questions :

1. From which distance the maximum number of students come? The answer is 3 km.
2. From which distance the maximum number of students come? The answer is 5 km.
3. How many students come from 4 km or more? The answer is 7 + 4 = 11
4. How many students come from less than 2 km? The answer is 5.
5. In all how many students are there in the class?

   Total number of students = 5 + 8 + 10 + 7 + 4 = 34

When the number of objects to be represented is large, we use a single symbol to represent a certain number of objects. Consider the following example.

In a shop, the sale of smart phones on different days of a week is given below :

Days	Monday	Tuesday	Wednesday	Thursday	Friday	Saturday
Number of smart phones sold	10	20	35	25	15	20

Here, the number of smart phones sold is large, so, we cannot represent each phone by a symbol. So, we shorten it by using the symbol 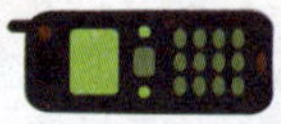 for 5 smart phones. So, the pictograph can be drawn as below.

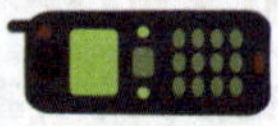 = 5 smart phones

Days	Number of smart phones
Monday	
Tuesday	
Wednesday	
Thursday	
Friday	
Saturday	

Exercise 13B

Apply and Learn

A The modes of travelling to school by the students of a class are given below:

Mode	Bus	Car	Scooter	Cycle	Walking
Number of students	10	3	4	10	12

Draw a pictograph to represent the above data.

B The different types of trees planted in a park are given below :

Name of the tree	Mango tree	Banyan tree	Neem tree	Guava tree
Number of trees	4	2	6	5

Draw a pictograph to represent the above data.

C The sale of toys in a toy shop during the weekdays of a particular week is given below. Draw a pictograph to represent the following data.

Day	Monday	Tuesday	Wednesday	Thursday	Friday	Saturday
Number of toys sold	20	12	32	16	24	20

D The total number of animals in five villages are given below :

Village	I	II	III	IV	V
Number of animals	90	60	120	100	80

Draw a pictograph to represent the above data.

Explore and Learn

CODE-p11M

Bar Graphs

A **bar graph** is a visual representation of given data with the help of bars. It displays information visually, through **rectangular bars** of equal width with equal space between them. The height of each bar represents the number of given data elements.

A bar graph can be drawn **vertically** or **horizontally**.

A bar graph always has a title. Therefore, by looking at the title, we can interpret the information depicted by it.

Look at the bar graph. Here, 2 squares represent 5 students. Now, let us try to answer the following questions :

1. What is the title of the bar graph?

   This bar graph depicts about the different subjects liked by the students.

Subjects liked by the students

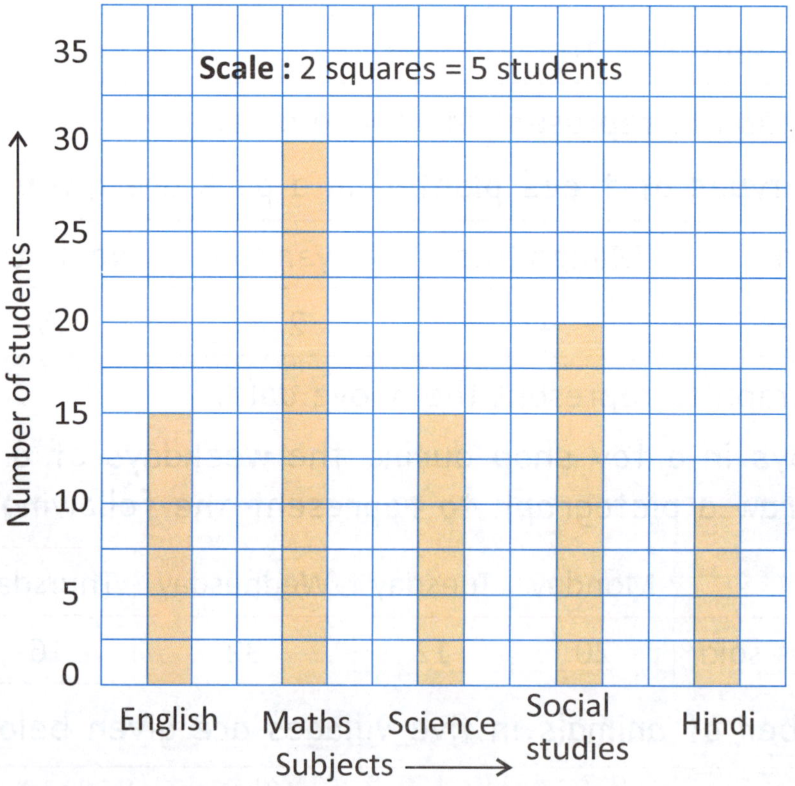

2. Which subject is liked by most of the students?

   Since, height of bars represent number of students, therefore the **tallest bar** represents largest number in the data. We observe that bar for **Maths** is the tallest. So, Maths is liked by most of the students.

3. Which subject is liked by least number of students?

   Since the bar for Hindi is the shortest, so Hindi is liked by the least number of students.

   From the above bar graph, we can also answer the following questions :

   (i) How many students like Maths? 30

   (ii) How many students like English? 15

   (iii) Which subject is liked by 20 students? Social Studies

   (iv) What is the total number of students in the group?

   Total number of students = 15 + 30 + 15 + 20 + 10 = 90

Exercise 13C

Apply and Learn

A The following bar graph shows the favourite picnic spots of children of a class. Look at the bar graph and answer the following questions.

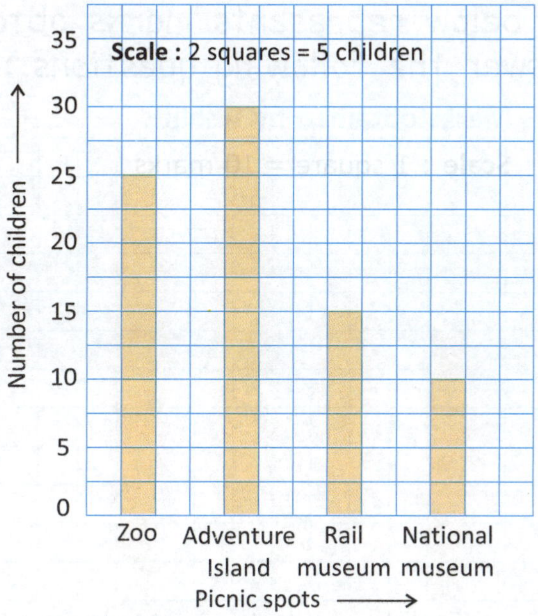

1. How many children would like to go to Rail Museum?
2. How many children would like to go to Zoo?
3. How many children would like to go to Adventure island?
4. How many children are there in the class?
5. Which destination is liked by the maximum number of children?

B The bar graph shown here represents different means of transport used by students of class IV-A to come to school.

Means of transport used by students of class IV-A

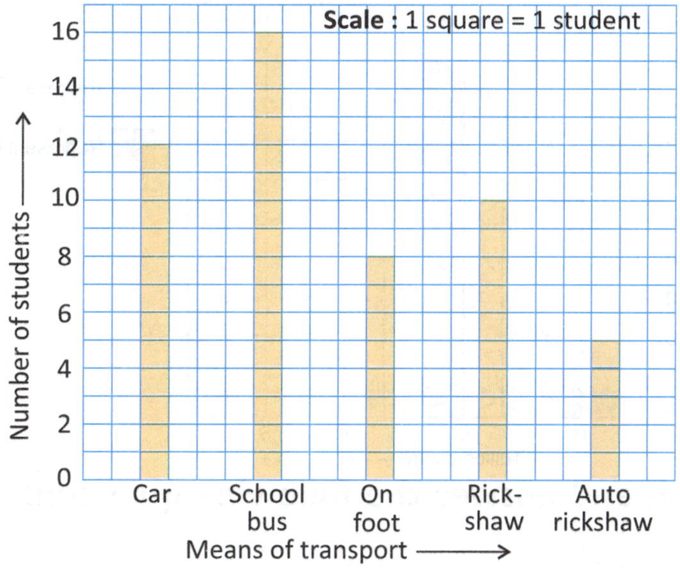

Study the bar graph and answer the following questions.

1. Which mode of transport is used by maximum number of students? ________
2. How many students come to school by car? ________
3. How many students come to school on foot? ________
4. How many students come to school by autorickshaw? ________

C The bar graph shown below represents marks obtained by Abhijit. Look at the bar graph and answer the following questions :

Marks obtained by Abhijit

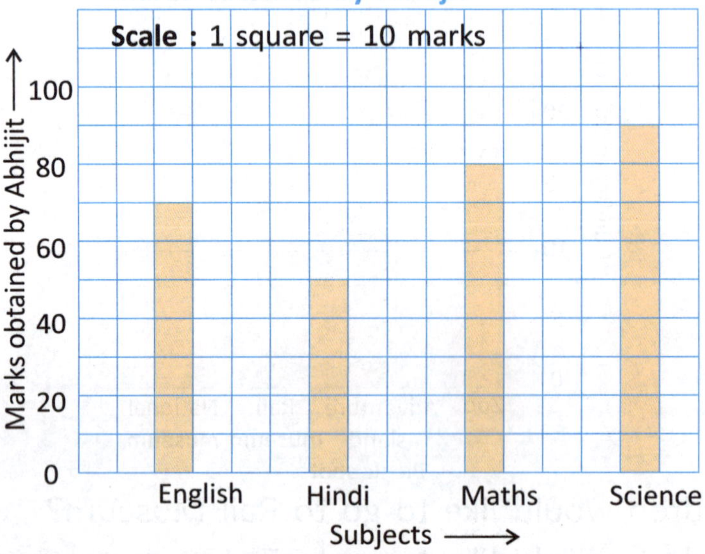

1. In which subject Abhijit got the highest marks?
2. In which subject Abhijit got the lowest marks?
3. Find the total marks obtained by him out of 400.

Fun With Maths

1. The given graph shows the number of boys and girls enrolled at four tuition centres.

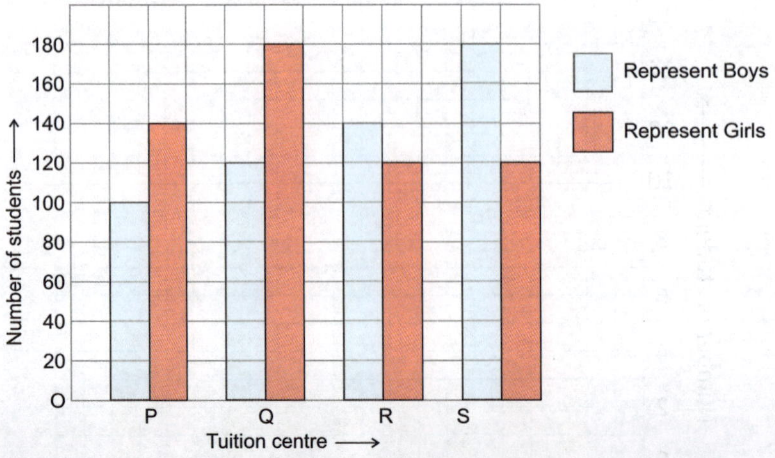

Observe the given graph and answer the following questions:

(i) How many boys are enrolled in all four tuition centres?

(a) 500 (b) 540 (c) 560 (d) 660

(ii) How many girls are enrolled in all four tuition centres?

(a) 500 (b) 540 (c) 560 (d) 580

(iii) The total number of students in the tuition centre Q is.

(a) 300 (b) 400 (c) 360 (d) 430

(iv) Which tuition centre has the lowest enrollment of students?

(a) P (b) Q (c) R (d) S

(v) What would be the total number of students at tuition centre P, if another 46 students want to enrol in it?

(a) 256 (b) 346 (c) 286 (d) 356

2. The given list shows the number of cars of each colour in a parking lot.

- There are 27 pink cars.
- There are 24 blue cars.
- There are 9 black cars.
- There are 15 green cars.

Pink	
Blue	
Black	
Green	

Cars in Parking Lot

Which key correctly completes the pictograph?

(a) Each  means 3 cars.

(b) Each  means 4 cars.

(c) Each  means 5 cars.

(d) Each  means 6 cars.

To get worksheet on this chapter scan this QR code

CODE-LLCr

Maths Lab Activity

Objective : To collect and represent data in the form of a bar graph.

Materials Required : Coloured papers, sketch pens, a pair of scissors, and glue stick.

Procedure/Demonstration :

1. Record the number of hours spent by each student in the class during a day in watching TV in the table shown below.

Name	Number of hours

Name	Number of hours

2. Write the names of the students along the horizontal line at equal distances and time spent (in hours) along the vertical line.
3. Now make strips of uniform width of different colours, for each student, of length according to time (in hours) spent by a child in watching TV. Paste these strips to form a bar graph.

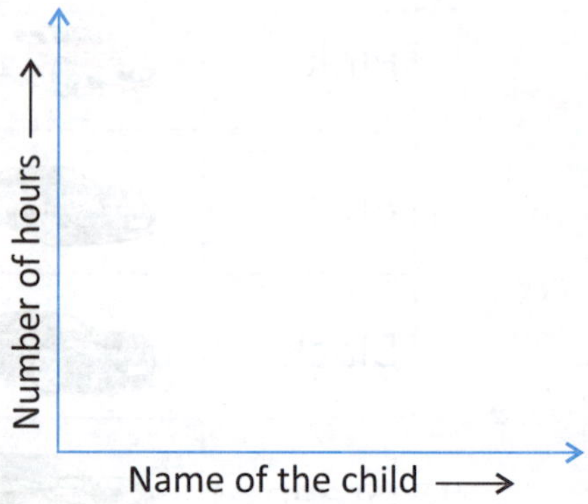

Now, answer the following questions :

(a) The numbers of students who spent 2 to 3 hours in watching TV a day is/are ______________

(b) The name(s) of student(s) who spent more than 6 hours a day watching TV is/are ______________

(c) The name(s) of the student(s) who spent maximum time in watching TV is/ are ______________

(d) The name(s) of the student(s) who spent exactly 2 hours a day in watching TV is/are ______________

Collect the data for other activities such as time spent in doing homework (in a week) by each student of your class and draw a bar graph for the data.

14

THEME 7 : PATTERNS
Patterns

Learning Target

Understanding patterns

I Can

- **I can** identify and extend patterns.
- **I can** solve questions on image patterns, number patterns and alphabet patterns.

Let Us Recall

In the previous class, we have read about patterns. Let us have a quick review of what we have read so far.

Exercise 14A

A Draw the next figures that follow the patterns :

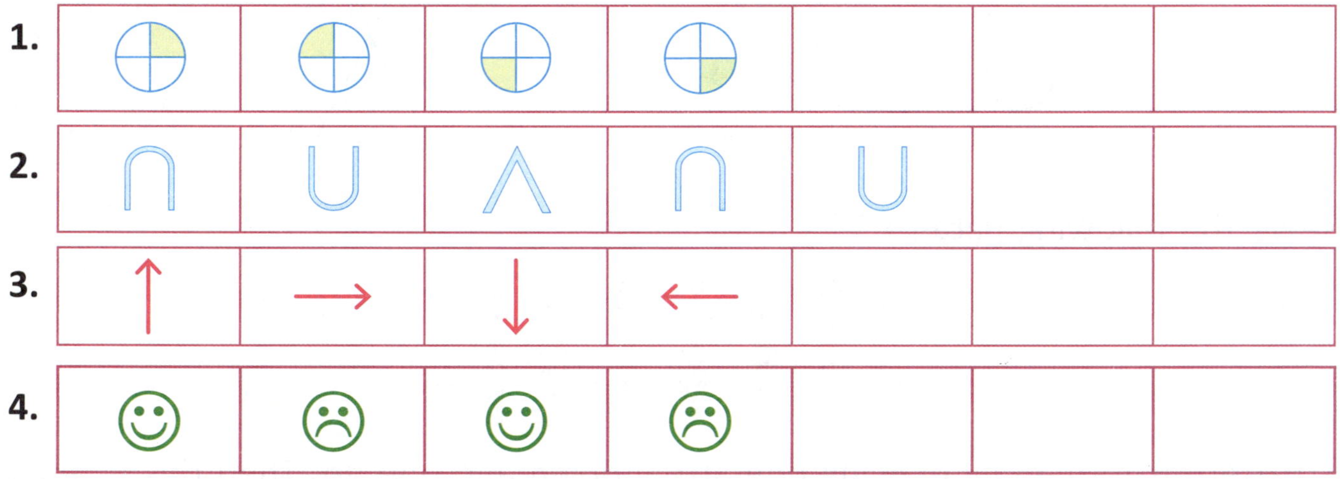

B Identify the rule and write the next three terms of each pattern :

1. 901, 802, 703, 604, ________, ________, ________

2. 110, 220, 330, 440, ________, ________, ________

3. A12, B23, C34, D45, ________, ________, ________

4. X, Y, X, Y, ________, ________, ________

Explore and Learn

In our daily life, we see so many patterns around us.

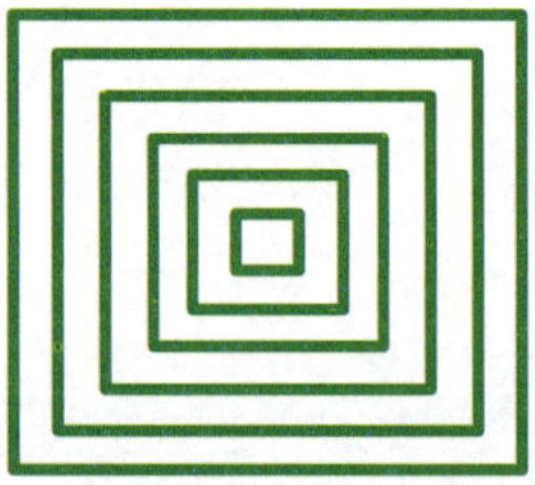

Patterns can be formed by drawing an image and its reflected image.

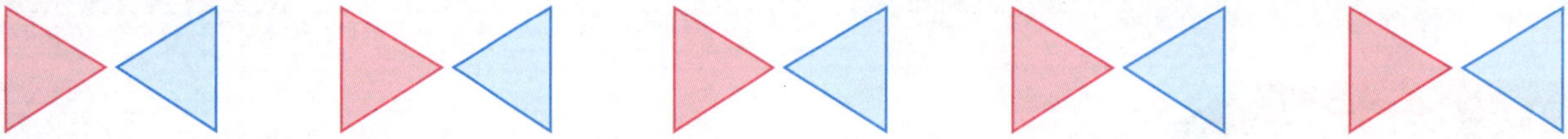

Patterns can be formed using any shape.

So, patterns are formed using geometrical shapes and designs.

We know that patterns are made by repeating a unit or block again and again.

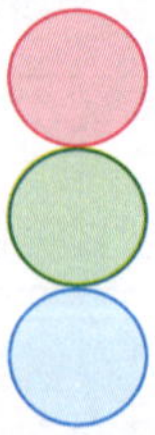

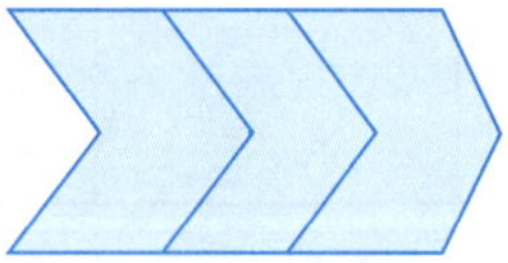

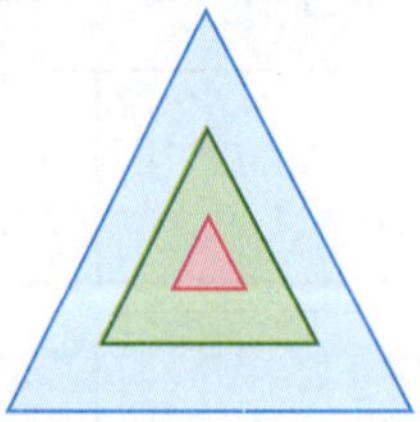

Observe the following pattern :

This pattern is formed by drawing one arrow down and one up. Then this is repeated.

A pattern formed by repetition of a single unit or shape which fills a plane by leaving no gaps and no overlaps is called a **tessellation**.

The brick wall is an example of a 3-D cuboid being placed one above the other to form a tessellation.

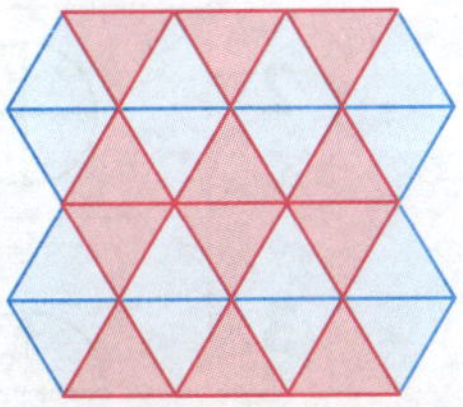

Tessellations are used to make pretty patterns for floor tiles.

Patterns can also be created using letters.

These letters can be arranged in different order :

AB, BC, CD, DE, EF, FG, ...

AC, BD, CE, DF, EG, ...

We can also make patterns using numbers like

12, 34, 56, 78, 910, ...

We can also make patterns using letters and numbers like

1A, 2B, 3C, 4D, 5E, 6F, 7G, 8H, ...

90A, 88B, 86C, 84D, 82E, 80F, 78G, 76H, 74I, 72J ...

Exercise 14B

Apply and Learn

A Make a tessellation pattern using the following blocks :

1. 

2. 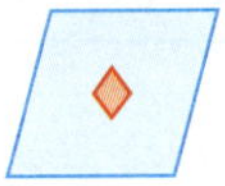

3. 

B Make a pattern using following blocks :

1. 

2. 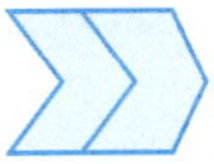

3. 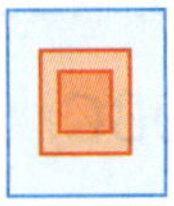

C Make a pattern with the blocks given below :

1. 

2. 

3. 

D Continue the patterns :

1.	↑	↓	↑↑	↓↓			

2.
3.
4.
5.
6.

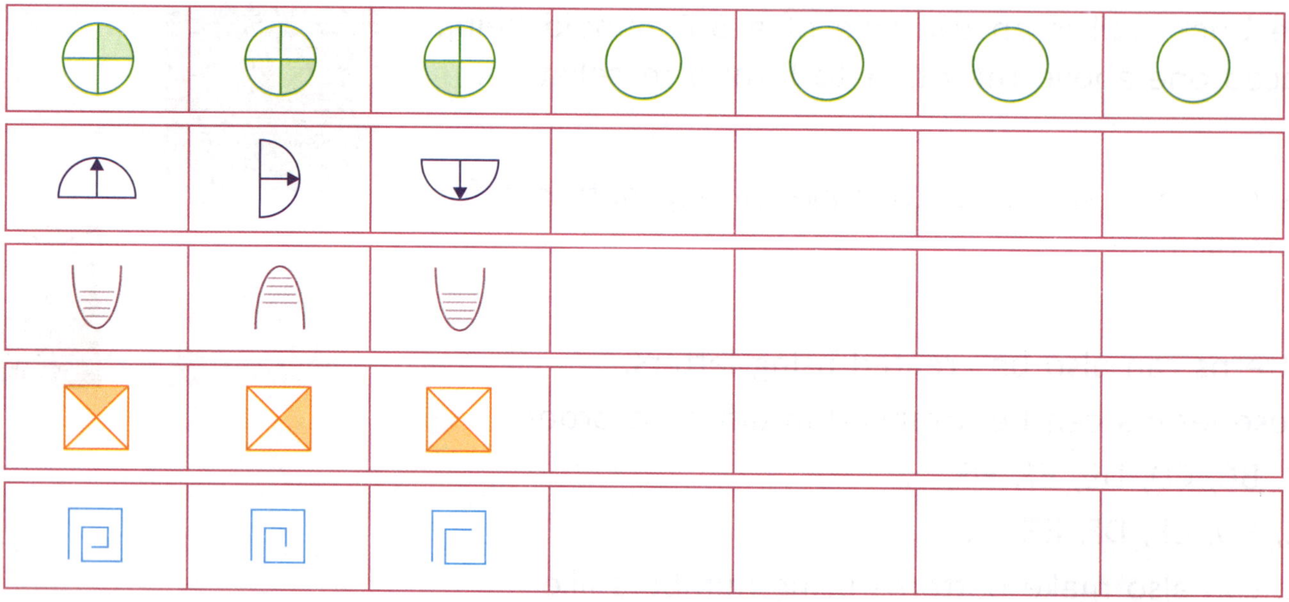

7. B, D, F, H, ________, ________, ________.

8. Y, W, U, S, ________, ________, ________.

9. QR, OP, MN, KL, ________, ________, ________.

10. KL9, LM8, MN7, ________, ________, ________.

11. 10, 20, 30, 40, 50, 60, ________, ________, ________.

12. 13, 23, 33, 43, 53, ________, ________, ________.

13. 2, 5, 10, 17, ________, ________, ________.

14. 51, 56, 61, 66, ________, ________, ________.

15. 8, 16, 24, ________, ________, ________.

16. 12A, 13B, 14C, ________, ________, ________.

17. 102B, 99D, 96F, ________, ________, ________.

18. 425A, 415B, 405C, ________, ________, ________.

19. 536AB, 530BC, 524CD, ________, ________, ________.

20. 616AA, 527BB, 438CC, ________, ________, ________.

Review and Refresh

A Write the next three terms of each pattern :

1. 1, 2, 4, 7, 11, ________, ________, ________.

2. 9A1, 8B2, 7C3, ________, ________, ________.

3. 415, 417, 419, ______, ______, ______.

4. B, E, H, K, ______, ______, ______.

B Write the next three terms of each pattern :

1. 491, 482, 473, 464, ______, ______, ______.

2. 4, 8, 12, 16, ______, ______, ______.

3. 9, 10, 12, 15, ______, ______, ______.

4. A1, C2, E3, G4, ______, ______, ______.

Mental Maths

1. The next term of the pattern 1, 2, 3, 5, 8, ... is ______.
2. The next term of the pattern LCD, MEF, NGH, ... is ______.
3. The next term of the pattern GGV, FFU,EET, ... is ______.
4. The next term of the pattern 7104, 8114, 9124, 10134, ... is ______.
5. The next term of the pattern A41, Z43, B45, Y47, ... is ______.
6. The next term of the pattern AA9B, BB8C, CC7D, DD6E, ... is ______.
7. Study the pattern carefully and complete it.

$1 \times 1 \times 1 = 1$

$2 \times 2 \times 2 = 8 = 3 + 5$

$3 \times 3 \times 3 = 27 = 7 + 9 + 11$

$4 \times 4 \times 4 = 64 = 13 + 15 + 17 + 19$

$5 \times 5 \times 5 = 125 = 21 + 23 +$ ______ + ______ + ______.

$6 \times 6 \times 6 = 216 =$ ______ + ______ + ______ + ______ + ______ + ______.

$7 \times 7 \times 7 = 343 =$ ______ + ______ + ______ + ______ + ______ + ______ + ______.

$8 \times 8 \times 8 =$ ______ = ______ + ______ + ______ + ______ + ______ + ______ + ______ + ______.

Fun With Maths

1. In the adjoining 4 × 4 square, four objects have been placed in such a way that no two objects are in the same row, column or diagonal. Subject to the same condition, find a solution for a 5 × 5 square using 5 objects and a 6 × 6 square 6 objects.

	X		
			X
X			
		X	

2. Three triangles are shown alongside. The numbers follow a certain pattern. You are required to identify that pattern and state the number behind question mark.

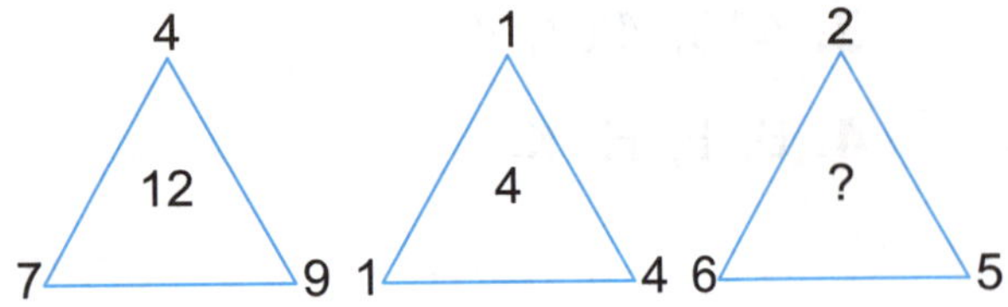

Which number replaces the question mark?

(a) 6 (b) 7 (c) 8 (d) 9

3. A number line is shown below. Here the numbers follow a certain pattern.

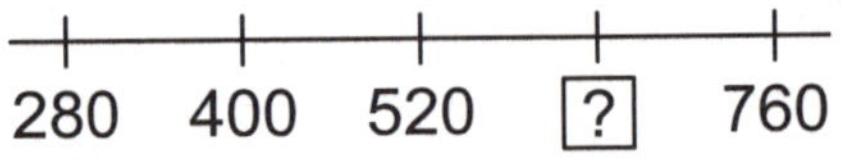

What is the missing number?

(a) 580 (b) 640 (c) 720 (d) 760

4. Following numbers follow a certain pattern the missing number is :

(a) 9000 (b) 8100 (c) 9100 (d) 10100

5. Five T-shirts are displayed at a shop. The numbers follow a pattern that needs to be identified.

Which of the following numbers is wrong in the above pattern?

(a) 14678 (b) 15678 (c) 16676 (d) 17878

To get worksheet on this chapter scan this QR code

CODE-tyyb

Maths Lab Activity

Objective : Understanding patterns in a calendar.

Materials Required : A calendar of any month.

Procedure/Demonstration :

1. Take a calendar of any month and mark a 3 × 3 box (9 dates) on it.
2. Add the 9 numbers of this box.

   10 + 11 + 12 + 17 + 18 + 19 + 24 + 25 + 26 = 162
3. Find the smallest number of the box Here it is 10.
4. Add 8 to it. So, 10 + 8 = 18.
5. Multiply the sum by 9. So, 18 × 9 = 162.
6. We can get the sum of the numbers of the selected box (obtained in step 2) without adding. To do so, simply multiply the middle number by 9. So, 18 × 9 = 162.
7. Do the above process for another 3 × 3 box and see whether it always works or not.

M	T	W	T	F	S	S
1	2	3	4	5	6	7
8	9	10	11	12	13	14
15	16	17	18	19	20	21
22	23	24	25	26	27	28
29	30	31				

CHECK YOUR PACE

(Based on Chapters 13, 14)

A The number of different subject books in a school library is given in the following table :

Subject	Hindi	English	Science	Mathematics	Social Science
Number of books	120	140	90	80	110

Draw a pictograph to represent the above data.

B The following bar graph shows the marks obtained by Vivek in 5 subjects in an annual examination. Study the bar graph and answer the following questions :

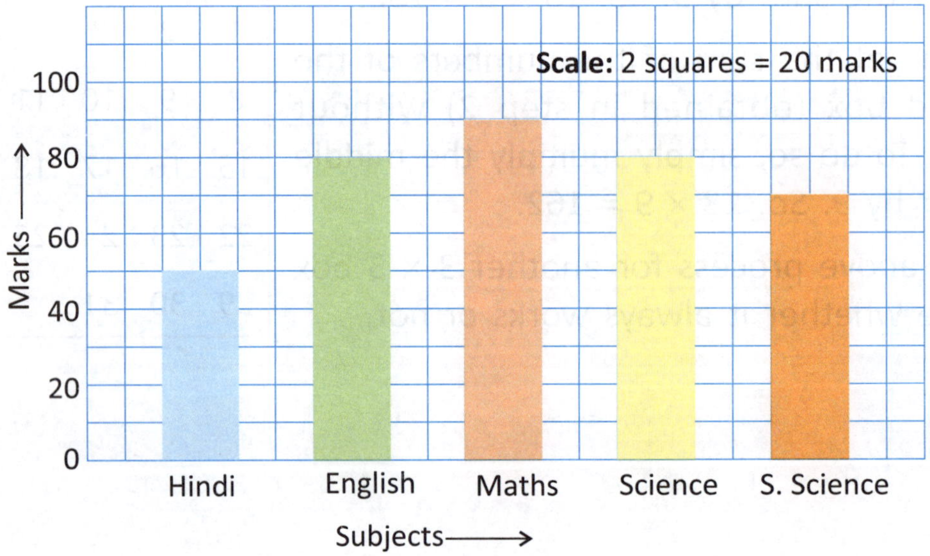

1. In which subject Vivek gets highest marks?
2. In which subject Vivek gets lowest marks?
3. In which two subjects Vivek gets equal marks?
4. In how many subjects does Vivek get 80 or more than 80 marks?
5. In how many subjects does Vivek get 50 or less than 50 marks?

C Write the next three terms of the patterns :

1. 109, 208, 307, 406, ________, ________, ________
2. 98, 87, 76, ________, ________, ________
3. AB9, CD8, EF7, ________, ________, ________
4. 1Z, 2Y, 3X, 4W, ________, ________, ________

MODEL TEST PAPER-1

[For Half Yearly Examination]
(Based on Chapters 1 to 6)

1. Fill in the blanks :

(a) In 8,07,623, 0 is at __________ place.

(b) The place value of __________ remains same whatever place it occupies in the place value chart.

(c) The predecessor the smallest 6-digit number is __________.

(d) The Hindu-Arabic numeral for XXXIX is __________.

(e) The fraction equivalent to $\frac{8}{9}$ with denominator 36 is __________.

(f) 85 × 85 = __________.

(g) Rounding 4603 to the nearest thousands gives __________.

2. Write T for true and F for false statements :

(a) A 5-digit number is always greater than a 4-digit number. __________

(b) The smallest 5-digit number using the digits 6, 0, 1, 8, 4 only once is 14,068. __________

(c) 100 thousands make ten lakhs. __________

(d) In Roman numeration system, we cannot write 0. __________

(e) $\frac{2}{3}$ of 15 is 10. __________

(f) $\frac{4}{7}$ is greater than $\frac{4}{9}$. __________

(g) $\frac{10}{10}$ is an improper fraction. __________

(h) 124 × 4000 is same as 1204 × 400. __________

3. Write the following numbers in figures :

(a) Three lakh eight thousand five. __________

(b) Nine lakh twenty seven. __________

4. Write the smallest 5-digit number using 3 different digits :

____

5. Reduce to the lowest terms :

(a) $\frac{24}{64}$ ______________________

(b) $\frac{24}{45}$ ______________________

6. Convert into mixed fractions :

(a) $\frac{47}{6}$ ______________ (b) $\frac{72}{5}$ ______________

7. Add / subtract :

(a) $\frac{5}{17} + \frac{1}{17} + \frac{3}{17} =$ ______________________

(b) $\frac{8}{21} - \frac{3}{21} =$ ______________________

8. Supply the mising digits :

(a)

	2		5	
+		6	4	5
	6	5		3

(b)

		6	0	5
+	2	5		8
	5		3	

9. Multiply :

(a) 4257 × 48

____

____

____

(b) 3124 × 152

____

____

____

10. Solve the following word problems :

(a) Find the number which is 2,148 more than 5,910

____

____

(b) The sum of two numbers is 8504. If one of the numbers is 3725, find the other.

____

____

MODEL TEST PAPER-2

[For Annual Examination]
(Based on Chapters 7 to 14)

1. Fill in the blanks :

(a) In a division sum, the number by which we divide the dividend is called ____________.

(b) 6508 ÷ 100 gives quotient = ____________ and remainder = ____________.

(c) Multiples of a number are ____________.

(d) Every non-zero number is a factor of ____________.

(e) The smallest composite number is ____________.

(f) A 4-sided polygon is called a ____________.

(g) A line has ____________ end points.

(h) Area is expressed in ____________ units of length.

2. Write T for true and F for false statements :

(a) The time between 12 mid-night and 12 noon is denoted as a.m. ____________

(b) The next term of the pattern
A1C, C2E, E3G, __ __ __ is G4H. ____________

(c) In a division sum, we have
Dividend = divisor × remainder + quotient. ____________

(d) Every number is a multiple of itself. ____________

(e) 2 is a composite number. ____________

(f) Parallel lines never meet. ____________

(g) Circumference of a circle is twice its diameter. ____________

(h) Area of a rectangle = length × breadth. ____________

3. Divide : 57,284 ÷ 6

4. **Check whether 60,816 is divisible by :**

(a) 2 ______

(b) 3 ______

(c) 4 ______

(d) 5 ______

(e) 9 ______

5. **Find the of LCM of 30 and 45**

6. **Find the perimeter and the area of a rectangle whose dimensions are :**

2 m and 80 cm.

______

______

______

7. **Add / subtract :**

(a) 121 cm 205 m + 81 cm 816 m

(b) 26 *l* 472 *ml* – 15 *l* 608 *ml*

8. **Convert :**

(a) 92 days into months and days.

(b) 126 minutes into hours and minutes.

ANSWERS

CHAPTER-1

Exercise 1A

A. **1.** Four thousand nine hundred eighty-five **2.** Eight thousand one hundred twenty
3. Nine thousand five hundred

B. **1.** 2429 **2.** 3470 **3.** 9503

C. **1.** hundreds **2.** ones **3.** thousands **4.** tens

D. **1.** 500 **2.** 80 **3.** 1000 **4.** 0

E. **1.** 4000 + 300 + 80 + 7 **2.** 2000 + 800 + 90 + 3 **3.** 1000 + 400

F. **1.** 2584 **2.** 6058 **3.** 4061 **4.** 8102

G. **1.** 8600 **2.** 3601 **3.** 9999 **4.** 2100

H. **1.** 2999 **2.** 5936 **3.** 4009 **4.** 9998

I. **1.** 4256, 4325, 4526, 4569 **2.** 1007, 1050, 1070, 1700

J. **1.** 9814, 6005, 4531, 2916 **2.** 7348, 7308, 7304, 7038

Exercise 1B

A.

	Lakhs	Thousands		Ones		
	L	T-Th	Th	H	T	O
1.		6	5	4	9	4
2.	1	4	9	2	0	6
3.	2	5	1	3	6	2
4.	3	5	0	0	0	8
5.	9	5	0	0	0	4

B. **1.** Fifty-three thousand, twenty-six.
2. Four lakh, eighty thousand, nine.
3. Two lakh, fifteen thousand, sixty.
4. Three lakh, five thousand, four hundred seven.
5. Seven lakh, one thousand, eight hundred twenty-four.

C. **1.** Twenty-nine thousand, five hundred two.
2. Six lakh, eighty-three thousand, five hundred twenty-seven.
3. Six lakh, fifty-three thousand, eight.

4. Seven lakh, fifty-eight.

5. Seven lakh, ninety-five thousand, three hundred twenty-six.

D. **1.** 15,512 **2.** 1,21,219 **3.** 4,30,006 **4.** 2,05,053 **5.** 5,00,001

Exercise 1C

A. **1.** 1 **2.** 7 **3.** 6 **4.** 3

B. **1.** 30 **2.** 6,00,000 **3.** 40,000 **4.** 0

C. **1.** 700 **2.** 5,00,000 **3.** 6 **4.** 50,000

D. 9,24,300; 64,000

E. **1.** 5,005 **2.** 50,050 **3.** 50,500 **4.** 50,050

F. **1.** 79,992 **2.** 7,920 **3.** 7,920 **4.** 7,920

G. **1.** 6,000 + 500 + 90 + 4 **2.** 60,000 + 9,000 + 8

3. 1,00,000 + 80,000 + 5,000 + 500 + 40 + 1 **4.** 5,00,000 + 10,000 + 9,000 + 30

H. **1.** 5,343 **2.** 2,50,394 **3.** 6,42,107 **4.** 5,00,505 **5.** 2,40,093 **6.** 9,04,200

Exercise 1D

A. **1.** $>$ **2.** $<$ **3.** $>$ **4.** $>$ **5.** $<$ **6.** $>$ **7.** = **8.** $>$

B. **1.** 5,320 **2.** 6,30,271 **3.** 8,93,162 **4.** 7,20,163

C. **1.** 21,951 **2.** 8,19,570 **3.** 6,09,268 **4.** 2,51,367

D. **1.** 351; 1,678; 2,500; 6,135; 21,015

2. 19,007; 26,871; 45,341; 3,65,727; 4,78,051

E. **1.** 7,19,076; 4,54,839; 2,81,263; 2,35,245; 81,526

2. 6,53,192; 6,35, 294; 1,28, 193; 68,156; 6,346

F. **1.** 65,831 **2.** 12,600 **3.** 6,89,960 **4.** 5,00,000

G. **1.** 7,35,999 **2.** 5,72,991 **3.** 5,32,599 **4.** 4,00,309

H. **1.** 98,631; 13,689 **2.** 73,210; 10,237 **3.** 9,84,320; 2,03,489

I. **1.** 1,00,000 **2.** 99,999

3. (a) greatest → 88,752 smallest → 22,578

(b) greatest → 88,410 smallest → 10,048

(c) greatest → 99,743 smallest → 33,479

4. (a) 1,111 (b) 1,023 **5.** (a) 99,998 (b) 98,765

Review and Refresh

A. **1.** Forty-three thousand, five hundred seventy-five **2.** Six lakh, twenty-nine thousand, one

3. Five lakh, forty **4.** Five lakh, ninety thousand, three hundred four

5. Eight lakh, five thousand, nine hundred four

6. One lakh, fifty-four thousand, six hundred eighty-seven

7. Thirty-two thousand, five hundred eight **8.** Two lakh, eight

B. **1.** 12,524 **2.** 20,008 **3.** 4,00,223 **4.** 8,15,905

C. **1.** 5,000 **2.** 7,00,000 **3.** 0

D. **1.** 1,00,000 + 20,000 + 5,000 + 100 + 90 + 7 **2.** 2,00,000 + 80,000 + 3,000 + 5

3. 5,00,000 + 40,000 + 1,000 + 900 + 30 + 8

E. **1.** 6,03,850 **2.** 5,03,219 **3.** 7,00,308 **4.** 2,03,010

F. **1.** > **2.** < **3.** < **4.** <

G. **1.** 298; 15,324; 15,630; 1,13,542 **2.** 29,812; 31,854; 1,25,000; 1,85,000

H. **1.** 1,25,471; 94,371; 61,832; 25,192 **2.** 1,00,008; 62,917; 45,132; 36,472

I. 1,00,000 **J.** 1,057

Mental Maths

1. 6,00,400 **2.** 6 **3.** 2,000 **4.** 5,02,073 **5.** 9,99,999 **6.** 99,987

7. 900 **8.** yes **9.** 1,000 **10.** 3,69,510

Fun with Maths

1. 20 **2.** David – 5, Peter – 7 **3.** (c) **4.** (i) (d) (ii) (d) (iii) (a) (iv) (b)

CHAPTER-2

Exercise 2

A. **1.** 4 **2.** 9 **3.** 15 **4.** 16 **5.** 20 **6.** 27

7. 19 **8.** 14 **9.** 34 **10.** 38 **11.** 39 **12.** 25

13. 30 **14.** 24 **15.** 7

B. **1.** XXI **2.** XIV **3.** XXIII **4.** XXXVII **5.** XXVII **6.** XXIX

7. XXXVI **8.** XXXV **9.** XIX **10.** XXXIII **11.** XXXVIII **12.** XXVI

13. XVI **14.** XVIII **15.** XV

C. **1.** > **2.** = **3.** < **4.** > **5.** = **6.** <

D. **1.** XIIII **3.** XVV **5.** VX

E. **1.** (d) **2.** (b) **3.** (f) **4.** (a) **5.** (c) **6.** (e)

Mental Maths

1. yes **2.** V **3.** V **4.** XXII **5.** XXXV **6.** 7 **7.** 29 **8.** no **9.** XXXI **10.** 3 times

Fun with Maths

1. Turn the page upside down. **2.** (c)

CHAPTER-3

Exercise 3A

G. **1.** $\frac{1}{2}$ **2.** $\frac{1}{3}$ **3.** $\frac{1}{3}$ **4.** $\frac{1}{4}$ **5.** $\frac{1}{4}$ **6.** $\frac{1}{3}$

H. **1.**
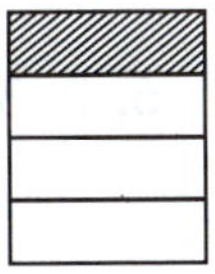
2.
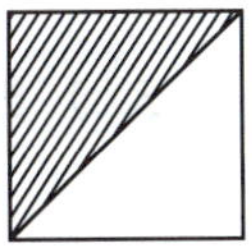
3.

4.
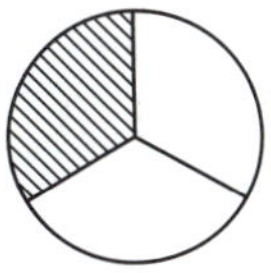
5.
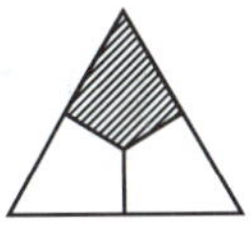
6.
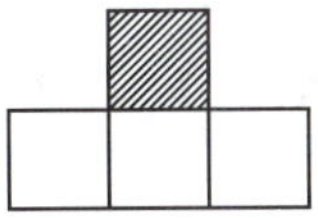

Exercise 3B

A. **2.** $\frac{5}{8}$, five-eighths **3.** $\frac{2}{6}$, two-sixths

4. $\frac{8}{9}$, eight-ninths **5.** $\frac{7}{12}$, seven-twelfths

B. **1.** $\frac{1}{7}$, one-seventh **2.** $\frac{3}{6}$, three-sixths **3.** $\frac{7}{10}$, seven-tenths

4. $\frac{3}{8}$, three-eighths **5.** $\frac{6}{15}$, six-fifteenths

C. **1.** 3, 11 **2.** 15, 16 **3.** 7, 9 **4.** 2, 15 **5.** 5, 11 **6.** 13, 22

D. **1.** $\frac{4}{7}$ **2.** $\frac{7}{15}$ **3.** $\frac{10}{21}$ **4.** $\frac{22}{35}$

E. 5 **F.** 6

G. **1.** 2 **2.** 3 **3.** 2 **4.** 4 **5.** 4 **6.** 15

H. **1.** 4 **2.** 3 **3.** 6 **4.** 6 **5.** 10 **6.** 8

Exercise 3C

A. **1.** $\frac{8}{10}, \frac{12}{15}, \frac{16}{20}$ **2.** $\frac{2}{8}, \frac{3}{12}, \frac{4}{16}$ **3.** $\frac{4}{6}, \frac{6}{9}, \frac{8}{12}$ **4.** $\frac{10}{18}, \frac{15}{27}, \frac{20}{36}$ **4.** $\frac{8}{20}, \frac{12}{30}, \frac{16}{40}$

B. **1.** 15 **2.** 8 **3.** 5 **4.** 3

C. **1.** 22 **2.** 40 **3.** 21 **4.** 9

D. **1.** $\frac{21}{28}$ **2.** $\frac{15}{20}$ **3.** $\frac{12}{16}$ **4.** $\frac{18}{24}$ **5.** $\frac{30}{40}$ **6.** $\frac{36}{48}$

E. **1.** equivalent **2.** not equivalent **3.** equivalent **4.** not equivalent **5.** not equivalent **6.** equivalent

Exercise 3D

A. **1.** no **2.** yes **3.** yes **4.** no **5.** yes **6.** no **7.** no **8.** yes

B. **1.** $\frac{4}{5}$ **2.** $\frac{4}{57}$ **3.** $\frac{8}{45}$

C. **1.** $\frac{1}{2}$ **2.** $\frac{3}{4}$ **3.** $\frac{5}{7}$ **4.** $\frac{3}{4}$ **5.** $\frac{3}{4}$ **6.** $\frac{2}{3}$

Exercise 3E

A. **1.** $<$ **2.** $>$ **3.** $>$ **4.** $>$ **5.** $<$ **6.** $<$

B. **1.** $\frac{5}{7}$ **2.** $\frac{3}{7}$ **3.** $\frac{8}{14}$ **4.** $\frac{9}{10}$

C. **1.** $\frac{3}{10}$ **2.** $\frac{3}{16}$ **3.** $\frac{2}{5}$ **4.** $\frac{1}{7}$

D. **1.** $<$ **2.** $>$ **3.** $>$

Exercise 3F

A. **1.** 1, 2, 3 **2.** 1, 2, 3 **3.** 3, 5, 8 **4.** 2, 4, 6 **5.** 1, 2, 2, 5 **6.** 2, 3, 5, 10

B. **1.** $\frac{3}{4}$ **2.** $\frac{2}{3}$ **3.** $\frac{15}{19}$ **4.** $\frac{11}{14}$ **5.** $\frac{3}{4}$ **6.** $\frac{13}{15}$

7. $\frac{3}{4}$ **8.** $\frac{22}{35}$

Exercise 3G

A. **1.** $\frac{4}{13}$ **2.** $\frac{2}{17}$ **3.** $\frac{2}{11}$ **4.** $\frac{1}{6}$ **5.** $\frac{3}{17}$ **6.** $\frac{2}{7}$

B. **1.** 11 **2.** 7 **3.** 4 **4.** 21 **5.** 7 **6.** 16

Exercise 3H

A. 1, 4 **B.** 1, 4 **C.** 1, 2, 4, 5 **D.** none **E.** 1, 2, 5, 7, 8, 9

F. **1.** $\frac{10}{3}$ **2.** $\frac{13}{2}$ **3.** $\frac{23}{3}$ **4.** $\frac{76}{9}$ **5.** $\frac{68}{7}$ **6.** $\frac{99}{8}$ **G.** **1.** $1\frac{1}{9}$ **2.** $3\frac{4}{5}$ **3.** $2\frac{5}{8}$ **4.** $6\frac{4}{9}$ **5.** $9\frac{2}{7}$ **6.** $18\frac{3}{5}$

Review and Refresh

A. **1.** $\frac{18}{45}$ **2.** $\frac{18}{21}$ **3.** $\frac{18}{28}$ **4.** $\frac{18}{48}$

B. **1.** $\frac{24}{32}$ **2.** $\frac{20}{32}$ **3.** $\frac{16}{32}$ **4.** $\frac{18}{32}$

C. **1.** $>$ **2.** $>$ **3.** $=$ **4.** $<$ **5.** $>$ **6.** $>$

D. **1.** $\frac{2}{3}$ **2.** $\frac{5}{9}$ **3.** $\frac{5}{7}$ **4.** $\frac{2}{3}$ **5.** $\frac{5}{7}$

E. **1.** $\frac{5}{4}$ **2.** $\frac{11}{10}$ **3.** $\frac{1}{2}$ **4.** $\frac{11}{14}$ **5.** $\frac{13}{18}$ **6.** $\frac{1}{3}$ **7.** $\frac{9}{14}$ **8.** $\frac{11}{15}$

F. **1.** $\frac{1}{10}$ **2.** $\frac{1}{3}$ **3.** $\frac{1}{3}$ **4.** $\frac{1}{12}$ **5.** $\frac{5}{14}$ **6.** $\frac{5}{12}$ **7.** $\frac{1}{30}$ **8.** $\frac{3}{34}$

Mental Maths

1. 3 **2.** 5, 11 **3.** $\frac{6}{19}$ **4.** $\frac{12}{27}$ **5.** yes **6.** $\frac{8}{15}$

7. $\frac{5}{9}$ **8.** $\frac{7}{7}$, 1 **9.** yes **10.** $\frac{6}{5}$

Fun with Maths

1. $\frac{6}{9}$ **2.** (i) (a) (ii) a) (iii) (d) (iv) (c) (v) (a)

3. (c)

Check Your Pace (Based on Chapters 1, 2, 3)

A. **1.** Forty thousand, two hundred fifty-seven **2.** Eighty thousand, five hundred six.

3. Seventy thousand, one **4.** Nine lakh, six thousand, one hundred sixteen.

5. Six lakh, ten thousand, fifty-three.

B. **1.** 21,004 **2.** 86,407 **3.** 7,09,008 **4.** 4,40,354

C. **1.** 70,000 **2.** 40 **3.** 1,000 **4.** 9,00,000

D. **1.** 40,000 + 700 + 30 + 6 **2.** 5,00,000 + 40,000 + 6,000 + 100 + 90 + 7

3. 9,00,000 + 80,000 + 3,000 + 200 + 10 + 6 **4.** 4,00,000 + 90,000 + 2,000 + 10 + 6

5. 7,00,000 + 5,000 + 200 + 90 + 3

E.

	Smallest number	Greatest number
1.	78,251	7,80,521
2.	65,437	6,50,437
3.	71,751	2,90,175

F. **1.** 14 **2.** 18 **3.** 21 **4.** 37

G. **1.** XII **2.** XIX **3.** XXV **4.** XXXIV

H. **1.** 15 **2.** XXXI **3.** XXIV

I. **1.** $\frac{15}{25}$ **2.** $\frac{4}{15}$

J. **1.** > **2.** < **3.** > **4.** <

K. **1.** $\frac{11}{15}$ **2.** $\frac{5}{8}$ **3.** $\frac{2}{3}$ **4.** $\frac{1}{2}$ **5.** $\frac{1}{3}$ **6.** $\frac{3}{7}$

L. **1.** $\frac{15}{7}$ **2.** $\frac{37}{8}$ **3.** $\frac{47}{9}$

CHAPTER-4

Exercise 4A

A. **1.** 784 **2.** 855 **3.** 735 **4.** 939 **5.** 989 **6.** 696

B. **1.** 914 **2.** 912 **3.** 655 **4.** 890

Exercise 4B

A. **1.** 9,885 **2.** 6,897 **3.** 8,779 **4.** 8,878 **5.** 5,792 **6.** 3,549

7. 6,838 **8.** 9,897 **9.** 8,989 **10.** 9,687 **11.** 7,967 **12.** 8,898

B. **1.** 8,649 **2.** 9,060 **3.** 8,069 **4.** 8,877

C. **1.**

	3	0	5	[7]
	5	6	[1]	0
+	[1]	2	0	2
	9	[8]	6	9

2.

	8	7	[2]	4
	0	1	4	[2]
+	1	[0]	1	3
	[9]	8	7	9

Exercise 4C

A. **1.** 9,938 **2.** 6,422 **3.** 8,302 **4.** 9,236 **5.** 9,406 **6.** 8,838

7. 9,437 **8.** 9,959

B. **1.** 8,709 **2.** 6,804 **3.** 8,378 **4.** 9,731

C. **1.**

	4	[4]	5	6
+	[2]	7	4	[8]
	7	2	[0]	4

2.

	5	0	[7]	5
+	3	[9]	7	[7]
	[9]	0	5	2

3.

		[4]	5	8
		5	[5]	4
+		6	4	[7]
	1	6	5	[9]

4.

	5	3	2	[0]
	[1]	9	0	8
+	2	5	[9]	3
	9	[8]	2	1

D. **1.** 1,999 **2.** 1,099 **3.** 8,632; 2,368; 11,000 **4.** 8,620; 2,068; 10,688

Exercise 4D

A. **1.** 8,272 **2.** 6,760 **3.** 8,644 **4.** 2,457 **5.** 2,739 **6.** 2,435

B. **1.** 2,369 **2.** 5,809 **3.** 8,409 **4.** 2,331 **5.** 3,775 **6.** 9,644

C. **1.** 3,821 **2.** 5,773 **3.** 7,232 **4.** 7,475 **5.** 9,275 **6.** 4,795

D. **1.** 8,326 **2.** 6,217 **3.** 7,382 **4.** 7,549 **5.** 9,939 **6.** 2,876

E. **1.** 5,775 **2.** 1,937 **3.** 2,699; 3042 **4.** 7923; 3142

Exercise 4E

1. ₹3,528 **2.** 4,297 **3.** 6,745 **4.** 9,416 **5.** 9,335 **6.** 6,525

7. 9,307 **8.** 7,603 **9.** 6,942 **10.** 7,565

Review and Refresh

A. **1.** 8,897 **2.** 9,941

B. **1.**

	5	[4]	6	0
+	2	5	[3]	8
	[7]	9	9	[8]

2.

	2	[7]	8	3
+	[5]	3	[2]	6
	8	1	0	[9]

C. 1,999 **D.** **1.** 8,754 **2.** 0 **3.** 9,351 **4.** 8,234 ; 1754

Mental Maths

1. 2,615, 6,038 **2.** 5,914 **3.** 0 **4.** 1,999 **5.** 1

6. 5,500 **7.** 8,539

Fun with Maths

1.

6	7	2
1	5	9
8	3	4

2. 23

CHAPTER-5

Exercise 5A

A. **1.** 272 **2.** 231 **3.** 155 **4.** 79 **5.** 148 **6.** 228

B. **1.** 25 **2.** 103 **3.** 130

C. **1.** 504 **2.** 269 **3.** 178

D. **1.** 540 **2.** 310

Exercise 5B

A. **1.** 1,155 **2.** 1,311 **3.** 4,354 **4.** 3,215 **5.** 1,213 **6.** 2,016
7. 2,202 **8.** 3,103 **9.** 1,202

B. **1.** 4,212 **2.** 3,123 **3.** 3,111 **4.** 2,325 **5.** 1,124 **6.** 2,220

C. **1.** 2,213 **2.** 3,571 **3.** 3,323 **4.** 4,212

D. **1.**

	[8]	5	7	[6]
−	6	[2]	1	3
	2	3	[6]	3

2.

	9	[8]	6	3
−	[5]	6	3	[0]
	4	2	[3]	3

Exercise 5C

A. **1.** 3,568 **2.** 3,491 **3.** 2,784 **4.** 1,793 **5.** 2,867 **6.** 1,729
7. 1,737 **8.** 1,729 **9.** 2,828

B. **1.** 3,369 **2.** 267 **3.** 1,388 **4.** 1,679 **5.** 2,863 **6.** 4,206

C. **1.** 5,223 **2.** 3,751 **3.** 1,997 **4.** 3,453 **5.** 1,891 **6.** 2,918

D. **1.**

	6	[3]	2	8
−	2	7	[2]	5
	[3]	6	0	[3]

2.

	[7]	4	3	[7]
−	4	[9]	6	4
	2	4	[7]	3

3.

	8	6	[1]	7
−	4	[2]	2	[3]
	[4]	3	9	4

4.

	5	[7]	[8]	2
−	[4]	7	3	8
	1	0	4	[4]

Exercise 5D

1. 115 **2.** 128 **3.** 481 **4.** 6,811 **5.** 4,862 **6.** 9,286 **7.** 0
8. 800 **9.** 0 **10.** 749 **11.** 1,657 **12.** 2,458 **13.** 796 **14.** 5,789
15. 90

Exercise 5E

1. 6,713 **2.** 8,703 **3.** 7,468 **4.** 2,849 **5.** 5,280 **6.** 1,553 **7.** 3,521
8. 2,851 **9.** 4,350

Exercise 5F

1. 2,558 **2.** 4,349 **3.** 5,551 **4.** 4,290 **5.** 5,061 **6.** 3,483
7. 4,879 **8.** 2,982 **9.** 3,685 **10.** 1,669

Review and Refresh

A. **1.** 2,655 **2.** 568 **3.** 4,053 **4.** 5,273

B. **1.**

$$\begin{array}{r} 8\ 7\ \boxed{1}\ 9 \\ -\ \boxed{3}\ 1\ 2\ \boxed{5} \\ \hline 5\ \boxed{5}\ 9\ 4 \\ \hline \end{array}$$

2.

$$\begin{array}{r} 6\ 0\ \boxed{7}\ 8 \\ -\ \boxed{6}\ 6\ \boxed{9} \\ \hline \boxed{5}\ 4\ 0\ 9 \\ \hline \end{array}$$

C. **1.** 8,999 **2.** 7,852 **3.** 856 **4.** 4,776

Mental Maths

1. 6,542; 2,260 **2.** Smallest, Largest **3.** 0 **4.** 3,600
5. 1 **6.** 1 **7.** 1,875 **8.** 2,329 **9.** 4,400 **10.** 5,000

Fun with Maths

1. 98 – 7 + 6 + 5 + 4 – 3 – 2 – 1, 98 – 7 – 6 – 5 – 4 + 3 + 21 **2.** (b)

CHAPTER-6

Exercise 6A

A. **1.** 196 **2.** 315 **3.** 198 **4.** 105 **5.** 621 **6.** 400
7. 544 **8.** 424

B. **1.** 54 **2.** 60 **3.** 200 **4.** 112 **5.** 126 **6.** 222
7. 450 **8.** 180 **9.** 270

Exercise 6B

A. **1.** 705 **2.** 936 **3.** 676 **4.** 2,891 **5.** 6,704 **6.** 6111
7. 4,008 **8.** 1,528

B. **1.** 16,989 **2.** 8,048 **3.** 9,990 **4.** 8,631 **5.** 7,480 **6.** 7,224
7. 9,134 **8.** 9,204

Exercise 6C

A. **1.** 336 **2.** 3,021 **3.** 10,044 **4.** 12,408 **5.** 21,850 **6.** 6,864

B. **1.** 1,260 **2.** 5,194 **3.** 5,712 **4.** 13,608

Exercise 6D

A. **1.** 2,44,224 **2.** 77,625 **3.** 8,40,048 **4.** 9,50,136 **5.** 4,04,040 **6.** 3,55,168

B. **1.** 2,81,874 **2.** 61,623 **3.** 7,55,055 **4.** 3,97,155

Exercise 6E

A. **1.** 518 **2.** 38 **3.** 1 **4.** 4,875 **5.** 1 **6.** 0
7. 0 **8.** 1 **9.** 0 **10.** 43,194 **11.** 1 **12.** 1,576
13. 600 **14.** 0

B. **1.** 1,26,350 **2.** 1,73,700 **3.** 2,08,880 **4.** 6,99,180 **5.** 3,63,500 **6.** 17,56,200
7. 1,68,300 **8.** 4,23,000 **9.** 4,34,000 **10.** 5,81,000 **11.** 9,60,000 **12.** 5,92,00

Exercise 6F

1. ₹ 29,876 **2.** 40,430 **3.** 85,100 **4.** ₹ 1,55,990 **5.** ₹ 11,20,875 **6.** 9,97,680
7. ₹ 2,13,520 **8.** 1,48,500 **9.** 2,97,110 **10.** 9,15,625 litres
11. 1,374 kg 750 g **12.** 184 kg

Exercise 6G

1. 1,225 **2.** 4,225 **3.** 7,225 **4.** 9,90,025 **5.** 6,32,025 **6.** 5,609
7. 9,016 **8.** 38,021 **9.** 2,45,009 **10.** 9,90,016

Exercise 6H

A. **1.** 50 **2.** 170 **3.** 400 **4.** 3,540 **5.** 29,830 **6.** 30
7. 470 **8.** 880 **9.** 9,280 **10.** 13,530
B. **1.** 200 **2.** 400 **3.** 6,900 **4.** 3,100 **5.** 38,500 **6.** 1,000
7. 800 **8.** 6,000 **9.** 4,400 **10.** 29,800
C. **1.** 9,000 **2.** 8,000 **3.** 34,000 **4.** 16,000 **5.** 87,000 **6.** 8,000
7. 5,000 **8.** 6,000 **9.** 87,000 **10.** 47,000

Exercise 6I

A. **1.** 80 **2.** 100 **3.** 90 **4.** 100
B. **1.** 400 **2.** 700 **3.** 700
C. **1.** 5,000 **2.** 9,000 **3.** 10,000
D. **(a)** **1.** 1,800 **2.** 5,240 **3.** 1,500
(b) **1.** 1,800 **2.** 5,300 **3.** 1,500
E. **1.** 2,400 **2.** 2,000 **3.** 2,400 **4.** 3,000

Review and Refresh

A. **1.** 4,896 **2.** 2,592 **3.** 1,224 **4.** 3,18,835 **5.** 91,812 **6.** 7,93,288
B. **1.** 29,350 **2.** 9,87,400 **3.** 7,97,500 **4.** 7,62,000
C. **1.** 1 **2.** 0 **3.** 4,532 **4.** 1,493
D. **1.** ₹ 1,23,975 **2.** 5,19,000

Mental Maths

1. 28 **2.** 2,845 **3.** 0, 0 **4.** 20; 1,592 **5.** 3,60,000 **6.** 99,000
7. 39,000 **8.** 2,19,000 **9.** 56,000 **10.** 5

Fun with Maths

1. Turn the page upside down **2.** (a) 101 (b) 10101 **3.** (b)

Check Your Pace (Based on Chapters 4, 5, 6)

A. **1.** 7,657 **2.** 8,525 **3.** 9,139 **4.** 8,166

B. **1.** 3,155 **2.** 5,843 **3.** 3,484 **4.** 1,633

C. **1.**

$$\begin{array}{r} 7\ \boxed{6}\ 2\ 6 \\ +\ 1\ 7\ 4\ \boxed{6} \\ \hline \boxed{9}\ 3\ \boxed{7}\ 2 \\ \hline \end{array}$$

2.

$$\begin{array}{r} \boxed{6}\ 3\ 0\ 4 \\ -\ 4\ \boxed{6}\ 3\ 7 \\ \hline 1\ 6\ \boxed{6}\ \boxed{7} \\ \hline \end{array}$$

D. **1.** 3,451 **2.** 7,605

E. **1.** 1,028 **2.** 4,160 **3.** 7,542 **4.** 17,094 **5.** 13,680 **6.** 45,593

F. **1.** 25,600 **2.** 4,39,000 **3.** 1,61,000

G. **1.** 580 **2.** 8,180 **3.** 190 **4.** 4,730

CHAPTER-7

Exercise 7A

1. 11 **2.** 9 **3.** 8 **4.** 9 **5.** 8 **6.** 7 **7.** 9
8. 4 **9.** 10

Exercise 7B

A. **1.** 3, 3 **2.** 3, 6 **3.** 7, 1 **4.** 5, 5 **5.** 5, 2

B. **1.** 6, 3 **2.** 9, 1 **3.** 7, 6 **4.** 8, 2 **5.** 9, 2

C. **1.** 21 **2.** 8 **3.** 41 **4.** 13 **5.** 13 **6.** 12
7. 14 **8.** 12 **9.** 26 **10.** 15

D. **1.** 11, 1 **2.** 22, 1 **3.** 32, 1 **4.** 17, 1 **5.** 17, 3 **6.** 7, 3
7. 8, 1 **8.** 10, 1 **9.** 13, 5 **10.** 15, 2

Exercise 7C

A. **1.** 312 **2.** 232 **3.** 110 **4.** 121 **5.** 195 **6.** 120
7. 159 **8.** 151 **9.** 88 **10.** 87

B. **1.** 52, 3 **2.** 64, 2 **3.** 36, 6 **4.** 44, 1 **5.** 89, 1 **6.** 81, 3
7. 77, 1 **8.** 69, 5 **9.** 33, 6 **10.** 53, 1

Exercise 7D

A. **1.** 169 **2.** 457 **3.** 681 **4.** 800 **5.** 520 **6.** 524
7. 1455 **8.** 630

B. **1.** Q = 1780, R = 1 **2.** Q = 1660, R = 3 **3.** Q = 279, R = 1
4. Q = 877, R = 2 **5.** Q = 585, R = 2 **6.** Q = 571, R = 4

C. **1.** odd **2.** odd **3.** even **4.** even

Exercise 7E

1. Q = 9, R = 1 **2.** Q = 16, R = 7 **3.** Q = 542, R = 8
4. Q = 791, R = 8 **5.** Q = 87, R = 32 **6.** Q = 40, R = 35
7. Q = 35, R = 0 **8.** Q = 85, R = 1

B. **1.** 9 **2.** 1 **3.** 0 **4.** 1 **5.** 1 **6.** 12 **7.** 21 **8.** 0 **9.** 16

Exercise 7F

1. ₹ 13 **2.** 6 **3.** 18 kg **4.** 70 **5.** 81 **6.** ₹ 125 **7.** 75 **8.** 4608 **9.** 145 **10.** 1225 **11.** ₹ 35, `₹525 **12.** 352 km

Review and Refresh

A. **1.** 45, 5, 9 **2.** 21, 7, 3 **3.** 152, 8, 19

B. **1.** Q = 120, R = 0 **2.** Q = 256, R = 0 **3.** Q = 795, R = 0 **4.** Q = 880, R = 0 **5.** Q = 420, R = 0 **6.** Q = 522, R = 1 **7.** Q = 451, R = 0 **8.** Q = 850, R = 4

C. **1.** Q = 3, R = 5 **2.** Q = 18, R = 5 **3.** Q = 17, R = 3 **4.** Q = 68, R = 15 **5.** Q = 41, R = 3 **6.** Q = 50, R = 10 **7.** Q = 31, R = 2 **8.** Q = 935, R = 8

D. **1.** 105 **2.** 9762 **3.** 2314 **4.** 0

E. **1.** ₹450 **2.** 105 km **3.** 2575

Mental Maths

1. 48 ÷ 8 = 6 and 48 ÷ 6 = 8 **2.** less **3.** 1000 **4.** 421, 8 **5.** 63, 8 **6.** 5926 **7.** 2895 **8.** 0 **9.** 1111 **10.** yes

Fun with Maths

1. (8,888 – 888) ÷ 8 = 1,000 **2.** (i) (b) (ii) (a) (iii) (b) (iv) (b) **3.** (b)

CHAPTER-8

Exercise 8A

A. **2.** ✓ **3.** × **4.** ✓ **5.** × **6.** ✓ **7.** × **8.** ✓ **9.** ✓ **10.** ×

B. **1.** 48, 60, 72, 84 **2.** 36, 45, 54, 63 **3.** 56, 70, 84, 98 **4.** 44, 55, 66, 77 **5.** 76, 95, 114, 133 **6.** 100, 125, 150, 175

C. **1.** yes **2.** yes **3.** yes **4.** no **5.** no **6.** 8, 16, 24, 32, 40 **7.** 14, 28, 42 **8.** 6, 12, 18, 24 **9.** 90 **10.** 60

D. **1.** 12, 8 **2.** 12, 13 **3.** 15, 18 **4.** 182 **5.** 240

Exercise 8B

A. **1.** ✓ **2.** ✓ **3.** ✓ **4.** × **5.** ✓ **6.** ✓ **7.** ✓ **8.** ✓ **9.** × **10.** ✓

B. **1.** yes **2.** yes **3.** no **4.** yes **5.** no **6.** 1, 5, 7, 35 **7.** 1, 2, 3, 6, 9, 18, 27, 54 **8.** 1, 2, 3, 6, 13, 26, 39, 78 **9.** 1, 2, 3, 4, 6, 8, 9, 12, 16, 18, 24, 36, 48, 72, 144 **10.** 1 and 125 **11.** 1 and 120

C. **1.** multiple, factors **2.** multiple, factors **3.** factors, multiple

Exercise 8C

1. 11, 13, 17, 19
2. 7, 11, 13, 17, 19, 23, 29, 31
3. 29, 31, 37, 41, 43, 47
4. 41, 43, 47, 53, 59, 61, 67, 71, 73
5. 61, 67, 71, 73, 79, 83, 89, 97
6. 4, 6, 8, 9, 10, 12, 14, 15, 16, 18
7. 52, 54, 55, 56, 57, 58, 60, 62, 63, 64, 65, 66, 68, 69
8. 19, 37, 61
9. 21, 39, 49, 51, 63, 91
10. 2
11. 2
12. 36, 38, 40, 42, 44, 46, 48, 50, 52, 54
13. 41, 43, 45, 47, 49, 51, 53, 55, 57, 59, 61, 63, 65, 67, 69
14. 58, 76, 104, 116
15. 25, 53, 69, 103, 115, 203
16. 1
17. no
18. (a) 18,976; 65,180; 7,854 (b) 7,962; 17,094; 1,79,622 (c) 7,008; 51,936; 2,56,068
(d) 8,325; 29,840; 8,74,265 (e) 5,886; 53,883 (f) 63,980; 25,000; 1,83,040
19. $2 \times 2 \times 2 \times 3$
20. $2 \times 2 \times 2 \times 3 \times 3$
21. $2 \times 2 \times 2 \times 2 \times 2 \times 3$
22. (a) $2 \times 2 \times 2 \times 3 \times 5$ (b) $2 \times 3 \times 5 \times 5$ (c) $2 \times 3 \times 5 \times 7$
23. (a)

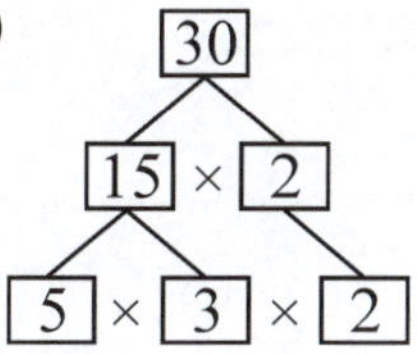

(b)

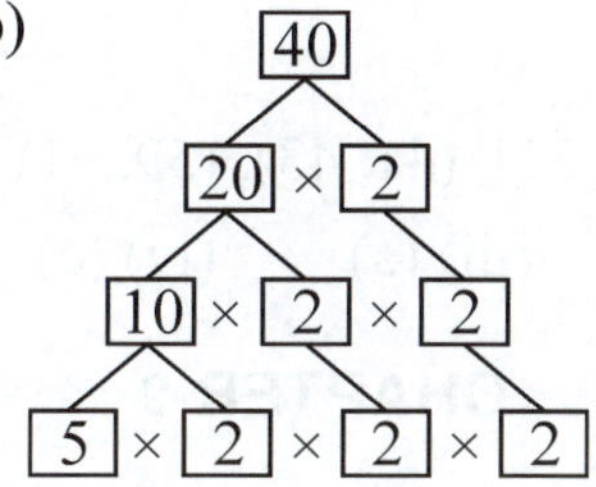

(c)

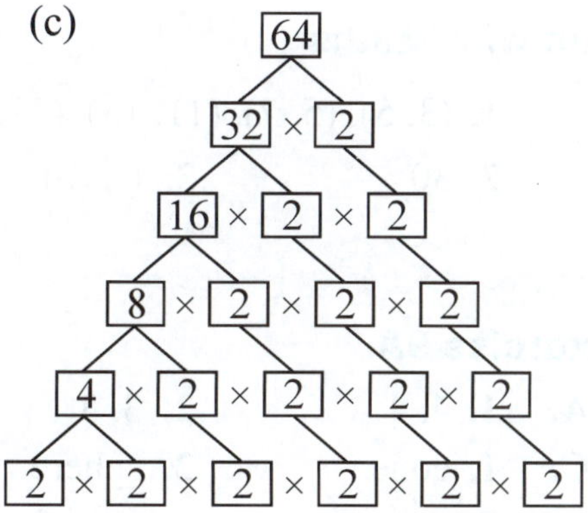

(d)

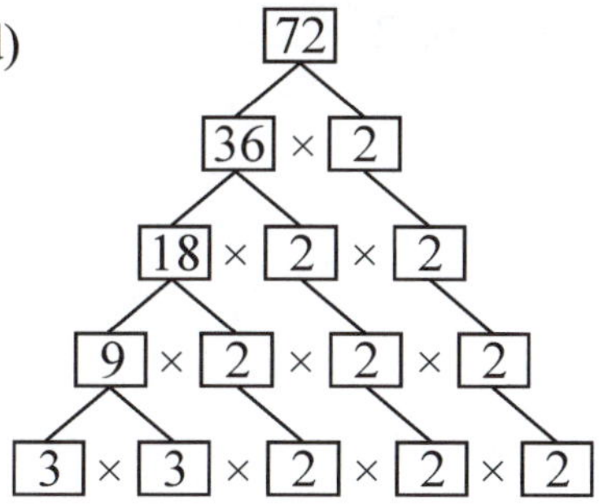

(e)

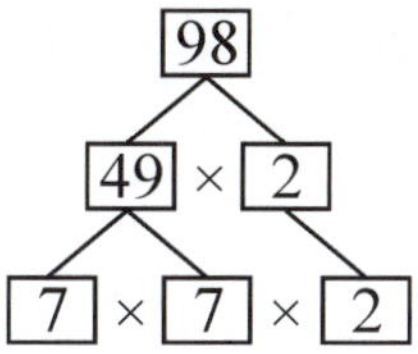

(f)

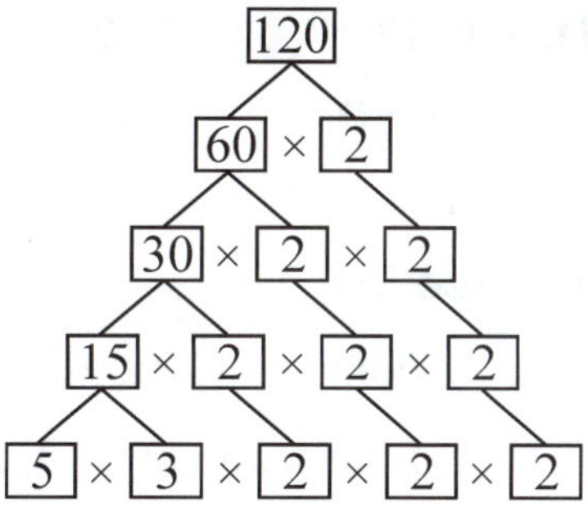

Exercise 8D

A. 1. 1, 3 2. 1, 2 3. 1, 3, 9 4. 1, 7 5. 1, 2, 5, 10
6. 1, 2, 4, 8

B. 1. 8 2. 5 3. 9 4. 16 5. 6 6. 15

C. 1. 9 2. 22 3. 9 4. 3 5. 9

Exercise 8E

A. 1. 30, 60 2. 20, 40, 60 3. 36, 72 4. 12, 24, 36, 48, 60

B. **1.** 30 **2.** 40 **3.** 60 **4.** 390 **5.** 40 **5.** 72

C. **1.** 90 **2.** 39 **3.** 60 **4.** 1,368 **5.** 792 **6.** 315 **7.** 360 **8.** 720

Review and Refresh

1. no **2.** yes **3.** yes **4.** 15, 30, 45, 60 **5.** 210

6. no **7.** yes **8.** yes **9.** 1, 2, 4, 5, 10, 20, 25, 50, 100 **10.** 1, 180

11. no **12.** 23,076; 52,056; 1,70,766 **13.** 17, 19, 23, 29, 31, 37

14. 46, 48, 49, 50, 51, 52, 54, 55, 56, 57, 58 **15.** 2 **16.** $2 \times 2 \times 2 \times 2 \times 2 \times 3$

17. $3 \times 5 \times 7$ **18.**

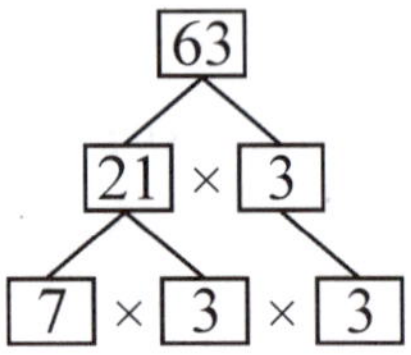

Mental Maths

1. yes **2.** 1 **3.** factors, multiple **4.** no **5.** 1, 5, 25

6. the number itself **7.** the number itself **8.** 2 **9.** 2 **10.** 1

Fun with Maths

1. (3, 5), (5, 7), (11, 13), (17, 19), (29, 31), (41, 43), (59, 61) and (71, 73)

2. 30 **3.** (i) (b) (ii) (d) (iii) (a) (iv) (c)

CHAPTER-9

Exercise 9A

A. **1.** 4, 4 **2.** 3, 3 **3.** 6, 8 **4.** 2 **5.** 2 **6.** 12

C. **1.** cone **2.** sphere **3.** cylinder **4.** sphere **5.** cuboid **6.** cylinder **7.** cube **8.** cylinder **9.** cylinder **10.** cylinder **11.** cuboid **12.** sphere

D. **1.** 12 **2.** 2 **3.** faces **4.** 0 **5.** 2

Exercise 9B

1. 5 **2.** 2

Exercise 9D

A. Point — 1, P and 5, D; Line — 2, $\overleftrightarrow{RS}$

Line segment — 3, $\overline{XY}$ and 6, $\overline{LM}$; Ray — 4, $\overrightarrow{AB}$

B. C, D, E, F, G and H

C. AE, AF, AB, EF, EB, FB

D. **1.** $\overline{AB}$, $\overline{BC}$, $\overline{CA}$ **2.** $\overline{PQ}$, $\overline{QR}$, $\overline{RS}$, $\overline{SP}$ **3.** $\overline{AB}$, $\overline{BC}$, $\overline{CD}$, $\overline{DE}$, $\overline{EF}$, $\overline{FA}$

4. $\overline{AB}$, $\overline{BC}$, $\overline{CD}$, $\overline{DE}$, $\overline{EF}$, $\overline{AF}$ **5.** $\overline{PQ}$, $\overline{QR}$, $\overline{RS}$, $\overline{ST}$, $\overline{PT}$ **6.** $\overline{AB}$, $\overline{BC}$, $\overline{CD}$, $\overline{DE}$, $\overline{EF}$, $\overline{AF}$

E. **1.** $\overline{AD}$, $\overline{DE}$, $\overline{DF}$, $\overline{CE}$ **2.** $\overrightarrow{AB}$, $\overrightarrow{EG}$, $\overrightarrow{DF}$, $\overrightarrow{AF}$

3. $\overleftrightarrow{CE}$, $\overleftrightarrow{AF}$ **4.** $\overleftrightarrow{CE}$ and $\overleftrightarrow{AF}$

F. **1.** $\overleftrightarrow{PS}$, $\overleftrightarrow{XY}$ and $\overleftrightarrow{AB}$, $\overleftrightarrow{QR}$ **2.** $\overline{AB}$, $\overline{XY}$, $\overline{PQ}$, $\overline{QR}$ **3.** $\overrightarrow{PA}$, $\overrightarrow{QB}$, $\overrightarrow{SX}$, $\overrightarrow{RY}$

G. **1.** T **2.** F **3.** F **4.** T **5.** T

Exercise 9E

A. **1.** yes **2.** yes **3.** yes **4.** no **5.** no **6.** yes

D. **1.** True **2.** False **3.** False **4.** True **5.** True

Exercise 9F

B. **1.** 4 cm **2.** 6 cm **3.** 7 cm **4.** 2 cm

C. **1.** 10 cm **2.** 16 cm **3.** 18 cm **4.** 6 cm

E.

Radius	3 cm	10 cm	3 m	5 m	15 mm
Diameter	6 cm	20 cm	6 m	10 m	30 mm

F. **1.** centre **2.** circumference **3.** twice **4.** chord **5.** chord

Review and Refresh

B. **1.** 5; $\overline{AB}$, $\overline{BC}$, $\overline{CD}$, $\overline{AD}$, $\overline{BD}$ **2.** 5; $\overline{PQ}$, $\overline{QR}$, $\overline{RS}$, $\overline{ST}$, $\overline{TU}$

C. **1.** line segments; $\overline{AC}$, $\overline{CD}$; Ray; $\overrightarrow{AB}$, $\overrightarrow{DE}$

2. line segments; $\overline{PR}$, $\overline{RT}$ Ray; $\overrightarrow{PQ}$, $\overrightarrow{RS}$, $\overrightarrow{TU}$

D. **1.** Q **2.** T **3.** Q **4.** T **5.** Q

F.

Radius	5 cm	8 cm	9 cm	7 cm	25 cm
Diameter	10 cm	16 cm	18 cm	14 cm	50 cm

H. **1.** T **2.** T **3.** F **4.** T **5.** F **6.** T

7. F **8.** F **9.** T

Mental Maths

1. No **2.** Yes **3.** No **4.** Yes **5.** No **6.** Yes

7. No **8.** No **9.** Yes **10.** No

Fun with Maths

2. (i) (b) (ii) (a) (iii) (a) (iv) (d) (v) (b) **3.** (d)

Check Your Pace (Based on Chapters 7, 8, 9)

A. **1.** Q = 14; R = 2 **2.** Q = 9; R = 8 **3.** Q = 59; R = 2

4. Q = 88; R = 4 **5.** Q = 208; R = 0 **6.** Q = 617; R = 0

7. Q = 946; R = 3 **8.** Q = 1,629 ; R = 3

B. **1.** Q = 59; R = 2 **2.** Q = 70; R = 6 **3.** Q = 832; R = 0

4. Q = 4; R = 32 **5.** Q = 8; R = 1 **6.** Q = 72; R = 19

C. **1.** 12, 24, 36, 48 **2.** 56 **3.** 150

D. **1.** 1 **2.** 24 **3.** 20

E. 31, 37, 41, 43, 47

F. 2, 7, 7

G. 3 H. 54 I. $\overline{AC}$, $\overrightarrow{AB}$, $\overrightarrow{CD}$

J. **1.** 7 cm **2.** 9 cm **3.** 12 cm

K. **1.** 8 cm **2.** 16 cm **3.** 20 cm

L. **1.** centre **2.** Circumference **3.** half **4.** longest **5.** equal **6.** triangle **7.** line segment **8.** plane **9.** parallel **10.** ray

CHAPTER-10

Exercise 10A

A. **1.** 16 cm **2.** 16 cm **3.** 18 cm **4.** 20 cm **5.** 16 cm **6.** 22 cm

B. **1.** 9 cm **2.** 14 cm **3.** 17 cm **4.** 16 cm **5.** 20 cm **6.** 28 cm **7.** 14 cm **8.** 26 cm **9.** 28 cm **10.** 19 cm **11.** 24 cm **12.** 20 cm

Exercise 10B

B. **1.** 4 sq cm **2.** 9 sq cm **3.** 16 sq cm **4.** 25 sq cm **5.** 49 sq cm **6.** 18 sq cm **7.** 8 sq cm **8.** 10 sq cm **9.** 8 sq cm **10.** 18 sq cm **11.** 18 sq cm **12.** 9 sq cm

C. **1.** 36 sq m **2.** 144 sq cm **3.** 400 sq cm

D. **1.** 10 sq cm **2.** 84 sq cm **3.** 150 sq cm

E. **1.** 5,000 sq m **2.** 48 sq cm **3.** 17,000 sq cm **4.** 20,900 sq cm **5.** 60,040 sq cm

F. **1.** 400 sq cm **2.** 49 sq cm **3.** 12,544 sq m **4.** 324 sq m **5.** 8464 sq dm **6.** 65,536 sq dm

G. **1.** 29 cm **2.** 34 cm **3.** 56 cm

Mental Maths

1. 1 sq cm **2.** 144 sq mm **3.** 2 sq m **4.** square **5.** length, breadth **6.** side × side **7.** 48 sq cm **8.** 1 sq cm

Fun with Maths

1.

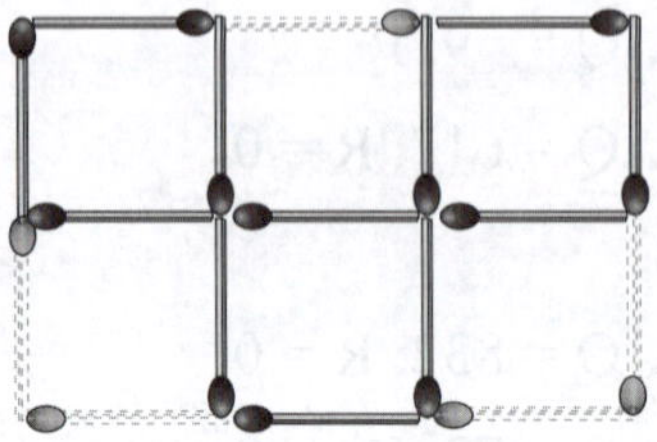

2. (b)

CHAPTER-11

Exercise 11A

A. **1.** 500 cm **2.** 1600 cm **3.** 820 cm **4.** 4550 cm

B. **1.** 2 m 5 cm **2.** 8 m 16 cm **3.** 16 m 25 cm **4.** 34 m 5 cm

C. **1.** 500 **2.** 1 kg **3.** 2 kg

D. **1.** 500 g

E. **1.** 10

F. **1.** 500 ml

Exercise 11B

A. **1.** 500 cm **2.** 1200 cm **3.** 9200 cm **4.** 15,200 cm **5.** 80 cm **6.** 160 cm **7.** 470 cm **8.** 540 cm **9.** 1665 cm **10.** 9605 cm **11.** 329 cm **12.** 62 cm

B. **1.** 4.75 m **2.** 17.50 m **3.** 24.65 m **4.** 39.86 m **5.** 7.3 m **6.** 11 m **7.** 17.2 m **8.** 20.5 m **9.** 48.3 m **10.** 51.9 m **11.** 1.55 m **12.** 2.90 m

C. **1.** 80 mm **2.** 190 mm **3.** 540 mm **4.** 730 mm **5.** 92 mm **6.** 639 mm **7.** 725 mm **8.** 978 mm

D. **1.** 7,000 m **2.** 12,000 m **3.** 12,050 m **4.** 26,212 m **5.** 1,08,208 m **6.** 2,16,080 m **7.** 4,93,196 m **8.** 5,00,050

E. **1.** 1 km 580 m **2.** 8 km 560 m **3.** 7 km 003 m **4.** 9 km 567 m

F. **1.** 95 cm **2.** 2 m 75 cm **3.** 6 m 18 cm **4.** 8 m 03 cm

G. **1.** 1 cm 6 mm **2.** 3 cm 7 mm **3.** 5 cm 2 mm **4.** 8 cm 3 mm

Exercise 11C

A. **1.** 38 cm 5 mm **2.** 66 cm 1 mm **3.** 20 m 7 cm **4.** 38 m 40 cm **5.** 171 km 634 m **6.** 210 km 858 m

B. **1.** 50 cm 9 mm **2.** 28 cm 7 mm **3.** 36 m 66 cm **4.** 56 m 56 cm **5.** 10 km 248 m **6.** 21 km 884 m

Exercise 11D

A. **1.** 48,000 g **2.** 63,000 g **3.** 84,000 g **4.** 1,91,000 g **5.** 7,050 g **6.** 16,325 g **7.** 42,980 g **8.** 75,105 g

B. **1.** 2 kg 456 g **2.** 3 kg 208 g **3.** 7 kg 562 g **4.** 8 kg 5 g **5.** 16 kg 892 g **6.** 18 kg 196 g **7.** 25 kg 008 g **8.** 32 kg 451 g

Exercise 11E

A. **1.** 9 kg 620 g **2.** 14 kg 85 g **3.** 81 kg 901 g **4.** 129 kg 695 g

B. **1.** 4 kg 225 g **2.** 2 kg 680 g **3.** 14 kg 560 g **4.** 47 kg 705 g

C. **1.** 7 kg 720 g **2.** 6 kg 780 g **3.** 34 kg 60 g **4.** 895 g **5.** 2 kg 425 g **6.** 23 kg 550 g

Exercise 11F

A. 1. 2,000 ml 2. 9,000 ml 3. 24,000 ml 4. 56,000 ml 5. 75,000 ml 6. 83,000 ml
7. 1,03,000 ml 8. 8,57,000 ml 9. 5,210 ml 10. 10,090 ml 11. 29,785 ml 12. 44,109 ml

B. 1. 1 *l* 309 ml 2. 18 *l* 596 ml 3. 2 *l* 645 ml 4. 8 *l* 345 ml 5. 56 *l* 210 ml 6. 83 *l* 218 ml
7. 90 *l* 003 ml 8. 96 *l* 352 ml

Exercise 11G

A. 1. 13 *l* 875 ml 2. 22 *l* 210 ml 3. 102 *l* 165 ml 4. 147 *l* 822 ml

B. 1. 3 *l* 625 ml 2. 4 *l* 705 ml 3. 4 *l* 200 ml 4. 5 *l* 686 ml
5. 39 *l* 750 ml 6. 28 *l* 681 ml

C. 1. 7 *l* 650 ml 2. 12 *l* 325 ml 3. 37 *l* 580 ml 4. 23 *l* 250 ml
5. 1 *l* 525 ml 6. 23 *l* 125 ml

Review and Refresh

A. 1. 700 cm 2. 90 cm 3. 436 cm 4. 782 cm

B. 1. 3 m 25 cm 2. 15 m 40 cm 3. 15 m 7 cm

C. 1. 5,000 m 2. 45,000 m 3. 87,000 m 4. 15,040 m
5. 25,215 m 6. 95,261 m 7. 1,00,010 m 8. 2,16,126 m

D. 1. 5 kg 627 g 2. 7 kg 15 g 3. 4 kg 7 g 4. 2 kg 10 g

E. 1. 4 *l* 278 ml 2. 3 *l* 96 ml 3. 2 *l* 8 ml 4. 6 *l* 397 ml

F. 1. 10 m 40 cm 2. 11 m 3. 14 km 120 m 4. 12 km 150 m
5. 15 kg 925 g 6. 7 kg 399 g 7. 12 *l* 450 ml 8. 28 *l* 166 ml

G. 1. 3 km 650 m 2. 4 km 650 m 3. 4 m 50 cm 4. 4 m 75 cm
5. 3 kg 675 g 6. 6 kg 265 g 7. 29 *l* 680 ml 8. 44 *l* 750 ml

Mental Maths

1. 228 2. 36,000; 36,00,000 3. 42,107 4. 15 5. 7, 5
6. 6 km 327 m 7. 472 8. 12,108 9. 26; 750 10. 12; 705

Fun with Maths

1. Both are equal. 2. yes 3. (d) 4. (b)

CHAPTER-12

Exercise 12A

A. 1. 4 : 00 2. 5 : 10 3. 4 : 40 4. 1 : 15 5. 1 : 30 6. 11 : 10 7. 6 : 55 8. 1 : 25

B. 1. 60 2. 366 3. June 4. September 5. August 6. 12 hours 7. 5 minutes

Exercise 12B

A. 1. 3 : 10 2. 4 : 15 3. 5 : 50 4. 6 : 25 5. 8 : 55 6. 9 : 40
7. 12 : 00 8. 12 : 45 9. 1 : 05 10. 7 : 20 11. 6 : 20 12. 10 : 25

Exercise 12C

A. **1.** a.m. **2.** p.m. **3.** p.m. **4.** p.m. **5.** a.m. **6.** p.m. **7.** p.m. **8.** p.m.

B. **1.** 5 : 45 p.m. **2.** 6 : 40 a.m. **3.** 12 : 05 a.m. **4.** 12 : 10 a.m. **5.** 2 : 40 a.m. **6.** 9 : 35 p.m. **7.** 8 : 15 a.m. **8.** 4 : 10 p.m. **9.** 11 : 30 p.m. **10.** 12 : 10 p.m. **11.** 1 : 10 a.m. **12.** 5 : 35 a.m. **13.** 11 : 50 a.m. **14.** 11 : 50 p.m.

C. **1.** 9 : 35 a.m. **2.** 11 : 00 p.m. **3.** 2 : 10 a.m. **4.** 11 : 00 p.m. **5.** 12 mid-night **6.** 12 noon **7.** 1 : 10 a.m. **8.** 12 : 50 p.m. **9.** 11 : 30 a.m. **10.** 7 : 00 a.m.

Exercise 12D

A. **1.** 720 seconds **2.** 900 seconds **3.** 1,380 seconds **4.** 1,920 seconds

B. **1.** 480 minutes **2.** 750 minutes **3.** 1,812 minutes **4.** 2,700 minutes

C. **1.** 68 hours **2.** 87 hours **3.** 108 hours

D. **1.** 504 hours **2.** 840 hours **3.** 672 hours

E. **1.** 60 months **2.** 72 months **3.** 128 months

F. **1.** 240 days **2.** 180 days **3.** 312 days

G. **1.** 12 minutes **2.** 50 minutes **3.** 6 minutes 40 seconds **4.** 12 minutes 30 seconds **5.** 27 minutes **6.** 30 minutes 40 seconds

H. **1.** 25 days **2.** 45 days **3.** 37 days 22 hours **4.** 41 days 16 hours **5.** 47 days 22 hours **6.** 50 days 5 hours

I. **1.** 1 week 3 days **2.** 52 weeks **3.** 4 weeks 2 days **4.** 12 weeks 1 day **5.** 14 weeks **6.** 14 weeks 2 days

J. **1.** 4 months and 1 day **2.** 12 months 20 days **3.** 2 months and 10 days **4.** 3 months and 22 days **5.** 12 months and 4 days **6.** 16 months 10 days

K. **1.** 10 years 8 months **2.** 30 years **3.** 33 years 4 months **4.** 45 years **5.** 79 years 2 months **6.** 83 years 4 months

Exercise 12E

A. **1.** 40 **2.** 35 **3.** 50

B. **1.** 1 hour 30 minutes **2.** 45 minutes **3.** 3 hours 40 minutes **4.** 1 hour 55 minutes **5.** 6 : 00 pm **6.** 12 : 35 pm **7.** 12 : 30 a.m.

Exercise 12F

1. 33 **2.** 27 **3.** 73 **4.** 28 October **5.** 11th May **6.** 16th May **7.** 35 **8.** 31 days **9.** 12th January **10.** 13th September

Review and Refresh

A. **1.** 2 : 05 **2.** 4 : 10 **3.** 8 : 30 **4.** 9 : 55 **5.** 10 : 00 **6.** 1 : 30 **7.** 5 : 55 **8.** 3 : 05

B. **1.** 6 : 30 a.m **2.** 8 : 10 a.m. **3.** 1 : 45 p.m. **4.** 12 : 20 a.m.

C. **1.** 1 minute 1 second **2.** 3 minutes 5 seconds **3.** 4 minutes 40 seconds **4.** 7 minutes 15 seconds

D. **1.** 1 hour 15 minutes **2.** 2 hours 5 minutes **3.** 3 hours 20 minutes **4.** 4 hours 7 minutes

E. **1.** 6 days 6 hours **2.** 30 days 10 hours **3.** 10 days 5 hours **4.** 22 days 12 hours

F. **1.** 6 years **2.** 4 years 2 months **3.** 8 years 4 months **4.** 5 years

Mental Maths

1. 24 **2.** a.m. **3.** p.m. **4.** 25 **5.** 7 : 30 **6.** 4 : 40

7. 3 : 40 **8.** 1 minute **9.** noon **10.** 1 : 30 p.m.

Check Your Pace (Based on Chapters 10, 11, 12)

A. **1.** 20 cm **2.** 30 cm **3.** 18 cm **4.** 20 cm

B. **1.** 6 sq. cm **2.** 12 sq.cm **3.** 10 sq.cm

C. **1.** 56 sq cm **2.** 100 sq.cm

D. **1.** 15 km 250 m **2.** 56 km 81 m **3.** 8 km 7 m **4.** 126 km 700 m

E. **1.** 2 kg 875 g **2.** 4 kg 83 g **3.** 26 kg 270g **4.** 15 kg 80 g

F. **1.** 8 *l* 35 ml **2.** 21 *l* 572 ml **3.** 81 *l* 80 ml **4.** 216 *l* 576 ml

G. **1.** 24 km 930 m **2.** 80 kg 201 g **3.** 56 *l* 975 ml **4.** 47 km 995 m

H. **1.** 1 : 30 p.m. **2.** 2 : 10 a.m. **3.** 11 : 05 a.m. **4.** 11 : 40 p.m.

I. **1.** 480 minutes **2.** 150 months **3.** 255 seconds **4.** 2 hours 16 minutes **5.** 8 days 18 hours **6.** 6 months 6 days

CHAPTER-13

Exercise 13A

A. **1.** 8 **2.** 3 **3.** Neha, Ridhima **4.** Shubham, 10 **5.** 31

B. **1.** Sleighing **2.** 30 **3.** Ice Skating

Exercise 13C

A. **1.** 15 **2.** 25 **3.** 30 **4.** 80 **5.** Adventure Island

B. **1.** School Bus **2.** 12 **3.** 8 **4.** 5

C. **1.** Science **2.** Hindi **3.** 290

Fun with Maths

1. (i) (b) (ii) (c) (iii) (a) (iv) (a) (v) (c) **2.** (a)

CHAPTER-14

Exercise 14A

A. **1.**

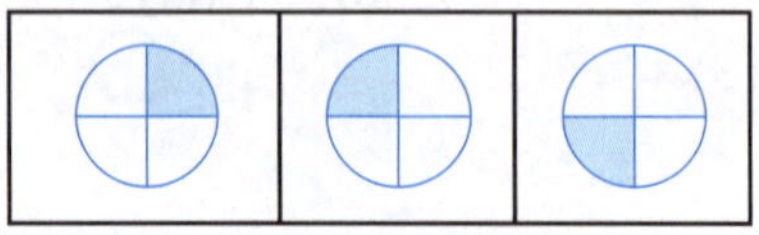

2.

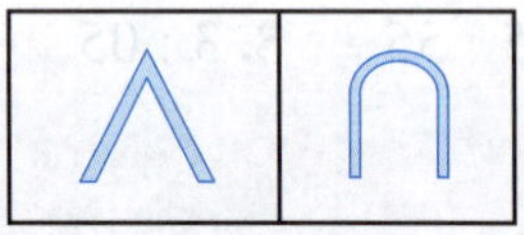

3. 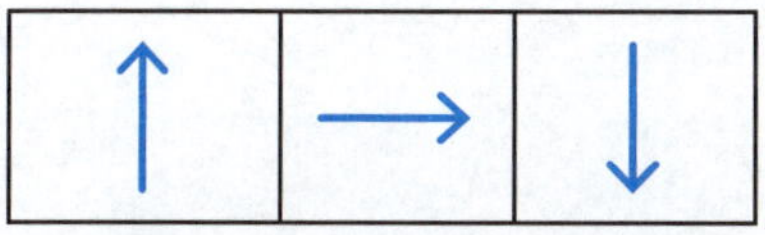

4. 

B. **1.** 505, 406, 307 **2.** 550, 660, 770
3. E56, F67, G78 **4.** X, Y, X.

Exercise 14B

D. **1.** 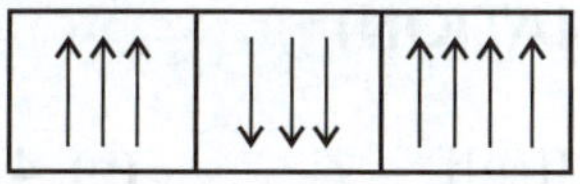

2. 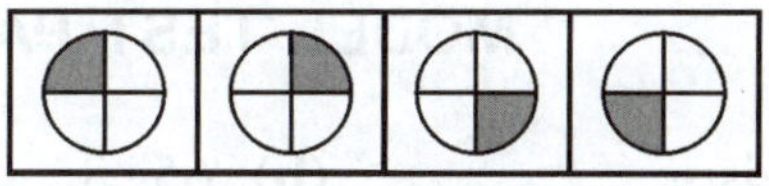

3. 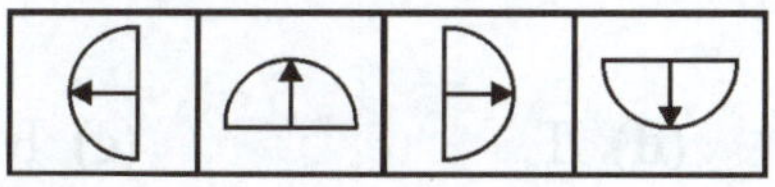

4. 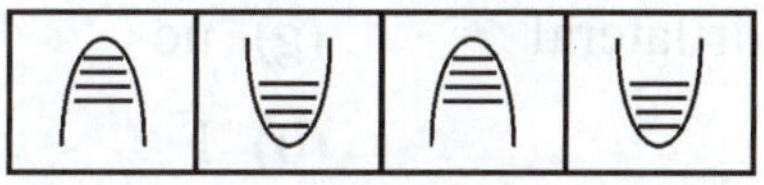

5. 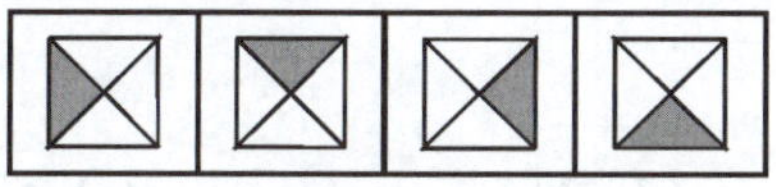

6. 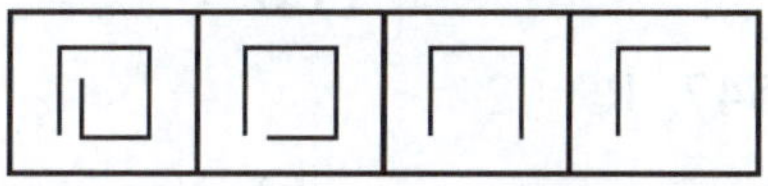

7. J, L, N **8.** Q, O, M **9.** IJ, GH, EF **10.** NO6, OP5, PQ4
11. 70, 80, 90 **12.** 63, 73, 83 **13.** 26, 37, 50 **14.** 71, 76, 81
15. 32, 40, 48 **16.** 15D, 16E, 17F **17.** 93H, 90J, 87L **18.** 395D, 385E, 375F
19. 518DE, 512EF, 506FG **20.** 349DD, 260EE, 171FF

Review and Refresh

A. **1.** 16, 22, 29 **2.** 6D4, 5E5, 4F6 **3.** 421, 423, 425 **4.** N,Q,T
B. **1.** 455, 446, 437 **2.** 20, 24, 28 **3.** 19, 24, 30 **4.** I5, K6, M7

Mental Maths

1. 13 **2.** OIJ **3.** DDS **4.** 11144 **5.** C49 **6.** EE5F

Fun with Maths

2. (d) **3.** (b) **4.** (c) **5.** (d)

Check Your Pace (Based on Chapters 13, 14)

B. **1.** Maths **2.** Hindi **3.** English, Science **4.** 3 **5.** 1
C. **1.** 505, 604, 703 **2.** 65, 54, 43 **3.** GH6, IJ5, KL4 **4.** 5V, 6U, 7T

MODEL TEST PAPER-1 (FOR HALF YEARLY EXAMINATION)

1. **(a)** Ten-Thousand **(b)** 0 **(c)** 99999 **(d)** 39 **(e)** 32
(f) 7225 **(g)** 5000

2. **(a)** T **(b)** F **(c)** F **(d)** T **(e)** T
(f) T **(g)** T **(h)** F

3. **(a)** 308005 **(b)** 900027

4. 10002

5. **(a)** $\frac{3}{8}$ **(b)** $\frac{8}{15}$

6. **(a)** $7\frac{5}{6}$ **(b)** $14\frac{2}{5}$

7. **(a)** $\frac{9}{17}$ **(b)** $\frac{5}{21}$

9. **(a)** 204336 **(b)** 474848

10. **(a)** 3762 **(b)** 4779

MODEL TEST PAPER-2 (FOR ANNUAL EXAMINATION)

1. **(a)** Divisor **(b)** 65, 8 **(c)** Infinite **(d)** Itself **(e)** 4
(f) quadrilateral **(g)** no **(h)** Square

2. **(a)** T **(b)** F **(c)** F **(d)** T **(e)** F
(f) T **(g)** F **(h)** T

3. Q = 9547, R = 2

4. **(a)** Yes **(b)** Yes **(c)** Yes **(d)** No **(e)** No

5. 90

6. Perimeter = 560 cm, Area = 16000 square cm

7. **(a)** 2 cm 1023 m **(b)** 10*l* 864 *ml*

8. **(a)** 3 months 2 days **(b)** 2 hours and 6 minutes